"Based on thorough and discerning scholarship, the book provides new evidence on the 'neglected' and 'hidden' history of Sharpeville. The authors are commended for this insightful narrative to dispel the one-sided and widely disseminated account of the Sharpeville Massacre by those who supported apartheid."

Chitja Twala, *University of Limpopo, South Africa*

"This compelling and thought-provoking book promotes the idea that the 'truth' in History as a discipline is itself based on shifting sand. Nancy Clark and William Worger prove that, if proof is needed, the production of history is a process of constant negotiation between evidence and interpretation where many questions are capable of a wide variety of answers."

Sifiso Mxolisi Ndlovu, *The University of South Africa*

"Sixty-three years after the apartheid killings at Sharpeville, the voices of the victims are heard, thanks to imaginative and dogged research by Nancy Clark and William Worger. And, startlingly, they report that the police count of 69 dead and 186 wounded – which has been accepted and endlessly repeated over the years – has always been a lie. This is a revelatory book."

Benjamin Pogrund, *former deputy-editor of the Rand Daily Mail, South Africa*

"Working intensively with Sharpeville's community, Clark and Worger aim here to right the wrongs of a past that has left many of the dead unrecognised and the injured disregarded. They reconstruct a history of Sharpeville as a place, as a community, and as a memory and an icon. After more than fifty years, Sharpeville remains the place where the anti-apartheid struggle went global: and with this lucid and compelling book, we at last know why."

David M. Anderson, *University of Warwick, UK*

Voices of Sharpeville

This is the first in-depth study of Sharpeville, the South African township that was the site of the infamous police massacre of 21 March 1960, the event that prompted the United Nations to declare apartheid a "crime against humanity."

Voices of Sharpeville brings to life the destruction of Sharpeville's predecessor, Top Location, and the careful planning of its isolated and carceral design by apartheid architects. A unique set of eyewitness testimonies from Sharpeville's inhabitants reveals how they coped with apartheid and why they rose up to protest this system, narrating this massacre for the first time in the words of the participants themselves. Previously understood only through the iconic photos of fleeing protestors and dead bodies, the timeline is reconstructed using an extensive archive of new documentary and oral sources including unused police records, personal interviews with survivors and their families, and maps and family photos. By identifying nearly all the victims, many omitted from earlier accounts, the authors upend the official narrative of the massacre.

Amid worldwide struggles against racial discrimination and efforts to give voices to protestors and victims of state violence, this book provides a deeper understanding of this pivotal event for a newly engaged international audience.

Nancy L. Clark is the Dean of the Honors College and Professor of History Emeritus at Louisiana State University. She is a Research Fellow at the University of the Free State.

William H. Worger is Professor of History Emeritus at the University of California Los Angeles. He is a Research Fellow at the University of the Free State.

Voices of Sharpeville
The Long History of Racial Injustice

Nancy L. Clark and William H. Worger

LONDON AND NEW YORK

Designed cover image: Detail from embroidery by Selina Makwana, "21 March 1960 Sharpeville Day For The Elimination of Racial Discrimination."

First published 2024
by Routledge
4 Park Square, Milton Park, Abingdon, Oxon OX14 4RN

and by Routledge
605 Third Avenue, New York, NY 10158

Routledge is an imprint of the Taylor & Francis Group, an informa business

© 2024 Nancy L. Clark and William H. Worger

The right of Nancy L. Clark and William H. Worger to be identified as authors of this work has been asserted in accordance with sections 77 and 78 of the Copyright, Designs and Patents Act 1988.

All rights reserved. No part of this book may be reprinted or reproduced or utilised in any form or by any electronic, mechanical, or other means, now known or hereafter invented, including photocopying and recording, or in any information storage or retrieval system, without permission in writing from the publishers.

Trademark notice: Product or corporate names may be trademarks or registered trademarks, and are used only for identification and explanation without intent to infringe.

British Library Cataloguing-in-Publication Data
A catalogue record for this book is available from the British Library

Library of Congress Cataloging-in-Publication Data
Names: Clark, Nancy L., author. | Worger, William H., author.
Title: Voices of Sharpeville : the long history of racial injustice / Nancy L. Clark and William H. Worger.
Other titles: Long history of racial injustice
Description: London ; New York : Routledge Taylor & Francis Group, 2024. | Includes bibliographical references and index.
Identifiers: LCCN 2023029272 (print) | LCCN 2023029273 (ebook) | ISBN 9781032191294 (hardback) | ISBN 9781032191300 (paperback) | ISBN 9781003257806 (ebook) | ISBN 9781003800705 (adobe pdf) | ISBN 9781003802105 (epub)
Subjects: LCSH: Sharpeville Massacre, Sharpeville, South Africa, 1960. | Apartheid--South Africa--Sharpeville--History--20th century. | Sharpeville (South Africa)--History--20th century. | Sharpeville (South Africa)--Race relations--History--20th century. | South Africa--Politics and government--1909-1948. | South Africa--Politics and government--1948-1961.
Classification: LCC DT1941 .C53 2024 (print) | LCC DT1941 (ebook) | DDC 968.22305--dc23/eng/20230621
LC record available at https://lccn.loc.gov/2023029272
LC ebook record available at https://lccn.loc.gov/2023029273

ISBN: 978-1-032-19129-4 (hbk)
ISBN: 978-1-032-19130-0 (pbk)
ISBN: 978-1-003-25780-6 (ebk)

DOI: 10.4324/9781003257806

Typeset in Sabon
by SPi Technologies India Pvt Ltd (Straive)

Contents

List of Figures   ix
Preface   xii

1 Contested Land: The Importance of Place   1
The Life of Emilia Mahlodi Pooe   16

2 A Company Town   20
The Company   21
Top Location   28
"Bad Noise" in Vereeniging   34
Moving a Location   41
The Women of Top Location   48

3 From Location to Township: Building Sharpeville   52
Planning a Racialised Town   52
Sharpeville   55
The Model Township: Lowering the Cost of Housing   58
The Apartheid Turn: Containing the Township   66
The Police Station   72
Racialised Spaces   80
Moving to Sharpeville   83

4 Life in Sharpeville   86
Strategies of Control   87
African Lives   89
Community   95
"My Life Struggle": Worker Activism   99
A Louder Voice: "As Arrogant as Truth"   102
Sharpeville Life: Faith and Hope   109

viii Contents

5 **21 March 1960** 114
   All of a Sudden the Crowd ... Had Been Flattened 114
   Sunday Night and Monday Morning: "The Dawn Has Come" 117
   Monday Morning, 21 March 1960 127
   The Aerial View 139

6 **The Massacre** 149
   The Vaal Triangle, 21 March 1960 149
   Sharpeville, Mid-Morning, 21 March 1960 151
   Monday Afternoon, 21 March 1960 158
   The Intersection 179

7 **A Family Tragedy** 189
   Let Us Start with the Children 189
   Counting the Victims 190
   Who Were the Victims? 197
   Trauma: Individual, Family, Community 201
   Surveillance 208
   Community 214
   Sana Benjamin 219

8 **Sharpeville and the World** 224
   African Witness 225
   Framing Sharpeville: The UN's "Session of Africa" 235
   "Listen to My Feelings" 241
   "Apartheid Is a Crime against Humanity" 248

9 **Coda: The Role of Memory** 260

Documents 265
   Document 1: Official Police List of the Dead, May 1960 265
   Document 2: Meriam Maine's Claim for the Loss of Her Son Naphtali Maine 266
   Document 3: Gilbert Dimo's Autopsy 268
   Document 4: Christina Motsepe's Life as Valued by an Actuary 269
   Document 5: Working List of Sharpeville Residents Killed by the Police on 21 March 1960 271
   Document 6: Working List of Sharpeville Residents Injured by the Police on 21 March 1960 274

Index 281

Figures

1.1	Photograph of approach to Sharpeville from the northwest, October 2018.	2
1.2	Map of earliest sites of human habitation and of intensive stone tool manufacture and rock art engravings in the Valley of the Three Rivers.	3
1.3	Drawings of rock engravings at Redan.	4
1.4	Drawing showing the distribution of +/− 30,000 African stone-walled, cattle-keeping communities, Gauteng c.1400s–1800s.	5
1.5	Drawing of typical stone-walled, cattle-keeping enclosure, Klipriviersberg, Gauteng, c.1400s–1800s.	6
1.6	Map of British garrisons and blockhouses, African concentration camps, and Boer farms using African labour during the South African War, 1899–1902.	13
2.1	Diagram showing the extent of coalfields mined by Cornelia Colliery in Vereeniging, 1933.	23
2.2	Map of Vereeniging Estates farms, including the location of coal and dolomite deposits, 1903.	24
2.3	Diagram showing Cornelia Colliery underground mining operations, 1933.	26
2.4	Map of Top Location drawn from memory by Petrus Tom, 2022.	30
2.5	Aerial photograph of Top Location, 1938.	31
2.6	Photograph of houses in Top Location, 1941.	32
2.7	Photograph of 450 Africans arrested in Top Location, 1937.	38
2.8	Map of proposed White housing in Duncanville on site of former Top Location, 1958.	46
2.9	Aerial photograph of Top Location after all residents had been "removed" and their homes demolished, 1969.	47
3.1	Aerial photograph of Sharpeville area, 1938.	56
3.2	Map of intended location of Sharpeville, 1937.	57
3.3	Allocation of space in Sharpeville by area and percentages, 1969.	60
3.4	Aerial photograph showing Sharpeville's first neighbourhoods, 1948.	61

x   *Figures*

3.5	Design of Sharpeville House, 1946.	64
3.6	Design of NE 51/9, 1955.	65
3.7	Photograph of Verwoerd at his farm, Stokkiedraai, on the Vaal River next to Vanderbijlpark.	67
3.8	Map of Vereeniging Town Planning Scheme, 1951.	69
3.9	Map of proposed Ethnic Zoning Plan with Buffer Zones, Sharpeville, 1957.	71
3.10	Photograph of example of site and service construction in Daveyton, 1956.	73
3.11	Diagram of street layout of Kwa-Thema Township, 1955.	77
3.12	Diagram of street layout of Lynville Township, 1955.	78
3.13	Diagram of street layout of Daveyton Township, 1957.	79
3.14	Aerial photograph of Sharpeville, 1968.	80
3.15	Map of Sharpeville's Town Centre, 1969 (identical to street layout in 1960).	81
3.16	Photograph of Sharpeville Memorial with families of victims, 21 March 2018.	82
4.1	Aerial photograph of Sharpeville, 1952.	87
4.2	Passbook photograph of Mohauli Solomon Masilo.	91
4.3	Passbook photograph of Monedalibe William Lesito.	92
4.4	Class photograph of African Police trainees, 1961.	93
4.5	Photograph of Anna Dhlamini, Mirima Theletsane, and Harriet Mahlonoko, Sharpeville, 8 March 1960.	104
4.6	Photograph of Mohauli Solomon Masilo's passbook showing the weekly signatures of the location superintendent.	106
4.7	Photograph of Mohauli Solomon Masilo's passbook showing the monthly signatures of his employer.	106
5.1	Nyakane Tsolo (identified by Michael Thekiso), bottom left, with the crowd outside the police station, around 1:10 pm, 21 March 1960.	140
5.2	Aerial photograph of the Sharpeville police station just after 11 am, 21 March 1960.	141
6.1	Photograph of crowd on no-name street around 1:10 pm, 21 March 1960, just after the Saracen convoy passed through and entered the police station.	158
6.2	Photograph of a Saracen and a van inside the Sharpeville police station fence around 1:15 pm opposite the crowd shown in Figure 6.1 on the no-name street around 1:10 pm, 21 March 1960.	161
6.3	Photograph of people running across the field north and northeast of the police station (building on left) and the clinic (building on right) around 1:45 pm, 21 March 1960.	171
6.4	Photographs taken within a few minutes of the conclusion of the shooting from inside the double gates of the police station looking out towards the intersection of the no-name street and Zwane, 21 March 1960.	173

7.1	Lydia Chalale official police diagram of injuries.	191
7.2	"Are there really dead bodies in those coffins? It looks as if they go into infinity." (Photograph.)	194
7.3	"A victim of the Sharpeville Massacre, who was only 11 years old at the time of the tragedy, is reminded daily of her severe injuries." (Photograph.)	198
7.4	Official mail received by Maine family at Stand No. 8554 in 1960 and still in their possession at the same address in 2019. (Photograph).	199
7.5	Map showing distribution of homes of Sharpeville residents shot by the police, 21 March 1960.	202
7.6	Ben Lechesa official police diagram of injuries.	206
9.1	Coffins of the Victims of the Massacre for burial 30 March 1960. Dlomo Dam in the distance. (Photograph.)	263

Preface

Write a book for us.[1]

This simple request made by the members of the Sharpeville community on a visit in 2018 started us on a journey to tell their story. On 21 March 1960, police opened fire on an unarmed crowd of protestors in Sharpeville and killed at least 91 people and injured at least 238 (not the police count of 69 dead and 180 injured that has been repeated ever since). The massacre that day was a pivotal event in the South African struggle against apartheid and an international turning point in the anti-apartheid movement. But since that time, Sharpeville itself has been largely forgotten in place of the other townships in the Vaal Triangle – Evaton and Sebokeng, Boipatong and Bophelong – and even the name Sharpeville commonly refers to the massacre rather than to the township. While the community has a history of its own, little has been written that puts the massacre in the context of Sharpeville itself, rather than as part of the South African struggle against apartheid. It has been our intention to put Sharpeville, the community and its history, at the centre of this story. To do so, we have followed the lead of the community by looking at those parts of their experience they most value: their long history in the area, the beginning of township life in Top Location and the later move to Sharpeville, their daily lives, and the trauma of the massacre.

When the massacre took place in 1960, Sharpeville was an important place, a lynchpin in the industrial development of the Vaal Triangle. The area included three major state-owned enterprises – Escom (electricity), Iscor (steel), and Sasol (oil from coal)[2] – as well as the Rand Water Board facilities that pumped water from the Vaal River to the all-important mines, factories, and communities to the north in Johannesburg. The industries which employed most of Sharpeville's residents were responsible for producing the machinery used throughout the factories and farms of the country and even

1 Mahasane Michael Thekiso and Moeletsi Vincent Thamae, interview by authors, Sharpeville, 11 October 2018.
2 Electricity Supply Commission established 1923, Iron and Steel Corporation established 1928, and South African Coal, Oil and Gas Corporation established 1950. Escom's name was officially changed to Elektrisiteitsvoorsieningkommissie (Eskom) in 1987.

in the rest of the African continent. In that same year, H. F. Verwoerd's government began in earnest the process of making South Africa a republic rather than a dominion of Great Britain, thereby intensifying the country's reliance on these local industries. It was the economic importance of this region that made its security so crucial. And the town of Vereeniging, due to the labyrinthine series of apartheid labour laws restricting African employment, was dependent on workers from its associated township, Sharpeville. That is why the Vereeniging police wanted, and got, a police station located in the middle of Sharpeville, the only one located inside any of the townships in the Vaal Triangle. The police at that station, who by mid-day on 21 March 1960 included the national leadership of both the Security Branch and the Uniformed Branch, took a fateful decision that shook the town, the country, and the world. Everything in Sharpeville's past led up to that moment, and everything that has happened in the community since has been a result of that event. The story of this community, that day, and the many years that followed is the story that we were asked to write.

Most scholars have continued to look at the events of 21 March 1960 as an unknowable mystery in which diametrically opposed forces struggled against one another – Africans vs. police, victims vs. perpetrators, left vs. right, good vs. evil – these dichotomies are all drawn from the texts that follow. The focus of these scholars on the event itself has been almost myopic, leading to descriptions of the actors present – the crowd and the police – rather than on how and why the situation had developed to such a point. Because of this focus, they have perpetuated a misleading image of Sharpeville and its residents: that it was composed of migrant workers when in fact the people had lived in the area for decades, often centuries; that it was full of disgruntled unemployed youth when in fact nearly everyone had jobs; that it was an insignificant town when in fact it was located at the centre of South Africa's industrial heartland.

The first and still the best book about the massacre was written by Ambrose Reeves, the Anglican bishop of Johannesburg. He went to Sharpeville the day after the massacre and participated actively in securing assistance for the families of those killed and injured, and in soliciting statements from as many as possible in order to develop a case against the police for presentation at the public hearings of the "Commission of Enquiry into Sharpeville (and other places)" in April, May, and June 1960. His book, *Shooting at Sharpeville: The Agony of South Africa*, summarised much of the evidence gathered, with a focus on the massacre itself and its immediate aftermath. Published at the end of 1960, it was immediately banned by Verwoerd's government and remained so until the 1990s. Few people in South Africa have ever seen or read it, and none in the Sharpeville community itself.[3]

---

3 *Shooting at Sharpeville: The Agony of South Africa* (Victor Gollancz: London, 1960). The book, including many of the photographs taken on the day of the massacre, is available as a digital download from the Historical Papers Research Archive at the University of the Witwatersrand, historicalpapers-atom.wits.ac.za/cpsa0003.

The only other books about the Sharpeville Massacre, both of them by political scientists focusing on the event rather than the community, were not written until after the end of apartheid and its repressive censorship practices. Philip Frankel's *An Ordinary Atrocity* (2001), its title suggested to him by "an aging but anonymous ex-police official," was researched in the late 1990s and relied heavily on what were then publicly inaccessible records in the Police Archive and interviews primarily with former policemen who spoke with him in exchange for anonymity. The combination of anonymity, a lack of citations for much of the text, and a bias towards the police – demonstrated by his remark that "the few preceding studies of the Sharpeville Massacre have been perhaps excessively sympathetic towards 'the victims'" – make it in our estimation an unreliable account both of the massacre and of the community.[4] Tom Lodge's 2011 *Sharpeville*, originally intended to be published on the 40th anniversary of the shooting in 2000, builds on his pioneering 1983 volume *Black Politics in South Africa Since 1945* and his 1984 PhD "Insurrectionism in South Africa: the Pan-Africanist Congress and the Poqo Movement, 1959–1965," each of which has a chapter devoted to PAC organising in Sharpeville. The 2011 book relies on his earlier documentary research, as well as several interviews conducted with survivors in the early 2000s, but on the whole follows Frankel's stress on the event rather than the community and also Frankel's misleading reconstruction of the massacre. Lodge does, however, provide considerable valuable material on the role that the event played in the development of the international anti-apartheid movement and on the ways the massacre has been memorialised.[5]

In contrast to the aforementioned works, the sole existing *historical* analysis of Sharpeville is by Matthew Chaskalson in an undergraduate research paper that he wrote in 1986. Chaskalson argued that "the question of why it was in Sharpeville as opposed to anywhere else in the Union that the PAC's campaign received its strongest response ... can only be answered by examining the local history that led up to the shootings."[6] His study was conducted at a time when archive restrictions and repeated enactments of states of emergency in the mid-1980s limited his access to government records in the National Archives (there was a 50-year closed period for "Native Affairs" records and none of the police records had been deposited). Instead, Chaskalson relied on the then-accessible records of the Vereeniging Town Council, leading him to paint a picture of a sympathetic town government undone by rising unemployment and dissatisfaction in Sharpeville. That

---

4 *An Ordinary Atrocity: Sharpeville and Its Massacre* (Yale University Press: New Haven, 2001). The quotations are from pages 15 and 18.
5 *Black Politics in South Africa Since 1945* (Longman: Harlow, 1983); "Insurrectionism in South Africa: the Pan-Africanist Congress and the Poqo movement, 1959–1965" (PhD dissertation, York University, 1984); *Sharpeville: An Anti-Apartheid Massacre and Its Consequences* (Oxford University Press: Oxford, 2011).
6 Matthew Chaskalson, "The Road to Sharpeville," African Studies Seminar Paper 199, African Studies Institute, University of the Witwatersrand, 22 September 1986.

picture becomes quite different when research in the police and "Native Affairs" records, now available, can be added to the mix.

Yet Chaskalson is quite correct in his fundamental point that focusing on the motivation of the protest – a reasonable response to oppression – rather than on the motivation for the oppression – literally overkill – itself does little to explain the singular outcome at Sharpeville. Without an understanding of Sharpeville's history, its economic importance, the reactions of Vereeniging's police to at least three previous "riots" (1933, 1937, 1940), as well as large-scale labour strikes in the area (1944, 1946, 1958), the actions of all concerned cannot make sense, hence the dichotomy of (peoples') protest vs. (police) panic.

As can be ascertained from the discussion of the historiography, little has been written about Sharpeville. It is one of those events that people assume that they know about, that much has been written about, and that no more needs to be done. The paucity of actual research accounts for the repetition in print and online of the little that has become a sort of received knowledge, that 69 people died, that 180 (sometimes 186) were injured, that it all happened so long ago that memories have been corrupted by time, and that no one can really know what happened. Few are likely aware of the only autobiography written by a Sharpeville resident, *My Life Struggle: The Story of Petrus Tom* (1985), or of the remarkable 45-page collection of Sharpeville interviews published by a young Dutch researcher in 2000, *Sharpeville Scars*. This probably explains why the most recent general history of South Africa, a multi-authored 700-page behemoth, repeats the same old errors, and even misplaces Sharpeville geographically in the eastern Rand![7]

The cold-blooded massacre of so many unarmed people begs an explanation. A thorough review of all records, the testimony, and the memories of survivors may not provide a definitive explanation of why such a tragedy took place, but it does reveal how the tragedy came about and unfolded on that day and in the following months and years. The records of the commission of enquiry into the massacre as well as the claims filed by the families of

---

7 Petrus Tom, *My Life Struggle: The Story of Petrus Tom* (Ravan Worker Series: Johannesburg, 1985), republished in Mandlenkosi Makhoba and Petrus Tom, *The Story of One Tells the Struggle of All: Metalworkers Under Apartheid* (Jacana: Auckland Park, 2018); Jasper van der Bliek, *Sharpeville Scars* (Tilburg-Lekoa Vaal Association: Tilburg, 2000); Herman Giliomee, Bernard Mbenga, and Bill Nasson, *A New History of South Africa* (Tafelberg: Cape Town, 2022). In the Giliomee et al volume, see page 477 for the discussion of Sharpeville, which in its entirety consists of the following: "Early in 1960 the PAC announced a campaign to defy the pass laws. One of the few centers where it was well organised was Sharpeville, an eastern Witwatersrand township [Sharpeville is in the southwest of the Rand] where blacks were particularly upset by the sharply increased rentals [on 21 March 1960 Sharpeville residents gathered to protest the pass laws]. On 21 March a PAC demonstration there turned into a major tragedy. A crowd had turned up at the police station. It was peaceful, with most simply wanting to heed the PAC instruction to be arrested without a pass. But the police were jumpy after a recent event in Durban where a crowd had murdered nine policemen [five of whom were African]. They panicked and fired into the crowd, killing 69 blacks."

victims provided us with a wealth of information that we could corroborate with the community. The testimony of those present at the massacre told a consistent story at odds with the "official" version of events, and the claims filed by the victims and their families explained the reality of their daily lives. These sources helped us to connect the event – the massacre – with the community, creating what is a new interpretation of both the event and the people of Sharpeville. They were not a nameless, faceless multitude without a voice, and they have never ceased to tell their stories about what happened that terrible Monday.

Indeed, our most valuable insights came from our interactions with the people of Sharpeville. Not enough can be said about the people who still live there, have always been there, and have always told their stories without much effect. In this book, we try to tell their stories with the hope that they can move forward and, in their own words, "memorialize this history properly."[8] We give special thanks to our primary guides to Sharpeville and its people, especially Mahasane Michael Thekiso and Moeletsi Vincent Thamae, who participated in all of our interviews and contributed their own questions and insights. They introduced us to over 30 Sharpeville residents who in turn shared with us their memories (all in Sesotho translated simultaneously by Vincent) including: Matlakala Mauleen Maine; Mphonyana Annetjie Matsabu; Mataeke Elizabeth Mokoena; Amelia Fantisi; Annacletta Mozomba; Ephraim Masilo; John Moeketsi Nteso; Mahlodi Caroline Lesito; Eucalphonia Mahanjane; Dikeledi Monnakgotla; Solobatsi Ishmael Poho; Difedile Machobane; Mapule Kgaole; Martha Masello Lepee; Sibonyile Rejoice Mgangane; Margaret Salanyane; Selina Motsepe; Minah Elizabeth Chabeli; Lydia Moahloli; Matshepo Maria Morobi; Madibe Catherine Koboekae; Buiswa Botha; Steven Papsy Masilo; Rosta Maratjwaneng Ramokgadi; Maggie Malema; Johannes Thutlo Ntjê; Machabedi Mirriam Lipale; Puseletso Elizabeth Sekate; Abram Mofokeng; Ntswaki Pauline Mathinye, M. Daphne Ramagole; Pulane Margaret Nkhi; Elizabeth Mono; Ntsoaki Ramodibe, Sello Kutoane; and Petrus Tom. Since our initial interviews, we were saddened to learn that three of the people who spoke with us have passed, Maria Thipe, Walter Phuteho, and Selina Mnguni.

Our first visit to Sharpeville in 2018 was facilitated through the good offices of Freedom Park where we enjoyed the support of Jane Mufamadi and Lubi Ndaba, and teamed up with Lillian Kekana, Jabulani Phelago, and Vincent Vilakazi to do an initial set of interviews. After that trip, Jabulani Phelago continued as a partner in our efforts to document the history of Sharpeville while pursuing his own scholarly interests in the history and memorialisation of the community. He joined us on our Sharpeville interviews in 2019 before the pandemic interrupted everyone's lives.

---

8 Nicho Ntema, email message to the authors, 2 December 2022.

When we returned to Sharpeville after the pandemic, Nicho Ntema, Sizwe Makaba, and Joseph Ngoaketsi, all Sharpeville people, helped us immeasurably in our endeavours, and we continue to work with them, with other members of the community, and with Jabulani Phelago to document more fully the events of 21 March 1960 and the long-term impact on Sharpeville and its citizens.

Archivists and librarians in South Africa, the United States, and the United Kingdom have been, as they are to every historian, of immeasurable assistance. We would like to give special thanks to Alexio Motsi, Mavis Xaba, and Mary Tshabangu at the National Archives in Pretoria; to Marlene Swanepoel at the Police Archive; and to Ruby Bell Gam at the University of California Los Angeles (UCLA) who joined us on some of our travels and made sure that much of the material on which this book is based was digitised for all to read, especially for the people of Sharpeville.

Benjamin Pogrund, Gail Gerhart, Tom Lodge, Matthew Chaskalson, Garth Benneyworth, and Karim Sadr have been generous and reliable email correspondents.

Ina Roos translated into English with meticulous care several hundred statements made by Sharpeville residents to the police in 1961 and 1962 and originally recorded in Afrikaans, as well as crucial parts of the testimonies given in Afrikaans by some of the witnesses appearing before the "Commission of Enquiry into the Occurrences at Sharpeville (and other places) on the 21st of March 1960," and at the Regina vs. Monyake and Others trial in 1960 and 1961.

Topanga Betke with her geographic information systems expertise shaped our raw documentary materials into lucid images for Figures 1.2, 1.4, 1.5, 1.6, and 7.5.

We give special thanks to Selina Makwana for her artistic vision and skill in creating the embroidery of which a detail is used as the cover of this book, and also to the Mapula Embroidery Trust, and especially Janétje van der Merwe, for their decades of work illuminating South Africa's history in thread.

The Routledge team has expertly brought to fruition the request of Sharpeville's residents that we write a book about their community. Gordon Martel and Eve Setch encouraged us from the beginning of the project, and Jennifer Morrow readied the manuscript for production with meticulous and welcome attention to detail.

Finally, a new generation of historians of South Africa has provided an intellectual sounding board and a great deal of collegiality for our work, and we will always be in their debt for many conversations: Professor Chitja Twala of the University of Limpopo, Professor Neo Lekgotla Laga Ramoupi of the University of the Free State, and Professor Sifiso Mxolisi Ndlovu and Professor Luvoyo Dondolo of Unisa.

1 Contested Land
The Importance of Place

> In the Transvaal we live in a province rich in memories of ancient human life.
> (Revil Mason)[1]

When one first approaches Sharpeville, there is little to mark the place as the site of continuous human history. Travelling south from Johannesburg, and approaching Sharpeville from the northwestern side of the community, one sees the first evidence of Sharpeville's surroundings: a massive industrial complex which is one of the largest steel mills in the world, six equally gigantic cooling towers of Eskom's Lethabo power station, and further on, open-cast coal mines gouged into the earth for miles. The industrial enterprise is far beyond human scale and dominates the otherwise barren and flat open countryside. One would be forgiven for mistaking the landscape for a scene from a dystopian science fiction film. There is little evidence of life. When entering Sharpeville itself, however, one is surprised at how small the town is compared to these surroundings, yet how packed it is with human activity. The story of these people is tied to their surroundings, and that history is a story of contest and conflict. The markers of a deep and tumultuous history are there, in the land (Figure 1.1).

The story of Sharpeville's people starts as long as one million years ago. Evidence of some of the earliest known human settlements on the continent has been found in this area, left by hunter-gatherer societies and followed by people who raised livestock and cultivated crops. The ancestors of the Sotho-Tswana peoples – who make up the majority of Sharpeville's population – covered the Highveld area from the Limpopo River to the Orange River for millennia before the invasions of the 19th century, first by the Ndebele peoples during the *Lifaqane* and then by the Dutch settlers during their Great Trek into the interior of the subcontinent. By the end of the 19th century, African chiefdoms were scattered, and most of their land was claimed by the Boers who then faced attack by the United Kingdom in a war over control of the newly discovered mineral wealth of the area. The city which had grown up at this site of ancient African history – Vereeniging – became an important staging area in this international war, including concentration camps for the Boers, as well as separate camps for the Africans who lived there. The city's oldest African "location" and the precursor to Sharpeville, itself the site of

DOI: 10.4324/9781003257806-1

2 *Contested Land*

Figure 1.1 Approaching Sharpeville from the northwest, you first see the industrial dystopia of the steel mills of Iscor (now ArcelorMittal) and the power lines of Eskom, October 2018.

Photo by authors.

one of the most significant archaeological discoveries on the continent, also served as a concentration camp for Africans.[2] Africans had lived here for millennia, fought off invaders of all types, and faced an international assault well before South Africa itself had even become a nation.

The earliest evidence of humans near Sharpeville is found in the rich valleys formed by the intersection of three rivers today known as the Vaal, the Klip, and the Suikerbosrand Rivers, where early stone age cultures hunted and lived off the land, leaving behind the remains of early tools dating from between one million and 500,000 years ago.[3] The Klip River valley connected this area to what is now known as the "Cradle of Humankind" where fossils of Australopithecus Africanus – 2.3 million years old and others even older, 3.5 million years old – are found (see Figure 1.2). These early humans lived in the limestone caves to the north and travelled south along the river, establishing camps as they hunted the game they found along the ancient plains and fashioning tools from the rocks and pebbles smoothed by the flow of the river. The modern name of the river – Klip – in fact translates to stone or rock in Afrikaans in recognition of its nature. The area near the confluence of the Klip, Vaal, and Suikerbosrand Rivers – the site of modern-day Sharpeville – attracted game and supplied fresh water as well as smooth pebbles to fashion hand axes and other tools, drawing early hunters to the site who left behind a rich trove of artefacts proving early human habitation.[4] The entire area surrounding Sharpeville rests on the dried-up bed of an ancient lake where excavations have recovered extinct fossil plants and ancient rock engravings. These engravings depict the animals the hunters pursued, as well as many abstract geometric patterns related to their beliefs about the cosmos (see Figure 1.3). These remnants of the Stone Age were first

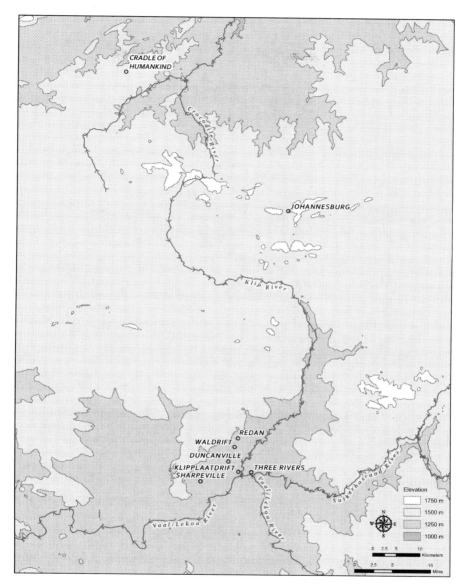

Figure 1.2 Map of earliest sites of human habitation and of intensive stone tool manufacture and rock art engravings in the Valley of the Three Rivers.

Based on Revil Mason, *Prehistory of the Transvaal: A Record of Human Activity* (Johannesburg: University of the Witwatersrand, 1962), 154, redrawn with updated information by Topanga Betke.

discovered by Europeans in the mid-19th century during investigations into the mineral deposits in the area. Unfortunately, most have since been covered by flooding from the damming of the Vaal River or have been destroyed through neglect and vandalism. Only one set of rock engravings remains today at Redan in the northern segment of the area.[5]

4 *Contested Land*

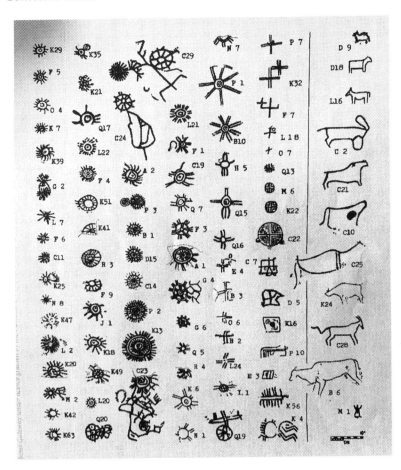

Figure 1.3 Drawings of rock engravings at Redan.
A. R. Wilcox and H. L. Pager, "The Petroglyphs of Redan, Transvaal," *South African Journal of Science* (November 1967): 495. CC BY 4.0.

Our earliest written records indicate that the culture associated with the Sotho-Tswana people, who now make up the majority of Sharpeville's inhabitants, began to take shape on the Highveld as early as the 14th century.[6] They comprised a large family of pastoral communities sharing similar languages in separate and diffuse chiefdoms throughout this region. They established thousands of stone-walled villages, only some of which have been excavated to the present. Less than 30 mi north of Sharpeville, for example, lie the sites of two major Sotho-Tswana settlements, one in the Klipriviersberg Nature Reserve and another known as Kweneng in the Suikerbosrand Nature Preserve (see Figures 1.4 and 1.5). People at both settlements engaged in crop cultivation and raised livestock, Kweneng, in particular, enjoying "extraordinary wealth."[7]

Contested Land 5

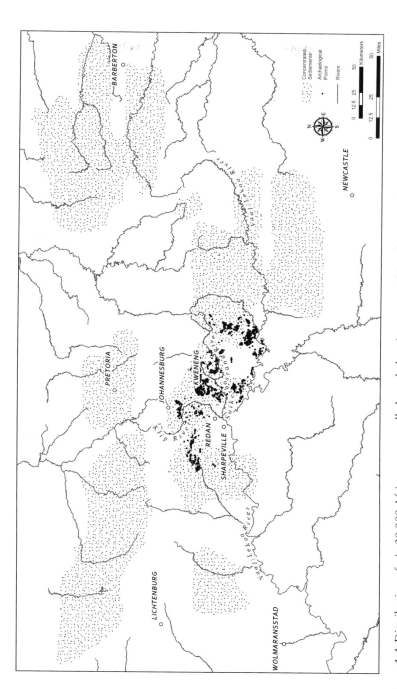

Figure 1.4 Distribution of +/- 30,000 African stone-walled, cattle-keeping communities, Gauteng c.1400s–1800s.

Based on R. J. Mason, "Transvaal and Natal Iron Age Settlement Revealed by Aerial Photography and Excavation," *African Studies* 27:4 (1968): Figure 4, 170. Copyright © University of Witwatersrand, reprinted by permission of Informa UK Limited, trading as Taylor & Francis Group, www.tandfonline.com on behalf of the University of Witwatersrand.[8] Redrawn with updated information by Topanga Betke.

6 Contested Land

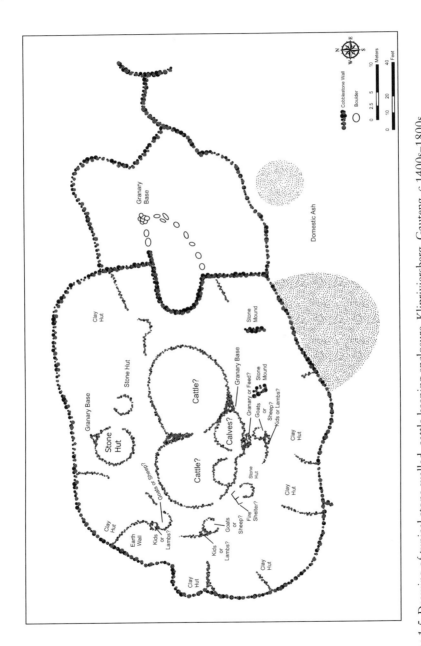

Figure 1.5 Drawing of typical stone-walled, cattle-keeping enclosure, Klipriviersberg, Gauteng, c.1400s–1800s.
Based on R. J. Mason, "Transvaal and Natal Iron Age Settlement Revealed by Aerial Photography and Excavation," *African Studies* 27:4 (1968), Figure 6, 171. Copyright © University of Witwatersrand[9], reprinted by permission of Informa UK Limited, trading as Taylor & Francis Group, www.tandfonline.com on behalf of the University of Witwatersrand. Redrawn by Topanga Betke.[9]

Over time, the Sotho-Tswana people divided into three groups: the Tswana in the west, the Pedi in the east, and the southern Sotho more properly known as the Basotho today. Stretching from the Limpopo River in the north to the Caledon River in the south, they occupied the land they knew as "*Lekoa*," their name for the Vaal River. As they expanded throughout the area, chiefdoms separated, forming new communities while retaining their language and customs. One such group, the Khudu, was settled in the Vaal/Klip River valley by the beginning of the 19th century, on the land today known as Vereeniging.

Despite their near continuous settlement of the area for centuries, the Basotho faced sudden and overwhelming attacks in the 19th century. Although there is still some debate over the causes, African polities throughout the region faced new pressures during this period, some due to environmental changes and some due to the increasing expansion of the Dutch settlers from the coastal areas. This period was marked by famine, with some "invaders," known as *fetcani*, an isiXhosa word for those who are weakened by hunger, seeking new lands. European missionaries, noting the expansion of the Zulu kingdom during this period under King Shaka, later described the overall dislocations of the early 19th century in more violent terms as the *Mfecane* (isiXhosa) or *Lifaqane* (Sesotho), roughly meaning crushing and scattering. At this time, the Sotho-Tswana chiefdoms were spread over hundreds of kilometres across the Highveld, but they were not united, and they lacked any concentrated military organisation to withstand invasions. The first to move into the Vaal River area from the east were the Ndebele (Nguni) under their leader, Mzilikazi. Whether or not the Sotho and Tswana chiefdoms were displaced by Mzilikazi, they faced the invasion by either fleeing (some Tswana groups) or more likely becoming incorporated into scattered Nguni groups as Mzilikazi moved north to the Pedi strongholds and even reached the Tswana chiefdoms west of the Harts River. Some Basotho fled south, like the Khudu who were settled in the Vereeniging area, many eventually grouping together under the leadership of the Basotho Chief Moshoeshoe, the founder of modern-day Lesotho.[10]

Into what one esteemed historian deemed a "scene of anarchy," the Basotho were faced with a more determined invasion by the Dutch settlers who were fleeing British rule further south and looking for land for their vast cattle herds.[11] The Boers, as the settlers were known, were less organised than the Nguni, arriving in various groups that criss-crossed the Highveld looking for vacant land. But they were better armed, and they engaged in attacks on Mzilikazi's forces, who appeared to be in control of most of the land, running them out of the area and north of the Limpopo into present-day Zimbabwe in 1837. In the short span of 30 years, the Ndebele and Boer invasions left the remaining Basotho scattered throughout the area and many holed up in the Caledon River Valley under the leadership of Moshoeshoe. The Boers were equally dispersed, but nonetheless claimed control over land, marking out farms in the 1840s on land previously occupied by the Basotho and establishing embryonic "states," one to the north of the Vaal, the *Zuid-Afrikaanse Republiek* (South African Republic, ZAR, 1852–1902) and the other to the south, the *Oranje Vrijstaat* (Orange Free State, OFS, 1854–1902).

The Boers claimed that the land was vacant, that the Basotho and other African groups were only recent arrivals on the scene, and that the land was God-given to them. While the British vacillated over whether to annex the land between the Orange and Vaal rivers which directly bordered the British Cape Colony, the land to the north of the Vaal was granted to the Boers under the Sand River Convention in 1852 and to the south of the Vaal in 1854. The British left the Boers in control of this land – to which neither group had any legal right – and gave them the "right to manage their own affairs and to govern themselves according to their own laws, without any interference on the part of the British government." Furthermore, the British also renounced "all alliances ... with ... the coloured nations to the north of the Vaal River," pledging to supply arms to the Boers for their protection against the Africans.[12] This left the Africans to the north of the Vaal on their own, while the British eventually granted the Basotho people to the south some protection under Moshoeshoe's rule in a limited area centred on the Caledon River Valley, modern-day Lesotho. Other groups on the edges of the Highveld – the Pedi and Venda to the north and some of the Tswana groups to the west – managed to retain their independence until the latter part of the 19th century when the Boers and the British succeeded in conquering the remaining African chiefdoms.[13]

In taking over this land, the Boers in the ZAR left no doubt who would be in control. One of the first documents produced by the government, an initial constitutional framework known as the Thirty-Three Articles, made clear that there would be no equality whatsoever between Black and White, and in 1855, it was further stipulated that Africans would not enjoy the rights of citizenship and in addition were not allowed to own land. By 1864, laws had been passed to compel Africans to provide labour to the Boers, to control African movement through the issuing of documents later known as "passes," and Africans were also taxed to provide funds for the administration of these laws. The Boers who had granted themselves control over the lands, marking out farms and registering ownership with their governments, also granted themselves control over the people they found there, being allowed to detain four African families on each of their farms to use as labourers.[14] In some cases, Africans were allowed to purchase land – the very land which they had originally owned – but only through missionaries on mission stations throughout the ZAR. There were several British and German mission stations in the territory where Africans undoubtedly resided and perhaps were able to buy land at least until 1887 when the ZAR enacted the Squatters Law, which prevented the practice. Although Africans could own the land through the missionaries, their legal claims were tenuous, and these parcels of land were eventually turned into "locations," as we shall see under a later British administration. Not surprisingly, many Africans fled the most densely settled Boer farming areas to escape the subservience demanded by the White farmers. In some cases, entire African communities moved out of the ZAR, as the Bakgatla did in 1870. Others who remained tried to evade the most exploitative situations by moving on to mission stations where they were granted some control over their labour and land.[15]

There was another alternative for Africans in the ZAR, to work for the speculative land companies that were purchasing land from both the government and the Boer farmers in the hopes that they would find more mineral wealth in the region. The massive diamond discoveries in Kimberley in 1867, followed by the even larger gold discoveries on the Rand in 1886, created a land rush throughout the region. The land companies were funded by overseas investors who had no interest in farming and were simply betting on future profits from mineral deposits that might be found in the future on this land. One such company operated on the banks of the Vaal River and was eventually responsible for the development of much of the area now known as the Vaal Triangle. The *Zuid-Afrikaansche en Orange Vrijstaatsche Koen en Mineralen Myn Vereeniging* – later known as the Vereeniging Estates company – was established in 1880, purchasing 22 farms in the area for the purpose of exploiting the coal deposits that had been found there. While the company mined the coal from underground, it also brought in African farmers as labour tenants to cultivate the land on the surface, planning to sell grain to the mines to feed their workers, as well as those in Johannesburg and elsewhere. There were eventually as many as 250 families on this property.

The plight of three families who ended up on the Vereeniging Estates farms illustrates the common pressures and circumstances which affected all Africans on the Highveld in the 19th century. Based on interviews with the descendants of these families – the Molefes, the Molopos, and the Mokales – they followed a familiar path from independence to servitude. Their families all originated in the area near the Magaliesberg mountain range where the bulk of Basotho were concentrated prior to the 19th century. Their families were all driven out during the Ndebele invasions of Mzilikazi and his troops, and they fled to the Caledon River Valley, the site of modern-day Lesotho, to seek protection in Moshoeshoe's chiefdom. A shortage of good arable land in the region led these families to leave in search of better land south of the Vaal River, and they found work on the farms of the White settlers providing labour in exchange for land on which to grow crops. They all eventually moved to the farms of the Vereeniging Estates on the banks of the Vaal River where they found more opportunities working as sharecroppers. These farms were owned by the company, not by Boer farmers, and since the company itself did no farming, the African sharecroppers were allowed to raise as many crops as they wanted and were only required to turn in a "share" to the company in return. The families prospered raising crops and livestock for their families as well as for the company. Their fate would change, however, as yet another invasion would cause havoc in this area.[16]

In addition to the farms of the Vereeniging Estates, some Africans also found sanctuary of sorts to the north of the city of Vereeniging, established in 1882, on an African "location." The ZAR established areas for African occupation, known as "locations," that were administered by Africans designated as chiefs or headmen and who were responsible for collecting taxes for the government from the inhabitants. In the case of Vereeniging, this land was located just north of the town and was known as Xaba's Location, most probably after the "chief" in charge. This was the very land that would later yield significant archaeological evidence of human habitation on the site from over 500,000 years ago.[17] The ZAR placed Africans there who were not employed by White farmers or merchants, but who were required to provide such labour when the government demanded. In practice, however, the government of the ZAR was manned by local farmers who often lacked the means or the interest in enforcing strict rule. These locations were not properly surveyed, and African land tenure was informally allowed. It is also possible that this land was purchased by Africans through White intermediaries – legal before 1887 – but it was later appropriated by the British administration when it was considered government property. Although of uncertain origin, Xaba's Location would survive as African-occupied land for half a century.[18]

Into this situation, international forces would once again completely transform settlement in the area. The area around present-day Sharpeville, situated roughly in the middle of the Highveld area, was soon to play a pivotal role in the greatest conflagration in the country's history: the South African War. While the Boers had established their own governments with British approval in the 1850s, after the discovery of diamonds (1867), and gold (1886) in Boer territory, the British government became increasingly frustrated with their control over these resources and the conditions of trade and investment demanded. After an unsuccessful British attempt to annex the ZAR, by the end of the 19th century, the standoff between Britain and the two Boer republics quickly turned to the declaration of war. The Boers had no standing army and scant access to sophisticated weaponry and their chances against the mighty British Empire appeared slim; however, they held on for 2½ years in a wasting battle that nearly destroyed their territories. The ongoing skirmishes played havoc around Vereeniging and drew the district's inhabitants into the destruction.

Vereeniging was located in a doubly precarious position. It was the site of a key strategic rail bridge across the Vaal River, and it also sat on the boundary between the ZAR and the OFS where British troops and Boer commandos crossed in battle. The combatants swept through the area, crossing where the river could accommodate animals and livestock. The rail line that ran through Vereeniging also connected the capitals of the two Boer republics – Bloemfontein and Pretoria – as well as connecting the British coastal ports with the important gold mines near British-occupied Johannesburg. The railways were a lifeline for both sides and were continually under attack by the

Boers. Despite some early military victories, Boer forces were quickly overwhelmed by the British troops and were forced to flee to the countryside. While retreating through the OFS and the ZAR, they made a stand at Vereeniging in May 1900, setting fire to the rail station and blowing up the rail bridge that crossed the Vaal River. As Lord Roberts led his troops through Vereeniging and on to Johannesburg, the Boers surrendered those towns, and soon also Pretoria, and the British annexed the ZAR as its own territory in September 1900.

But the war dragged on through an additional two years as the Boers switched to guerrilla tactics to try to break down supply lines and make the war as costly as possible for the British. The railway that went through Vereeniging was a favourite target, and the British built forts along the line as well as along the Vaal River to catch the Boer commandos. The British used their own unconventional tactics, destroying the farms, crops, and livestock that provided commandos with food and provisions, and also by removing any remaining family and workers from the farms and placing them in what were called "concentration camps." Unlike the deadly concentration camps of the Nazis, these camps were still prisons and became infamous for the high mortality rates suffered by women and children due to inadequate health care and sanitation. A large Boer camp was established south of the city of Vereeniging, on the banks of the Vaal River not far from present-day Sharpeville. Today, a small cemetery marked as the "Boer Concentration Camp Cemetery" sits just outside Vereeniging in a desolate area less than a mile east of Sharpeville where 108 children and 48 adults are buried. An unknown number of Africans in unmarked graves are buried nearby, as well as in a graveyard used later for Africans to the north of Top Location (see Chapter 2).[19]

The Africans who were working on farms in the vicinity – owned by Boers or the Vereeniging Estates Company – as well as those mining all-important coal for the railways at the newly opened mines in the area (see Chapter 2), were quickly commandeered by the British. As outlined by Lord Kitchener in March 1901, the British strategy of Total War included Africans:

> All natives living on farms should be collected and sent to the railway; if possible household natives should be permitted to accompany families or sent to the same station [to serve White families]. Supplies found on the farms should be sent in with the natives to feed them until their arrival at the railway. Additional supplies should be taken by the supply officers and the remainder destroyed. All standing crops are to be destroyed either by turning cattle into them or by burning. All forage is to be destroyed.[20]

In all, the British established at least 65 concentration camps for Africans during the war. Some were located adjacent to the Boer camps – required to be 1.6 km distance from the Boers to preserve racial separation – in order to provide "service" to the Whites. But they were all placed next to the railway lines that fed into the mining capital of Johannesburg rather than being randomly located around the country, near to where Africans lived and worked.[21] In this way, African men were sent to the mines to work, or drafted into the British Army as scouts or in other positions of military support. The location of the camps near the rail lines was also intended to provide support to British garrisons and "block houses," the armed outposts that protected the rail line. There was no cultivation of any kind within 1.5 km on either side of the line in order for the soldiers to have clear sight of any encroaching Boer commandos. Nevertheless, the African women, children, and elderly who were left in the camps were expected to work on the nearby farms that had been cleared by British troops, cultivating food for the troops. Since the British policy was to withhold food and medical support from the Africans in exchange for labour, Africans had little choice. The only way Africans in the camps could obtain food was to provide labour – the "no work no food" policy. Those Africans employed by the military or in the mines had the cost of feeding their families deducted from their salaries, while those who chose to resist and refused to work under such conditions were subject to the British policy of "let die," in other words, work or die.[22] The African concentration camps provided a labour reserve for the British Army to accomplish two of its most important goals through the use of free labour: reduce the costs of the war and get the all-important gold and coal mines back into operation.

The area between the Vaal and Klip Rivers had an especially concentrated series of camps along the rail line, and from Vereeniging south to Bloemfontein, there were an additional 23 camps sited along the rail line. As farms to the south in the OFS were cleared, the livestock was driven across the Vaal River headed up to Johannesburg where the sheep and cattle were slaughtered to feed workers on the mines. The British garrisons and blockhouses on the Vereeniging stretch, and their attendant African concentration camps, were sited to protect the herds as well as troops and arms that were laden on the trains passing through. Garrisons or blockhouses and their adjacent camps were located at the train stations along the route at the Vereeniging station, at Redan, Meyerton, Witkop, and Klip River stations. The largest African concentration camp in the area was established at the long-standing Xaba's Location, just north of the city. By October 1901, there were nearly 2,500 Africans housed at the camp in Vereeniging and a total of approximately 1,350 at the other smaller camps; by January 1902, all Africans in the area had been moved into concentration camps or military labour camps. In addition to serving the military installations, the Africans at these camps were also sent out to work on the surrounding farms: Rietfontein, Vlakfontein, Kookfontein, Waldrift, Houtkop, Vyffontein, and Klipplaatdrift (see Figure 1.6). By the end of the war, the British estimated that there were approximately 5,000 Africans in this area in the camps and working on farms.[23]

Contested Land 13

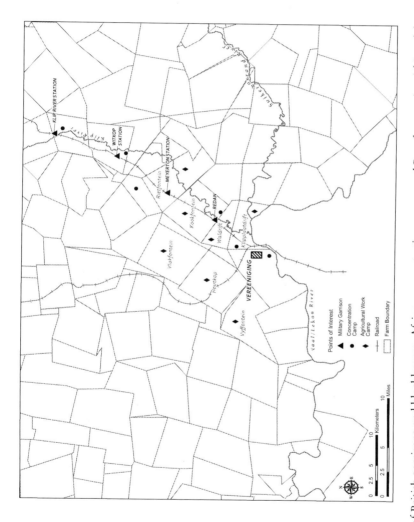

Figure 1.6 Map of British garrisons and blockhouses, African concentration camps, and Boer farms using African labour during the South African War, 1899–1902.

Based on the Map of the Greater Witwatersrand Gold Fields, Supplement, *South African Mining Year Book*, 1934/1935. Published by the S.A. Mining Journal Syndicate, Johannesburg, and the Argus South African Newspapers, Ltd., London. Issued August 1934, redrawn with updated information by Topanga Berke.

What was the experience of these prisoners, if they survived at all? Many Africans, as well as Boers, perished in the concentration camps due to unhygienic conditions and meagre rations. Although records are spotty, it is estimated that at least 20,000 Africans died in the camps. The experiences of the three families mentioned earlier – the Mokales, Molefes, and Molopos – tell us something about the fate of those who survived.

At the beginning of the war, the Mokales and Molefes both saw their men conscripted by the Boers and the women and children sent to concentration camps run by the British. Troops from both sides of the conflict confiscated the livestock held by these families, while the Molopos saved their cattle by sending their herd to Lesotho for safekeeping with relatives. For the Molefes, the Boers took all their cattle, fowls, and pigs and then set their huts and the corn fields on fire. The men were then taken off and served as grooms maintaining the horses used by the Boers, constantly moving with the troops as they evaded the British. While they were moving about the country, the women and children were in the concentration camps. Dinah Molopo recalled that her younger brothers and sisters died while in the camp at Kroonstad. Emilia Pooe née Molefe recalled her experiences in the camp as a struggle for survival on a day-to-day basis, with great difficulty in getting food to eat or even firewood for cooking or heat and being required to cultivate crops with bare hands and hoes. By the end of the war, Dinah Molopo recalled leaving the camps where her family had lost brothers, sisters, and children only to find their homes destroyed and relatives sick with smallpox, "flat on the ground and so ill as to scare anyone away."[24] Even those who survived the concentration camps faced a daunting recovery.

The overall destruction of the South African War cannot be minimised, described by the British as "scorched earth." The British had pitted nearly half a million troops against the 75,000 Boer commandos and spent £200 million to conquer the two rebel states. In the process, approximately 10 percent of the Boer population perished in the war. As British troops scoured the ZAR and OFS during the guerrilla phase of the war, they destroyed some 30,000 farms, burning all buildings and crops and killing at least 7 million livestock on the farms. All African farms and settlements were essentially wiped out, as well as the Boer farmsteads. The country was indeed a wasteland, save for the operating gold and coal mines in the ZAR. As the wave of destruction passed over the Highveld, how did Africans try once again to reclaim their land and rights?

When the war ended, the British proceeded to draw the new nation of South Africa into an international web of trade and investment that would completely transform the lives of its inhabitants. No longer constrained by the byzantine tax and transportation systems and trade regulations of the former Boer republics, South Africa would enter an economic union of sorts within the British Empire, trading gold, diamonds, and crops for advanced tools and machinery that could modernise everything from ploughing the fields to sending a telegram. The combination of industrialisation – started through the country's earlier mineral revolution – and commercialisation, especially when foreign investors could control their rates of return, transformed the country, including the countryside around Sharpeville.

The Molefes, Mokales, and Molopos returned from the concentration camps to find their homes destroyed and their livelihoods gone. The Mokales and Molefes resumed sharecropping on the farms of the Vereeniging Estates, and the company initially provided the farmers with loans to buy seeds and even cattle and oxen to help plough the fields. Destitute farmers worked on the company farms in far greater numbers following the war, up to 240 households as compared with 150 before the war. In this way, during the early years following the war, both families were able to rebuild their resources even though they were required to "share" their crops – 50/50 – with the Estates. But White tenants on the same farms, those Boers who owned no land, were able to recoup their fortunes much faster through easier and bigger loans, and the use of more livestock. Nevertheless, just as African farmers began to succeed, industrialisation and commercialisation took their toll, as well as the political considerations of the new South African government. The larger-scale White farmers in the area – who also included the remnants of the Boer political elite – began intensive cultivation and marketing to the lucrative mining enterprises in Johannesburg and on the Rand, squeezing out the smaller-scale sharecroppers. And they were also able to introduce the use of mechanised threshing machines rather than human labour to process their grain and tractors to replace the African-operated ploughs. If these factors were not enough to drive out the African farmers, in 1913, the South African parliament passed the Natives Land Act, which effectively outlawed sharecropping altogether and cut Africans out of trading their goods. From that point on, Africans were only allowed to work for wages, and they could only farm on land in the government-designated African reserves which constituted only 7 percent of the country's land.[25] Not surprisingly, many Africans left the countryside in the first two decades of the 20th century to find work in the cities.

Vereeniging played one last crucial part in the South African War when its founder, Sammy Marks, put the town "on the map" and in the history books by inducing both sides to meet there to agree to the terms which would end the war, later known as the Peace of Vereeniging, despite the fact that the treaty was signed in Pretoria, not Vereeniging. The town's site was central to all parties, especially to the Boer commandos who had been fighting throughout the ZAR and OFS. Marks had been friendly with both sides, eager to continue his Vereeniging businesses – which we will examine in the next chapter – no matter who won the war. Sixty representatives of the Boer commandos met in Vereeniging in May 1902 on the site of one of Marks' coal mines on the banks of the Vaal River. Tents were raised to house the delegates, and water and electricity were provided. Marks played some role in convincing the Boers that their cause was hopeless, and by the end of the month, they had agreed to terms, and the treaty itself was signed in Pretoria

16 Contested Land

on 31 May 1902. Under the terms of the treaty, the British granted the two territories self-government after a period of reconstruction, and by 1910, the self-governing Union of South Africa – including the Cape and Natal colonies as well as the Boer republics – came into being through an act of the British parliament. Under the South Africa Act of 1910, Britain noticeably did not extend voting rights to the African population, nor improve their situation to any degree.[26] The British moved in to secure the mining industry and the rail lines that carried the precious metals to the coast for sale abroad, and even helped to rebuild the devastated agricultural sector by supporting large landowners with loans and equipment. As long as the British could count on stability and profits in South Africa, the Boers were left to deal with their African neighbours as they pleased.

As the 20th century dawned, Lekoa – the territory of the Basotho for centuries – had truly been transformed. Over the course of the 19th century, the independent African chiefdoms of the Basotho had been scattered and their lands destroyed and stolen. A nation of farmers was being turned into a nation of wage earners. Nevertheless, they remained on their land even if they had limited access to its wealth and would spend the 20th century fighting to reclaim it.

When one approaches Sharpeville from the northwest via the N1, exiting off the R57, as described at the beginning of this chapter, there are few traces of human history, but when one leaves Sharpeville taking a different route via the northeast, the human markers of the area's history now appear very clearly. Leaving Sharpeville on the R28, you immediately pass the Boer Concentration Camp Cemetery; not far from the cemetery is the Vaal River site where the Peace of Vereeniging was negotiated, and further toward the river we know that the prehistoric fossil forests and early stone implements of the area's ancestors lie beneath the water. On the other side of the Vaal River is the site of the farms where the Molefes, Mokales, and Molopos worked, now destroyed by open-cast coal mining. Passing on through Vereeniging, the R59 highway intersects the excavation site of early African habitation, later known as Xaba's Location, used as an African concentration camp, and later to become Top Location, where thousands of Africans lived even before the South African War and until the 1950s. Today, that land is almost entirely vacant, save for a high school and museum. Continuing north, the highway parallels the rail line adjacent to the British garrisons and blockhouses, as well as additional African concentration camps. And near the suburb of Redan are located the rock engravings of some of Vereeniging's earliest inhabitants. A long history surrounds Sharpeville.

The Life of Emilia Mahlodi Pooe

The experience of Emilia Mahlodi Pooe, a member of the Molefe family, vividly describes the shifting terms upon which African lives existed in these times. She was born in 1882 on the farm where her parents worked as labourers for a Boer farmer. By the time she was 15, they had moved three times, finally settling on a farm where her father could work as a sharecropper, raising his own crops. In 1897, the country was hit by a cattle disease – rinderpest – which took out nearly 95 percent of all cattle, followed by a plague of red locusts, which took out most of the crops. Not long after, the South African War compounded their woes with Emelia and her family interred at the concentration camp in Vredefort, being fed porridge made of maize which had previously been fed to animals. Following the war, the family moved back to the Vereeniging Estates farms, and with some cash earned during the war, the Molefes were able to return to sharecropping but found that the terms for sharing the crop had changed; without their own oxen, they received only a third or quarter of their harvest. And when threshing machines were introduced to complete the harvest by separating the grain from the chaff, as opposed to hand threshing by the sharecropper, the landowners took even more control over determining shares. While Emelia's extended family worked together, pooling resources to succeed at sharecropping, in the wake of the passage of the 1913 Natives Land Act, sharecropping was essentially outlawed. And those farms that would allow the Pooes to farm demanded that they reduce their livestock. This was a common ploy of the Boer farmers to get the cattle at bargain prices. By 1930, her children were old enough to go out to work on their own, and they found better wages in the mining industry, on alluvial diggings on the Vaal River itself, in the Vereeniging coal mines, and in gold mines in Johannesburg. As sharecropping became more difficult, Mrs. Pooe's husband was demoted to overseer and finally to storeman on the farm and could plough only enough land for his family. He was pressured to sell his livestock as well and finally left the farm to live in Boipatong where his son worked in Vanderbijlpark.[27]

Notes

1 Revil Mason, *Prehistory of the Transvaal: A Record of Human Activity* (Johannesburg: University of the Witwatersrand, 1962), 440.
2 The term "location" was used as a term for "a tract of land with boundaries designated or marked out," in connection with "native settlements," in South Africa since the early 19th century and up to the mid-20th century when the term "township" was used interchangeably and ultimately replaced it as an official term. Jennifer Robinson, *The Power of Apartheid: State, Power and Space in South African Cities* (Oxford: Butterworth-Heinemann, 1996), 57.
3 H. J. Deacon and Janette Deacon, *Human Beginnings in South Africa: Uncovering the Secrets of the Stone Age* (Walnut Creek, CA: Altamira Press, 1999), 82.
4 Mason, *Prehistory of the Transvaal*, 23, 117, 153.
5 Marguerite Prins, "The Primordial Circle: The Prehistoric Rock Engravings of Redan, Vereeniging" (PhD diss. North-West University, Vaal Triangle, 2005), 37–39.
6 Mason, *Prehistory of the Transvaal*, 379. Although there are ruins of "thousands of stone walled villages" throughout the Highveld, archaeological research has been insufficient to establish a clear chronology.

7 Karim Sadr, "Kweneng: How to Lose a Precolonial City," *The South African Archaeological Bulletin*, June 2019; Paidamoyo Hazel Chingono, and Karim Sadr, "The Ash Heaps of Kweneng, South Africa," *African Archaeological Review*, December 2022.

8 Mason's original count from examining aerial photographs of 6,237 stone-walled communities has since been expanded to a figure of +/– 30,000 by a more exact recounting from the aerial photographs combined with the use of Google Earth and Lidar (Light detection and ranging which "sees through" vegetation). Personal communication, Karim Sadr, 27 April 2023.

9 The stone-walled community depicted by Mason is located in what is now the Klipriviersberg Reserve, about 50 km or 30 mi (a day's walk) from the areas where Top Location and then Sharpeville are established.

10 Julian Cobbing, "The Mfecane as an Alibi: Thoughts on Dithakong and Mbolompo," *Journal of African History* 29, 3 (1988): 487–519. Historical interpretations of the disruptions of the early 19th century have been subject to debate since Cobbing raised doubts about the accepted version of Zulu responsibility for much of the destruction of the period.

11 Leonard Thompson, "Cooperation and Conflict: The High Veld," in Monica Wilson and Leonard Thompson, eds., *The Oxford History of South Africa, Volume 1* (Oxford: Oxford University Press, 1969), 415.

12 Ibid., 421.

13 Ibid., 435.

14 The Plakkerswetten, or Squatters Law, limited landlords to no more than five families on a farm. Stanley Trapido, "Putting a Plough to the Ground: A History of Tenant Production on the Vereeniging Estates, 1896–1920," in William Beinart, Peter Delius, and Stanley Trapido, eds., *Putting a Plough to the Ground: Accumulation and Dispossession in Rural South Africa 1850–1930* (Johannesburg: Ravan Press, 1986), 340.

15 Stanley Trapido, "Landlord and Tenant in a Colonial Economy: The Transvaal 1880–1910," *Journal of Southern African Studies*, Vol. 5, No. 1 (Oct. 1978): 26–58.

16 Trapido, "Putting a Plough to the Ground," 336–372.

17 H. Breuil, C. van Riet Lowe, A.L. du Toit, *Early Man in the Vaal River Basin*, Archaeological Survey, Archaeological Series 6 (Pretoria: Union of South Africa, 1948). In 1943, van Riet Lowe undertook extensive excavations in Duncanville, in the area where Top Location was situated, and found artefacts from the earliest stages of the stone age on this property.

18 Thompson, "Cooperation and Conflict," 436; Garth Benneyworth, "A Case Study of Four South African War (1899–1902) Black Concentration Camps," *New Contree* No. 84: 74–91.

19 Visit by authors, Vereeniging, October 2022.

20 Quote from Lord H.H. Kitchener, March 1901, *Circular Memorandum 31*, as cited in Benneyworth, "Case Study," 76.

21 Stowell Kessler, *The Black Concentration Camps of the Anglo-Boer War, 1899–1902* (Bloemfontein: War Museum of the Boer Republics, 2012), 12.

22 Military Governor Pretoria, 27 May 1901, Vol. 245 as cited in Benneyworth, "Case Study," 79.

23 Benneyworth, "Case Study," 88.

24 Trapido, "Putting a Plough to the Ground," 347–349; Ted Matsetela, "The Life Story of Nkgono Mma-Pooe: Aspects of Sharecropping and Proletarianization in the Northern Orange Free State, 1890–1930," in Shula Marks and Richard Rathbone, eds., *Industrialisation and Social Change in South Africa: African*

Class Formation, Culture, and Consciousness, 1870–1930 (New York: Longman, 1982), 219–220.
25 This percentage was later increased to 13 percent under the Natives Trust and Land Act No. 18 of 1936.
26 The Cape province had a non-racial franchise for all males based on education and property ownership which was extended for a time but abandoned under a series of laws that moved them off the common voter rolls. Coloureds, Africans, and Indians were allowed to elect a limited number of White representatives to parliament under the Representation of Natives Act No. 12 of 1936, the Asiatic Land Tenure and Indian Representation Act No. 24 of 1946, The Separate Representation of Voters Act No. 46 of 1951, the South Africa Act Amendment Act No. 9 of 1956, and the Separate Representation of Voters Amendment Act No. 30 of 1956.
27 Matsetela, "The Life Story of Nkgono Mma-Pooe," passim.

Bibliography

Benneyworth, Garth. "A Case Study of Four South African War (1899–1902) Black Concentration Camps." *New Contree*, Vol. 84 (July 2020): 74–91.

Bergh, J.S. *Geskiedenis Atlas van Suid Africa, die Vier Noordelike Provinsies*. Pretoria: J.L. van Schaik, 1998.

Chingono, Paidamoyo Hazel, and Karim Sadr, "The Ash Heaps of Kweneng, South Africa." *African Archaeological Review*, December 2022: 73–87.

Kessler, Stowell. *The Black Concentration Camps of the Anglo-Boer War, 1899–1902*. Bloemfontein: War Museum of the Boer Republics, 2012.

Matsetela, Ted. "The Life Story of Nkgono Mma-Pooe: Aspects of Sharecropping and Proletarianization in the Northern Orange Free State, 1890–1930." In *Industrialisation and Social Change in South Africa: African class formation, culture and consciousness, 1870–1930*, edited by Shula Marks and Richard Rathbone, 212–237. New York: Longman, 1982.

Prins, Marguerite. "The Primordial Circle: The Prehistoric Rock Engravings of Redan, Vereeniging." PhD diss., North-West University, Vaal Triangle, 2005.

Robinson, Jennifer. *The Power of Apartheid: State, Power and Space in South African Cities*. Oxford: Butterworth-Heinemann, 1996.

Sadr, Karim. "Kweneng: How to Lose a Precolonial City." *The South African Archaeological Bulletin*, June 2019: 56–62.

Thompson, Leonard. "Cooperation and Conflict: The High Veld." In *The Oxford History of South Africa, Volume 1*, edited by Monica Wilson and Leonard Thompson, 391–446. Oxford: Oxford University Press, 1969.

Trapido, Stanley. "Landlord and Tenant in a Colonial Economy: The Transvaal 1880–1910." *Journal of Southern African Studies*, Vol. 5, No. 1 (1978): 26–58.

Trapido, Stanley. "Putting a Plough to the Ground: A History of Tenant Production on the Vereeniging Estates, 1896–1920." In *Putting a Plough to the Ground: Accumulation and Dispossession in Rural South Africa 1850–1930*, edited by William Beinart, Peter Delius, and Stanley Trapido, 336–372. Johannesburg: Ravan Press, 1986.

2 A Company Town

> *De Zuid Afrikaansche en Oranje Vrijstaatsche Kolen en Mineralen Vereeniging.*
> On July 4, 1882, the Volksraad approved the township plans and the name chosen for the village, Vereeniging, [was] the last word of the company's title which in Dutch means association.
>
> (Official History of Vereeniging)[1]

Beneath the surface of Sharpeville's contested land lay the key to the total transformation of the area from a farming backwater to the industrial centre of South Africa. Coal was discovered underneath that land along both sides of the Vaal River – the remnants of the prehistoric forests that drew humans there for centuries. The coal attracted the establishment of an electrical power station on the Vaal River, the manufacture of steel nearby, and by the 1930s a thriving engineering industry that fuelled South Africa's booming industrial development. Within the first 30 years of the 20th century, coal stacks and power lines sprang up amidst the devastated postwar landscape, and what would become known as the Vaal Triangle was born.

As the new town of Vereeniging grew, so too did another town, Top Location. This is where the majority of Vereeniging's residents lived, the Africans, who would always outnumber the Whites in Vereeniging. They had always, in fact, lived there, as demonstrated in 1943 when the noted archaeologist C. van Riet Lowe discovered artefacts from the earliest stages of the stone age on this property.[2] By the 19th century, it had been designated as Xaba's Location under the Zuid-Afrikaanse Republiek (South African Republic, ZAR), and the same land was later used as an African concentration camp by the British during the South African War. Top Location became a home for the region's displaced African communities and the source of Vereeniging's industrial workforce. As more and more Africans lost their land during the wars of the 19th century and were pushed off remaining lands by White farmers, they were forced to come to town to look for work. They were not allowed to live wherever they chose but were directed to Top Location where they could build their own homes on plots of land designated for Africans. As the population grew, the size of the location more than doubled and by 1936 the municipality decided to build a bigger location, farther away from the White community, to be known as Sharpeville. Thus, the

DOI: 10.4324/9781003257806-2

nucleus of Sharpeville developed out of Top Location where Africans had lived for centuries and built their homes, and they now created a new way of life. And in the process, they built the massive industrial complex known as the Vaal Triangle. Vereeniging could not exist without Top Location, or later on, Sharpeville.

The Company

In the mid-19th century, no site seemed more improbable to spawn a massive industrial complex than Vereeniging. Land had been claimed by the Boers in the aftermath of the *Lifaqane*, but the area was so sparsely populated that it did not even include one of the church mission stations established by the various European religious denominations that were busy ministering to Boer and African alike. There was, in fact, little to distinguish Vereeniging's future site from the vast empty landscape that surrounded it. As the English novelist Anthony Trollope described the area,

> Here and there it was stony, – but for the most part capable of cultivation. None of it, however, was cultivated with the exception of small patches round the farmhouses. These would be at any rate ten miles distant one from each other, and probably more. The roads are altogether unmade, and the "spruits" or streams are unbridged.[3]

This was the same land where the metropolitan centres of Johannesburg and Vereeniging would later emerge, but in the 19th century, South Africa's Highveld was a bleak, nearly empty reminder of the wars that had swept through Lekoa.

There were signs of life further south where diamonds were discovered in the even more barren landscape of the semidesert northeast corner of the British Cape Colony. Diamonds were discovered in a dry riverbed in what would become the town of Kimberley in 1867 and the diamond diggings soon drew miners and investors from around the world. By 1879, Kimberley was producing nearly £3 million worth of diamonds per year and was responsible for approximately 20 percent of the colony's revenue.[4] In the hopes of also striking it rich, the neighbouring Oranje Vrijstaat (Orange Free State, OFS) government commissioned a survey of its lands in 1876 to look for similar signs of mineral wealth. Instead of diamonds, however, the geologist George William Stow discovered a resource of a different kind: a major coal field that spanned the Vaal River. The Vereeniging-Clydesdale Coalfield, originally estimated to encompass 200 sq mi, in fact, extended over 600 sq mi, reaching north of the Vaal River approximately 6 mi and south for 20 mi. The entire area is underlaid with seams of coal of varying widths and quality and covers all the area beneath Vereeniging, from Meyerton in the north to Clydesdale in the south, including the ground where Top Location once existed as well as where Sharpeville sits today. A cross-section diagram from 1933 of the coalfields mined in 1933 by Vereeniging's largest colliery, the Cornelia Colliery, demonstrates its reach and depth (see Figure 2.1).

While the OFS government was not interested in pursuing a discovery it doubted could draw the same interest as Kimberley's diamonds, foreign investors saw an opportunity. South Africa had started to attract the interest of investors and speculators around the world following the diamond discoveries, and by the end of the 19th century, foreign investment in South Africa outpaced European investment in the rest of the African continent combined. Since the local Boer farmers had little to no capital to invest, it was foreigners who brought the money, equipment, and know-how to South Africa to make something happen. Sammy Marks was one such investor. Born in Lithuania in 1844, he moved to England and later left for Kimberley in 1869 to pursue his fortune at the diamond diggings and with his cousin Isaac Lewis operated as diamond merchants – buying and selling diamonds at Kimberley – accumulating enough profits to buy some of the coal-bearing land in Vereeniging. The more famous Cecil Rhodes, an Englishman who came to South Africa at the age of 17 to improve his health, also got his start at the Kimberley diamond diggings and initially bought land in Vereeniging as well hoping to use that coal to power his operations in Kimberley. But as he proceeded to acquire diamond claims in Kimberley, eventually forming a monopoly of diamond trading through his company, De Beers, Rhodes lost interest in Vereeniging and sold his share of the coal property preferring to focus on diamonds, as well as the new emerging goldfields to the north in Johannesburg. Lewis and Marks remained at Vereeniging, forming an investment company, African and European Investments, which traded on the London Stock Exchange. As their business expanded, Isaac Lewis left South Africa to run their financial offices from London while Sammy Marks stayed in South Africa to oversee their mining operations.

Marks had big plans for Vereeniging. He envisioned that the area would become the industrial centre of South Africa, what he called a "new Sheffield," comparing it to the British steel town. Not only was there an abundance of coal, but Vereeniging sat on the banks of one of the country's largest rivers, the Vaal River, which would later supply the country's entire industrial complex. Marks and Isaac Lewis quickly formed a local company – *De Zuid Afrikaansche en Oranje Vrijstaatsche Kolen en Mineralen Vereeniging* (South African and Orange Free State Coal and Mineral Mining Association) – and in 1880 bought up 22 plots of land along the Vaal River from local Boers who had only recently appropriated what they saw as "empty" land, a total of 126,000 acres 75 percent of which had coal deposits (see Figure 2.2). The land had not been cultivated and was barely populated, most of the White farmers having merely laid claim to the land farming it on a subsistence level. Wasting no time, Marks also gained approval from the ZAR government in 1882 to establish a town there between the Vaal and Klip Rivers on the site of the earliest human habitation in the area but which lay empty at this time.

A Company Town 23

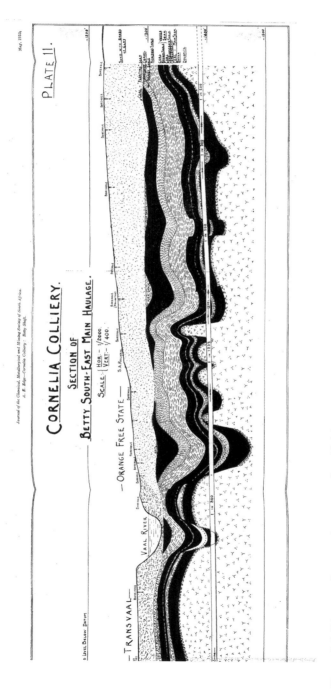

Figure 2.1 Diagram showing the extent of coalfields mined by Cornelia Colliery in Vereeniging, 1933.
A. E. Edge, "The Cornelia Colliery: Betty Shaft," *Journal of the Chemical, Metallurgical and Mining Society of South Africa* (May 1933): 355.

24 A Company Town

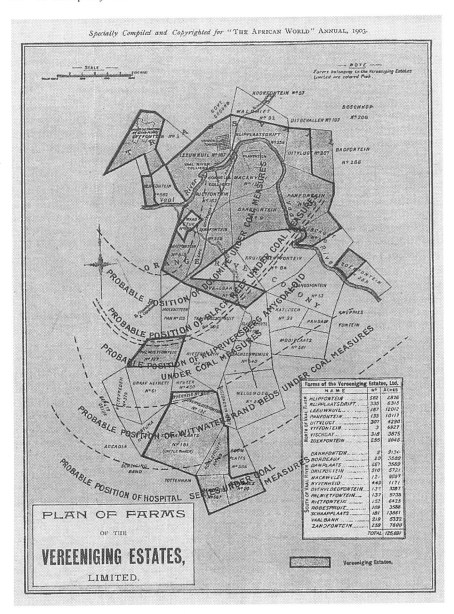

Figure 2.2 Map of Vereeniging Estates farms, including the location of coal and dolomite deposits, *The African World*, 1903.
Courtesy of the British Library, General Reference Collection P.P.1423.cii. 1903–.

For convenience's sake, the Volksraad named the town Vereeniging after the Lewis and Marks company. When gold was discovered in 1886 only 30 mi to the north in Johannesburg, Marks saw that Vereeniging's coal would have an even greater and closer market than Kimberley's diamond mines. The town sat on the Vaal River, which was the boundary between the ZAR and the OFS, and by 1892, the rail line connecting the gold fields, the diamond fields, and the coastal port of Cape Town was completed, running directly through Vereeniging and adjacent to Marks' coal mines. The Vereeniging coal fields suddenly sat at the crux of South Africa's industrial development.

Marks moved quickly on all fronts, but his first concern was to start mining coal on a profitable basis. He had already started in 1879 to sink mine shafts deep into the ground on the north bank of the Vaal River finally settling on an area – just south of the current town of Sharpeville – to establish what was then called the Central Mine. By 1892, the Central Mine employed 650 African workers, and 50 Whites, comprising most of the residents of Vereeniging. Owing to various problems, however, including fluctuating prices, the poor quality of the coal, and finally a catastrophic explosion in 1905 that killed 17 miners, the Central Mine was shut down in 1911. Instead, mining would follow the veins of coal as they spread under the Vaal River into the OFS where Marks could tap the same body of coal under more stable conditions. Since mining equipment and operations were already based on the northern side of the river, next to the growing town of Vereeniging, coal was moved from the southern bank coal mines by rail over a bridge to the new processing plant, until 1931, when the coal company simply built an incline shaft under the river to bring the southern bank coal to the northern bank near present-day Sharpeville (see Figure 2.3). The Cornelia Colliery, as it was named, enjoyed great success supplying coal to the most important electricity station in the Transvaal, the Victoria Falls and Power Company's (VFPC) station on the Vaal River. The private power company, initially given sole concession rights in the ZAR, held an exclusive contract to supply power to the gold mines on the Rand. By 1920, the Cornelia Mine employed 1,800 African miners and 130 White overseers and managers. Eventually, the company undertook serious operations directly on the southern part of their property and over time produced approximately 65 million tons of coal from that area. Coal would form the basis of all industries in the area and the very foundations of the town.[5]

Vereeniging was destined to be more than a mining town since its abundant coal could be used in many industries and was in fact a principal source of industrial power until the middle of the 20th century when petroleum and natural gas began to be used more widely. Coal was burned to produce steam to power engines and the electricity generators at the local power stations (as it still is), and its chemical composition was also used to turn iron ore into steel. In Vereeniging, coal would be used for both purposes.[6] The VFPC built a power station in Vereeniging in 1912 when Marks offered the company free land, cheap coal, and plenty of water from the Vaal River. The power

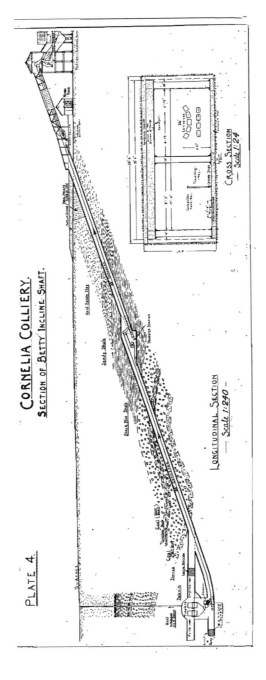

Figure 2.3 Diagram showing Cornelia Colliery underground mining operations, 1933. Edge, "The Cornelia Colliery," 343.

company then supplied the Vereeniging-Johannesburg rail line and more importantly carried the electricity via cables 30 mi north to the gold mines, a fact that would make Vereeniging of great strategic importance.[7] The year after reaching the arrangement with the power company, Marks entered into a similar agreement on much the same terms to establish a steel mill adjacent to the power station, the Union Steel Corporation, and in 1925 Union Steel established an additional plant in a new industrial enclave on the northern side of Vereeniging, called Peacehaven. Marks even had the foresight to use clay found while mining the coal to start making bricks and later a range of products; that company still exists today as Vereeniging Refractories (formerly Vereeniging Brick and Tile). In later years, the Vereeniging area became the site of three major state-owned industries: the largest steel mill on the African continent operated by the South African Iron and Steel Corporation (Iscor), power stations run by the Electricity Supply Commission (Escom, later changed to Eskom in 1987), and the South African Coal, Oil and Gas Corporation (Sasol). This early development, still evident today, was focused on the banks of the Vaal River near the present community of Sharpeville.

This was not the sum of all his endeavours in Vereeniging; Marks also established farms south of the Vaal River where, as we learned in Chapter 1, he pursued an agricultural project. Rather than sell the grain produced there, Marks used it to support two of his other business ventures, feeding his African workers on the coal mines, and using it to produce alcohol at his distillery in Pretoria. The Hatherley Distillery was nearly 70 mi away in Pretoria, but Marks planned to make his gin and brandy with Vereeniging farms' fruit and grains. The distillery catered primarily to the Johannesburg gold mines whose owners provided the alcohol to their workers, but Hatherley was never much of a success and closed during the South African War. Farming also came to an end by 1923, but the forests that were planted on what was known as Maccauvlei Forest – a commercial effort to manufacture timber mine props – stood until they were removed in 1985 to make way for open-cast coal mining of what remained of the Cornelia deposits. Nevertheless, by the time he died in 1920, Sammy Marks and his partners were involved in all the major industries in Vereeniging – coal mining, electricity, steel, bricks, and grain mills. Vereeniging was truly a town created through the activities of the "company."

As can be imagined, all this activity led to the creation of an ever-growing town of miners, craftsmen, engineers, workers of all sorts, and their families. And like Sheffield, the very nature of the town was based on all this industrial and commercial activity. Fittingly, the White leaders of the new town represented a sort of industrial aristocracy, most of them immigrants from overseas. Vereeniging's first mayor, T. N. Leslie, came to South Africa from his birthplace in England in 1881 and by 1891 was working for Marks at his Hatherley Distillery in Pretoria before moving to Vereeniging to work at the Cornelia Mine. The White population of the town, overwhelmingly from Europe, numbered less than 2,000 even by 1921. Most of the mayors until the 1940s were likewise foreign-born industrialists brought to Vereeniging to work for the foreign firms such as Stewarts and Lloyds (Scotland), Babcock and Wilcox (United States), Irvine Chapman (Ireland), and Massey-Ferguson (United States). John Lille Sharpe, for whom Sharpeville would be named, was born in Glasgow and came to Vereeniging to run the Stewarts and Lloyds factory there in 1927, serving as mayor from 1934 to 1937. It was only in the 1930s that the White population began to expand, reaching nearly 7,000 by 1936, still vastly outnumbered by over 13,000 Africans. But even as more local Whites came to the town, their connections to industry remained clear with men who worked at the large foreign enterprises serving as mayors. The town had been founded by industry and remained a company town.[8]

Thus, within the span of 40 years, Lekoa's land had been turned inside out. Now what lay beneath the soil, the coal, limestone, and clay, had been brought to the surface to be transformed into bricks, steel, and electricity. In traversing the landscape, coal mines, quarries, kilns, turbines, and rail lines now dominated the surface of the land that still held the early artefacts of Lekoa's history and had seen the conflicts of the *Lifaqane* and the South African War. And a town was quickly emerging from the dust, peopled by Africans working in the factories and mines, foreign workers running the industrial enterprises, and a smattering of Boers who were without land or trades yet still privileged by virtue of their race. Initiated by foreign investors drawn to South Africa's gold and diamonds, like Sammy Marks, the industrial transformation of South African land was well underway, replacing corn fields with coal fields and creating a new social order.

Top Location

That new social order would certainly be a racial order; Vereeniging was laid out as a segregated city from its very beginning. When Sammy Marks first drew up his plans for the town of Vereeniging in 1892, he divided the land into a grid pattern of approximately 1,000 "stands" or plots of land, for sale to Whites only, where they could build their own houses. And separately, approximately a mile distant from the area proclaimed as Vereeniging, there was already a much smaller, isolated area where Africans were to live, Top Location. As in every other town in early 20th century South Africa, Africans were sent to the outskirts of town to build their own dwellings and fend for themselves. The old ZAR had prohibited Africans from owning land since 1855, and in 1913, the new Union government demarcated only 7 percent of the total land area of South Africa for African community ownership, adding an additional 6 percent of some of the poorest land in the country in 1936. None of this land included any of the country's industrial areas or even major cities. And in 1923 under the Natives (Urban Areas) Act, the government made it clear that Africans in the cities would not be allowed any freedom to choose their housing but would be restricted to racially segregated "locations" in municipal and even in some rural areas. The town of Vereeniging was never a free place for Africans to live.

Nevertheless, as the African population became more concentrated around Vereeniging, a variety of living arrangements emerged and overlapped. Some Africans continued to live in the countryside on White-owned farms where they worked. Others lived in the company compounds erected on the coal mines, as well as next to factories such as the Brick and Tile works just south of present-day Sharpeville, but these compounds were restricted to single males, no families were allowed. The new industrial factories including Union Steel and the British-owned engineering firm Stewarts and Lloyds housed their workers under little to no government supervision or regulation. The housing at Brick and Tile, as pictured in the report of the Vereeniging municipal health inspector in 1942, clearly consisted of little more than tin shacks with a "bucket system" for disposing of waste. In total, there were eight such industrial compounds in Vereeniging housing over 8,000 people by 1942. In addition, the municipality erected some "hostels" not attached to specific factories for workers who could not find housing. There were additional living quarters referred to as "back-yard slums" in Vereeniging and even pitched tents along the Vaal River for those who could find no other available housing.[9]

Others found housing in Top Location. The land that eventually became Top Location had been the site of human settlement for centuries; in 1881, the Lewis and Marks company purchased it as part of their original purchase of land. During the South African War, the location was used as one of several concentration camps for Africans in the area where British troops moved people who could either not work on nearby farms (old people and children) or families whose men were working in the mines, on railways, or with the military. After the end of the war, in 1903 the Vereeniging administration requested that the British not dismantle the camp, but rather allow them to take it over as a municipal location.[10] In 1910, under the new Union government, an agreement was reached with the Lewis and Marks company, which still owned the land, to designate the area as a municipal location while the company retained mining rights to the land. It was declared "Top Location," approximately 1½ mile north of the town of Vereeniging, and the city took over the administration of the property in 1913.[11]

The conditions under which Africans lived in the British concentration camps were deplorable, leaving the newly designated Top Location in a questionable state. During the war, the British troops had swept Africans off all the nearby farms, cramming them into the camp with little in the way of services. In most cases, Africans were simply dropped off at these camps with their belongings and had to construct their own makeshift shelters and find water. Once under municipal control after the war, 188 plots on approximately 30 acres of land were demarcated for African occupation. Africans were told to build their own houses on this land, houses which they legally owned although they could only rent the land beneath the house from the town. The earliest census figures for the location show 576 people living on the 188 stands.[12] But by 1932 as more and more Africans were forced off

30 *A Company Town*

their land and into town, Top Location expanded to quadruple its original size. By that time, the municipality had built only 42 houses and added 9 "hostels" for single workers – 6 to house 120 single males, and 3 for 20 females – while there were more than 400 houses that were built and owned by Africans. Adhering to segregationist policy, 367 "Coloureds" were allowed to live in a separate neighbourhood in the southernmost area of Top Location, while a similar number of Indians and Chinese were housed in an area on the eastern border of the location referred to as the "Asiatic Bazaar" (see Figures 2.4 through 2.6). When all building was stopped in 1937 in

Figure 2.4 Map of Top Location drawn from memory by Petrus Tom, 2022.

A Company Town 31

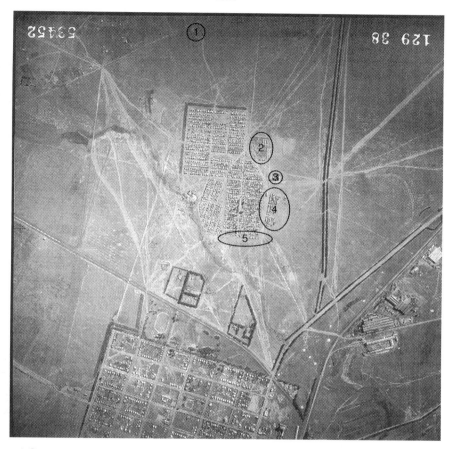

1. Cemetery 2. Hostels 3. Superintendent's house
4. Asiatic Bazaar 5. Coloured Neighbourhood

Figure 2.5 Aerial photograph of Top Location, 1938.

Source: © Chief Directorate: National Geospatial Information (NGI), Department of Agriculture, Land Reform & Rural Development, Republic of South Africa. Reproduced under Government Printer's Authorisation (Authorisation No. 11900) dated 6 June 2023.

anticipation of the move to the new location being built in Vereeniging – Sharpeville – there were over 800 residential plots of land housing over 8,000 people.[13]

Later residents of Sharpeville traced their family roots to Top Location and before that to the countryside. Interviewed in the 1980s, these Sharpeville residents all had similar stories. Chris Jana's family had been tenants on a farm in the OFS, but they finally left because the Boer farmer, in a common move, kept appropriating the family's stock – cattle, sheep, chickens – or

32   A Company Town

Figure 2.6 Houses in Top Location, 1941. Health Report for 1941–1942, NTS 4178, 33/313 Vol. IV, SAB.
Source: National Archives and Records Service of South Africa.

slaughtered the animals claiming that they were overgrazing his land. Jana's grandfather left the farm and found work at Vereeniging Brick and Tile, one of the earliest factories in town, and he managed to establish his family in Top Location rather than in the company's location. Peter Mathibela, who was born in Top Location in 1952 and moved to Sharpeville in 1980, came from a family that was likewise forced off a farm in the OFS but whose father found employment in Vereeniging with the South African Railways. Others followed their commercial employers to Vereeniging like the father of the famous boxer Sexton Mabena (see Chapter 3) who moved his family to Top Location in 1933.[14] These families were the fortunate ones to find work and a place to live in Vereeniging.

The municipality laid on a minimum of services, enough it was hoped to keep the population healthy and removed from the White community. The city built a medical clinic just outside the location that focused on providing maternity care and treating cases of tuberculosis and venereal disease. And the city set aside playing grounds for soccer and tennis and built a "communal hall" for township meetings. But crucial sanitation service was substandard. By 1937, with over 8,000 residents, water was accessible at only 26 communal standpipes where the lack of proper drainage led to muddy pools of standing water. Since there was no plumbing inside the houses, all waste was disposed of through a "bucket system" whereby the municipality arranged to collect and dispose of the waste three times per week. There were public facilities for 20 showers and 3 public lavatories with 4 flush toilets each, but no facilities for washing clothes. Water used for residential purposes routinely pooled in roads and ditches due to a lack of drains, and not surprisingly, typhoid and gastroenteritis were common in the location.[15] For the most part, residents had to provide many of their own services. The city allowed the residents to build six churches where schooling could be provided for Top Location children, and residents were allowed to open some commercial shops to sell groceries and provide services such as tailoring and shoe repairs. Although the municipality welcomed the labour these residents provided, it shirked any duty to properly house them while at the same time prohibiting them from determining their own living arrangements.

Located close enough for residents to walk to work in Vereeniging or to the growing number of factories in the area, Top Location was a convenient place for these workers to live. Both Petrus Tom and Nyakane Tsolo worked at the nearby African Cables factory, where both men were involved in establishing one of the first African trade unions in Vereeniging. In one of the earliest images of Top Location, an aerial photograph from 1938, the paths taken by the Top Location residents to their places of work – shown by worn footpaths – are clear (see Figure 2.5). The many paths also connected to nearby farms to the north and east where residents could find additional work or visit family members on the farms.

Life in Top Location consisted of more than work, as the residents developed a new lifestyle more geared to urban life, a development that would later worry the White town council. Soccer, picked up from the church schools for youth, became intensely popular, as it remains today. Some of the first soccer clubs in the Transvaal were formed in Top Location as early as 1912. One of the first, the Transvaal Jumpers, grew out of the local schools where the students could train and play on the school grounds. In the 1930s, the Vereeniging Bantu Football Association was established and joined the larger Johannesburg Bantu Football Association where in 1943, the Transvaal Jumpers won their division and started competing against the Orlando Pirates and Moroka Swallows, teams which are famous to this day. And many of the soccer players also trained with the boxing club, the Central Boys Club, established in 1946. The boxing club was even allowed to use one office in the municipal building as a makeshift gymnasium. Some of these boxers gained national fame later when the members and the club were moved to Sharpeville in the 1950s. And gangs, at this stage more like the clubs and without serious criminal activities, emerged in Top Location. One of the most successful bands to come out of Sharpeville – the Sharpetown Swingsters – was originally formed in Top Location by schoolboys at the Methodist Mission School bugle band. Enthralled by jazz music as well as some American dance movies with Fred Astaire, which were very popular in South Africa in the 1930s and 1940s, they formed the band in 1953 and later recorded with Columbia Records.[16] The social and cultural life of Top Location was heavily influenced by American and European culture, but residents were developing a distinctively African style of urban life unlike that in the rural areas.[17]

The government was alarmed at the development of an urban African culture, referring to urban Africans as "detribalised," and worried that urban Africans would become permanent residents of the White cities. Municipal officials in Vereeniging specifically saw the increasing immigration of women into the city as a sign that African workers were there to stay to establish families and raise their children. The government had hoped – and would go on hoping for many years – that African males could come into the cities to work on an intermittent basis while leaving their families in the rural areas to support themselves through farming. But Africans were being squeezed out of any useful land to make way for White farmers, making survival in the countryside impossible. And families that were torn apart when the men spent 11 months of every year in the cities working in mines or factories sought any way to stay together, even courting arrest in the cities. Families that could not survive in the countryside had no choice but to move into the cities, such as Vereeniging. Women came to the cities – and to Top Location – sometimes by themselves to survive and to construct new lives and new families.[18] The growth of these arrangements signified a settled and permanent African population in what the government considered the "White" cities.

The plight of such families is well illustrated by the experience of Petrus Tom, born in Top Location in 1935. His father died soon after his birth, and his mother struggled as a domestic worker, or maid, working for White families in Vereeniging for as little as £2 per month. While his mother was required to stay at her employer's property during the week – under legal requirements "domestic workers" were not allowed to bring a child or husband – Petrus lived instead with his grandmother and his siblings in Top Location. The family scraped by with money from his mother, from an uncle who was serving in the South African Army during World War II, from odd jobs that Petrus found as a child, and from his grandmother's brewing of traditional African beer, a popular staple from the rural areas. Finding money for his schooling was a struggle, and he left school with a primary education to find work to help his family. For many, life in the towns was a constant struggle, while the rural areas no longer offered a possibility of survival.[19] This struggle would soon emerge in open confrontation between residents and the police in Vereeniging's Top Location.

"Bad Noise" in Vereeniging[20]

Vereeniging's officials took drastic action in the 1930s to deal with a growing crisis in housing for both Black and White communities. The town had simply grown so fast that it was impossible to keep up with the demand for accommodation. By 1936, there were at least 14 major industrial employers in the area and a population of over 13,000 Africans and 6,700 Whites. The town government was alarmed that incoming local Whites were in some cases living in "slums" and moved quickly to build an additional 70 houses for them.[21] But they were also concerned that Africans in search of housing might intrude on the segregated, White areas of the town. The city administrators were loath to accommodate the incoming Africans by spending the money to expand Top Location, to build another location, or to open White areas to African housing. The answer, they felt, was to scour the location for Africans who were not employed at any of these valuable businesses and to kick them out. In order to roust what was deemed "surplus labour" out of the town and especially Top Location, police raids began to intensify at this time.

In charge of carrying out such policies, the superintendent in charge of Top Location personally conducted weekly raids during the 1930s to arrest and deport any "surplus" Africans from the township. Patrolling the neighbourhood on his bicycle with an African assistant, the superintendent D. B. Naude would check whether Africans had the proper documents that entitled them to live in Top Location, to see if they had paid their taxes or the special fees owed to the municipality, and he would also search for alcohol which was strictly prohibited. The sale and consumption of alcohol by Africans had been prohibited in the Transvaal since 1896; nevertheless, African women, like Petrus Tom's grandmother, continued to brew beverages made from sorghum, maize, and other grains which had traditionally been consumed at various ceremonies and on certain occasions for ritual and social purposes. Under strict prohibitions, these traditional activities were made illicit and resulted in the criminalisation of otherwise normal activities. Moreover, as women were singled out as the culprits for brewing the beer, the prohibitions also resulted in turning the women into criminals – criminal because they had broken a law that was manifestly unjust – who could then be ejected from the townships with their children and sent to the rural areas to try to survive. Another way the women were targeted was through the requirement that they provide specific official documentation – hard to come by under traditional customs – that they were married to a male who had a legal permit to reside in the location; otherwise, they could not stay. By his own admission, Naude proudly stated that he ejected as many as 50 Africans per month, especially women. He admitted that he "could never understand the policy of why we should allow a surplus lot of unattached women to remain [in the location]."[22]

His aggressive enforcement and prosecution methods were deeply resented by the women. In 1933, there was a demonstration against him and what the women considered was his continual harassment of them by approximately 150 women in Top Location. Although it was later alleged that he "was very nearly murdered ... by these native women whom he was turning out of the location in batches," this was somewhat of an exaggeration since no assistance was required by the police in subduing the demonstration.[23] It is unclear how violent or threatening they behaved, but the women were nonetheless charged before the Magistrate and fined for unruly behaviour. Naude defended his ongoing treatment of the residents in Top Location and claimed that the attack was "attributable to these women," who he described using an all too familiar racist stereotype of African women as "loose women," coming into the location to find husbands, brew beer, and engage in prostitution, as if these activities reflected their inherent nature rather than their desperate attempts to survive.[24] The town council, fearful of violence as well as any action that threatened to disrupt the city's labour supply or the fees it collected from the residents, instead prohibited Naude from such raids and left matters solely to the police. In the wake of the attack and what he felt was a lack of support from the council, Naude left Vereeniging shortly after the incident.

Following Naude's departure, the South African Police took over what they openly called "beer raids," foregoing the pretense that they were doing anything other than targeting the women they blamed for brewing beer. Using a patrol van rather than the bicycle used by Naude, they routinely raided houses in Top Location, looking for beer or any other pretext to arrest residents. As Petrus Tom recalled,

> Police raids took place day and night. Sometimes we would wake up and see members of the S.A. Police and municipal police, black and white, going from house to house searching for beer, passes, taxes, stolen goods, permits, and illegal residents.[25]

Not surprisingly, the number of arrests grew by at least 150 percent. Further, the method of arrest changed significantly. Whereas police had previously required those arrested to come into court the following day, police immediately took those charged away in the van to jail. And arrests were often made harshly with attendant physical assaults. Many women who were arrested in this manner resented not only the brutality of the officers but also the embarrassment of being thrown into the van in front of family and neighbours.[26] As one woman, Elizabeth Pululu, commented, "We are used to [rough handling]. When the police arrest natives they handle them roughly." But she especially resented police body searches of the women, "I say it is indecent because it is not nice for a man to feel a woman."[27]

When a new police chief, Head Constable Snyman, assumed duty as the South African Police (SAP) commander at Vereeniging in September 1937 and "received reports of the laxity of the location control as regards beer and dissolute women," he immediately decided to launch a raid for "beer, pass-less Natives and tax receipts."[28] While he was based at police headquarters in the town of Vereeniging, nearly 2 mi from Top Location, he quickly decided to visit the location on 15 September, patrolling the streets in the police van, known as the "pick-up" van for its primary purpose of arresting Africans. In the course of that visit the police entered several homes and arrested a number of women for brewing beer, handling the women in a rough manner. He returned three days later, on Saturday, 18 September, and again patrolled the location making several arrests and placing the women in the van to be taken to the superintendent's office to be charged with brewing beer. He also attempted to arrest a man near the central public square in the location, and after some rough treatment of the intended prisoner, the police were attacked with stones by onlookers. As they drove off, one of the policemen fired at the residents.

The following day, Sunday 19 September, Snyman returned with reinforcements from the nearby towns of Heidelberg, Evaton, and Klip River with a total of 31 SAP and 7 municipal police from Vereeniging. It was clear that the police retreat the previous day was seen as a loss for Snyman, and he intended to retaliate with a show of force on Sunday to erase any impression of weakness on the part of the police. This force fanned out across the location and brought all those arrested for beer, taxes, and pass offences to the central square in the location. In addition, Snyman called for all location residents to come to the central square so that he could individually check their passes and tax receipts, an absurd request considering that over 8,000 people lived in the location. Snyman personally drove through the location in the van to make this announcement on a bullhorn, and eventually, approximately 2,000 residents came to the square. When they saw the van arrive at the square, the residents began to throw stones at the vehicle. At that point, Snyman ordered the police to fire, and "many rounds of ammunition were expended by the Police." When the police ran out of ammunition, they turned and "raced"[29] on foot to the superintendent's office immediately outside the location for protection. More rifles and ammunition were obtained from the police station in Vereeniging, but when the police re-entered the location, they found the van tangled in a wire fence with Constable Pienaar inside severely wounded, and Constable Greyling lying nearby, dead. A third White constable, van Staden, had become detached from the main group and was found dead elsewhere, and two African constables were found seriously wounded.[30] That evening, police reinforcements from Heidelberg were called and surrounded the location. The following day, the entire location was searched and 450 Africans were arrested (Figure 2.7).

In the wake of the violence, many of those residents who had not been arrested fled in fear of being detained, leaving many of Vereeniging's businesses without workers. Among those who fled were most probably some who had been injured by the police fusillade and feared that their injuries would prompt the police to assume that they were guilty in the attack and detain them as well. Between those who fled and those who were arrested, reportedly thousands of Africans left Vereeniging, leaving the local industries without workers. Operations at the VFPC electrical power station that serviced the Johannesburg gold mines, as well as at the Union Steel Corporation and other factories, were thus seriously threatened. Vereeniging was primarily an industrial town of great importance, and any dislocation of economic activity had a serious impact on the national economy, as well as tarnished the growing reputation for productivity that the town council had encouraged. The town had already dealt with a serious strike the month before (August) at the Springfield Colliery that supplied coal to the gold mines as well as to a new power station on the Klip River. Control over the workforce was an ongoing balancing act that could cost the town and the employers

38   A Company Town

Figure 2.7 Photograph of 450 Africans arrested in Top Location, 1937.
The Bantu World, 25 September 1937.

dearly. A telegram from Deputy Prime Minister Smuts the day following the arrests ordered the police to release those not directly involved in the violence, thereby restoring workplace activity, but this move was bitterly resented by the local White community.[31]

In addition to threatening the strategic industries in the region, the murder of two White constables by a group of Africans caused panic among Vereeniging's White community. The Greyshirts, a pro-Hitler South African fascist group, immediately called a meeting in Vereeniging's town square attended by 1,500 local Whites. Farmers from the surrounding area felt that Africans had no right to be in Vereeniging at all and should instead remain as servile – and necessary – labour on the farms. They demanded stricter control over the location, blaming what they saw as the "liberalism" of the government administration for the deaths of the White police. Some asserted the "right of every European to shoot down any black savage who has the temerity to raise his hand against a white person" and called for the use of tear gas and even a display of force by military planes over the locations (a suggestion that later became relevant in 1960). Prime Minister J.B.M. Hertzog threatened the introduction of even stricter laws, claiming that "it is demanded from him [African] that he shall respect the white man and obey the laws of the country." Recalling a familiar trope of Boer mythology that recounted the brutal slaying of White settlers by the Zulu, the clergyman officiating at the funeral for the two deceased White policemen declared, "It was heathendom that killed [Piet] Retief and his men at Dingaan's kraal … and it was heathendom that killed Constables van Staden and Greyling."[32] The White community of Vereeniging could not make any clearer their belief that Africans had no right to the land.

The riot would leave quite a different impression on one young woman who would commit her life to fighting apartheid: Adelaide Tambo, later to become the wife of African National Congress president Oliver Tambo. Born Matlala Adelaide Frances Tshukudu in Top Location, she was seven years old when the police came to her house on 20 September at 4 am to search for "agitators" from the previous day. Her 82-year-old grandfather was the only male at home, her father and uncle having already left for work at Union Steel, and the police grabbed him and marched him to the town square with the others to be publicly whipped until he collapsed. Adelaide insisted on following her grandfather to the square where other men had been lined up for arrest, and she ran home for help. She would never forget the experience, saying "His brutal and humiliating treatment at the hands of the police was the trigger, the deciding factor" in becoming politically active.[33]

And yet, despite clear evidence that police behaviour and the enforcement of intolerable laws were responsible for the violence, the government instead concluded that women – again characterised as loose, undesirable, and depraved – were the culprits. Although testimony in the official enquiry into events repeatedly identified police conduct as the problem, the report concluded that "it is these unattached women who carry on the illicit liquor traffic and prostitution," creating "a rowdy and hooligan element with which the present Police Force is unable to cope."[34] The only action taken by the municipality to rein in the police was to officially prohibit them from carrying sjamboks, a heavy leather whip shaped like a rod normally used as a cattle prod, although this practice continued until at least 1960. Instead, a series of new regulations regarding alcohol possession and consumption were issued along with the intensification of efforts to remove "surplus" Africans. The location was surrounded by a high wire fence so that police could check the permits of anyone entering, floodlighting was installed for easier night-time surveillance, and four more police were hired.[35] Finally, in a futile effort to undermine the beer brewers, the town council erected a municipal beer hall just outside the location in 1938 to divert alcohol sales away from the women and into the municipal treasury. Residents and even local hostel dwellers universally boycotted the beer hall, and the municipality suffered huge financial losses as a result.[36]

Regardless of the increased security measures and restrictions imposed by the police, Vereeniging's officials still felt that the Top Location residents, and especially the women, remained a great threat. Increasing harassment led to another confrontation when in 1940, Location Superintendent Herbert Davidson claimed that a crowd of African women attempted to murder his assistant during a beer raid. Davidson had been superintendent during the previous violence in 1937 for which he had been criticised by officials at that time for being "rather a weak man [who] does not exercise sufficient control over the location," and he had also been counselled by the native commissioner at that time to "try and tighten up things in the location with a view to stopping the brewing of large quantities of liquor in the location which was having a very bad effect on the industrial workers in this area."[37] Accordingly, on 20 November 1940, Davidson's assistant, Eric MacKenzie embarked on a beer raid in the location with three African constables, entering at least five houses looking for beer and destroying some liquor in three of the houses. By the time he and the constables entered the sixth house that was occupied by a woman, Minnie Mofokeng, who had only recently been charged and fined for illegal liquor, a crowd of women gathered outside the home and began shouting. While there were conflicting reports of what was shouted (a war cry or a welcome), how many women were in the crowd (1,000 or 400), or what their intent was (murder or celebration), MacKenzie and his subordinates became frightened. In their later testimony, it was clear that they feared the crowd – despite the absence of weapons of any kind – remembering the deaths of the constables in 1937. MacKenzie dramatically described the confrontation with the crowd:

> I heard a native war cry; it appeared to be made by a woman ... men and women converged on me from the West; there was a good thousand of them; they stood for a few moments and came on again towards me; they were jumping, screaming and shouting ... this is a sign that they were out to kill.[38]

Clearly, MacKenzie was scared, and it is surprising that he and the constables did not panic and fire on the crowd. Constable Ben Pitsi, a veteran of the 1937 incident, admitted to being "terror-struck," saying "I was afraid they would kill us."[39] In fact, other than shriek and yell, the women did nothing to attack the men who were armed, including MacKenzie who was carrying a revolver.

While no one was injured, the location superintendent, Davidson, decided to take a hard line; his response was to identify supposed ringleaders and try to kick them out of the location altogether, sending them who knows where – a far more disastrous penalty than levying a fine or even requiring jail time.[40] He called the women who were identified as the so-called ringleaders of the disturbance to his office where he threatened at least three of them – Paulina Sakoeni, Julia Debogo, and Anostasia Thabanetu – with being ejected from the location and for good measure physically menaced them as Paulina Sakoeni testified: he "pointed the revolver at me; he took out two bullets out of the revolver and asked me whether I knew what they were; he said that one day I will find them inside my stomach."[41] Rather than being intimidated into silence and quietly leaving the location, the women instead made a formal objection to the native commissioner. At that point, realising that his threats had no effect, Davidson retaliated by charging them with incitement to murder and violence and took them to court. In what must have been a great embarrassment for Davidson, the eight women were all acquitted of incitement to commit murder, while one was found guilty of incitement to violence.

Shortly after this incident, Davidson resigned, and his assistant Eric MacKenzie – who was responsible for the 1940 debacle – was promoted to superintendent of the location. He held on to his belief that all problems in the location stemmed from the women, saying, "[T]oday there is no control of the location because we have between 400 and 500 skokiaan queens," a derogatory term for women who sold illicit alcohol. And he also held on to a fear of the women, saying "There is always in the back of the mind of everybody that nasty riot we had in 1937," remembering the death of the constables while raiding the location for beer. Nevertheless, he managed to arrest nearly 300 women for possession of alcohol in his first year as superintendent, fining them nearly £700. The beer raids intensified once the municipality built its own "beer hall," the only legal place for Africans to drink the beer brewed and sold by the municipality. As in other towns in South Africa, this arrangement brought in revenue to the municipality that was used to administer the locations so that the residents were responsible for paying for their own services without any contribution from White businesses or residents. As the location superintendent, MacKenzie had a vested interest in the success of the beer hall and the correlated decline of homebrew, earning him the nickname, "beer man" from the residents for the zealousness of his raids.[42]

But the Vereeniging Town Council wanted a more permanent solution to stem what they saw as the dangerous unrest in the location. In order to more closely supervise the residents, especially by conducting regular raids for illegal beer, the council wanted to build a police station – manned by the SAP rather than municipal constables – right inside the location. The existing police station was located almost two miles away in Vereeniging, and the police had to be summoned by the superintendent to the location when trouble broke out. The SAP, a national body responsible for serious criminal activity, resisted such requests, arguing that the municipal constables who were normally responsible for enforcing local laws should be responsible.[43] By 1942, however, the Native Affairs Commission finally agreed with the municipality, describing Top Location as "a difficult location" and noting that "control can only be re-established in the location if the women are permanently removed ... [and] that the assistance of the South African Police be provided so far as this may be requisite to deal with the brewing and sale of illicit liquor."[44] This determination would have to wait, however, as the town council sought an even more dramatic solution: the demolition of Top Location altogether.

Moving a Location

As early as 1935, the town council started negotiations to do away with Top Location and to open that land for commercial development. The location sat less than 2 mi from Vereeniging's downtown along the road that travelled north to Johannesburg, and it was less than a mile from the rail line. Factories and White housing started opening along the rail line on the eastern side opposite the location in the community of Peacehaven in the 1930s, followed by more housing further east in Three Rivers in the 1940s. The municipality saw an opportunity to attract more development in the area north of Vereeniging by clearing out Top Location. By 1937 – even before the "riot" of that year – the town wanted to make way for even more factories on the land occupied by these workers in Top Location. The mayor John Lille Sharpe was also the general manager of one of the major firms, Stewarts and Lloyds, and he declared that "the location now is retarding the European development of the town." He saw the industrial compounds for workers at his and other factories as preferable to the more expensive housing in the location and because they allowed only African males there, they could also eliminate the possibility of African families establishing themselves in the town. As he explained in 1937, his firm was in the process of expanding their compound to "accommodate 1,000 which will be taken away from the Municipal location [Top Location]."[45] His preference was to open the land for White development and to house workers, but not their families, at the work site as long as their labour was needed. The town council agreed and argued that under the Slum Clearance Act (1934) they could remove Top Location as a health hazard, but the municipal health officer objected, saying, "[I]t is to be pointed out that the majority of the houses cannot be looked upon as slum properties, except in so far as they are overcrowded."[46] Mayor Sharpe instead petitioned the provincial administration to allow the municipality to remove the residents to another location rather than move them to the company hostels; but also to appropriate all Top Location land in order to develop it for White businesses and housing. With government approval, the fate of the location was sealed and plans for its demolition proceeded quickly.

But the actual demolition of the houses in Top Location, and the transformation of that land into Duncanville, took an extraordinarily long time. There were several reasons for the delay, foremost being the fact that the town did not actually own the land. Vereeniging Estates – the Lewis and Marks company that had founded Vereeniging in the 19th century – still owned the land, only allowing the city surface use. The city had to purchase the land in order to develop it into the commercial and residential neighbourhood it envisioned. Negotiations with the company dragged on for over ten years with the deal finally concluded in 1946: the city paid the company £240,000 for two pieces of land, one was Top Location to become Duncanville, the other a swampy piece of land to the southwest of the city to be Sharpeville. The actual removal of the residents and their transition to Sharpeville would take another 13 years, not complete until 1959. Not all residents were anxious to move, and many demanded recompense for the houses they had built. Since the overwhelming number of houses in Top Location had been constructed by the residents themselves – and they had legal ownership of the structures – the Vereeniging Town Council was required to pay residents the value of the houses if they were demolished or alternatively agree to move the materials for their use at Sharpeville. Valuation of the structures was contested by the residents as being too low, and the process was lengthy and tedious. Although the city government did not hesitate to move these people about with little regard for their wishes, the process of doing so was nevertheless complicated and drawn out.

Some of the residents were moved out of the Vereeniging area altogether, including many who lived from rents paid by lodgers in their houses or were engaged in their own businesses such as transport driving, dairies, and slaughtering, and even pastors and ministers. With housing at a premium, renting out rooms or even building additional structures on one's lot was common. In many cases, the rent provided all the income the stand holder received. When the structures at Top were demolished, these people lost their livelihood, and in many cases their right to live in the township. Under the increasingly stringent requirements for permission to live in the townships, many women did not qualify for residence if they did not have a male head of household. The move was especially hard for widows. When Aletta Mako, a widow, lost her home in Top Location, she also lost £5 month she received in rent, and she was given £32 in compensation for her home from the municipality. Eliza Matzumo, also a widow, lost £1.8.0 in rent and received £30 compensation for her house, while the municipality also took the iron roof from the house. Another widow lost £3.10.0 in rent, was given £50, and the municipality took all of her building materials, evidently for resale.[47] None of these women were allowed to move to Sharpeville. Clearly, the Vereeniging Town Council hoped that this process would reshape the location into an ideal labour reservoir of workers employed by the White-owned factories nearby that would provide sufficient revenue and reduce all challenges to control over the inhabitants. When demolition of the old location was finally completed in 1959, the remaining residents who were not employed – old people on pensions, widows, and the infirm – were denied residence in Sharpe, and instead, they were told to return to their "original homes,"[48] the very term used by H. F. Verwoerd – minister of Native Affairs (1950–1958) and prime minister (1958–1966) – to describe the ethnically determined "Bantustans," which formed the core of his concept of separate development. By 1959, when the final structures were demolished, this meant exile into the Bantustans, now slated for self-government, but in which most Top residents had never lived or even visited. True to Apartheid policy, Africans "should only be allowed to enter urban areas ... to minister to the needs of the white man,"[49] the most vulnerable in Top would be cast out because they could no longer so minister.

But many of those with what were considered "legal rights" to live in Sharpeville, were nevertheless not granted access. The first residents started to move to Sharpeville in 1943, but by 1946, there were still nearly 13,000 people living in Top Location largely due to the municipality's reluctance to grant all residents access to Sharpeville.[50] The officials were especially anxious to evict lodgers and prevent them from moving to Sharpeville. As early as 1944, a lodger Michael Mokoteli and his family were evicted from Top despite his obtaining employment at the new Sharpe Public School. His experience illustrates the byzantine implementation of this process. Mr. Mokoteli, a schoolteacher, moved to Top Location in 1939 and lived there as a lodger with his family. He was eventually offered a teaching post in Bothaville, approximately 100 mi to the southwest of Vereeniging across the Vaal River in the OFS. There was no available housing there, and he was forced to share a room with two other men, leaving his family in Vereeniging. When he obtained a teaching position in Sharpeville at the Public School, he discovered that his family had been evicted from Top Location by the location superintendent and that they were then denied residence in Sharpeville by the manager for the Vereeniging municipal locations. Writing to the secretary for Native Affairs, he lamented, "I really fail to see what I can do with my family at this juncture as they have been rendered homeless and cannot live in an open air, and I think I have been treated very unfairly."[51] In fact, the Mokotelis were victims of a policy instituted by the town council barring Top lodgers from obtaining permits to live in Sharpeville, specifically with the intent to deny the lodgers any rights to houses in Sharpe. "Every permit granted for permanent residence in the Old Location [Top] means that the council is assuming the obligation of providing an additional house in the new (Sharpe) Location for the holder of that permit."[52] The specific objection was that the council would incur "additional expenses and loss on this sub-economic scheme."[53]

The case of the Mokoteli's was far from unusual. As residents in Top were routinely evicted for any late payments on their permits, even those born in the location found themselves homeless. Jan Mofisane was born in Top Location but was evicted in 1953 by the location superintendant. Mofisane had attempted to pay for his permit on 30 June 1951 but was informed that he was late making the June payment. After eviction, he was allowed to move to nearby Evaton but was eventually sent back to Vereeniging because that was his birthplace. Upon his return, he was arrested for being in Top Location without a permit, and he was fined £1. Initially evicted for dubious reasons, he was denied the right apparently to live anywhere. In requesting some assistance from the native commissioner, he explained, "I am forbidden from entering either Evaton or my home Vereeniging. I fear that without your assistance I shall be continually arrested as there is no other place I could go."[54]

While the move from Top Location continued throughout the 1940s and 1950s, the municipality nevertheless forged on with the development of Duncanville as a White residential and industrial township. The demolition of houses in Top Location had started even before the land was fully under municipal ownership with some 76 torn down by the end of 1946. As soon as the sale was finalised, the city began to sell plots of land skirting what still remained of Top Location. It laid in new water, sewer, and power lines for the White businesses between 1947 and 1951 as well as railway sidings connected to the Johannesburg rail line for the new industrial factories that began to spring up on the outskirts of Top Location, now called Duncanville. The American engineering firm, Babcock and Wilcox purchased 45 acres there in 1949 and began operations soon after. In 1952, Duncanville was officially proclaimed an "industrial township," and more large-scale factories producing steel products began to ring the outskirts of the old location. In the late 1950s, the city expanded the new White township even further, with Duncanville Extension 1 to the north to accommodate a new residential area, and Extension 2 to the south for even more factories (see Figure 2.8). When all the houses – and residents – had finally been removed from Top Location, an Afrikaans school was built over the northernmost areas of Top's residential space to serve the White families who had moved into Duncanville Extension 1. By 1959, only the houses in the "Asiatic Bazaar" remained with their residents awaiting the construction of an "Asians-only" township to accord with the apartheid separation of all racial groups. Within a decade, all would be gone (see Figure 2.9).

Leaving Vereeniging along the eastern road to Johannesburg, motorists pass the factories that sprang to life in Duncanville before and after the removal of Top Location. Those factories – African Cables, Scaw Metals, McKinnon Chain, and Union Steel (now ArcelorMittal), among others, are still in operation. The buildings still stand, although some businesses have come and gone in the past 90 years. And yet the core land of Top Location, where the houses sat, has been left empty. The site of some of the earliest human habitation in South Africa, as well as the soccer games, schools, boxing matches, homes, grocery stores, and churches of Top Location, is now entirely empty. Two new schools sit on the edges of the former neighbourhood, the Krugerlaan School and the Phoenix High School, and a museum built in 1992 sits approximately on the former site of the location superintendent's house. The lane that connects the museum to the R42 highway to Johannesburg runs along the area of the former "Asiatic Bazaar," which was removed in the 1960s. The museum, the Vaal Teknorama, houses exhibits detailing Vereeniging's history including its prehistory, its role in the South African War, and the Sharpeville Massacre, but not one word about Top Location. Even the old Top Location cemetery, at 69 Senator Rood near the M61, is unmarked and undeveloped, squeezed between some small shops and a Dutch Reformed church. Are the over 3,000 bodies that filled the cemetery to overflowing in 1938 still there today? There are no markers at the old Top Location that would let anyone know that over 13,000 people once lived there, and nothing to explain that these people were moved to Sharpeville where they became the first residents of that township.

46   A Company Town

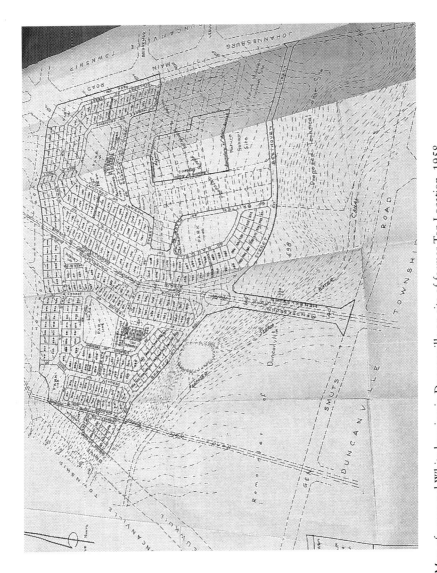

Figure 2.8 Map of proposed White housing in Duncanville on site of former Top Location, 1958. NTS 6523, 33/313 (T)(21), SAB. Source: National Archives and Records Service of South Africa. Photo by authors.

A Company Town 47

1969

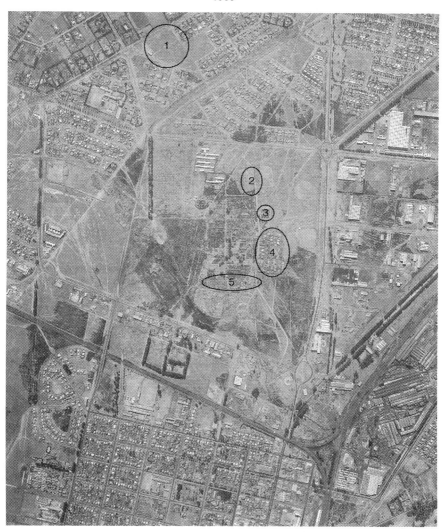

1. Cemetery (unmarked)
2. Hostels (demolished)
3. Superintendent's house (demolished)
4. Asiatic Bazaar (awaiting demolition)
5. Coloured Neighbourhood (demolished)

Figure 2.9 Aerial photograph of Top Location after all residents had been "removed" and their homes demolished, 1969.

Source: © Chief Directorate: NGI, Department of Agriculture, Land Reform & Rural Development, Republic of South Africa. Reproduced under Government Printer's Authorisation (Authorisation No. 11900) dated 6 June 2023.

The Women of Top Location

The day of the 1940 disturbance was a day like any other for these women. Emily Magkotse, who had been renting a room in Top Location for nine months, was returning from the nearby farm of a White owner where her family stayed while she worked in Vereeniging. When she got back to the location, she went to the public ablution blocks "to go and wash my body." She was later arrested and sent to jail for participating in the riot. Jemina Sapola, also a "lodger," had been in Top Location for ten months. She was also outside the location that day, "I was in Vereeniging town. I went to do washing that day. I did not find the missus there; I went to do washing for my sister. Two children accompanied me [her sister's children], I did not find the missus there and I went back to the location." When she was told by the superintendent to leave the location on suspicion of leading the riot, "I went home to pack my things. I took the things outside the location, I went to the Johannesburg road." She was later arrested and put in jail. Sophia Kodi had only been in Top Location for two weeks. On the day of the disturbance, "I was in town looking for work. I came back in the afternoon. I asked for work among houses on the North side of town [White residential area]." She was also arrested. And even Anostasia Thabanetu, a resident of Top Location for eight years who lived in one of the better houses built by the municipality, was not spared harassment by the police. Her house was searched for beer, and later she was taken to the superintendent's office where she "saw the Superintendent shooting with a revolver; he said he would show us how he shoots a native woman."[55] The police continued to abuse women in these raids. In 1942, a woman who police identified only as "Mamashiya" was arrested for being in possession of six gallons of beer. She was sent to jail to await trial, and later that same day, she gave birth to twins, one of whom died. In defence, the police claimed, "There is no evidence of neglect of this prisoner after her condition had become known," inferring that somehow, they had been unaware that a woman pregnant with twins was about to give birth. As a show of mercy, she was removed from the jail and sent to the hospital that evening; all charges were dropped.[56] It was on behalf of such women that Matlala Adelaide Frances Tshukudu, later to be known as Adelaide Tambo, fought against the police, saying, "I'm going to get these white boys. When I'm grown up, I am going to get them. It doesn't matter what it takes."[57]

Notes

1 Ramon Lewis Leigh, *Vereeniging, South Africa* (Johannesburg: Courier-Gazette, 1968), 21; Richard Mendelsohn, *Sammy Marks: 'The Uncrowned King of the Transvaal'* (Cape Town: David Philip, 1991), 55.
2 H. Breuil, C. van Riet Lowe, A.L. du Toit, *Early Man in the Vaal River Basin*, Archaeological Survey, Archaeological Series 6, (Pretoria: Union of South Africa, 1948).

3 Anthony Trollope, *South Africa, Volume II* (London: Chapman and Hall, 1878), 118.
4 William Worger, *South Africa's City of Diamonds: Mine Workers and Monopoly Capitalism in Kimberley, 1867–1895* (New Haven: Yale University Press, 1987), 28, 42.
5 Leigh, *Vereeniging*, 112–116.
6 Nancy L. Clark, *Manufacturing Apartheid: State Corporations in South Africa* (New Haven: Yale University Press, 1994), 150–163. In 1942, Iscor would establish its major steel plant next door in Vanderbijlpark, and in 1954, Sasol would locate its first oil from coal plant just south of Vereeniging in Sasolburg.
7 In 1903, the government-regulated Rand Water Board took control over water distribution from the Vaal River.
8 Leigh, *Vereeniging*, 73–75, 142.
9 Vereeniging Municipality, July 1942, "Annual Report of the Acting Medical Officer of Health for 1941–1942," Native Affairs Department (hereafter NTS) vol. 4178, file 33/313 IV, Central Government Archives Since 1910 (hereafter SAB).
10 Garth Benneyworth, "A Case Study of Four South African War (1899-1902) Black Concentration Camps," *New Contree* No. 84 (July 2020): 90.
11 Controlling Officer (Urban Areas), 20 November 1959, "Vereeniging: Application for Establishment of Duncanville Extension 2 Township," NTS vol. 6523, file 33/313(T)(21), SAB.
12 G.R. Sanders, 16 October 1937, Minutes of Evidence 387–397, Vereeniging Native Riots Commission, NTS vol. 7671, file 87/332, SAB.
13 Inspector of Urban Locations, 2 February 1937, "Report on Inspection at Vereeniging," NTS vol. 4178, file 33/313 III, SAB.
14 Ian Jeffrey, "Cultural Trends and Community Formation in a South African Township: Sharpeville, 1943–1985" (MA thesis, University of the Witwatersrand, 1991), 48–49.
15 Inspector of Urban Locations, 2 February 1937, "Report on Inspection at Vereeniging," NTS vol. 4178, file 33/313 III, SAB.
16 Their recordings can be found here: https://samap.ukzn.ac.za/taxonomy/term/7417/all.
17 Ian Jeffrey, "Life in the New Township: The Expression of Area Rivalry, 1943–1960," in "Cultural Trends and Community Formation," 68–121.
18 Philip Bonner, "'Desirable or Undesirable Basotho Women?' Liquor, Prostitution and the Migration of Basotho Women to the Rand, 1920–1945," in *Women and Gender in Southern Africa to 1945*, ed. Cherryl Walker (Cape Town: David Philip, 1990), 221–250.
19 Petrus Tom, *My Life Struggle* (Johannesburg: Ravan Press, 1991), 1–4.
20 "Isidumo Esibi E Vereeniging," *The Bantu World*, 25 September 1937.
21 Vereeniging Municipality, July 1942, "Annual Report of the Acting Medical Officer of Health for 1941–1942," NTS vol. 4178, file 33/313 IV, SAB.
22 D.B. Naude, 14 October 1937, "Vereeniging Native Riots Commission, Minutes of Evidence," 293, NTS vol. 7671, file 87/332, SAB.
23 J.L. Sharpe, 11 October 1937, "Vereeniging Native Riots Commission, Minutes of Evidence," 14, SAB.
24 D.B. Naude, 14 October 1937, "Vereeniging Native Riots Commission, Minutes of Evidence," 290, SAB.
25 Petrus Tom, *My Life Struggle*, 6.
26 "[Draft] Report of the Vereeniging Location Riots (1937) Commission: The Patrol Van," 26-29, NTS vol. 7671, file 87/332 II, SAB.
27 Elizabeth Pululu, 15 October 1937, "Minutes of Evidence, Vereeniging Native Riots Commission," 312, SAB.

28 "[Draft] Report of the Vereeniging Location Riots (1937) Commission: Disturbance on Saturday 18 September 1937," 60–61, SAB.
29 F.C. McMaster, 23 September 1937, "Vereeniging Municipal Location: Assault on Police," NTS vol. 7671, file 87/332 I, SAB.
30 "[Draft] Report of the Vereeniging Location Riots (1937) Commission: Disturbance on Sunday," 62–65, SAB.
31 Edward Roux, *Time Longer than Rope: A History of the Black Man's Struggle for Freedom in South Africa* (Madison: University of Wisconsin Press, 1967), 283.
32 Baruch Hirson, *Yours for the Union: Class and Community Struggles in South Africa* (Johannesburg: Witwatersrand University Press, 1990), 63–72; Roux, *Time Longer Than Rope*, 283–285.
33 Luli Callinicos, *Oliver Tambo: Beyond the Engeli Mountains* (Cape Town: David Philip, 2005), 201–202; David Beresford, "Adelaide Tambo: Heroine of South Africa's anti-apartheid struggle through the exile years," *The Guardian*, 1 February 2007.
34 "[Draft] Report of the Vereeniging Location Riots (1937) Commission: Control of the Location," 10, 13, SAB.
35 Town Clerk, Vereeniging to Secretary for Native Affairs, 19 January 1938, NTS vol. 7671, file 87/332 I, SAB.
36 Town Clerk, Vereeniging to Secretary for Native Affairs, 15 March 1941, NTS vol. 5391, file 33/331 (G) 3, SAB.
37 F.C. McMaster to Director of Native Labour, Johannesburg, 23 September 1937, NTS vol. 7671, file 87/332 I, SAB.
38 Testimony of Eric MacKenzie, 28 November 1940, *King vs. Paulina Sakoeni and others*, 1-3, NTS vol. 5391, file 33/331 (G) 3, SAB.
39 Testimony of Ben Pitsi, 13 December 1940, *King vs. Paulina Sakoeni and others*, 35–36, SAB.
40 Testimony of Herbert Davidson, 17 December 1940, *King vs. Paulina Sakoeni and others*, 46, SAB.
41 Testimony of Paulina Sakoani, Julia Debogo, and Anostasia Thabanetu, 24 December 1940, *King vs. Paulina Sakoeni and others*, 59–68.
42 G. Heaton Nicholls to Minister of Native Affairs, 6 October 1942, "Native Affairs Commission: Third Interim Report, Vereeniging Location," South African Police vol. 365, file 48/4/41, SAB.
43 E. Verster to Commissioner of South African Police, 19 March 1941, South African Police vol. 365, file 48/4/41, SAB.
44 Nicholls to Minister of Native Affairs, 6 October 1942, "Native Affairs Commission: Third Interim Report, Vereeniging Location," SAB.
45 J.L. Sharpe, 11 October 1937, "Minutes of Evidence, Vereeniging Native Riots Commission," 13, SAB.
46 "Report on Inspection of Proposed Site for New Native Location at Vereeniging," October 1938, NTS vol. 4178, file 33/313 III, SAB.
47 "Note of Interview with a Deputation from Vereeniging Consisting of Members of the Native Advisory Board," 3 September 1943, NTS vol. 5898, file 33/313(N) II, SAB.
48 J. Ramahlola to Secretary of Native Affairs, 16 June 1958, "Re-ejection of People from the Old Location Vereeniging to Their Original Homes," NTS vol. 4179, file 33/313(F) VI, SAB.
49 Ivan Evans, *Bureaucracy and Race: Native Administration in South Africa* (Berkeley: University of California Press, 1997), 31.
50 Synopsis Health Report for Vereeniging, 20 September 1946, NTS vol. 4179, file 33/313(F) V, SAB.

51 Michael Mokoteli to Secretary of Native Affairs, 8 September 1944, "My Ejection from Top Location," NTS vol. 4178, file 33/313 IV, SAB.
52 I.P. O'Driscoll to Director of Native Labour, 12 September 1947, "Complaint by Natives of the Old Location – Vereeniging," NTS vol. 4179, file 33/313(F) V, SAB.
53 I.P. O'Driscoll to Director of Native Labour, 5 November 1947, "Vereeniging Location," NTS vol. 4179, file 33/313(F) V, SAB.
54 Jan Mafisane statement, 4 February 1957, NTS vol. 6271, file 33/313(P) 5, SAB.
55 Testimony of Paulina Sakoani, Julia Debogo, and Anostasia Thabanetu, 24 December 1940, *King vs. Paulina Sakoeni and others*, 59–68, SAB.
56 Nicholls to Minister of Native Affairs, 6 October 1942, "Native Affairs Commission: Third Interim Report, Vereeniging Location," SAB.
57 Callinicos, *Oliver Tambo, Beyond the Engeli Mountains*, p. 200.

Bibliography

Callinicos, Luli. *Oliver Tambo: Beyond the Engeli Mountains*. Cape Town: David Philip, 2005.

Clark, Nancy L. *Manufacturing Apartheid: State Corporations in South Africa*. New Haven: Yale University Press, 1994.

Evans, Ivan. *Bureaucracy and Race: Native Administration in South Africa*. Berkeley: University of California Press, 1997.

Hirson, Baruch. *Yours for the Union: Class and Community Struggles in South Africa*. Johannesburg: Witwatersrand University Press, 1990.

Jeffrey, Ian. "Cultural Trends and Community Formation in a South African Township: Sharpeville, 1943–1985." MA dissertation, University of the Witwatersrand, 1991.

Kessler, Stowell. *The Black Concentration Camps of the Anglo-Boer War, 1899–1902*. Bloemfontein: War Museum of the Boer Republics, 2012.

Leigh, Ramon Lewis. *Vereeniging, South Africa*. Johannesburg: Courier-Gazette, 1968.

Mendelsohn, Richard. *Sammy Marks: 'The Uncrowned King of the Transvaal'*. Cape Town: David Philip, 1991.

Roux, Edward. *Time Longer than Rope: A History of the Black Man's Struggle for Freedom in South Africa*. Madison: University of Wisconsin Press, 1967.

Tom, Petrus. *My Life Struggle*. Johannesburg: Ravan Press, 1985.

Trollope, Anthony. *South Africa, Volume II*. London: Chapman and Hall, 1878.

Worger, William. *South Africa's City of Diamonds: Mine Workers and Monopoly Capitalism in Kimberley, 1867–1895*. New Haven: Yale University Press, 1987.

3 From Location to Township
Building Sharpeville

> A simple scheme of "town planning" should be applied to every new Native Village which should form a town planner's paradise, as they are among the rare instances of the deliberate construction of a new village as part of a concerted, centrally directed plan, with no initial mistakes to complicate matters.
> (Edgar Brookes)[1]

Sharpeville is the physical embodiment of its past, standing today as it did in March 1960 on the day of the massacre. The streets and the buildings have not changed and remain as they were laid out by apartheid engineers nearly 80 years ago. Today, they look run down and are in some cases abandoned; the place could be regarded as one more deteriorating town for the poor, a sad but not uncommon reality around the world. But these streets and buildings are also a guide to understanding the history of this place, the clear intentions of the apartheid planners, and the failure of those plans. Sharpeville was in fact held up as a "model" township which countless other South African townships would emulate. But while Sharpeville was meant to be a controlled and isolated town for Africans, the very layout and organisation of the township helped to create the circumstances that culminated in the police massacre of 1960. Intent on keeping control over the residents, and cutting costs in all areas, Sharpeville's planners trapped the inhabitants in a community with few amenities but one central police station. In this chapter, we will trace the physical development of Sharpeville and the goals and plans developed by the apartheid government, before examining in the next chapter how its residents created their own worlds within these boundaries.

Planning a Racialised Town

The creation of Sharpeville was the outcome of conceptions of racial identity that played a major role in the design of cities that still exist in South Africa, as well as in the rest of the post-colonial world. The inversion of Africans from insiders – belonging to the place – to outsiders who did not belong, was nowhere more apparent than in the cities which Whites assumed as their own territory. The South African government over several decades made clear

DOI: 10.4324/9781003257806-3

that Africans could only live in these cities if they served the White population, and although Africans could occupy the townships, they were never allowed to consider these places their own. Hendrik Verwoerd, minister of Native Affairs and later prime minister, succinctly defined this formulation in 1956 when he stated,

> The native residential areas, the locations, in the European cities and towns are not native territory. They are parts of the European area. ... The native residential area in the town is only a place where the European in his part of the country provides a temporary dwelling for those who require it of him because they work for him and thus earn their living in his service.[2]

Creating racially defined places, determining where, when, and even how Africans could occupy land, was not only a function of racial separation and domination; it also constituted a mechanism of constant coercion and control over an entire population. In this manner, it was much easier for officials to exert control over a geographically defined group than enforcing such control on scattered individuals. As early as 1905, one police chief in Durban explained his problems of controlling Africans who could live anywhere, saying, "How on earth can I take charge of Natives that are allowed to squat in every yard, hole and corner."[3] It would be much easier for him if they were all in one place. Thus, South African society was shaped along racial lines in concrete ways, through the built environment, as well as through legal mechanisms strictly enforced by the state.

Ordering the places in which Africans were required to live was serious business for the South African government, eager not only to separate but to control this population. There were towns like Top Location everywhere in South Africa that had grown organically through population increase and the continual alienation of African lands by Whites. The growth of mining and industrialisation, concentrated in cities like Vereeniging that had been established to serve industry, intensified the process and by 1942, 267 locations similar to Top Location were scattered throughout the country. The planning and building of Sharpeville was not an isolated phenomenon but was instead an instructive example of the type of urban arrangement designed in South Africa and in much of the post-colonial world. Furthermore, it is singularly important because for a short time, it came to embody the ideal South African township. Rather than being an outlier, in South Africa or the world, Sharpeville is literally a concrete example of the racially ordered city.

A familiar pattern developed in South Africa up to the 1940s whereby original haphazard locations such as Top Location were replaced by relatively small locations further out of town until much larger "townships" were built even further from the White areas in the 1950s. The cumulative effects of rural displacement – through the Natives Land Act, the expansion of White commercial farming, and intense industrialisation – led to the almost doubling of the African population in the towns in 15 years (1921–1936). The central government repeatedly enacted legislation to stem or even reverse the tide of African immigration to the cities, but employers welcomed a surplus of workers who were eager to take whatever wages they could get. The government issued what were called "model regulations" for the locations, beginning with the Natives (Urban Areas) Act in 1923, but the rules were little more than guidelines as to what municipalities were allowed to do such as erect buildings and hire employees, and enact restrictions on brewing beer and keeping livestock.

The locations were planned and built under the control of local municipalities, despite the efforts of local architects to design liveable environments. In the 1930s and into the 1940s, some South African architects looked abroad to find models for the country's growing towns, but there was an implicit understanding that even the thought of designing towns on a race-blind basis was dismissed out of hand; as one government engineer put it,

> In designing a township for Africans, it will be seen that no preconceived ideas, however well they have been employed in European townships, should be applied to non-European townships ... the low state of civilization of the African demands a different treatment.[4]

For example, the White suburbs next door to Sharpeville in Vanderbijlpark embodied the British architect Ebenezer Howard's concept of "Garden Cities" with self-contained neighbourhoods, parks, and green belts surrounding an urban commercial centre, while the town's African location, Bophelong, followed a different design, attempting to create a "traditional" African setting with houses grouped together in a "kraal" formation.[5] In 1937, a group of South African architecture students unsuccessfully proposed plans for a housing development for 20,000 Africans based on the concept of the "Radiant City" developed by the Swiss architect Le Corbusier, with a "simple and classical contrast between buildings and nature ... order and repose, besides its many material advantages, have a very positive effect on the human mind."[6] Instead, location planning would be guided by twin concerns over cost and control. The Garden Cities ideal was never really considered for Africans on both counts: the provision of services such as sewage was costly, and the layout of the roads would confound rapid security response. The Radiant City was also rejected on both counts, as multi-story buildings cost more and took longer to build than single-unit dwellings, and surveillance of individuals would be nearly impossible in interior hallways and staircases. Instead, municipal engineers would build the housing without regard to architectural standards. By 1943, one of the architects responsible for the Le Corbusier–inspired location design, Roy Kantorowich, lamented, "Sub-economic schemes [for African housing] are almost exclusively handled by municipal departments, not, as one would imagine under the control of the city architect (a non-existent personality) but under the city engineer!"[7]

The new locations would be built according to the most basic considerations of cost and convenience by White administrators.

Rather than acknowledge the natural expansion of communities and the development of South African society, African communities were instead separated and isolated from White South Africa. The "location strategy" to order African lives, always meant to separate Black from White, became more granular as the cities grew and by the 1950s, control was as important as separation.[8] Through complex rules and regulations that channelled behaviour through the built environment of the townships and the punitive consequences of transgression, the townships that emerged in South Africa in the 1950s were designed to imprint Africans into a controlled mould. Sharpeville was not only one of the earliest of these new townships; it became a sanctioned model for the rest of the country.

Sharpeville

In 1936, the Vereeniging Municipality identified a piece of land to the west of the city that was available for the town's new location. Since Vereeniging was a relatively small town that was still surrounded by open farmland, finding a suitable spot well away from White neighbourhoods did not seem to pose a problem, and a swampy patch of land 2½ miles outside of town was identified as a likely spot for what would be called Sharpeville Native Township. It was empty and served as an area for the run-off of water from the nearby farms, which emptied into a pan, or small lake. An existing farm road skirted the property, connecting it with the town to the east and the industrial area to the south on the banks of the Vaal where the Central Mine and the Vereeniging Brick and Tile factory were located, and which would allow workers from the location to walk to their jobs without entering Vereeniging. An uneven row of dwellings was scattered along a footpath rimming the lake, and other footpaths connected these dwellings with the town, the factories to the south, and farms to the north and west (see Figure 3.1). There were also natural barriers separating the intended location from the White town. The area to the east between this parcel and the town of Vereeniging had been used since 1931 as a run-off area for wastewater from the city, pumped there to run off onto the open fields. The new location would be surrounded by the Vaal River to the south, the sewage run-off area to the east, and open farmland to the north and west. The town councillors, all of whom worked for the important business interests in the town, were pleased that workers would be available but would be physically separated from the White town.

The initial design of Sharpeville's layout relied heavily on the topography and development of the space prior to its creation. The boundaries were fixed in 1937 along some pre-existing roads, paths, and property lines, no doubt for convenience but also to avoid the cost of building new roads. The northern boundary ran along a road connected to a new farming project, Roods Gardens, opened in 1932 for "poor working-class Whites."[9] The eastern

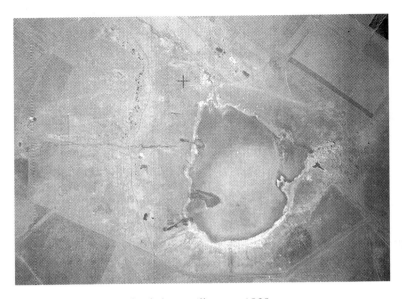

Figure 3.1 Aerial photograph of Sharpeville area, 1938.

Source: © Chief Directorate: National Geospatial Information (NGI), Department of Agriculture, Land Reform & Rural Development, Republic of South Africa. Reproduced under Government Printer's Authorisation (Authorisation No. 11900) dated 6 June 2023.

boundary was fixed on a path connecting the Roods road to Vereeniging. The existing group of dwellings that faced the lake formed the southern boundary. The western boundary was relatively open facing unrestricted access to open land (see Figure 3.2). What would become one of the township's main streets, Zwane Street, was the extension of a pre-existing country road connected to the Vaal River industrial area and Vereeniging. The other main road, Seeiso Street, was drawn in a straight line from the existing pathway to Vereeniging on the eastern end of the township to Zwane Street on the western end. The street names were also drawn from some idea of pre-existing communities gleaned from anthropologists in the Native Affairs Department, Seeiso being a Sotho surname, and Zwane an Nguni surname. None of the African residents of Vereeniging were consulted on any of these decisions regarding the township – its location, boundaries, or street names – so it is not likely they concurred or approved in any meaningful way.

Once these rudimentary boundaries and streets were laid out, the question became how to organise the neighbourhoods inside the township. The location of the two main streets (Seeiso and Zwane) and their point of intersection formed the basis of the distinctive grid pattern of streets and buildings which exists to the present, as well as the tilted orientation of the entire township lying in a southwest-northeast direction. With these two streets forming the axis of the development, subsidiary streets were laid out in

From Location to Township 57

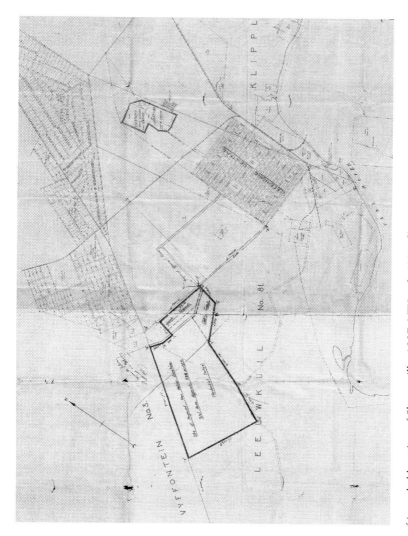

Figure 3.2 Map of intended location of Sharpeville, 1937. NTS vol. 5898, file 33/313N vol. I, SAB.
Source: National Archives and Records Service of South Africa.

perpendicular lines to the two main streets, intersecting the outer boundaries of the township at angles of approximately 25 degrees. This arrangement gives the entire layout the configuration of an arrow pointing to the southwest, culminating in the intersection of Seeiso and Zwane, the exact location of the 1960 massacre. The street layout of Sharpeville was based on these limitations and a belief that straight streets, as opposed to curved streets, were preferable for issues of cost – services such as rubbish collection and water reticulation would be cheaper on straight streets – and control through the easier routes for police vans.

The Model Township: Lowering the Cost of Housing

As one of the few housing projects undertaken during World War II, Sharpeville was later looked upon as a housing model for construction undertaken in the postwar period.[10] Unlike most other municipalities, Vereeniging had already secured funding from the government for African housing in 1941, before most government spending that was not war-related was halted. As a result, Vereeniging could therefore proceed with construction during the war, important as housing was critical for the influx of war workers into the area. All the existing engineering firms in Vereeniging, including Union Steel, African Cables, Dunswarts, and Stewarts and Lloyds, were called upon to meet the military's demand for war materiel and desperately needed these workers. In addition, the state-owned South African Iron and Steel Corporation (Iscor) began building a massive steel mill to the west of Vereeniging and created a new town, Vanderbijlpark, that hemmed Sharpeville in from the west and would eventually dwarf Vereeniging. In the meantime, workers brought in to build the Iscor plant were also creating pressure on local housing. The town could not eject these newcomers who were vital to local production. Instead, new housing was rushed into production.

Planning had been underway since the early 1940s to build Sharpeville's first houses. Initially, the municipality decided to make housing inside Sharpeville available to the Whites who were flooding the town looking for work, as well as the Coloureds who were being moved from Top Location. In 1942, plans were made to demarcate an area for White occupation on the easternmost edge of Sharpeville nearest to Vereeniging and the South African Railways (SAR) marshalling yard, on the assumption that White SAR employees would live there. Fifty houses were built by the Knap Construction Company – the same company responsible for building municipal housing in Top Location – "for letting, in the first instance, to European residents in the town; the dwellings eventually to be incorporated into the Native Location."[11] An area on the other end of Seeiso Street near the intersection with Zwane Street, was likewise set aside for the relatively small Coloured population that was among the first group being moved from Top Location. They had lived in a similarly separate neighbourhood in Top. And despite a reluctance to allow Africans to own their houses, as they had in Top Location, the town council agreed to set aside 416 plots for a "Native Village" adjacent to the Coloured area where Africans could construct their own houses under the supervision of the town engineer and lease the land.[12]

The town was eager to recoup as much money as possible on the project, in particular by increasing the density of housing. Each plot of land that was occupied by a rent-paying resident meant revenue for the municipality; any land that was used for schools, churches, parks, shops, clinics, creches, ablution blocks, and even the roads, did not accrue any revenue for the municipality but rather incurred costs in terms of initial outlay and maintenance. Even more important, the loans that allowed the municipalities to build the townships, provided through the National Housing and Planning Commission (NHPC), could only be used on housing. Funding for schools, clinics, community halls, and even road construction had to come from other sources, usually from revenue extracted from the township residents for rents, fees, and permits once their houses were completed and occupied, as well as the sale of municipal beer. The Vereeniging Town Council was adamant that no funds from general revenue accounts – those provided by White ratepayers and businesses – should be spent on the township. The size of the location had already been reduced in 1943 through the elimination of a large piece of land to the northeast that had been earlier demarcated for a sports field and an area to the south adjacent to the lake/dam that had originally been set aside for a "cattle camp," thereby reducing the amount of land available for either services or housing.[13] Thereafter, spaces for services were further reduced – replaced with rent-paying lots – due to a concern over the "capital costs of services"; the more houses built the lower the costs for the municipality (see Figure 3.3).

Services were at a minimum from the beginning. For the approximately 330 houses first completed in the location by 1943, the city provided only two ablution blocks for showering and laundry, 13 standpipes scattered throughout the area for water supply, and 338 individual "pails" for night soil removal. The council decided to provide only a "bucket" system for human waste disposal rather than an intended "pit" system due to concerns by the Rand Water Board that drainage from the pits would leak into the Vaal River, polluting the water supply to the city and beyond. The first group of residents removed from Top Location arrived in Sharpeville in 1943 to occupy the houses in the neighbourhood that came to be known as Putsoastene, or Putswao, a reference to the greyish colour of the roofs. Even by 1946 as Putsoastene expanded and nearly 5,000 people lived there, they were only provided with 1 additional ablution block (making 3), and a total of 70 water standpipes and 1,067 "pails" for disposal.[14]

As time passed, even the initial plans for minimal services were reduced. The township's earliest plans showed a cluster of services at the Seeiso Street entrance – shops, a community hall, a clinic, and a creche – as well as an administration building, a beer hall, and hostels for single male workers. These latter services were the only ones ever built. The clinic and the

60 *From Location to Township*

LEGEND			
description	reference	area in morgen	% of total area
RESIDENTIAL		273.04	39.37
ROAD RESERVES		139.05	20.04
OPEN SPACE			
• parks		56.75	8.18
• sports area		40.45	5.83
SCHOOLS			
• primary		23.49	3.40
• secondary		14.80	2.14
MUNICIPAL PUR.		16.20	2.34
HOSTELS		12.04	1.74
UNDETERMINED		7.74	1.12
BUSINESS		5.63	0.81
CHURCH SITES		7.61	1.09
BREWERY BEERHALL ETC.		2.93	0.42
ABLUTION BLOCKS		2.02	0.29
GOVERNMENT		1.30	0.18
CRECHE		0.52	0.07
POLYCLINIC		0.54	0.08
EXISTING CEMETERY		3.90	0.56
BUFFER STRIP		85.57	12.34
TOTAL AREA		693.58	100.00

Figure 3.3 Allocation of space in Sharpeville by area and percentages, 1969, detail, BAO vol. 9488, file 19/1718/1 Part III, SAB.

Source: National Archives and Records Service of South Africa.

community hall were eventually built at the intersection of Zwane and Seeiso – next to the police station – and the provision of shops was greatly reduced under pressure from commercial interests in Vereeniging to steer Sharpeville's residents into town to spend their money. Early plans also included three administrative offices to be located at intervals throughout the location in addition to the superintendent's office located immediately outside Sharpeville, one at the easternmost Seeiso Street entrance, one in the centre of the location at the intersection of Seeiso and Zwane, and another at the far western tip of the location for an assistant superintendent. The town council had determined, "The inadvisability of the grouping of public buildings, shops etc. at the entrance to the location in view of the distance to the farthest end of the location"[15] and thus planned to spread them out. Nevertheless, they changed their minds once the town determined that it would be more economical to concentrate all administrative offices in one location – at the Seeiso Street entrance – cutting down the costs of duplication across the township. When new neighbourhoods were planned in the westernmost area of the township in the late 1950s, they were well beyond the intersection of Seeiso and Zwane, as far as 3 mi away from the offices at the township entrance.[16] Density and the elimination of "duplication" of services were paramount cost-cutting strategies.

When the core neighbourhoods along Seeiso and Zwane had been established and there were over 10,000 residents in Sharpeville by 1948, little in the way of services were yet delivered. The aerial photograph from 1948 shows Putsoastene, Rooistene, and Vergenoeg (see Figure 3.4). A row of houses for Whites lines the northern angled border, the Coloured area is parallel to Seeiso Street near the intersection with Zwane Street and the superintendent's residence, administrative offices, and hostel quarters are at the Seeiso Street entrance to Sharpeville. One lone shop was opened near the

Figure 3.4 Aerial photograph showing Sharpeville's first neighbourhoods, 1948.
Source: © Chief Directorate: NGI, Department of Agriculture, Land Reform & Rural Development, Republic of South Africa. Reproduced under Government Printer's Authorisation (Authorisation No. 11900) dated 6 June 2023.

Seeiso-Zwane intersection that still stands today, as well as two schools along Seeiso (later known by residents as "School Square"). Sharpeville was a "model location," providing isolated, cheap housing and little else.

At the same time, the government was eager to find the cheapest way possible to build houses that would be needed in the postwar period throughout the country. Municipalities could only build the houses by obtaining huge loans from the government, creating a strain on the national budget. Eager to reduce the outlay for African housing planned for the postwar period, the NHPC responsible for approving the loans completed a study on the Minimum Standards of Housing Accommodation for Non-Europeans in 1949 as a guideline for all postwar municipal projects. The report argued both that these standards should be the very least that could be done and that they also were the maximum that would be financed: "A minimum standard had been laid down and ... would be the highest cost that would be allowed in respect of Native housing."[17] Soon after, the government's Council for Scientific and Industrial Research (CSIR) began to investigate "ways and means of reducing the costs of building urban Bantu houses which conform with accepted minimum standards of accommodation and which provide the minimum requirements for stability, weather resistance, durability and thermal sufficiency."[18] Standards at a minimum and even greater reduced costs were the guidelines for African housing.

Not surprisingly, Sharpeville emerged as the project that was used as the model adopted by the government for all other township dwellings in the country. An elaborate series of tests were conducted by the National Building Research Institute (NBRI), an arm of the CSIR, from 1952 to 1954 on the houses built in Sharpeville. Why Sharpeville? As noted in the report, "This particular scheme was chosen because it was reputed to be one of the lowest-cost Bantu housing schemes in the country."[19] In recognition of Vereeniging's accomplishment, the town engineer, P.E. Klarer, was even appointed to the investigative committee. The final hefty report, running nearly 300 pages with an additional appendix listing 22 specialised reports on each factor of Sharpeville's construction, included the study of ventilation, strength of walls, thermal conditions, foundation construction, use of bricks vs. blocks, and the use of White vs. African labour. It is worthwhile noting the central role played by the Sharpeville houses as described in the report:

> As a start to the investigation, and in order to obtain an idea of current costs of urban Bantu housing, the Sub-committee made arrangements for the detailed examination and analysis of one thousand houses constructed by the Vereeniging Municipality over the years 1947-1951. ... This led to the development of cost norms for urban Bantu housing, the cost norm for any centre in the Union being defined as the cost of building the NE 51/9 house. ... These cost norms have been arrived at by taking the labour (European artisans) and material requirements as measured at Vereeniging and calculating the costs of these in various

centres at the ruling rates for materials and labour as found in the particular centres concerned. The same percentage for overheads as measured at Vereeniging, is also assumed to apply in each centre. **This approach supposes that in the use of labour and materials, any local authority in the Union can achieve an efficiency at least equal to that obtaining at Vereeniging at the time the cost norm studies were made.**[20]

(Authors' bold)

The house design used in Sharpeville since 1946 was thus adopted as the now ubiquitous NE 51/9 model upon which all cost estimates and plans were used throughout the country[21] (see Figures 3.5 and 3.6). The plan had been approved by the chief research officer at the NBRI, D.M. Calderwood, over other African house plans used in Johannesburg, Pretoria, Port Elizabeth, Pietermaritzburg, and Boksburg and was officially adopted as a model in 1953. Calderwood found the Sharpeville plan "admirable," while the others were deemed either too large or lacking in some aspects of privacy, circulation between rooms, or even aesthetics. The Sharpeville model was one of the smallest two-bedroom models at 528 sq ft, comprising two bedrooms and a living room of approximately 100 sq ft each, a 91 sq ft kitchen, and a bathroom area of 46 sq ft There was no indoor plumbing, water supply, or electricity inside the house and no storage or porch areas outside the house. The eventual NE 51/9 model was expanded slightly to 580 sq ft with larger areas for the bedrooms and the living area. A number of other plans were produced for smaller and larger houses, their costs all likewise based on cost norms from the Sharpeville NE 51/9, which became the most common housing in South Africa.[22]

Vereeniging proved to be an ideal area for further experimentation in cost reductions. The town's earliest industries first established by Lewis and Marks had already given the town its greatest advantages in terms of building costs as many of the primary materials used in building, specifically bricks from the nearby Brick and Tile works, steel products from Union Steel, and local limestone were already available. The NBRI committee conducted more experiments at Sharpeville and found that costs could be cut even further by using corrugated iron roofs instead of cement asbestos roofs and by reducing the height of the houses by 6½ inches. The committee noted that although the use of the corrugated iron roofs decreased insulation in the houses – making them warmer in summer and colder in winter – the committee was not bothered since the resulting temperatures did not surpass the "thermal limits for health as distinct from the thermal limits for comfort."[23] Uncomfortable, but not unhealthy. But the biggest reduction in the overall costs of the houses was in the use of African labour. Vereeniging had a substantial industrial African workforce which had been used to build the nearby Iscor plant. By using "Native operators," under the supervision of White workers and by training the operators on the job, labour costs were reduced by as much as 47 percent.[24] This was especially effective when

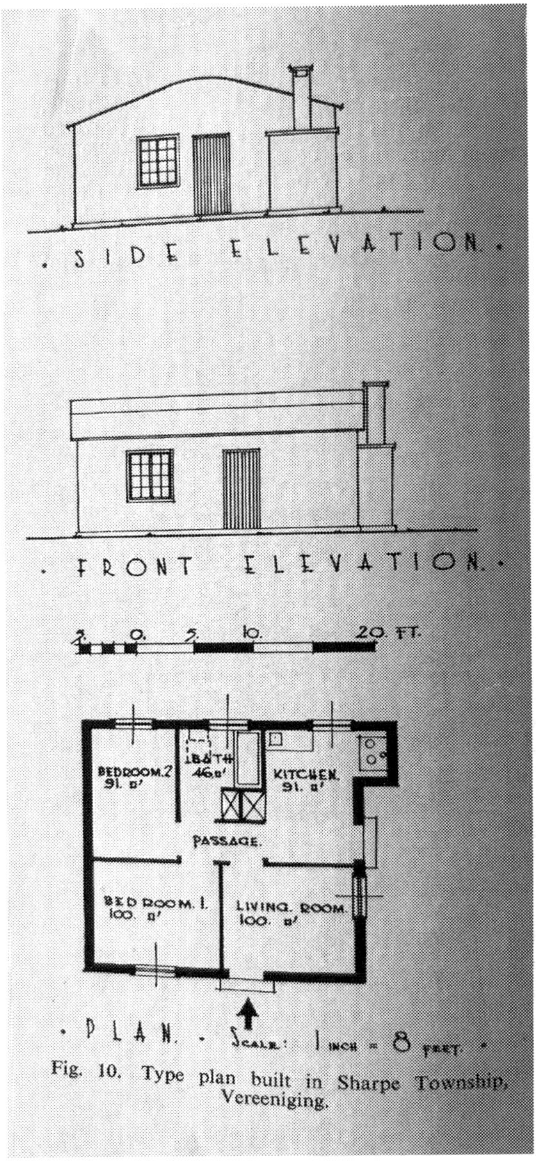

Figure 3.5 Design of Sharpeville House, 1946.

D. M. Calderwood, *Native Housing in South Africa* (Johannesburg: University of the Witwatersrand, 1955), 20.

constructing the houses with cement blocks rather than bricks, which required skilled bricklayers. Although the committee found that no single item used in the construction of the houses could, by itself, reduce costs, the use of African labour could affect reductions throughout the entire construction process.

From Location to Township 65

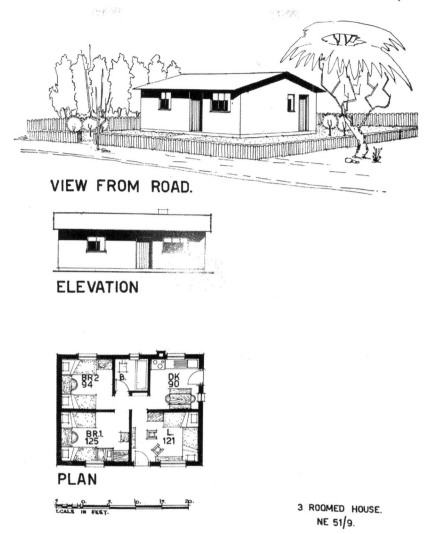

Figure 3.6 Design of NE 51/9, 1955.
D.M. Calderwood, *Native Housing in South Africa* (Johannesburg: University of the Witwatersrand, 1955), 31.

Vereeniging had cut costs to the minimum in Sharpeville, creating what the government believed would be a sustainable model for the rest of the country. Housing density was high, and construction costs were the lowest. But in the years to come, more radical notions of what constituted the model location would come about based less on costs than on control. Sharpeville would be caught in a situation where although it met every criterion for a model location, it was simply built in the wrong place at the wrong time.

The Apartheid Turn: Containing the Township

The presence of Africans in the cities was a major issue in the election of the National Party government in 1948. While the sitting government of the United Party was preoccupied with the costs of housing, it also saw room for African ownership of houses and property in the cities at the discretion of the White municipalities in recognition of varying views of segregation throughout the country. The rival National Party was unequivocal in its opposition to such measures, stating that Africans "will never be able to own real estate in the [urban] areas," and outspoken in its commitment to "preserve the white character of our cities."[25] When the new government took office in 1948, it proceeded to find ways to implement this ideal without further discussion or debate; apartheid was a given; all else was execution of the ideal. As Vereeniging's town engineer P. E. Klarer put the finishing touches on the last 1,000 experimental houses in Sharpeville in 1952, the new minister of Native Affairs, H. F. Verwoerd, took the floor in parliament to enunciate the government's guidelines for African locations going forward. While Sharpeville already embodied most of these requirements, Verwoerd's plans would spell the end for Sharpeville.

The focus of Verwoerd's concern was White security. His "conditions for the approval of location sites" centred on the means to entirely separate the African population from the Whites and therefore the locations must be an "adequate distance from the white township," and just to be safe, they should be separated from the Whites by an industrial area. In addition, there should be "buffer zones" on all sides of the location, with entirely vacant land that might also include barriers such as railroad tracks or power lines. While there should be easy transport into the White city, it should be by rail – segregated by race – rather than road, but if a road was necessary, it should pass through an industrial area where presumably Africans would work. The African township itself should be "a considerable distance from main, and more particularly national roads, the use of which as local transport routes should be discouraged." In other words, even the roads would be racially segregated with some for Whites and others for Africans. These stipulations concerning roads would lead to significant transportation costs for Africans and construction costs for municipalities required to build separate roads for Africans. Vereeniging itself eventually built two separate roads for Africans. Most importantly for Sharpeville, Verwoerd foresaw the consolidation of townships to prevent their proliferation among and between White properties: "Regional planning of racial areas is required," and he envisioned "mega" townships rather than the relatively smaller ones like Sharpeville. Verwoerd drew special attention to the southern area of the Transvaal where he owned a farm (see Figure 3.7), Stokkiedraai, on the banks of the Vaal River not far from Sharpeville, saying,

> I feel that in so far as the Southern Transvaal is concerned, the whole area from Vereeniging to the other side of Pretoria, and from Springs to a long way beyond Krugersdorp, should in this respect be planned as a single great area.[26]

From Location to Township 67

Figure 3.7 Photograph of Verwoerd at his farm, Stokkiedraai, on the Vaal River next to Vanderbijlpark.

December 1965. *Hendrik Frensch Verwoerd, Fotobiografie Pictorial Biography 1901–1966* (Pretoria: Voortrekkerspers, n.d.), 121.

Soon after making this statement, Verwoerd appointed a committee to do just that, to examine racial zoning in the southern Transvaal.

In the fall of 1952, the Witwatersrand Native Areas Planning Committee, known as the Mentz Committee after the chairman, F. E. Mentz, began its investigations into African residences in five regions of the southern Transvaal including Vereeniging. The question it faced was where to house the growing African population in Vereeniging and neighbouring Vanderbijlpark which together had a population of over 85,000 Africans. The Vereeniging Town Council had already decided to build another location 6 mi to the northeast of the town and had paid £100,000 for nearly 3,000 morgen, five times the size of Sharpeville. Council planning had accounted for all of Verwoerd's regulations with buffer zones and special roads but had not foreseen a new objection to what the committee termed "dispersed residential areas." Looking at the proposed location – Mafube – in the northeast of the region and the established freehold township of Evaton to the northwest, the Mentz Committee noted one of two unsatisfactory scenarios: either the White neighbourhoods in between the two would be surrounded by "Native areas," or the two townships would tend to grow towards each other and merge, forcing out White neighbourhoods and, worrying for strategic reasons, crossing the main rail line between Vereeniging and Johannesburg (see Figure 3.8). The government was especially concerned that African neighbourhoods did not surround any transportation routes – rail lines or roads – or the power stations or water lines (in the case of Vereeniging sending water and electricity to Johannesburg) for fear that such services could be disrupted through attacks by Africans. Instead, the committee decided that the future African residential area for the region would sit between the major transportation routes to Johannesburg – a rail line in the east and a provincial road on the west – and stretch from Evaton in the north to just south of Sharpeville as one large "mega" township surrounded by White areas. Although this plan included the added costs of constructing an 8-mile-long road that would link the proposed African township of Sebokeng to Vereeniging in order to prevent Africans from travelling on White roads, the government felt that preserving White areas and consolidating African housing was worth the cost.[27] The road would be called "Houtkop" road, an Afrikaans derogatory term for Africans.[28]

The existing townships were clearly in jeopardy. It was expected that Vanderbijlpark's location, Bophelong, be removed and the population relocated to the new township, Sebokeng, but at this point in 1954, it was still assumed that Sharpeville would remain and form the southernmost portion of the new township. Vereeniging was quickly granted the rights to extend Sharpeville to the southwest to the border with Vanderbijlpark in November 1952 in order to complete the southernmost part of the proposed African residential area. The area known as Extension 1 and locally as Vuka, added less than 200 acres, a fraction of what Vereeniging needed for housing. The parcel of land it had already bought to establish Mafube was now considered useless. However, a different government commission that met in 1952 to address the problem of housing for Coloureds and Indians, the Murray Commission, determined that each of these groups must be housed in their own, separate locations in order to meet the legal requirements of the Group Areas Act (1950) which stipulated separate residential areas for each racial group. To meet these requirements, Vereeniging would eventually revisit Mafube and divide it into two locations, Rust-ter-Vaal for Coloureds, and Roshnee for Indians. Coloureds would be removed from Sharpeville and Indians from what was left of Top Location, both in 1967 to these new neighbourhoods.

Although the town had been granted additional space in Sharpeville, it would now also need to meet the evolving regulations demanded by Verwoerd's government before construction of new housing could begin. The next five years would find the city scrambling to find a solution for Sharpeville. The first plan submitted by P. E. Klarer in 1951 in anticipation of building Extension 1, included an additional administrative centre on the westernmost side of the township; a rail line adjacent to the southern boundary,

From Location to Township 69

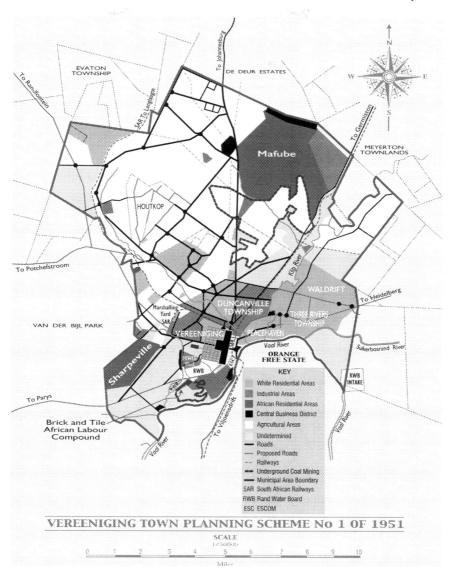

Figure 3.8 Map of Vereeniging Town Planning Scheme, 1951.

Proposed African township of Mafube (dark grey) to the northeast, Evaton to the northwest outside the municipal boundaries of Vereeniging, Sharpeville (dark grey) to the southwest. Municipality of Vereeniging, Town Engineer's Department, 24 October 1951, "Vereeniging Town Planning Scheme," NTS vol. 5899, file 33/313(N), SAB. Source: National Archives and Records Service of South Africa.

separating the township from the "national road" and cutting through the township; and a direct connection to the national road via Seeiso Street. This plan was rejected by the Native Affairs Department due to the limited boundary included between Sharpeville and the White areas of Vanderbijlpark, which consisted of a 50-foot-wide tree belt, the government at that time requiring a 200-yard buffer. When the map was redrawn in 1954 removing the township's development next to Vanderbijlpark, it was again rejected on the grounds that there was an inadequate buffer to the south next to the national road. Nevertheless, a new plan for the neighbourhoods in Extension 1 was finally accepted in 1957, including a 1,500-foot buffer zone next to the highway, no rail line, and a 600-foot buffer along the boundary with Vanderbijlpark. These would be the boundaries that would constrain any further development of Sharpeville to the present. The city also changed the number of access roads in and out of Sharpeville after having initially planned four roads leading out of the township and connecting with White areas. But Verwoerd required that there be "only one main access road through the nearest point to the town for the exclusive use of the location residents," meaning the extension of Seeiso Street at the easternmost point of the township would be the only way into or out of the township.[29]

There were even more fundamental changes embodied in the 1957 plans. Verwoerd also insisted that the neighbourhoods within Sharpeville be zoned for specific African ethnic groups (see Figure 3.9). Apartheid legislation had already stipulated that each racial group – Whites, Coloureds, Asians (Indian and Chinese), and Africans – live in its own "area," and he wanted to divide Africans even further into specific language groups (although, notably, he did not stipulate such a division between English and Afrikaans-speaking Whites or between Indians and Chinese who were lumped together as "Asians") for a number of reasons. In 1953, Verwoerd introduced the concept of "Bantu education," under which Africans received education in their "mother tongue," and dividing the township neighbourhoods accordingly would locate the residents near the relevant schools. Verwoerd also wanted to connect these urban neighbourhoods with the African "homelands" he designated in the rural areas and thus not only encourage separate identities among the African population but also introduce traditional leaders in the homelands as "authorities" over the urban population. In 1951, the government laid the groundwork for claiming that separate rural areas were the real "homelands" for Africans based on ethnicity – one for Zulu, one for Tswana, etc.[30] In 1959, the Promotion of Bantu Self-Government Act legislated this fiction, transferring all political rights for Africans to government-appointed "tribal" leaders in the "homelands" who would in turn appoint a "representative of the Territorial authority... [to] look after the interests of the Bantu people living in the urban area who belong to the particular national unit by which he was appointed." In a speech delivered to Africans in Vanderbijlpark at the end of 1959, Native Affairs Commissioner R. A. Bowen made clear the government's aim to reverse the "detribalisation" which Verwoerd abhorred:

From Location to Township 71

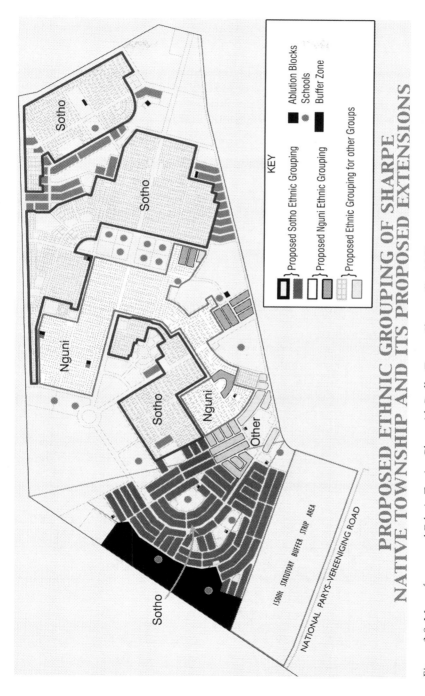

Figure 3.9 Map of proposed Ethnic Zoning Plan with Buffer Zones, Sharpeville, 1957.
Municipality of Vereeniging, Town Engineer's Department, "Proposed Ethnic Grouping of Sharpe Native Township and its Proposed Extensions," 2 August 1957, NTS vol. 5613, file 33/313 I, SAB. Source: National Archives and Records Service of South Africa.

"These areas are the recognized homelands of the Bantu people just as the remaining extent of South Africa is the homeland of the white people."[31] The fiction of considering Africans as outsiders and Whites as insiders was to be made a reality. In Sharpeville, this meant that the neighbourhoods were divided between Sotho-speaking and Nguni-speaking neighbourhoods, with a small space reserved for "other" groups. It is unclear how such divisions were made, or whether massive relocations took place, but the new town engineer, R. A. Fone, included the designations in the 1957 plan which was personally approved by Verwoerd.

Nevertheless, the long-term development of Sharpeville was in doubt. With the construction of the mega township at Sebokeng, Verwoerd still sought to consolidate all African housing into one location. That would mean eventually moving the inhabitants of Sharpeville to Sebokeng, just as Top Location had been destroyed and its inhabitants moved to Sharpeville. With his own farm, Stokkiedraai, close by on the Vaal River, Verwoerd wanted to eliminate both Sharpeville and Vanderbijlpark's township of Bophelong to make room for the further expansion of the growing nexus of government-owned and controlled industries in the area. In addition to the government steel corporation, Iscor, in Vanderbijlpark, and the state-owned Electricity Supply Corporation (Escom, now known as Eskom) power stations in Vereeniging, the government had also embarked on the establishment of the South African Coal, Oil, and Gas Corporation (Sasol), the oil-from-coal enterprise, on the opposite bank of the Vaal River where the new company town of Sasolberg would be constructed. The three communities – Vereeniging, Vanderbijlpark, and Sasolberg – would form a powerful state-owned industrial complex known as the Vaal Triangle.

Consequently, there was little incentive to fund more than the absolute minimum requirements in Sharpeville. Any new housing in the township would only be provided through a programme of "site and service" accommodation under which Africans were moved to a vacant lot in a township, given minimal shelter, and then required to build a house on the lot within five years (see Figure 3.10). Verwoerd used the programme to clear out makeshift communities – so-called squatter camps – where Africans erected their own shelters wherever they could throughout the country. Thus, the new housing erected in Extension 1 would all be constructed as a "site and service" neighbourhood, with approximately 9,000 Top residents moved there in 1959. This would be the end of housing construction in Sharpeville.

The Police Station

One of the last buildings constructed in Sharpeville, and perhaps the most consequential, was the police station. The city fathers had long desired to establish a police station inside the township rather than continuing to rely on police from the town of Vereeniging to provide control. They had not forgotten the incidents in Top Location in the 1930s, including the deaths of

Figure 3.10 Photograph of example of site and service construction in Daveyton, 1956.

Note self-made "shacks" where residents lived while constructing new houses. J. E. Mathewson, *The Establishment of an Urban Bantu Township* (Pretoria: J. L. van Schaik, 1957), Annexure L(4).

two White policemen at the hands of the residents. Since that time, Vereeniging's White officials had ceaselessly asked the South African Police (SAP) to establish a station inside the location – first at Top and then at Sharpeville. As early as 1941, following an incident involving the assistant superintendent and the women in Top Location, the town council asked the SAP to establish a post inside the location "to maintain proper discipline and control." While the SAP declined, not wanting to admit responsibility for control in Top Location, the deputy commissioner of the Transvaal Division also noted that "the lay-out does not make for efficient control."[32] Top Location had grown in increments with sections added in a piecemeal fashion and without major streets traversing the area. There was no central site or main roads that would have made patrolling the area effective. In this context, the SAP looked to the completion of the new location – Sharpeville – perhaps providing a better layout. While it would not be until 1959 that a police station was finally established inside Sharpeville, with disastrous effect, the town council insisted in 1942 that the location superintendent should at least establish a "hostel for the accommodation of native police" inside the township.[33] The superintendent's house was located just outside the Seeiso Street entrance to Sharpeville and his administrative offices and a hostel for single males employed in Vereeniging were immediately on the other side of the border, approximately 200–300 yd away from his house, a perfect location for housing the African constables. These policemen conducted raids inside Sharpeville under the supervision of the superintendent, looking for liquor, which Africans were not allowed to possess, as well as to check on overdue rent and permits to reside in the township.

In 1948, the new manager of non-European affairs in Vereeniging, I. P. Ferreira, took over control of the police and the raids, intent on the establishment of a bona fide police station inside the township. When he discovered in early 1952 that the SAP had started a programme of training African police and placing them in police stations inside some of the townships on the Rand, he was eager to include Vereeniging. The townships where this had been tried already had local police stations inside their boundaries that were being turned over to the SAP, which required that a station meet certain requirements, including prisoner cells and barracks for the police. Ferreira pleaded with the SAP to include Vereeniging, promising "that they [Vereeniging officials] would do all in their power to meet the requirements of the Police in this connection." He was especially interested in whether the prisoners could be held at the station or even be transferred to the Native Commissioner Courts, which handled those accused of pass offences – that is, lacking the documentation to prove they had a right to be in the township. These courts were notorious for immediately dispatching detainees to jails and work farms, creating an assembly line from arrest to incarceration. For Ferreira, the advantages of having the police station inside the township were twofold: there would be SAP available at any time to conduct raids in the township, and those arrested would be held in Sharpeville rather than transported into Vereeniging to be held in the municipal jail. Eager to separate Sharpeville's Africans from the jails and courts of White Vereeniging, Ferreira saw a chance to isolate his prisoners within the township.[34]

Still concerned about possible unrest in Sharpeville, the Vereeniging Town Council sought greater police powers within the township as the Campaign for the Defiance of Unjust Laws, known as the Defiance Campaign, gained steam in the southern Transvaal in 1952. The campaign was organised by a broad range of political groups representing Africans, Coloureds, Indians, and Whites, whose volunteers defied apartheid laws by using "Whites-only" amenities or areas, or travelling without their passbooks, the documents that controlled their movements. The campaign was peaceful, with volunteers singing, giving the "thumbs-up" sign, and shouting "Afrika" and "Mayibuye" (meaning "come back, Africa"), actions which would later be repeated in 1960. By the fall of 1952, some campaign organisers had entered Sharpeville to inform the residents about the campaign, without effect, but their presence alarmed the Vereeniging officials. In particular, the council was concerned that "Many undesirable natives, who could be classed as agitators, are resident in the Evaton Area [north of Sharpeville] and it is believed that they will attempt to hold meetings in Sharpe Native Township." The town council wanted the government to ban all meetings in Sharpeville, as had been done in Evaton and other areas throughout the country, in order to prevent "the incitement of natives." At this time, the local Native commissioner, I. P. O'Driscoll, who had served for years in this area, did not believe it was necessary to take action against the Sharpeville residents, noting that those who supported the campaign "form a relatively small percentage of the Native population of these locations."[35] In the end, no action was taken, and no disturbances occurred.

It should be noted that the council was especially concerned that "In view of the strategic position of Vereeniging as regards water, power and communications, it is essential to take all possible steps to prevent any disturbances or disruption of the essential works." Vereeniging – the company town – provided electrical power to the gold mines in Johannesburg via two Escom power stations, the Vaal Station, and the Klip Power Station which was the largest coal-powered station in the world at the time. Johannesburg also relied on water supplies from the Vaal River via the Rand Water Board pumping station located in Vereeniging. And the major rail lines connecting the mines with the coast ran through Vereeniging. Any disturbances in Vereeniging would indeed threaten the heart of South Africa's economy.

Whether the SAP finally recognised the strategic importance of Vereeniging or the government generally felt an increasing need to police the townships, in 1957, Vereeniging was finally granted the right to establish a police station inside Sharpeville. Approval took place at the same time that Verwoerd approved the plans for Extension 1 and the ethnic reorganisation of Sharpeville, and the size of the proposed police station, very small in relation to other stations, may have been a temporary measure. Nevertheless, it would be manned by Native police trained by the SAP and the Native Affairs Department stipulated that "no person other than a Native may ... reside on the site."[36] The city was required to erect the station, funded through loans provided by the Native Affairs Department and according to certain SAP standards, and then to lease the building to the Department of Public Works for use by the SAP. It was up to the city of Vereeniging to build and pay for the station. It would house both African police and African prisoners.

By this time, more townships were being built in the postwar period, reflecting different ideas about how to implement control – Verwoerd's preoccupation – over Africans. Three of the townships to the north in the industrial areas of the Rand – Lynville in Witbank, Kwa-Thema in Springs, and Daveyton in Benoni – were built in the early 1950s and each included the houses which were first tested in Sharpeville and priced according to the Sharpeville norm. All were surrounded by the same buffers – open land, streams, or railroads – that were required by the apartheid government. There was an even more striking similarity in their shapes, a sort of irregular triangle with two straight borders ending in a narrow juncture with a third either concave or convex curve. Since the borders were built around existing physical boundaries on site, it is difficult to attribute their shape entirely to a plan. Nevertheless, the shapes were similar to Sharpeville's boundaries. But what was different was the placement of the entry to the townships and the police station site. In the three newer townships, the main road entered the township not on one end as in Sharpeville, but straight into the middle of the concave/convex side where the community centre, including the police station, was located, very much in a central position in the township. And there were two roads, rather than one, in and out of the townships (see Figures 3.11 through 3.14). By moving the entry to a more central position, the new townships could consolidate administrative functions and effectively surveil the residents from a central location while providing easy access for official entry in case of an emergency.

The Sharpeville station was ultimately located in the centre of Sharpeville, along with the only clinic, creche, and community hall as well as most shops in the township, similar to the layouts in Daveyton, Kwa-Thema, and Lynville, but with one major difference. Rather than being positioned in both the centre and at the entrance to the township, the Sharpeville police station essentially sat at a dead end surrounded by residential neighbourhoods nearly 2 mi from the entrance. In order to follow the same plan as the other three townships, Zwane Street should have been extended to the south and made the entrance to Sharpeville as well as to the north to connect with Vanderbijlpark, but Verwoerd had stipulated that the roads used by Africans should not intersect with the national highway (to the south) and that the entrance to the townships should lie closest to the neighbouring White town, in this case, Vereeniging, making the Seeiso Street entrance the only choice. By the time the police station was erected in late 1959, the area at Zwane and Seeiso streets was one of the last areas developed in Sharpeville, having originally been reserved for a park in 1941 and later a school in 1943. When the township was expanded with the addition of Extension 1, the site suddenly became much more central to the entire location. Making the police station more central to the township would facilitate quicker responses for raids and arrests and the transport of prisoners to the jail there. But the location of the police station was also a problem for the police, surrounded by residential neighbourhoods with no easy exit. The town layout, originally drawn up 20 years earlier, was based on the existing topography of the land, with roads following old farm roads and skirting the drainage lake and now entirely unsuitable for the type of racialised control demanded under apartheid.

The expanded presence of the police nevertheless was intended not only to increase surveillance but also the residents' awareness of that surveillance. The station was built on Zwane Street, next to a small lane that led to Seeiso Street less than a block away. The township clinic was built on the opposite side of the lane, next to the community hall, and there was a block of shops nearby, a busy place for the residents (see Figure 3.15). The buses that carried residents to work in Vereeniging travelled along Seeiso to Zwane Street turning around again, passing near the police station, before heading back to the Seeiso Street exit. The station included cells for prisoners and a barracks for

From Location to Township 77

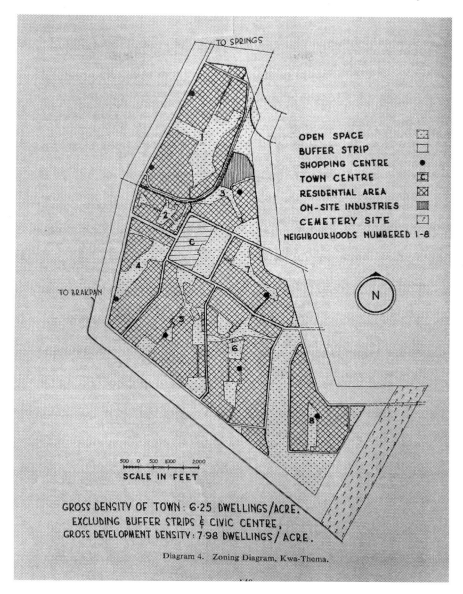

Figure 3.11 Diagram of street layout of Kwa-Thema Township, 1955.
Calderwood, *Native Housing in South Africa* (Johannesburg: University of the Witwatersrand, 1955), 148.

the single constables that were stationed there. Housing next to the station along Zwane Street was made available for the married officers, dubbed "Scotland Yard," by the residents. The station opened in October 1959 much to Ferreira's satisfaction.

78   From Location to Township

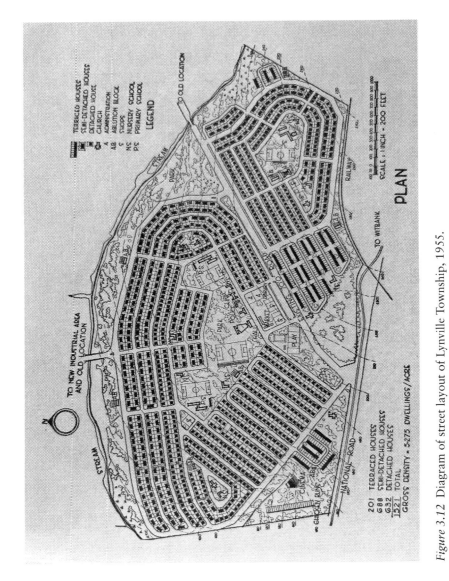

Figure 3.12 Diagram of street layout of Lynville Township, 1955.
Calderwood, *Native Housing in South Africa* (Johannesburg: University of the Witwatersrand, 1955), 121.

From Location to Township 79

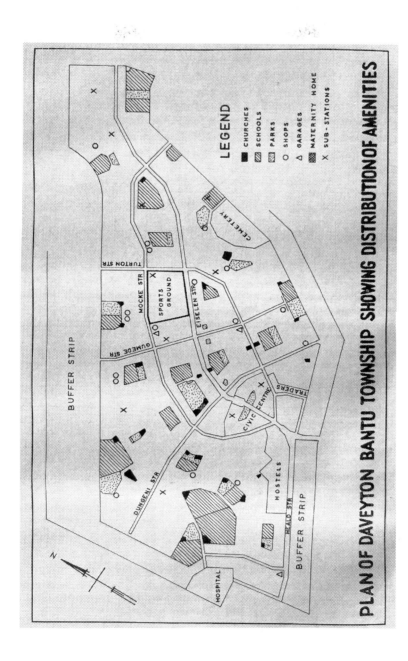

Figure 3.13 Diagram of street layout of Daveyton Township, 1957.
J. E. Mathewson, *The Establishment of an Urban Bantu Township* (Pretoria: J. L. van Schaik, 1957), Annexure G.

80 *From Location to Township*

Figure 3.14 Aerial photograph of Sharpeville, 1968.

Source: © Chief Directorate: NGI, Department of Agriculture, Land Reform & Rural Development, Republic of South Africa. Reproduced under Government Printer's Authorisation (Authorisation No. 11900) dated 6 June 2023.

Racialised Spaces

The organisation of these townships, Sharpeville included, was clearly based on concerns of cost but also of security. The French philosopher Michel Foucault has described how some of the techniques used in prisons can more generally spread throughout society and in towns, creating a "carceral" effect of ongoing surveillance. Foucault's concept is based on a 19th-century model of incarceration, the panopticon, in which prison cells were monitored from a central tower or vantage point from which the guards could easily see each cell and each inmate and record – and punish – misbehaviour. With its fences, police station, and identical arrangement of houses, Sharpeville's "inmates," so termed by the director of Native Affairs, lived in something like an extended jail. Residents were under constant surveillance and checked every day as they left the township for work and returned home at the end of the day, especially after a fence was erected around Sharpeville in 1958 to cut off unauthorised entrance to the township. Police raids of their homes – searching for illegal beer, demanding permits, tax receipts, and documentation – took place at any time, usually in the middle of the night, leaving the residents in a constant state of apprehension. The raids were facilitated not only by the

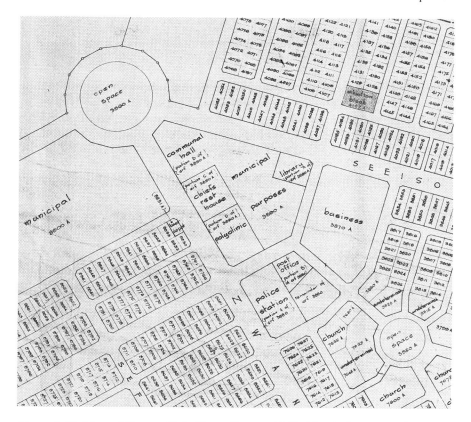

Figure 3.15 Map of Sharpeville's Town Centre, 1969 (identical to street layout in 1960), detail, BAO vol. 9488, file 19/1718/1, vol. III, SAB.
Source: National Archives and Records Service of South Africa.

ability of the police to reach all areas of the township quickly from the new centrally located station but also by the very layout of the streets – straight streets at straight angles – and the monotony of the NE 51/9 houses against which any unusual behaviour could be noticed. When speaking of the 19th-century prison system, Foucault argued that such circumstances "induce in the inmate a state of conscious and permanent visibility that assures the automatic functioning of power."[37] In other words, the fear that one was being watched or could be apprehended at any time produced the compliant behaviour demanded by the police. Indeed, this was certainly the intention of the apartheid government that Verwoerd – now prime minister – wanted to use to not only apprehend lawbreakers but to prevent their entry and residence in what he deemed to be the White areas of South Africa. Africans would be made aware, every minute of the day, that the cities belonged to

Whites. As the South African sociologist Ivan Evans notes, "[C]oercion in the urban areas was always constant but not always direct."[38]

Today when you visit Sharpeville, the layout of the buildings remains the same, although their uses have changed. The first buildings you see are what remains of the original administrative offices where police were first housed, next to what appear to be row houses, originally the location hostels for single male workers. An abandoned four-story building across the street from the hostels was the municipal brewery and what appears to be a lake is in fact the drainage pool for the area. There is a new police station located behind one of the schools along Seeiso Street, much closer to the entrance to the township, but the old police station, the site of the massacre, is now repurposed as a community development centre. Otherwise, most of the township remains as it was in 1960 although the homes – including the original site and service dwellings – are now owned by the inhabitants who have modernised, expanded, and otherwise improved the original NE 51/9 structures in most cases. But the "buffer" zones between Sharpeville and neighbouring Vanderbijlpark – now consisting of cemeteries – still maintain distance, and the municipal sewage treatment plant built in 1956 separates Vereeniging from the township on the eastern border. Although there is now an extension of Zwane Street to the national road, it also connects to a closer, parallel road built earlier for Africans to take into Vereeniging rather than travel on the national road. Most amenities remain outside the narrow boundaries of Sharpeville, especially a large shopping centre located midway between the township and the national road. The most notable structure in the township today is at the intersection of Seeiso and Zwane, the Sharpeville Memorial, housing an exhibition recounting the town's history next to an open space marking the 69 officially recognised victims of the massacre (see Figure 3.16).

Figure 3.16 Sharpeville Memorial with families of victims, 21 March 2018. Photo by authors.

Sharpeville remains physically circumscribed by its apartheid past but filled with emotional meaning for its inhabitants.

Moving to Sharpeville

In 1959, Petrus Tom, who was born in Top Location in 1935 and had lived there his whole life, was moved to Sharpeville with his family. They were sent to the site and service area of Sharpeville known as Vukazenzele, meaning "get up and do it yourself." Houses in Top Location were removed row by row so that

> we knew which day we were going to be removed to Sharpeville. Each household was given a number. ... We had lunch at twelve o-clock and then found that all our belongings were no longer there. They'd already moved them to Sharpeville. We'd got a number in Sharpeville but we didn't know Sharpeville very well. ... In Sharpeville we didn't know where to look for our number. I asked some people who gave me directions. We spent one or two hours looking for our new home. The next day one still got lost because one was not used to the place. It took us about two weeks to learn how to get home, where to get off the bus and where to board the bus to town. We did not use buses in Top Location. We used bicycles or simply walked because Top Location was next to the factories.[39]

Notes

1 Edgar H. Brookes, "Some Municipal Problems," *Race Relations*, vol. 1, No. 2 (1934): 14.
2 A. N. Pelzer (ed.), *Verwoerd Speaks: Speeches 1948–1966* (Johannesburg: APB Publishers, 1966), 128.
3 Jennifer Robinson, *The Power of Apartheid: State, Power, and Space in South African Cities* (Oxford: Butterworth-Heinemann, 1996), 43.
4 A. J. Cutten, 25 May 1948, "The Planning of Native Townships and Locations," South African Institute of Race Relations Collection, Historical Papers Research Archive AD1715, University of the Witwatersrand.
5 Ebenezer Howard, *Garden Cities of Tomorrow* (Boston: MIT Press, 1965); Vanderbijlpark Estate Company, 12 December 1952, "Layout Plan of Native Location," Native Affairs Department (hereafter NTS) vol. 6150, Central Government Archives Since 1910 (hereafter SAB).
6 LeCorbusier, *The City of To-morrow and its Planning* (New York: Dover Publications, 1987); F. J. Wepener, "Part II: Psychological Approach," in P. H. Connell, C. Irvine-Smith, K. Jonas, R. Kantorowich, and F. J. Wepener, *Native Housing: A Collective Thesis* (Johannesburg: Witwatersrand University Press, 1939), 85.
7 R. Kantorowich, "The Architect in Society," *South African Architectural Record* (October 1943): 256.
8 "The location was to remain central to state urban policy for much of the twentieth century," Robinson, *The Power of Apartheid*, 56.

84 *From Location to Township*

9   Ramon Lewis Leigh, *Vereeniging, South Africa* (Johannesburg: Courier-Gazette, 1968), 87.
10 Sharpeville was the first of several townships with similar layouts and construction that were completed in the 1950s before the inauguration of the megatownships, including Lynville, Kwa-Thema, and Daveyton. All were deemed "model" townships, a designation routinely used for those townships or locations that followed the "model regulations" outlined by the government. See Figures 3.11–3.14.
11 "Special European Housing Scheme," *Vereeniging Recorder*, 2 December 1942.
12 P. E. Klarer, 1946, "Notes on Sharpe Native Village Scheme," NTS vol. 5898, file 33/313(N)II, SAB.
13 See layout plans, 1943, NTS vol. 5898, file 33/313(N)II; 1957, NTS vol. 5613, file 33/313 I; 1969, Bantu Affairs Department (BAO) vol. 9488, file 19//1718/1, III, SAB.
14 Association of Administrators of Non-European Affairs, 26 January 1951, "Minutes of Meeting," NTS vol. 4651, file 120/313(15), SAB.
15 Town Clerk Vereeniging, 7 December 1944, "Notes of the Proceedings of a Meeting between Representatives of the Council and the Native Affairs Department," NTS vol. 5898, file 33/313(N)II, SAB.
16 F. Rodseth, 19 July 1952, "Zoning of Urban Native Areas," NTS vol. 4533, file 633/313 III, SAB.
17 Association of Administrators of Non-European Affairs, 26 January 1951, "Minutes of Meeting," NTS vol. 4651, file 120/313(15), SAB.
18 National Building Research Institute, *Research Studies on the Costs of Urban Bantu Housing* (Pretoria: South African. Council for Scientific and Industrial Research, 1954), 1.
19 Ibid., 127.
20 Ibid., 21.
21 Meaning: Non-European 1951 plan 9 of at least 27.
22 D. M. Calderwood, *Native Housing in South Africa* (Cape Town: Cape Times, Ltd., 1953), 20.
23 "Report of the Sub-committee on the Technical Elements in Urban Bantu Houses," in National Building Research Institute, *Research Studies on the Costs of Urban Bantu Housing*, 104.
24 A. L. Glen, "Time Studies of Labour Employed on the Building of Urban Bantu Houses Using Native Building Workers on an Operative Basis," *NBRI Bulletin*, no. 12: 26.
25 In Afrikaans: "hulle nooit in die gebiede vaste eiendomme sal kan besit nie"and "Die Party will die blanke karakter van ons stede bewaar," *Verslag van die Kleurvraagstuk-Kommissie van die Herenigde Party*, 1948.
26 H. F. Verwoerd, 30 May 1952, "Policy of the Minister of Native Affairs," in *Verwoerd Speaks: Speeches 1948–1966*, ed. A.N. Pelzer, 42–43.
27 F. E. Mentz, 22 December 1952, *Verslag van die Komitee aangestel om die vraagstuk van woongebiede vir naturelle in die omgewing van die Witwatersrand en Vereeniging te ondersoek. Part V: Vereeniging Gebied*, NTS vol. 5899, file 33/313(N)I, SAB.
28 *Houtkop* in Afrikaans: wooden head. The road also bordered the site of Top Location. White residents of Vereeniging later claimed that the term instead meant "hilltop."
29 See layout plans for 1951, 1954, and 1957 in NTS vol. 5613, file 33/313 I, SAB.
30 The Bantu Authorities Act, No. 68 of 1951. The Promotion of Bantu Self-Government Act, No. 46 of 1959, later established eight "national Bantu units"

under a system of tribal authorities with "ambassadors" assigned to urban areas of South Africa.
31 R. A. Bowen, "Self-Government for the Bantu: A Talk Delivered to the Urban Bantu inhabitants of the urban locations of Vanderbijlpark, Meyerton and Vereeniging: October, November 1959," NTS vol. 4179 file 33/313(F)VI, SAB. The Director of Non-European Affairs for Vereeniging, I. P. Ferreira refused to allow Bowen to address the residents of Sharpeville in October 1959 on the grounds that there was no precedent for such action.
32 E. Verster to Commissioner of the South African Police, 19 March 1941, "Vereeniging Native Location," South African Police, vol. 365, file 48/4/41, SAB.
33 Town Council of Vereeniging, 30 November 1942, "Extract of Minutes of the Ordinary Monthly Meeting," NTS vol. 5898, file 33/331(N)I, SAB.
34 "Extract from Minutes of Meeting of Association of Administrators of Non-European Affairs, 21 February 1952," South African Police vol. 365, file 48/4/41, SAB.
35 Acting Town Clerk, Vereeniging, 19 December 1952, "Control of Meetings, Gatherings or Assemblies and Prohibition of Incitement of Natives in Certain Areas," NTS vol. 4179, file 33/313(F) VI, SAB.
36 Secretary for Native Affairs, 13 December 1957, "Vereeniging: Sharpe Naturelledorp: Voorgenome Newe Polisiestasie," NTS vol. 5899, file 33/313 (N) II, SAB.
37 Michel Foucault, *Discipline and Punish: The Birth of the Prison* (New York: Vintage Books, 1977), 201.
38 Evans, *Bureaucracy and Race*, p. 121.
39 Petrus Tom, *My Life Struggle*, 22–23.

Bibliography

Calderwood, D.M. *Native Housing in South Africa*. Cape Town: Cape Times, 1955.

Foucault, Michel. *Discipline and Punish: The Birth of the Prison*. New York: Vintage Press, 1977.

Howard, Ebenezer. *Garden Cities of Tomorrow*. Boston: MIT Press, 1965.

Le Corbusier. *The City of To-morrow and Its Planning*. New York: Dover Publications, 1987.

Mathewson, J.E. *The Establishment of an Urban Bantu Township*. Pretoria: J.L. van Schaik, 1957.

Pelzer, A.N. (ed). *Verwoerd Speaks: Speeches 1948–1966*. Johannesburg: APB Publishers, 1966.

Robinson, Jennifer. *The Power of Apartheid: State, Power and Space in South African Cities*. Oxford: Butterworth-Heinemann, 1996.

4 Life in Sharpeville

> We still enjoy our lives, celebrations, and traditional events gathered with our families and friends. We still enjoy life.
>
> (Maggie Malema)[1]

Verwoerd intended the townships to separate and isolate Africans, denying them an urban identity other than as workers with only precarious rights in the cities. He especially reviled those who in his words were "detribalised" and who had lost touch with their "own" rural communities while in the White cities, resulting in their "degeneration."[2] He did not want Africans seeing themselves as South Africans – but instead as Sotho, Zulu, Xhosa, etc. – nor believing they belonged anywhere other than in the "homelands" he created. But those Africans in the urban areas were instead expanding and elaborating their own cultures within the cities, despite all official efforts to stop such development. The design of the townships and an increasing number of restrictive laws were ultimately futile attempts to stop a process which was centuries old as Africans continued to exist in the spaces now claimed by Whites and to adapt their cultures to their new lives. They were, as Maggie Malema says, enjoying their lives. And as the South African writer Jacob Dlamini has argued in his own memoir recounting growing up in Katlehong, a township approximately 30 mi north of Sharpeville, "What does it mean to say that black life under apartheid was not all doom and gloom and that there was a lot of which black South Africans could be, and indeed were proud?"[3]

One way that the people of Sharpeville responded to Verwoerd's efforts to control their lives, as embodied in the "panoptican" like design of Sharpeville, was to engage in the "surreptitious creativities" which as Michel de Certeau, a critic of Foucault's explained, "elude discipline without being outside the field in which it is exercised."[4] In other words, if the government had a strategy to impose control through laws, surveillance, and even the physical layout of the town, then Africans developed tactics to create their own freedoms without putting themselves in jeopardy. In a physical sense, residents could evade the lines drawn for them on the plans and maps that laid out Sharpeville; they could enter and leave the township as they pleased as is obvious in Figure 4.1. We can observe the ways in which Sharpeville's residents

DOI: 10.4324/9781003257806-4

Life in Sharpeville 87

Figure 4.1 Aerial photograph of Sharpeville, 1952.
Source: © Chief Directorate: National Geospatial Information (NGI), Department of Agriculture, Land Reform & Rural Development, Republic of South Africa. Reproduced under Government Printer's Authorisation (Authorisation No. 11900) dated 6 June 2023.

physically forged their own paths through the township and outside of it eschewing the buffers and fencing designed to limit their movements. Instead of focusing on the neat grids of blocks and roads, we can see the myriad footpaths through the neighbourhoods and those leaving Sharpeville to connect with other roads and carry residents to the outside world. In the same way, they could evade restrictions and quietly engage in activities that were not entirely illegal but gave them some freedoms. More importantly, they could also engage in those activities and institutions deemed "White," or European, and make them their own. This was most worrisome for Verwoerd, as such an African urban culture represented the permanent "detribalisation" that he so feared and that would eventually lead Sharpeville's residents to active protest.

Strategies of Control

One of the most basic ways in which the municipality tried to control the new township was to pick and choose who would be allowed to live there. Although it was always argued by the town council that the new township was necessary in order to re-house the residents of Top Location, it also became clear that not all who lost their homes would be allowed to live in Sharpeville. One requirement that would disqualify a considerable number of Top Location residents was employment at one of the town's valued firms, such as Stewarts and Lloyds, African Cables, South African Farm Implements (Safim), Brick and Tile, and Union Steel. Another preference implemented by the location superintendent was to allow "as far as possible only married couples with families shall be removed [to Sharpeville]." And also that "natives occupying houses in the new location shall be strictly prohibited from keeping lodgers," that is, those who rented rooms from the standholder. As the houses were built, Location Superintendent Michiel Andries Labuschagne would personally select those who would be moved from Top, key to populating the area with "desirable" tenants.[5]

The town council, as well as Verwoerd's government, was adamant that Africans should be strictly prohibited from any claim to ownership of land or homes in the White cities, and that the municipality would be the only landlord in the township. Africans would live in the houses that were built by the municipality and would pay rent to that body without any rights to ownership or even residence; they would be turned into tenants of the state overnight. The Top residents wanted at least to be allowed to use the materials from their homes in Top to construct new dwellings in Sharpeville so that they would owe rent only on the lot and not on the home. The municipality firmly opposed this path, fearing that "if they allowed the people to erect their own dwellings in the new location the new municipal houses [that accrued rent] would be left vacant."[6] The municipality also feared that homeowners would build extra rooms so that they could rent them out to lodgers, a situation that had developed at Top Location. Officials had trouble keeping track of the lodgers and also opposed homeowners earning income other than from the town's White businesses. Nevertheless, the municipality was ultimately forced to relent on these restrictions. In 1948, lodgers were admitted in response to a housing crisis when even Vereeniging's most valued workers could not find housing. By 1959, there were 2,281 lodgers in Sharpeville out of a total population of 30,974. Likewise, the town eventually allowed a restricted number of residents to build their own homes. The municipality was also forced to offer some compensation for the houses in Top Location as they were destroyed. By 1947, the municipality had paid nearly 200 families for the demolition of their homes in amounts from £132 down to £9, the amounts agreed to by Manager of Non-European Affairs I. P. Ferreira in consultation with valuators selected by the residents and the town council. By 1959, when the removals were completed, 619 lots had been designated for owner-built houses out of the total 3,561 houses in Sharpeville, but fewer than 100 had been built.[7] That area became known as the "Stands," primarily because it stood vacant for so many years without any houses or semblance to what the government called a "Native Village."

In addition to the physical ordering of the location, apartheid laws were also instituted to further control the residents, providing a clue as to African social behaviour. Laws in any country reflect ongoing activities that are deemed unacceptable by the government; in other words, they reflect real behaviours, perhaps uncommon, that are judged dangerous or undesirable by the sovereign state. It is therefore instructive to consider some apartheid laws in this light, as revealing not only state ideology but also African activity. For example, the Bantu Education Act, which decreed that the state would provide a curriculum for Africans that was different from that of Whites and that was suited to their "place in society," was enacted as the first generation of highly educated Africans – including Nelson Mandela, Robert Sobukwe, and others – began to challenge the government. Freedom of speech was also increasingly restricted as these leaders spoke out.[8] In the same sense, most laws enacted in the 1950s were aimed at identifying and separating all races, revealing not only a virulent racism but also implying that the races were beginning to comingle.[9] And a number of laws began to limit African rights to live in urban areas, as the African urban population outnumbered urban Whites for the first time in the 1950s.[10] The local Vereeniging administration also revised their previously somewhat lax location regulations in 1956, trying to "tighten" control over the growing community. The new regulations included a flurry of restrictions: every visitor required a permit; "foreign" Africans, meaning those from Lesotho, were no longer granted residential permits; residents could be ejected from the location if they were unemployed, working outside of Vereeniging, or gone for one month; widows no longer had a guarantee to keep their homes if there was no adult employed male in the house; and location officials could enter any house at any time to search for liquor or to check permits without a warrant.[11] Vereeniging officials were especially concerned to project to the growing business community a reputation for peace and stability in the location. These new regulations reflected official worries that Sharpeville's residents were enjoying what officials believed were too many rights of residence and privacy.

African Lives[12]

Sharpeville's residents were moved into the new houses as they were built, with groups of people who may have been from various areas in Top Location suddenly thrown together as neighbours. As the residents moved into the available houses, they created community identities by giving a name to each tract of houses the administration otherwise intended to be nameless, identical, and anonymous. The first groups were those who had settled their claims for compensation for their homes in Top and some who may have been eager to move. According to Petrus Tom, who was in one of the last groups to move in 1959, "It was not a forced removal at first. In Top Location they were jumping from place to place taking only those people who wanted to move."[13] Thus the residents of Sharpeville were made up of disparate groups held together only by the timing of their move, but they nevertheless quickly formed new neighbourhoods.

Four clearly identified neighbourhoods had been completed by 1952 despite the slow pace of building during the war. Their names were initially meant by the residents to help them find their new homes; as Petrus Tom noted, the new residents were each given only a number for their new home; the streets were not even named. Identifying areas by neighbourhoods eased the search process but also created community identities. The first, Putsoastene, was closest to the entrance to the township and lined Seeiso Street for 12 blocks, ending at the area set aside for schools. The name came about as a description of the initial grey slate roofs on the houses (*putsoa*: grey in Sesotho; *stene*: stone in Afrikaans). For at least four years, Putsoastene stood as the only neighbourhood in the location with approximately 850 houses but with few amenities. The second neighbourhood, Rooistene, was similarly named for the colour of the bricks on the houses (*rooi*: red, and *stene*: stone, both in Afrikaans) and continued the development of the housing along Seeiso Street, adding approximately 1,100 houses by 1948. In that year, Vergenoeg ("far enough" in Afrikaans) was also completed, stretching along the southern side of Zwane Street, and by 1952, the fourth neighbourhood Phelindaba ("finish the story" in Zulu) bordering the northeastern boundary of the location (see Figure 4.1). By this time, there were over 3,000 houses in Sharpeville with over 20,000 residents. Housing construction would pause at this point, with the remaining neighbourhoods finished later: Stands in the area north of Rooistene (the owner-built houses), Phomolong (resting in Sesotho) north of Putsoastene, and Vukazenzele ("get up and do it yourself" in isiXhosa) the site and service neighbourhood south of Vergenoeg.

These residents were well established and industrious, and by municipal design, almost universally employed; they were not the "temporary" migrant workers who came into the cities on limited contracts, leaving their families behind in the rural areas. The people of Sharpeville found multiple ways to make a living, feed and educate their families, and build a life. They worked in a variety of occupations, many at the local factories, others at White businesses in Vereeniging, and some at businesses inside Sharpeville itself. There were also a significant number who ran their own businesses, independent of White employers. Some sold coal or milk in the neighbourhood. Some were transport drivers with horses and carts or started their own taxi businesses. And most of the women took on the only work they could find, cleaning homes and washing the laundry for Vereeniging's White families or brewing African beer to sell in the township. In this manner, the people of Sharpeville showed their endless creativity not only to survive but to succeed in apartheid South Africa.

The most independent Sharpeville residents started their own businesses, catering to the needs of the vast population in the township. Some were coal merchants, like the Tsolos, Mofokengs, and Ntesos, or sold milk like the

Life in Sharpeville 91

Tshabalalas. There were others like Ramadiro John Thipe who worked as a plumber in the township, repairing the zinc tubs used for washing and bathing and making tin pots used for cooking. The Thipes were one of the first families to move to Sharpeville into the first neighbourhood, Putsoastene, and their house #917 faced directly onto Seeiso Street, where his daughter Maria still lived in 2019. She was born in Top Location in 1936 and was 9 years old when they moved to Sharpeville in 1945. The Thipes had four children, two girls and two boys. John Thipe made approximately R25 per month, and his wife earned another R12 per month doing "domestic work" in a White home in nearby Vereeniging. Another family, the Masilos (see Figure 4.2), worked together as an extended family with two brothers running a taxi service and a third working as a panel beater. The family had lived in Top Location since 1924 and moved to Sharpeville in 1947 after receiving £20 in compensation for their house in Top Location. Eventually, the three brothers and their families spread out with the two taxi drivers Simon in Putsoastene and Ezekiel on Seeiso Street in Rooistene, while the panel beater, John, lived in Phomolong where the residents had been allowed to build their own houses. Ezekiel's wife Constance also worked as a teacher, earning R27.66 per month in addition to her husband's earnings of approximately R20 per month. Their cousins, the Sepengs also moved from Top in 1946 after receiving £31.9 for their house and settled in Vergenoeg near the area known as Church Square. Daniel Sepeng worked at the Metro Bioscope in Vereeniging while his brother John worked at African Cables. Relying on family cooperation and with some savings from their properties in Top Location, these families were able to achieve a certain amount of independence and success.

Figure 4.2 Passbook photograph of Mohauli Solomon Masilo.
Courtesy of the Masilo family. Photo by authors.

92 *Life in Sharpeville*

Others, like Daniel Sepeng, worked at the small businesses in Sharpeville and Vereeniging that served the town's growing population. Sampson Mathinye, a father of five, worked at the Vaal Meat Supply making R6.75 per week while his wife, Eva, earned R5 per month doing laundry for a White family in Vereeniging. They were married in the Methodist Church in 1945 when Sampson was living in Evaton and Eva lived on Houtkop farm north of Vereeniging. Soon after they wed, they moved to 8603 Sharpeville in Vergenoeg where their daughter Paulina still lives. The Lesito family, with seven children, was supported by the father Monedalibe William who worked at Broderick Engineering Works while his oldest son, Mohauli Solomon, worked at Broderick Motors, one of the first Volkswagen dealerships in Africa (see Figure 4.3). And there were also residents who worked at the only mortuary in Vereeniging, Bosman and Son, which offered racially segregated "separate and identical facilities" for Africans with a staff of three Africans to serve the "bereaved."[14] Elias Molotsi worked at the funeral home in Vereeniging while Azael Kutoane was one of the three Africans employed to write policies and collect monthly premiums for the burial society from Sharpeville's policy holders. Many of Sharpeville's residents held a variety of jobs at Vereeniging's small businesses – Vaal Paint, Lubner Furnishings, the Vereeniging Steam Bakery, Roet's Dry Cleaners, Wolmarans Butchery, Fair Wear Stores, etc. – regularly travelling into the town to provide basic services for the community.

Still others worked directly for the Vereeniging Municipality in positions which sometimes put them at odds with their neighbours. Petrus Nthoasane

Figure 4.3 Passbook photograph of Monedalibe William Lesito.
Courtesy of the Lesito family. Photo by authors.

worked at the Sharpeville Beer Hall, located directly across Seiso Street from the superintendent's office and the adjacent workers' hostel. New location regulations promulgated in 1956 stipulated that municipalities had the sole right to brew beer, drawing deep resentment from Sharpeville residents. The beer hall produced beer that provided a significant amount of revenue for the Sharpeville administration and was also intended to supplant the "home-brew" that the government had outlawed and which formed the object of most of the hated police raids in the township. There were also a number of residents who worked as policemen stationed in Vereeniging prior to the erection of the Sharpeville police station in October 1959. Known to the other residents as "blackjacks," and referred to by the administration as "Non-European" or "Native" police, they were usually the ones sent on the nighttime raids and were themselves often mistreated by the White police (see Figure 4.4). Samuel Moathlhodi worked for the Vereeniging police and supported his wife, child, and his father who was a pensioner. When he was dismissed by the police, he moved to Standerton where he obtained another

Figure 4.4 Class photograph of African police trainees, 1961.
Courtesy of the Ralebakeng family. Sello Ralebakeng, the father of Santutu J. Ralebakeng (top-left corner of the class photo), died in police custody after the massacre. Santutu Ralebakang was later forced out of the police force because his peers learned of his father's death being related to the Sharpeville massacre. Photo by authors.

job as a policeman but returned to Sharpeville where his family still lived. Despite his status, he was one of the victims of the police massacre 21 March 1960, when he was shot dead. Similarly, relatives of other Sharpeville police including the Ralebakengs and the Mbeles were killed that day, while their police relatives were forced to identify their bodies.

But other government workers had a more positive experience. Elizabeth Setlhatlole and her family moved from Top Location in 1946 after receiving £83 for her house, an unusually large amount. She worked at the Vereeniging general post office beginning in 1949 just before becoming widowed in 1950. Although she never remarried, Elizabeth was able to keep the house in her name and raise her two children, Jacob and Willemina. She lived two doors down from Zwane Street in Vergenoeg, directly across the street from the police station. Even more fortunate were the Musibis, who were both teachers, with Lechael beginning in 1943 at the Moeli Higher Primary School where he earned R70 per month and his wife at a private school where she made R20 per month. They lived in the old Putsoastene neighbourhood near the school square where they raised six children. The Setlhatloles and Musibis – along with the taxi-driving Masilos – were some of the township's more successful families.

Otherwise, most of Sharpeville's residents worked at Vereeniging's well-known industrial factories that proliferated near vacant Top Location – Stewarts and Lloyds, African Cables, Union Steel, Safim – and at Vereeniging Brick and Tile, adjacent to the new location. These were the firms that had, in essence, created the "company town" of Vereeniging and which had the highest demand for workers. They needed stable workers who were trained to operate the machinery that manufactured equipment for the mining industry, the railways, and especially after World War II for the proliferating engineering firms in the Pretoria-Witwatersrand-Vereeniging (PWV) area. As production techniques had changed during the war, there was a greater demand for what were termed "operatives" who ran the machines in a repetitive process rather than the skilled craftsmen who had worked in the pre-war factories. Although the African workers in Sharpeville were still labelled "general labourers" by law with relatively low pay compared to the White craftsmen, many of their jobs were in fact semi-skilled positions requiring significant training and for which employers desired stability.[15] Sharpeville had been created to provide just such workers, stable family men (African women were not allowed to work in the factories) who were reliable and had some education.

Some of Sharpeville's workers were lucky enough to work at factories that were near the new township, close to the Vaal River to the south. Joel Raboroko worked at the nearby Union Steel Vaal works, a little over 3 mi from Sharpeville but easily accessible on his bicycle, as he said, "I take, as all the others, the gravel road past the lake to the location [on the way home]." In other words, workers travelling to work near the river or accessing Vereeniging from the south were evading the "official" entry and exit point on Seeiso Street next to the administrator's offices. Likewise, many of Sharpeville's residents worked even closer to the township at the Brick and Tile factory, which was directly south of the township less than half the distance to the Union Steel plant. Hophny Morobe, a young man married but without children, was earning R46 per month at Brick and Tile, a relatively high salary. An ambitious man, he also enrolled in a correspondence beekeeping class with the Institute of Beekeeping in London, obviously hoping to increase his income and gain some financial independence. He and his wife had moved to the site and service section of Sharpeville where he had relatives nearby, and like Joel Raboroko, he regularly travelled to work on his bicycle. Not only was it more convenient to travel by bicycle but also cheaper since they could avoid paying bus fares.

And some of Sharpeville's residents were those who travelled the nearly 5 mi back to their old neighbourhood near Top Location to work at the growing number of plants in surrounding areas of Peacehaven and Duncanville. Some employees, like Emmanuel Fantisi who had four children at home in Sharpeville, rode their bicycles the entire way to their workplace at Safim. Others, like Piet Seeri, were not so lucky living with his brother in Sharpeville while his wife and children remained nearly 30 mi away in Fochville, unable to find enough housing for the entire family. And some workers were forced to live in Sharpeville's hostel for the same reason, such as Ephraim Thaba, whose wife and five children remained in the northern part of the country, in Pietersburg, over 200 mi away. He worked at African Cables, one of the oldest and largest plants in Vereeniging, producing electrical cables for power transmission from the Electricity Supply Commission (Escom, now known as Eskom) stations in Vereeniging – one of which was the largest coal-fuelled power station in the world at the time. Most of these workers travelled by bus to work, adding to the costs of moving away from the centrally located Top Location.

These were the people who made Sharpeville their new home and who fashioned a community in their neighbourhoods and the township. Despite all attempts by the government, they could still claim the city as their home.

Community

Other than claiming their neighbourhoods and providing a living for their families, Sharpeville's residents also participated in and created the normal activities associated with any community. There were schools and churches, sports for the growing youth population, music and dancing, as well as the youth gangs that would later worry Vereeniging's officials. Throughout the 1950s, Sharpeville's population grew, and those residents increasingly developed a culture that further tied them to urban life.

One of their most important priorities, other than housing and jobs, was education for their children. Unfortunately, the first schools in Sharpeville were slow in coming. They were initially clustered in a central location on either side of Seeiso Street, approximately 13 blocks from the entrance to the township. Dubbed "School Square," the first school built there was the Matsie Steyn Lower Primary School. Others came at an especially slow rate, with most children continuing to attend schools in Top Location and elsewhere until those in Sharpeville were completed. Some instruction even took place in private homes as recalled by Joseph Mabena, "In Sharpeville there were no schools at that time. School used to be in houses. We didn't have schools, we didn't have lights, anything."

But this did not discourage Sharpeville's parents from educating their children. Mabena was sent to Soweto for schooling: "I did not go to school here, I went to Orlando High to further my studies."[16] Likewise, Gilbert Dimo sent his oldest son to school in Pretoria, while Maggie Malema remembers attending a mission school in Alexandra just as Adelaide Tambo did. The first proper schools built in Sharpeville were affiliated with some of the major church denominations, with the Matsie Steyn Lower Primary School run by the Dutch Reformed Church, Moeli Higher Primary School run by the Methodist Church, Boitso Higher Primary School run by the Anglican Church, and Stewart Higher Primary School run by the Presbyterian Church. Martha Lepee still fondly recalls attending Matsie Steyn when the children were entertained – rather than frightened – by marching drills put on by the local police at the school, compared with more austere treatment later. By 1956, there were approximately 3,000 children attending five schools in Sharpeville – three higher primary, two lower primary – with another 1,300 students still travelling back to Top Location to attend school there. In particular, the only high school available to Africans in Sharpeville, the Lekoa Shandu, was still located in Top, making it more difficult for Sharpeville youth to continue their education. By 1959 there were only 307 pupils enrolled in Lekoa Shandu out of a population of nearly 15,000 youth (under 18) in Sharpeville.[17]

Some of the churches that offered schooling found that option increasingly difficult. Clustered around "Church Square" near the intersection of Seeiso and Zwane streets, many were mission-oriented organisations that had historically operated African schools. The Paris Evangelical Mission, Lutheran Berlin Mission, and the South African Baptist Missionary Society all opened churches in Sharpeville, but with the passage of the Bantu Education Act in 1953, their efforts at education were discouraged in favour of government-run schools. Government subsidies for the mission schools were withdrawn, making it nearly impossible for them to operate, and over the course of the 1950s, most throughout the country were forced to close down unless they agreed "to provide education to conform with the Departmental syllabus in respect of all subjects with the exception of Religious instruction."[18] Instead, government schools would emerge to teach Africans in their "mother tongue" at the lower levels, seeking to entrench notions of ethnic identity between African groups while at the same time severely limiting proficiency in English or Afrikaans, necessary for academic success at the higher levels. To make matters worse, all schools were required to adhere to government-designed curricula, which differed on the basis of race with Africans limited to learning only those skills that corresponded to their place in society; that is, as manual labourers. Some of the major church denominations, especially the Catholic Church, were able to continue their schools without the government subsidy, as did the Dutch Reformed Church, but they were required to stick to the government curriculum.

Nevertheless, by 1959, there were 18 churches operating in Sharpeville. As the educational mission of many of the larger churches faded, other churches more closely identified with Africans emerged, including some wholly independent from the major denominations. Both the Ethiopian Church and the African Methodist Episcopal Church came to Sharpeville by 1956 and still operate there, as do some specifically African offshoots of the major denominations, the African Methodist Church, African Catholic, Presbyterian Church of Africa, and the (now) Uniting Reformed Churches in Southern Africa, a combination of the racially separated sections of the Dutch Reformed Church for Africans and Coloureds. The pastor of the Presbyterian Church of Africa, the Reverend Maja, played a critical role on 21 March 1960, helping to transport the wounded to the hospital. The pastor of the African Methodist Church, E. E. Mahabane, was the brother of Z. R. Mahabane who was the former president of the African National Congress. E. E. Mahabane also played a major role in the relief efforts following the 1960 massacre and later became president of the South African Institute of Race Relations, one of the most important nonpolitical anti-apartheid organisations in the country. Catering more to the spiritual and social needs of Sharpeville residents rather than their educational training, the churches began to represent a more African religious orientation than the original mission churches. Clearly, Africans were adapting western institutions to their own needs.

Sharpeville's residents also created a social community in their new neighbourhoods and leisure activities, outside of the rigours of work, became popular. Not surprisingly, Putsoastene and Rooistene were the first to import some activities from their Top neighbourhoods, in particular boxing and soccer. Both sports had been well established in Top Location, especially the soccer teams which were affiliated with the schools. When George Thabe moved to Putsoastene in 1946, he quickly formed the Young Rangers club there which was soon followed by the Mighty Blues. Likewise, another club, the Transvaal Jumpers which was founded in Top Location in 1933 and trained at the Methodist School there moved in 1959 when their founder, Sam Ngwenya, moved to Sharpeville. He based the club in the new Vukazenzele neighbourhood. Sharpeville soon had over a dozen teams based in the different neighbourhoods – Naughty Boys (Phelindaba), Basutoland Stars (Phomolong), Dangerous Lions (Putsoastene), among others – playing against each other as well as other teams in the Transvaal province. Thabe eventually became chairman of the Vaal Triangle Community Council and president of the South African National Football Association, with the

Sharpeville stadium named after him. In the 1960s, some of the best players in Sharpeville joined to form the Vaal Professionals, a nationally recognised team.[19]

The early soccer clubs also spawned an interest in boxing, which would add to Sharpeville's fame. In the early years, many of the soccer players joined one of Sharpeville's two boxing clubs, primarily to keep in shape. The Central Boys' Club had been established in Top Location in 1946 and was allowed to use a room in the municipal offices there for training, and when they moved to Sharpeville in 1954, they used facilities in the hostel and drew from neighbourhoods on the eastern side of the township, Putsoastene as well as nearby Phelindaba and Phomolong. The rival club, Ferreira Boxing Club, was formed in 1955 by residents in the neighbourhoods on the western side of the township, Rooistene and Vergenoeg, and used the communal hall, next to the library and clinic, for training. They named the club after Vereeniging's director of Non-European Affairs, I. P. Ferreira, in order to curry favour with him so that he would allow them to train in the hall. Both clubs included boxers and football players, but boxing quickly became Sharpeville's most popular sport.[20]

By 1956, the fame of Sharpeville's boxers began to spread with the sportswriter for *Drum* magazine, J. Arthur Maimane proclaiming it "Boom Town" for boxing. "Vereeniging's gymnasiums are crowded. The local boys have got the professional boxing bug. They all want to be fighters."[21] John Mtimkulu was the first Sharpeville boxer to gain national attention, winning the Flyweight title in 1955 and later the Bantamweight championship in 1961. He was born in Top Location in 1939 and moved to Phelindaba in 1952, joining the Central Boys' Club. His early victory helped to interest more young men in boxing, as evidenced by Maimane's declaration of Sharpeville as "Boom Town," and soon another local boxer, Sexton Mabena, earned the national Bantamweight title in 1956. Dubbed "Wonder Boy" by the press, he was described as "this 18-year-old high school student, who has had only four professional fights to date, [is] in the maestro class."[22] Indeed, Mabena would later go on to win the Featherweight class in 1959, and the Lightweight class in 1961. He was so successful that he was sent overseas to fight five matches in England, three of which he won, against fighters from Scotland, England, Nigeria, and Jamaica. Since his titles in South Africa – as with all African fighters – were restricted to a "non-European" category, his success against the British fighters meant a great deal. And his trip came at a time of great tension in the township – he was gone from October 1959 until April 1960 – placing him in London on 21 March, 1960. For a time in the 1950s and 1960s, Sharpeville became a major centre of the African boxing world in South Africa.

But life in Sharpeville did not revolve solely around a male-oriented sports culture. The Sharpetown Swingsters, whose members moved from Top Location to Sharpeville in 1953, played at local events including weddings and parties, and were successful enough to record over 20 records with Columbia Records in the 1950s. They also played at the local shebeens – the informal and illegal "clubs" in the township that served alcohol – such as

Sidwell's Place in Putsoastene. A more formal type of entertainment was offered by the Vereeniging Ballroom Dance Club, which taught members the waltz and foxtrot at Sharpeville's Community Hall, while the Vereeniging Non-European Social and Cultural Club arranged fashion shows and beauty contests there. In 1958, a graduate of St. Cyprian's Anglican school in Sharpeville, Betty Mkgome, was crowned Miss Vereeniging (non-European), also at the Community Hall. Movies were shown there, usually a good selection of American films, including westerns, musicals, and noir gangster films. Influenced by the films, some of the young men began to dress like their stars, "We used to watch films at the communal hall, film [stars] like Richard Widmark and John Dillinger, Ricky Nelson. You name them, there were so many ... therefore we had to buy [clothes] from America." They would engage in fashion contests of their own, with jazz records as the prize.[23] Some of these youth gangs had originated in Top Location such as the Indians who were based in Putsoastene; others were established after the move including the Berlins, Meadowlands, and Cocktails who later vied for positions in the hall while watching films. Although accused of being gangsters by the municipal officials, or *tsotsis* in South African parlance, the anthropologist Ian Jeffrey concluded that at this stage in the 1950s, the different "gangs" competed with each other in sports and dress and sometimes fought one another, but that it was only after 1960 that more criminally oriented "robbery" and prison-based gangs emerged.[24] In this earlier period, Sharpeville remained a primarily working-class community.

During the 1950s, Sharpeville grew into a cohesive community which organised itself into different neighbourhoods and developed a new urban culture. Although much if not most of this culture was western-oriented with education, religion, sports, dress, films, and music based on European and American forms, it was significant that these were made into uniquely African cultural expressions. Taking music as one example, as the ethnomusicologist David B. Coplan explains, South African music from the earliest days of European settlement, infused choral, religious, minstrel, vaudeville, and later jazz and currently hip-hop music with uniquely African forms.[25] Sharpeville was no exception. More importantly, these expressions eluded and confounded the apartheid goal to keep Africans from becoming "detribalised," one of Verwoerd's great fears. While apartheid sought to cement African identities in the "homelands," declaring urban areas in particular as owned by Whites, the residents of Sharpeville were claiming the town as their own community. As such, Sharpeville's culture embodied the "surreptitious creativities" that undermined the strategies of apartheid without endangering the residents.

"My Life Struggle": Worker Activism[26]

The arena in which Africans most directly challenged the inequities and strictures of segregation and apartheid was the workplace. While most of

Sharpeville's earliest residents enjoyed a moderate livelihood, they were not hesitant to organise and protest against their working conditions. Unequal pay, dangerous working conditions, long hours, etc., were the order of the day. Although limited by legal prohibitions against African unions and strike activities, they still found ways to organise, craft effective actions and articulate their demands. They were the backbone of Vereeniging's industries, an increasingly important area of strategic value which included three state-owned corporations – the Electricity Supply Commission (Escom), the South African Iron and Steel Corporation (Iscor), and the South African Coal, Oil and Gas Corporation (Sasol) – as well as the source of the water pumped from the Vaal River to Johannesburg by the Rand Water Board. As such, authorities were nervous about any protests that could put production at risk. Nevertheless, Vereeniging's workers also realised some leverage in this situation, especially the workers in Sharpeville who had skills that were not easily replaced. Worker activism in Sharpeville would eventually demonstrate the effectiveness of unified protests in the political realm as well.

The area had historically experienced worker activism by miners at the nearby coal mines, who in 1939 went so far as to desert the Springfield Colliery and with 600 workers march to Johannesburg to protest their working conditions. Most of these workers were contract migrants from Mozambique, but more skilled local workers who operated the drills and jackhammers also joined in this strike, and another in 1945 when a fellow miner was assaulted by a White overseer and later died. More representative of Sharpeville's workers were those who worked at the local industrial factories – Brick and Tile, Stewarts and Lloyds, Union Steel, African Cables, and the power stations at two locations owned by Escom. In 1944, more than 2,000 members of the African Gas and Power Workers' Union went out on strike at the Vereeniging power stations as well as at the Escom stations adjacent to the gold mines on the Rand. This huge strike imperilled gold production on the Rand during wartime and the government sent in troops to man the power stations and quickly put down the strike.[27] But the next year, another African union – the Transvaal Brick and Tile African Workers Union – called on its members in Vereeniging, Johannesburg, and Pretoria to go out on strike over low wages. In this case, the Brick and Tile workers living in Sharpeville formed a powerful force in the strike but again to no avail.

In 1946, a confluence of workers from several firms in Vereeniging went out on strike, nearly shutting down all industrial production in the town. The action began when timber workers at the nearby Vereeniging Estates Maccauvlei forest went out on strike for six weeks before being beaten up by the local police and replaced with scab workers. Next, over 2,500 workers at Stewarts and Lloyds – formerly chaired by Mayor John Lille Sharpe for whom Sharpeville was named, and the country's major shell factory during the war – went out on strike over their low wages. The employees living in Sharpeville demanded a 100 percent increase in their salaries, rejected out of hand by the company. They also requested to be paid at the end of the month because the municipality required them "to pay their room and house rentals monthly and [they] found that being paid at the end of every 30 shifts carried their pay day so far over the end of each month that they were unable to meet their financial obligations on the due date" and were therefore fined.[28] This request was granted by the company. But this action was quickly followed by an even larger protest at both of Union Steel's Vereeniging plants – producing bombs, bolts, nuts, and copper wire for the military – with both location residents and compound workers joining together to protest their work conditions. Union Steel's compounded workers lived in an industrial hostel near the plant that was also used by other companies and the Union Steel employees – including those living in Sharpeville – quickly combined with workers from Safim, African Cables, McKinnon Chain, SA Nuts and Bolts, and African Metals to join the strike. Nearly 3,000 workers camped out on the still open area near Top Location and "moved en masse towards the industrial area." Town officials feared the worst when the strikers called on workers from Stewarts and Lloyds and Escom to join them, estimating that "had they succeeded in this about 10,000 natives would have been involved."[29] The Transvaal Non-European Iron, Steel, and Metal Workers Union which represented workers in Vereeniging, Germiston, Benoni, and Pretoria attempted to negotiate with the companies which refused to recognise the union. Police force was used once again to force the workers back to their posts while the companies fired those deemed to be the ringleaders. These strikes, as well as those affecting the power supply, threatened the heart of South Africa's industrial production and alerted local officials to the need to clamp down tightly on worker unrest. Subsequently, legislation barring Africans from going on strike or joining multiracial unions and prohibiting African unions from joining into trade confederations was passed in the postwar period to blunt the power of African workers.[30]

But the spirit of protest was not destroyed in Vereeniging despite all efforts. Worker activity at African Cables provides a telling example. The firm was one of the largest in Vereeniging and produced all sorts of electrical cables that were used for wiring in telephones and ignitions as well as the huge power cables that carried electricity from the power stations in Vereeniging to the mines in Johannesburg. The workers had reason to complain about their conditions, especially when they discovered that White workers were receiving a special allowance for work on the night shift whereas African workers were not. They refused to return from a lunch break one evening until management explained the problem, whereupon they were threatened and ultimately charged with "refusing to work." They were taken to court, and although they were not members of any union, the workers hired their own attorney. The case was heard in the Vereeniging courthouse where "the court was so packed with workers that there were no spectators, even where the whites usually sit. From the prosecutor's desk upwards, there were just workers. Those who came to listen to the case had to stand outside."[31] It became clear that the company had disregarded industry agreements, but nevertheless, the workers were found guilty, given a suspended sentence, and then granted the shift allowance after all. That was not the end of problems at African Cables, however, and in the next year, workers had to protest again for a factory canteen and later instigate a "go-slow" to receive their wages in a timely manner.[32]

One of the workers involved at African Cables would later use the experience to help organise African opposition to a number of growing restrictions on African life, including the pass laws. Nyakane Tsolo, who was later credited with leading the Sharpeville protest on 21 March 1960, was born in Coalbrook in 1939 and moved to Sharpeville in 1944 to attend school. His father Philemon was a coal merchant and also ran Shop No. 12 on Stand Number 2068A in the Stands area of Sharpeville according to an application for malt used to brew beer; the family lived at Stand 2767 just off Seeiso Street in Rooistene.[33] Nyakane attended primary school in Sharpeville and secondary school at Lekoa Shandu earning a junior certificate in 1958. As his wife later recounted, "[I]f he was to proceed to Standard 10 [matriculation] he would have been required to go to boarding school." Since the family could not afford to send him away, he instead got a job at African Cables. He soon became involved with the strike action there, and according to one of his friends, he began to try to organise a union at the factory.[34] Friends and relatives remember him as a charismatic, dynamic personality who naturally drew followers; at the same time, he was becoming increasingly interested in problems outside the factory with a more political slant. By 1959, he was in touch with members of the Pan Africanist Congress (PAC) in Evaton, and he began to organise a local PAC branch in Sharpeville. Drawing on his former classmates and colleagues at African Cables, he and his brother Job – together with his girlfriend Suzan Tshukudu, Adelaide Tambo's sister – began to organise a group of young people in Sharpeville who were likewise discontented not only with their working conditions but also with the increasingly restrictive interference of the government, and especially the police, in their lives.[35] Designing their own lives, evading the controls of the state, and enjoying some respite from apartheid's burdens was becoming impossible.

A Louder Voice: "As Arrogant as Truth"[36]

In many ways, Sharpeville embodied the tensions and contradictions inherent in apartheid ideology, and indeed in systems of imperial and colonial control everywhere: the incorporation of subject peoples into systems of exploitation, absent the possibility of their assimilation into the ruling classes. The people of Sharpeville were fashioning their own lives and culture, speaking up for their rights in the workplace, and moving into western institutions of learning and religion on their own terms, yet these were not the goals of apartheid. Instead, the South African government, and the Vereeniging Municipality, cared little for these accomplishments and were focused on the separation, compliance, and subjugation of a racially defined and low-cost labour force. The municipality required that all costs of construction, administration, and policing of the township be borne solely by its residents and not by the White population or even the local companies that reaped huge profits from the exploitation of Sharpeville's workers.[37] And the government – parliamentary and administrative – enacted law after law in the 1950s to further enforce restrictions and limitations on Africans. By the time that Nyakane Tsolo and his colleagues came of age in Sharpeville, the relationship between the government's "strategies" of control, and the "tactics" of Sharpeville's residents to exert independence had nearly come to a standstill as each became intolerable for the other.

Whether through the concerted effort to restrict Africans, the design of the township, or press censorship, challenges from Sharpeville's residents were seldom reported, although they certainly took place. There had been a group of women demanding housing who camped out at the superintendent's office in 1944, banging pots and pans for several days until they were finally given some accommodation.[38] And in 1951, over 1,000 residents attended a meeting in the open to protest against regulations that would prohibit keeping cattle in the township.[39] The prohibition threatened the livelihood of transport carriers, the provision of milk for some families, and even the traditional practice of lobola, a bride price paid in cattle. Authorities eventually relented somewhat but sold off what they deemed surplus livestock to local White farmers.[40] While there were no major demonstrations in Sharpeville during the Defiance Campaign of 1952 organised by the African National Congress (ANC), 49 passive resisters were arrested there while police noted evidence of serious support from most residents.[41]

But official efforts to suppress news of a demonstration of sorts that took place in 1960 – only two weeks before the massacre – suggest that officials may well have routinely covered up complaints by residents. On 8 March 1960, 150 African women gathered outside the superintendent's office to complain about high rents. A story in the newspaper, *New Age*, included pictures of three of the women – Anna Dhlamini, Mirima Theletsane, and Harriet Mahlonoko – who explained that their anger over the rents came to a head over the municipality's refusal to permit a family to bury a corpse in the Sharpeville cemetery because they had not been able to pay their rent for two months[42] (see Figure 4.5). Another account of the protest appeared in *The Star* newspaper including further details that the women also complained about the municipal beer hall leading to drunkenness among their husbands and a claim that the women were especially angry with the superintendent, Mr. Labuschagne, and may have pushed his car. But the story was transformed by I. P. Ferreira, the manager of Non-European Affairs, who claimed that the women – less than 70 in his story – had actually come to him to complain that they had been threatened by the ANC and PAC that if they did not protest against the rents, their houses would be burnt down. In his version, he needed to protect the women from these political organisations and

104 *Life in Sharpeville*

These three women led the deputation against the high rents in Vereeniging's Sharpeville Location. From left to right: Mesdames Anna Dhlamini, Mirima Teletsane and Harriet Mahlonoko.

Figure 4.5 Photograph of Anna Dhlamini, Mirima Theletsane, and Harriet Mahlonoko, Sharpeville, 8 March 1960, *New Age*, 24 March 1960.

not the other way around. Events would soon put the lie to the picture of contentment and submission painted by Ferreira.

By March 1960, there were in fact many Sharpeville residents who were ready to launch serious, if peaceful, protests against the growing state intrusion in their lives. As Ferreira and Labuschagne were well aware, political groups had been active in Sharpeville for years and had their followers. As early as 1952, the Society of Young Africa (SOYA), had a chapter in Sharpeville which Nyakane Tsolo's older brother, Job, helped to establish.[43] This organisation viewed Africans' problems in South Africa as a double oppression – that is, both a racial and a class struggle, a threatening analysis for Vereeniging's industries. It held secret meetings in Sharpeville that were quickly banned by Superintendent Labuschagne and later faded from the scene as national disagreements weakened its structure.[44] At the same time, the ANC was also active in Sharpeville with a relatively small membership, and Michael Thekiso can still remember travelling to Kliptown in 1955 as a 15-year-old to attend the Congress of the People. Organised by four groups representing Africans, Coloureds, Indians, and Whites, as well as a trade union organisation, the Congress of the People ratified the Freedom Charter, a broad vision of a future multiracial democracy in South Africa.[45] But by 1956, these groups experienced a leadership vacuum of sorts at the national level as their leaders were put on trial for their participation in the Congress of the People in the infamous Treason Trial, which lasted until 1961 when all charges were finally dismissed. Whether through government harassment, lack of official organisation, or waning local interest, the ANC in Sharpeville remained a presence although a quiet one throughout the 1950s.

By 1959, a breakaway group of the ANC, the newly formed PAC led by Robert Sobukwe, was formed and a local branch was launched in Sharpeville. Committed to a more activist role than the ANC had taken against White domination, the PAC attracted a young group of factory workers in Sharpeville.[46] The PAC represented the "Africanist" faction in African politics, a group that had steadfastly argued and identified with the struggle of all African countries against colonialism and racism, with the slogan "Africa for the Africans." They were described by the writer Bloke Modisane as "a new generation of nationalist Africans, the young intellectuals who are as arrogant as truth ... [who believe that] To liberate himself the African must destroy white domination and smash the myth of white superiority."[47] The PAC wanted to move quickly and decisively to initiate a mass movement against the apartheid government. The PAC leadership chose to wage a campaign against the country's pass laws, perhaps the most infuriating injustice Africans experienced on a daily basis.

Since the earliest days of colonial rule in South Africa, Africans had been required to carry a "pass" to prove that they had a legal right to be in any particular place in South Africa.[48] Police could demand to see a pass at any time or place and arrest anyone who could not prove the legality of their position. In 1957, the government announced that women, for the first time, would also be required to carry passes, a hotly contested issue that had provoked widespread demonstrations in South Africa, beginning as early as 1913.[49] In a sense, the pass laws were a culmination of all other controls, since the passbook contained information about every facet of an individual's life: their age, gender, ethnicity, place of birth, place of work, address, and even receipts for their taxes, rents, and permits paid to the location superintendent. If any one of these pieces of information was out of line, the pass holder could be arrested, fined, jailed, and even evicted from their homes. In order to grasp the depth of intrusion into everyday life, see a copy of some of the pages from Mohauli Solomon Masilo's passbook, especially those pages that required regular signatures by the local superintendent (weekly) and his employer (monthly) (Figures 4.6 and 4.7). His general tax receipt was recorded yearly. It is not difficult to imagine how many ways anyone could fail to keep every piece of information "in order."

Sharpeville residents found the pass restrictions not only infuriating but also a serious obstacle when it came to finding better jobs; they were not allowed to work outside Vereeniging and still retain the right to live in Sharpeville. White urban administrators, including those in the Vereeniging Municipality, objected to allowing residents whose labour supported other towns to live in their townships. The only Africans with legal rights to live permanently in a specific urban area were those who worked there but also who were born there, had lived there continuously for 15 years, or had worked continuously for the same employer for 10 years. Under the pass laws, any Sharpeville resident who found a better job in Johannesburg or Sasolburg or even next door in Vanderbijlpark was required to relinquish

106 *Life in Sharpeville*

Figure 4.6 Photograph of Mohauli Solomon Masilo's passbook showing the weekly signatures of the location superintendent.
Courtesy of the Masilo family. Photo by authors.

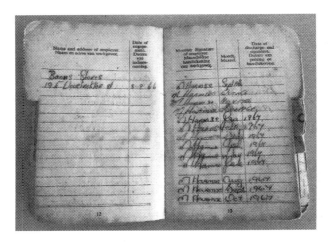

Figure 4.7 Photograph of Mohauli Solomon Masilo's passbook showing the monthly signatures of his employer.
Courtesy of the Masilo family. Photo by authors.

their rights to live in Sharpeville and risk re-establishing rights in another township such as Soweto in Johannesburg, Zamdela in Sasolberg or Bophelong in Vanderbijlpark. An increasing number of Africans risked moving to better jobs anyway and were arrested under the pass laws throughout the 1950s, reaching a national peak of 413,639 in 1959. Most were convicted for failing to produce the reference book on demand or having the book "imperfectly completed," in other words for being in a location without permission, failing to pay taxes, or seeking work without permission.[50]

Equally worrying were the restrictions placed on Sharpeville residents looking for work even in Vereeniging. Verwoerd's government enacted the Native Laws Amendment Act in 1952, which established a labour bureau system, requiring the permission of the "local" labour bureau for an African to be employed anywhere. This system was meant to produce what Verwoerd saw as a "rational" distribution of labour by expelling "surplus" labour from some areas and shuttling such workers to other labour regions or more likely to the so-called homelands where there were no jobs. Sharpeville resident Gladwin Mekhoe explained what this process was like:

> When you report at the Vereeniging Pass Office [Labour Bureau] as a work seeker you are not given permission to go yourself to go and make enquiries with different factories and houses ... you cannot get a job on your own. Even if you go [to Vanderbijlpark or Springs or Johannesburg] on your own and do find employment you will not be granted permission. ... If you are a tenant or a resident of the location and you are in arrear with your rental then you are arrested [and expelled].[51]

The Vereeniging Town Council became concerned that those who could not find work in the town would simply become troublemakers; they were especially concerned that younger residents would turn to crime and protest. This interpretation was later promoted by the police as a major cause of the 21 March protest, and it has also found its way into scholarly analyses as well.[52] However, as we will see in the next chapter, and as Gladwin Mekhoe explained, "The majority who are out of employment are the elderly people. My group [he was 23 years old] is only a small group which is out of employment."[53] And the actual incidence of unemployment was certainly overstated by the town council since even according to the reports of Manager of Non-European Affairs I. P. Ferreira, the average rate of unemployment for males over the age of 18 was only 5 percent, a fairly modest average despite the government's goal of allowing only employed Africans to live in the cities.[54]

Unemployment was not the central concern of the PAC, but rather the overall systems of control that plagued all Africans. Nyakane Tsolo, by all indications the de facto leader of the PAC in Sharpeville, attended the organisation's national inaugural convention in April 1959 where he met PAC president Robert Sobukwe. As Tsolo later explained his commitment to the PAC,

> Our aim is to unite the people on the basis of African nationality, to create and assert the African personality and to restore the black man's human dignity. ... We all want one unity, shall I say, the feeling of Afrika![55]

Hophny Morobe was also attracted to the PAC message "to unite the African people... I just know that we loved unity, to let [us] stand as a nation, as a race."[56] He joined with Tsolo and David Ramagole (listed in police documents as Ramodibe) in September to establish a branch, learning that Thomas More also had a group that wanted to join. Although a dispute over money caused a split – Morobe resigning and leaving the group – Tsolo and More went on to recruit more members and by the end of the year had approximately 100 formally enrolled. At that time, Sobukwe announced a plan for "positive action" in the coming year and called on all PAC branches to participate.

The Sharpeville branch had been meeting regularly since April 1959 and began some preparations for action. They printed PAC lapel tags for members, stamped with the organisation's slogan "Africa for Africans," and in March 1960 started to distribute PAC pamphlets calling on residents to "play your role in the positive and final act against the pass laws." Tsolo and the branch members blanketed the neighbourhoods with the pamphlets which continued throughout the month. The second pamphlet read, "Passes must go now. No bail, no defence, no fine," calling on the residents to report to the police without their passes and crowd the jails with those arrested rather than accept bail to be released. The third pamphlet stated "Anyone who gets this circular should keep it. He will have got hold of history," building excitement for the fourth pamphlet, released on 18 March, which finally announced the date of action: 21 March 1960.[57] The Sharpeville branch, only one small branch of over 100 in the country, was determined to answer Sobukwe's call. What could the people of Sharpeville expect?

Travelling into the heart of Sharpeville, one still sees remnants of the life that was carved out of apartheid's restrictions. School Square stands on either side of Seeiso Street with the Matsie Steyn School still in operation, faced by Assumpta Catholic private school. And the churches still line Church Square between Zwane and Seeiso, St. Cyprian's Anglican Church, St. Luke's Methodist Church, the Uniting Reformed Church (formerly the Dutch Reformed Church), and to the north of Seeiso Street the Assemblies of God where the Rev. Molefe preached (see the following section). The Community Hall where so many boxing matches as well as social dances took place still stands at the intersection of Zwane and Seeiso, across from the sports grounds – now named after George Thabe – where the soccer matches took place and still take place. But there are also things that have disappeared, replaced by a new South Africa. The municipal beer halls and depots that were scattered through the township have been replaced by bottle stores and nightclubs, and shebeens are now legal and proudly display their names and blare music into the streets. Seeiso Street still hosts most of the shops in the township, including a mid-size grocery market, and the first set of shops built in Sharpeville near the main intersection still stands. But otherwise, the commercial life of the township is now centred in a large discount mall to the south on Kariba Street, built as the "black" road into Vereeniging, with a hypermarket and Makro store with more goods and closer than any shops in Vereeniging itself. But Sharpeville residents still identify themselves as residents of their specific neighbourhoods, Putsoastene, Vuka, Phomolong, etc., their first claim to community in the township. And they still recall the most significant day in the life of the community, 21 March 1960.

Sharpeville Life: Faith and Hope

One of the first churches in Sharpeville was the Assemblies of God, the largest Pentecostal denomination in the world. It preaches healing and miracles and was described in 1954 in *Drum* magazine as follows,

> HUNDREDS CROWD THE VEREENIGING CHURCH TO HEAR THE YOUNG REV. MOLEFE'S MOVING SERMONS. THEY SING WITH FERVOUR. THEY PRAY DEVOUTLY. THEY LOOK UP TO GOD. THEY PROCLAIM THEIR FAITH TO THE ALMIGHTY. Vereeniging has a rare preacher in 27-year-old Rev. Philip Molefe. He is one of those preachers who doesn't send his listeners to sleep or induces wandering of the mind. Instead, with every sermon he preaches at the new Assemblies of God Church which has been built in Sharpeville Location, more people crowd the church and fill the yard at the evening gospel meetings to hear him advise them on a new life... The church building is not one of those modern buildings, artfully decorated to attract people inside. It is a bare hall with planks supported on bricks for benches; and a bare platform for a pulpit. Nor does he wear any of the colourful cassocks associated with priests. And he has moved them. Every evening he holds a gospel meeting, and every evening hundreds flocked to listen to him. Sometimes the crowds overflowed into the church grounds from where they listened to his preaching through amplifiers. They have listened and followed him, many giving up their old churches – and giving their uniforms to him – to be baptized by him in the nearby Vaal River.[58]

Notes

1 Maggie Malema (trans. Moeletsi Vincent Thamae), interview with authors, Sharpeville, October 2019.
2 H. F. Verwoerd, "The Policy of Apartheid, September 3, 1948," in *Verwoerd Speaks, Speeches 1948–1966*, edited by A.N. Pelzer (Johannesburg: APB Publishers, 1966), 9–10.
3 Jacob Dlamini, *Native Nostalgia* (Johannesburg: Jacana Press, 2010), 13.
4 Michel de Certeau, *The Practice of Everyday Life* (Berkeley: University of California Press, 1984), 96.
5 Town Council of Vereeniging, 30 November 1942, "Extract of Minutes of the Ordinary Monthly Meeting," Native Affairs Department (hereafter NTS) vol. 5898, file 33/331(N)I, South African National Archives Repository (hereafter SAB).
6 "Note of Interview with a deputation from Vereeniging consisting of members of the Native Advisory Board," 3 September 1943, NTS vol. 5898, file 33/313(N)II, SAB.

7 Department of Native Affairs, 15 September 1959, "Vraelys wat ten opsigte van die stadsgebied Vereeniging voltooi moet word," NTS vol. 4179, file 33/313(F)VI, SAB.
8 See the Suppression of Communism Act 44 of 1950, Public Safety Act 3 of 1953, Criminal Law Amendment Act 8 of 1953, Riotous Assemblies Act 15 of 1954, and Prohibition of Interdicts Act 64 of 1956.
9 See Prohibition of Mixed Marriages Act 55 of 1949, Population Registration Act 30 of 1950, Immorality Act 21 of 1950, Reservation of Separate Amenities Act 49 of 1953.
10 See Group Areas Act 41 of 1950, Illegal Squatting Act 52 of 1951, and the Native Laws Amendment Act 54 of 1952, which introduced conditions for African rights to live in urban areas. There were also a number of laws passed to create separate "homelands" in rural areas to which Africans were assigned citizenship based on their ethnicity: Bantu Authorities Act 68 of 1951, and the Promotion of Bantu Self Government Act 46 of 1959.
11 15 August 1956, "Municipalities of Vereeniging, Randfontein, and Westmaria, Location Regulations," Administrators Notice No. 664, *Government Gazette*, South Africa.
12 Information about the families described in this section was gathered from statements made to the police and held in the archival collection of the South African Police vols. SAP 616-622, SAB; "Commission of Enquiry into the Occurrences at Sharpeville (and other places) on the 21st March 1960" (hereafter Commission); *Regina vs. Monyake and Others* trial, Case No. R. 58/1960 in the Court of the Magistrate of the Regional Division of South Transvaal, held at Vereeniging (hereafter Court Case). All wage figures are reproduced as listed in the original documents, varying from South African Rand to British pound sterling.
13 Petrus Tom, *My Life Struggle* (Johannesburg: Ravan Press, 1985), 21.
14 Ramon Lewis Leigh, *Vereeniging, South Africa* (Johannesburg: Courier-Gazette, 1968), 289.
15 Nancy L. Clark, "Gendering Production in Wartime South Africa," *The American Historical Review* Vol. 106, No. 4, (October 2001): 1181–1213.
16 Ian Jeffrey, "Cultural Trends and Community Formation in a South African Township: Sharpeville, 1943–1985" (MA dissertation, University of the Witwatersrand, 1991), 99–100.
17 Department of Native Affairs, 15 September 1959, "Vraelys wat ten opsigte van die stadsgebied Vereeniging voltooi moet word," NTS vol. 4179, file 33/313(F)VI, SAB.
18 Fatima Industrial School R.C., Sharpeville, "Registration of Schools," 30 August 1957, OEO vol. 3/48 file A305, SAB.
19 See an interview with former members of the Vaal Professionals: https://www.youtube.com/watch?v=HU9vOB5o3ns.
20 Ian Jeffrey, "Street Rivalry and Patron Managers," *African Studies* Vol 51:1 (1992): 69–94.
21 "Boxing boom bursts on Vereeniging," *Drum*, April 1956.
22 "Mabena will beat all our bantams!," *Drum*, July 1956.
23 Jeffrey, "Cultural Trends and Community Formation," 126.
24 Ibid., 194; Matthew Chaskalson, "The Road to Sharpeville," in *Regions and Repertoires: Topics in South African Politics and Culture*, ed. Stephen Clingman (Johannesburg: Ravan Press, 1991), 131, alternatively claims that youth gangs "operated from the beerhalls and now expanded their activities to include the regular robbing of school pupils on buses and between the bus terminus and Lekoa Shandu Secondary School in Top Location." Chaskalson's description is based on minutes of meetings of the Vereeniging Non-European Affairs Committee

18 January 1958, and minutes of the Sharpeville Advisory Board meeting 22 November 1957. These records are no longer available.
25 See David B. Coplan, *In Township Tonight: South Africa's Black City Music and Theatre* (Chicago: University of Chicago Press, 2008).
26 Taken from the title of the autobiography of Petrus Tom who was born in Top Location, moved to Sharpeville in 1959, and worked in the union movement for over 25 years.
27 Nancy L. Clark, *Manufacturing Apartheid: State Corporations in South Africa* (New Haven: Yale University Press, 1994), 126.
28 I. P. O'Driscoll to Director of Native Labour, 31 January 1946, "Strike of Natives at Stewarts and Lloyds," NTS vol. 7686, file 248/332, SAB.
29 District Commandant (Johannesburg) to Deputy Commissioner South African Police Witwatersrand Division, 12 July 1946, "Strike of African Steel, Iron and Metal Workers employed by Union Steel Corporation: Vereeniging," and Additional Native Commissioner, Vereeniging to Director of Native Labour, Johannesburg, 15 July 1946, NTS vol. 7686, file 261/332, SAB.
30 Industrial Conciliation Act 36 of 1937, Native Labour (Settlement of Disputes) Act 48 of 1953, Industrial Conciliation Act 28 of 1956.
31 Petrus Tom, *My Life Struggle*, 18; Mahasane Michael Thekiso, interview by authors, Sharpeville, October 2018.
32 Petrus Tom, *My Life Struggle*, 19–20.
33 "Application for Malt. Sharpeville Location," no date, NTS vol. 5391, file 33/313(G)V, SAB.
34 Mahasane Michael Thekiso, interview by authors, Sharpeville, October 2018.
35 Gladys Qabukile Nzimande-Tsolo, "The Sharpeville Leader: Michael Nyakane Tsolo," 24 March 2020, Consciousness.co.za. https://consciousness.co.za/the-sharpeville-leader-michael-nyakane-tsolo/.
36 Bloke Modisane, *Blame Me on History* (New York: E. P. Dutton, 1963), 232.
37 The exception was the Native Services Levy Act of 1952, which allowed local authorities to collect funds from local employers for the provision of services in the locations. According to the Vereeniging Town Council, the council began collecting the levy in 1953, collecting an average of £60,000 per year. By 1958, it held £237,841 in a separate fund, compared to total income for the year of £361,059. "Vraelys wat ten opsigte van die stadsgebied Vereeniging voltooi moet word," 15 September 1959, NTS vol. 4179, file 33/313(F)VI, SAB. Monthly figures recorded by the Vereeniging Town Council provided to the authors by Matthew Chaskalson.
38 "Memo," 13 July 1944, NTS vol. 4178, file 33/313IV, SAB.
39 Chaskalson, "Road to Sharpeville," 15.
40 Native Commissioner Vereeniging to Town Clerk Vereeniging, 16 January 1951, "Amendment to Location Regulations – restrictions on number of animals that may be kept in locations," NTS vol. 6270, file 33/313(P)III; Native Commissioner Vereeniging to Director of Native Labour Johannesburg, 30 January 1951, "Amendment to Location Regulations – Restriction on number of animals that may be kept in locations," and Native Commissioner Vereeniging to Director of Native Labour Johannesburg, 15 February 1951, "Amendment to Location Regulations: restriction on number of animals that may be kept in locations," NTS vol. 6270, file 33/313(P)IV, SAB.
41 Acting Town Clerk Vereeniging to Secretary for Native Affairs, 19 December 1952, "Control of Meetings, Gatherings or Assemblies and Prohibition of Incitement of Natives in Certain Areas," NTS vol. 4179, file 33/313(F)VI, SAB.
42 "Sharpeville Women's Rent Protest," *New Age*, 24 March 1960.

43 Z.A.T. Makaba, "Reflections on Nyakane Tsolo – a forgotten political figure in the struggle annals of South African history" (BA Hons thesis, North-West University, 2019), 36.
44 Tom Lodge, *Sharpeville: An Apartheid Massacre and Its Consequences* (New York: Oxford University Press, 2011), 82.
45 The African National Congress (ANC), the Coloured Peoples Congress (CPC), the South African Indian Congress (SAIC), the Congress of Democrats (COD), and the South African Congress of Trade Unions (SACTU).
46 For a fuller discussion of African politics in this period, see Gail Gerhart, *Black Power in South Africa: The Evolution of an Ideology* (Berkeley: University of California Press, 1979); and Tom Lodge, *Black Politics in South Africa since 1945* (Johannesburg: Ravan Press, 1983).
47 Bloke Modisane, *Blame Me on History*, 232.
48 The laws relevant to the 1950s were the Abolition of Passes and Coordination of Documents Act 67 of 1952, and the Native Laws Further Amendment Act 79 of 1957. For a good historical overview of laws and policies concerning passes, see Doug Hindson, *Pass Controls and the Urban African Proletariat* (Johannesburg: Ravan Press, 1987).
49 Native Laws Further Amendment Act 79 of 1957.
50 Muriel Horrell, *A Survey of Race Relations in South Africa 1963*, (Johannesburg: South African Institute of Race Relations, 1964), 137.
51 Testimony of Gladwin Mekhoe, 5 January 1961, Court Case, 2669–2671.
52 The argument that youth unemployment led to gang activity and was ultimately one of the contributory factors in the March 21 protest can be found in Gerhart, *Black Power in South Africa*, Philip Frankel, *An Ordinary Atrocity: Sharpeville and its Massacre* (Yale University Press: New Haven, 2001), and Lodge, *Sharpeville*.
53 Testimony of Gladwin Mekhoe, 5 January 1961, Court Case, 2672.
54 Notes on the Reports of the Manager of Non-European Affairs, Vereeniging, 1953-1956, provided to the authors by Matthew Chaskalson. These reports included the number of registered workers, those placed, and those unemployed as per the records of the local Labour Bureau.
55 Testimony of Nyakane Tsolo, 24 May 1960, Commission, 2500, 2501, 2504.
56 Testimony of Hophny Morobe, 2 May 1960, Commission, 3156.
57 Court Case, 25–28.
58 "Tsotsis Repent!," November 1954, *Drum*, 36–37. Rev. Molefe was one of the priests who presided over the mass burial of the Sharpeville massacre victims and later became a leading figure in the Pentecostal movement. He was active in the South African Council of Churches and was chairman of the Vaal Council of Churches during the Vaal uprisings of 1984. His son, Vernon was politically active and was later killed under mysterious circumstances in 1992, and another son, Phil Molefe, is a journalist and former chief of news at SABC. Rev. Molefe died at the age of 92 in 2020.

Bibliography

Chaskalson, Matthew. "The Road to Sharpeville." In *Regions and Repertoires: Topics in South African Politics and Culture*, edited by Stephen Clingman, 116–146. Johannesburg: Ravan Press, 1991.

Clark, Nancy L. *Manufacturing Apartheid: State Corporations in South Africa*. New Haven: Yale University Press, 1994.

Clark, Nancy L. "Gendering Production in Wartime South Africa." *The American Historical Review* Vol. 106, No. 4 (October 2001): 1181–1213.

Coplan, David B. *In Township Tonight: South Africa's Black City Music and Theatre.* Chicago: University of Chicago Press, 2008.

Cornell, Margaret. "The Statutory Background of Apartheid: A Chronological Survey of South African Legislation." *The World Today* Vol. 16, No. 5 (May 1960): 181–194.

de Certeau, Michel. *The Practice of Everyday Life.* Berkeley: University of California Press, 1984.

Dlamini, Jacob. *Native Nostalgia.* Johannesburg: Jacana Press, 2010.

Gerhart, Gail. *Black Power in South Africa: The Evolution of an Ideology.* Berkeley: University of California Press, 1979.

Hindson, Doug. *Pass Controls and the Urban African Proletariat.* Johannesburg: Ravan Press, 1987.

Jeffrey, Ian. "Cultural Trends and Community Formation in a South African Township: Sharpeville, 1943–1985." MA dissertation, University of the Witwatersrand, 1991.

Leigh, Ramon Lewis. *Vereeniging, South Africa.* Johannesburg: Courier-Gazette, 1968.

Lodge, Tom. *Black Politics in South Africa Since 1945.* Johannesburg: Ravan Press, 1983.

Lodge, Tom. *Sharpeville: An Apartheid Massacre and Its Consequences.* New York: Oxford University Press, 2011.

Modisane, Bloke. *Blame Me on History.* New York: E.P. Dutton, 1963.

5   21 March 1960

All of a Sudden the Crowd … Had Been Flattened[1]

When the sun rose in Sharpeville on 21 March 1960, few would have believed that the day would end with at least 91 dead and 238 and more injured. The community was poised for a peaceful protest against the pass laws which so restricted their lives and made it increasingly difficult to survive, but while they expected arrest and imprisonment, none of their leaders anticipated the ferocious reaction of the police. Since that day, the community has searched for answers to this tragedy and, aside from police justifications and an inconclusive official investigation, none can provide an explanation to fit the enormity of the tragedy. In this and subsequent chapters, we will try to work towards an answer by constructing a narrative of the event by the people who lived through it, the people of Sharpeville, who told their stories time and again without being heard.

By 1960, not only Vereeniging but the surrounding towns of Vanderbijlpark and Sasolburg – known collectively as the Vaal Triangle – had become the centre of industrial activity which underpinned the South African economy. Three major state enterprises – Escom, Iscor, and Sasol – were located in the region. Four of Escom's largest power stations – Taaibos, Highveld, Klip, and Vaal – generated the electricity that powered the Johannesburg gold mines. Iscor's plant in Vanderbijlpark produced 70 percent of the country's steel in a raw form, that was then processed by Vereeniging firms – Stewarts and Lloyds, Amcor, Vecor, African Cables, etc. – into tubes, pipes, cables, and heavy machinery for the mining and manufacturing industries. And the newest state enterprise, Sasol, sited on the opposite side of the Vaal River from Vanderbijlpark, used the huge local coal reserves to produce the precious oil that the government deemed essential to make the country independent of outside suppliers.[2]

Perhaps the most important resource provided through Vereeniging was water for the entire Rand. The Rand Water Board pumped 250 million gallons of water per day to Johannesburg and Pretoria from stations located on the Vaal River in Vereeniging.[3] In a drought-prone country with few major river systems, the entire Rand and its people and industries could not have

DOI: 10.4324/9781003257806-5

survived without this water for even a day. Moreover, the main rail line linking Cape Town, Kimberley (with its diamonds), and the Rand ran directly through Vereeniging and within a few hundred metres of Sharpeville. Taken all together, the Vaal region was key to the economic survival of South Africa, and any disruption to these industries, especially through the interruption of labour, would be crippling. The Vereeniging Town Council had already noted in 1952, "In view of the strategic position of Vereeniging as regards water, power and communications, it is essential to take all possible steps to prevent any disturbances or disruption of the essential works."[4]

In January and February of 1960, Special Branch (SB) officers were already active in the Vaal Triangle at the scene of the Coalbrook mining disaster 15 mi south of Vereeniging where a mining collapse on 21 January killed 437 miners and closed down operations.[5] The officers were there to ensure that the surviving miners would continue to work despite the dangerous conditions. The Coalbrook mine supplied Escom's two newest stations, Taaibos and Highveld, that along with the existing Vaal power stations were responsible for supplying Johannesburg's gold mining industry with over 1 million kilowatts of power per day. All of these stations were designed to burn the type of coal found in the Vereeniging coalfield; consequently, the Cornelia Colliery in Vereeniging was tasked with increasing production for all of the power plants in order to make up the shortfall from Coalbrook. Two police officers, Lieutenant Colonel Gideon Daniel Pienaar, Divisional Inspector at the Witwatersrand Police Headquarters, and Colonel Abraham Theodorus Spengler, Deputy Commander of the SB, were at Coalbrook to see that the surviving miners would continue to work despite the dangerous conditions and "to ensure that there is no agitation among the miners in the compound" so that production could resume promptly.[6] Spengler, like the Vereeniging Town Council almost a decade earlier, recognised the strategic importance of the Vaal Triangle. "[T]he steel factories, the four major power supply stations, the water supply and the coal mines had to be protected because they formed the base of the country's economy." If the labour supply was ever "withheld from essential industries in the Vereeniging and Vanderbijlpark area … the economy of the whole country could have been seriously affected."[7] Both Pienaar and Spengler would later play key roles in the Sharpeville massacre.

The potential for a critical collapse of the industrial economy had been made evident. The emergency measures to obtain additional supplies of coal "were costly," the simultaneous closing of two collieries (the north and south portions of Coalbrook) was "without precedent," the shortage of electricity meant that residents of the Vaal region and Johannesburg had to experience load shedding for a week, and full production of electricity did not resume until 19 March almost a month after the initial accident. As an Escom press release stated at the time, "[I]t is hoped that there will not be any further instance of reduction of supply due to the loss of coal supplies."[8]

When the buses that daily brought Sharpeville's workers to their Vereeniging jobs did not arrive by 5:30 am on 21 March 1960, it appeared to local officials that their fears had been realised. PAC leaders had targeted the bus drivers, preventing them from going to work to provide transportation for Vereeniging's workforce. The first police on the spot were the local Vereeniging officers, but they were soon joined at 6:30 am by members of the "SB" of the police, the unit involved in the surveillance of political groups and trade unions that the government targeted as "troublemakers." Such groups were prosecuted as "communists" under South African law, which legally defined as communists any individuals or groups advocating "any political, industrial, social or economic change by the promotion of disturbances or disorder, by unlawful acts of omissions or by the threat of such acts and omissions."[9]

As the morning of 21 March progressed, it became apparent that Vereeniging and Vanderbijlpark would be without their African workers; as the *Rand Daily Mail* reported, "At least 80 percent of shops and offices in the towns were without African labor." The *New Age* reported "Monday's events marked virtually a general strike in the Vereeniging and Vanderbijl Park area. Iscor suspended operations due to the absence of its African labour force." Factories including Metal Box and Dorman Long in Vanderbijlpark closed down for lack of workers, while South African Farm Implement Manufacturers (Safim, the largest farm machinery manufacturer in South Africa), Union Steel, and Stewarts and Lloyds in Vereeniging worked with skeleton crews.[10] Africans were instead supporting the PAC campaign by marching to police stations in the Vaal Triangle to demand arrest for not carrying their passes. Those in Evaton and Vanderbijlpark marched to their closest police stations, which were in the White areas adjacent to the African townships. They were met with baton charges by the police and even low-flying jets which successfully moved the crowds into a retreat back to the two townships in Vanderbijlpark (Bophelong and Boipatong; Boipatong was also known as Tsirela) and to a large field adjacent to the police station in the case of Evaton where the crowds continued to wave "Away with passes" signs until the middle of the day. The police resorted to similar tactics in Sharpeville, pushing a crowd back from the road that led to Vereeniging in the early morning with tear gas and a baton charge, but while barring any movement into the White areas, these tactics did nothing to prevent a crowd from gathering at the Sharpeville Police Station which, unlike those in Vanderbijlpark and Evaton, stood in the middle of the township.

By 10 am, the head of the South African Police (SAP) in Vereeniging (and district commandant for the entire Vereeniging-Vanderbijlpark-Evaton region), Major Willem van Zyl began to fear the worst. He called his immediate superior Lieutenant Colonel Pienaar to request more police be sent to Sharpeville. Pienaar had been tasked by his uniformed branch superiors with coordinating the Witwatersrand SAP response to the PAC pass demonstrations on 21 March. Testifying to the subsequent "Commission of Enquiry into the Occurrences at Sharpeville (and other places) on the 21st of March 1960," van Zyl said, "I believed that there would be a bloodbath. I saw no other way out. That is how it looked to me and I am convinced that it would have happened."[11] By 1:00 pm, reinforcements had come from throughout the Witwatersrand area to Sharpeville, including Lieutenant Colonel Pienaar, Colonel Spengler, and the latter's boss Colonel Willem Carl Ernst Prinsloo, the national head of the SB. Within half an hour, two leaders of the national police from Pretoria also arrived, Brigadier Cornelius Johannes Els and General Hendrik Jacobus du Plooy, respectively, assistant commissioner and deputy commissioner (third and second in command) of the SAP. There was now a total of almost 300 armed police officers at the Sharpeville police station and four Saracen armoured vehicles, each equipped with Browning machine guns capable of shooting 400–600 rounds a minute. Unable to isolate Africans as they had in Bophelong and Evaton, the police were themselves surrounded in the police station, though always linked to their main command at the entrance to the township by a fifth Saracen. Although not a single policeman sustained a serious injury (the subsequent commission of enquiry concluded that the police injuries were inconsequential, with three policemen only sustaining slight injuries and only one of them needing any medical attention for a graze), within the hour, over 300 Africans (and perhaps more) were shot in less than one minute, falling to the ground in a machine gun fusillade so powerful that, as Petrus Tom remembers to this day, "All of a sudden the crowd had gone because they had been flattened." How did such events unfold? Let us hear from the eyewitnesses.

The following re-telling of the events of 20 and 21 March 1960 is based on the testimonies of over 400 eyewitnesses whose accounts were recorded in detail within days, weeks, and months of those events, and interviews that we recorded with survivors and family members in 2018, 2019, and 2022. Sharpeville residents have spoken again and again about March 1960, especially after the advent of a majority-elected government in 1994 released them from fear of state-enforced violence, yet they feel that no one listens. In this chapter and in Chapter 6, we have attempted to listen to their voices, to tell the story as they told it in their own words, and to give identity and agency to the people who otherwise remain largely an anonymous and unidentified mass of "victims" in the published accounts of the Sharpeville police massacre.[12]

Sunday Night and Monday Morning: "The Dawn Has Come"

> Father [*Tata*, a term of respect], we want to tell you that all the men should go out into the street.
>
> (Nyakane Ramabele Michael Tsolo)[13]

Around 8 pm on Sunday evening, 20 March 1960, Elias Lidia gets on his bicycle and rides a few hundred yards from his home on Zwane Street just southeast of the police station to the newest neighbourhood in Sharpeville, the prosaically named "Site and Service" area known locally as Vuka, situated to the southwest of the police station, the shops, the clinic, the library, and the community hall. He has heard that a leader of the PAC is going to speak, and he wants to learn about the newly formed organisation. He has also heard "that there would be something in Sharpeville, like an anti-pass campaign." A dressmaker and fashion designer by trade, Elias Lidia keeps a diary and plans to write a book about life in South Africa.[14]

Like other residents of Sharpeville, Elias Lidia has read the four PAC pamphlets left under people's doors during the week before 21 March, but he does not know much about the organisation or its specific plans for Monday. He has attended a few of their meetings in people's homes in Sharpeville but thought it a "weak organisation." He only knows personally three members, an acquaintance of his he knows as Qwadi (Khoali Teketsi), Nyakane Tsolo, and a third person whose name he does not know. But he also knows that it has a growing influence in the community. It "had a very strong hold over the young people of Sharpeville, they [the young people] could almost do nothing that was out of line. ... Nothing bad." Moreover, like the ANC, the PAC is "fighting for one thing, and that is freedom," and Lidia believes "very strongly" in the importance of that struggle.[15]

Excited by the ideas he has read in the pamphlets, Elias Lidia gets to the eastern side of Vuka where he finds 200 people drawn by the same narrative of freedom. It is a half-moon that night, providing enough illumination for people to recognise one another. Lidia's estimate of the crowd size is based on his years of experience putting on fashion shows and counting the number of potential customers present. Teketsi, married with three young children, in his 20s, a machine operator for African Cables, and a resident of Vuka, is the main speaker and talks about how things are going to be organised once dawn comes: the PAC campaign will be launched, people who "wished to support the campaign, would have to stay away from work; that was only on Monday – and surrender to the Police." Lidia thinks that based on the questions asked by the audience, most of them are finding out about the PAC for the first time.[16]

The "gathering," as Lidia refers to it, lasts for several hours until it is brought to a sudden halt by the arrival of two vehicles loaded with policemen. Lidia does not recognise any of them. The leader of the police calls out to the crowd "*Gaan julle weg?*" Though posed as a question, "Are you going away?" Lidia knows "it was an order." Teketsi steps forward and tries to speak to the police. He is immediately struck with a baton as the police charge and disperse the entire crowd. The police are "very contemptuous" thinks Lidia, treating "everybody and every way which we tried to say to them, with contempt." He gets on his bicycle and rides "straight back home."[17]

The rest of the town is quiet as the police disperse Teketsi's meeting on the southwestern side of Sharpeville. Over to the eastern side, David Ntsame, a municipal gatekeeper, walks down the main street Seeiso to begin his 10 pm shift in charge of the single chain link that stretches across the one tarred and guarded entry to Sharpeville, "the Gate" as it is known. There is nothing unusual taking place as he walks to work in the pale moonlight: "The people I came across were the usual people going to work [night shifts like his] and returning from work and proceeding to their homes."[18]

But Tsolo and fellow PAC members are already busy organising for the next day. Lucas Mosheledi, a 21-year-old liquor deliveryman and member of the PAC, has his instructions: go house to house and gather supporters, and form groups of about 20 people to go to the police station the next morning and be arrested for not having reference books. Each group will have its own leader, all will be against passes, and only men shall form the groups, not women or children. "These groups would go about and meet, and the group would grow bigger and bigger, as the groups were meeting." Late on Sunday evening, Mosheledi wakes up "his followers" and begins going door to door, knocking and asking people to join them, aiming to gather first at Putsoastene, the oldest neighbourhood in Sharpeville, and then walk up Seeiso to the football field, northwest of the police station. "All those of the Pan-Africanists [understood] ... that ... there was no violence to be done or to fight with the Police or anything like that," everyone knew that. When Nyakane Tsolo and another man knocked on the door of Francis Motshoahole (sometimes written Motshole) on Khabasheane Street, almost at the centre of Sharpeville, at around 11:30 pm, Motshoahole recognises him immediately because he knows Tsolo's father and brothers since they live only three streets away. Tsolo and his partner say to Motshoahole, "Father [*Tata*, a term of respect], we want to tell you that all the men should go out into the street." Annoyed at first because some other youths arriving before Tsolo had broken one of his windows that night, Motshoahole is reassured when Tsolo tells him that he will fix the window the next day. He agrees to join the group of 15 or so men, young and old, gathered in his yard and proceeds to meet up with other groups going to different homes until there are about 250 men who walk over to Seeiso Street.[19]

The same process is repeated throughout Sharpeville for an hour or two before midnight into the early hours of Monday morning. Richard Mtimkulu who lives near Seeiso two blocks west of the school square in the Rooistene neighbourhood, gets woken up by a young man he knows as Dlamini, "[h]e is a tall boy with side-whiskers, as well as the way he cuts his hair, he cuts them in a certain fashion," who tells him to come along to the football field. Izak Rampai is woken up by young men in a hurry who knock and keep on moving, shouting as they leave his house, "Let's go, let's go," we are going to the sports ground. Caiphus Papa Motsepe's wife Mita asks the men who knock on their door "what they wanted to do with my husband and they told me that I had to tell him to come and he then went out." Christian Khumalo answers his door and tells those who have knocked that he is a member of the SAP; "they replied that it did not matter whether I was a Policeman or whether I was a Minister of Religion; but the main object is that I should not carry a reference book." They insist that he accompany them, and he does so. Likewise with Bernard Xingwana, who tells the people knocking on his door that he is an employee of the municipal "Native Affairs" department, and they reply that he is "just the sort of person they wanted to have with them." When Piet Kok a sergeant with the Vereeniging Municipal Police who because he is officially designated as Coloured (Griqua) is required to live in Sharpeville, answers the door of his mother's house in Putsoastene and says he is a policeman, the young men do not insist that he go with them, but both of Kok's brothers choose to join the group in the street. Some people like Samuel Mahlasi and Piet Mokoena ignore the knock on the door, and the PAC people "passed on"; some, as has been the case with Francis Motshoahole, claim their windows have been damaged, and they have been threatened. Mosheledi and Tsolo put these cases down to a few bad actors, with Mosheledi noting that in "any organization there are always people who try to '*verongeluk*' it [to mess things up]," and Tsolo stating that any people doing such actions "are not of our people. ... Our people are disciplined people. They know what it is."[20]

There is a constant movement of people, most gathering on Seeiso and walking to the football field, some on the lower western side like Vuka walking along side streets to the same destination. All are told that eventually they will be going to the police station. Some decide to go there directly to offer themselves for arrest while leaving their passes in their homes, like Jan Nyepisi who has a limp from a workplace injury and cannot keep up with his group. On arrival at the police station around midnight, he finds Jan Motsei who has been told by his nighttime visitors that he "should leave my pass on the table and that we should go to the Police Station," and Jan Salanyane whose visitors told him "[l]eave your pass and greet your children and accompany us," and Azael Mabote who simply hears a loud announcement in the street about going to the police station and leaving his pass behind. The African police at the station ask them why they have come and take down their names. Then they sit on a bench outside, 10 or 15 of them in total, waiting to be arrested.[21]

Larger numbers are gathering at the football field 500 m northwest of the police station, just beyond the circle where Seeiso loops around to join Zwane. Thomas More, the vice chairman of the PAC, plans to address them. More is 25 years old, a junior certificate graduate who works for the main bicycle manufacturer in Vereeniging, Raleigh Industries. He is married and is the sole support of his family, his elderly mother, and his six sisters. Like Teketsi earlier in the evening, he plans to talk to those gathered about the aims of the PAC and explain the details of the proposed actions that will begin soon after dawn. Many in the audience know that PAC members Teketsi and Salanyane Steven Lepee burned their passes at the bus terminus on Friday. Would they have to do the same? By around 11:30 pm or so there are roughly 150 to 200 people gathered to listen to More, and others are arriving all the time. More and a few others are wearing the paper lapel badges that Thaddea Ntoampe had printed after hours at African Cables a few weeks previously, badges that read "Africa for Africans. P.A.C." or "Away with passes! P.A.C." or simply "P.A.C."[22]

A little before 11 pm on Sunday, the African sergeant on duty at the Sharpeville police station, concerned about the unusual activities taking place, decides to call Sergeant David Mokabela (who lives on Zwane diagonally opposite from Elias Lidia's house), who had finished his Sunday shift less than an hour earlier, and have him patrol the town with some constables. The duty sergeant then phones his superiors in Vereeniging to alert them about the situation. He first reaches his immediate superior, Sergeant Johannes Grobler, the commander of the Sharpeville police, who being White lives in Vereeniging, and then the sergeant on duty at the Vereeniging police station who relays the message to his superiors – that Africans are walking about Sharpeville "molesting" people and forcing them to leave their homes. The police reaction is swift. Captain Edward Cawood, the second in command of the Vereeniging SAP, immediately gathers a group of policemen and sets off for Sharpeville, Cawood has been in the SAP for 25 years, stationed for the past ten months in Vereeniging but before that for the previous six years "in what is commonly known as the black spots, Orlando, Kliptown, Moroka, Newlands, those spots," all in Soweto. He has with him Lieutenant Quartus Fourie and Head Constable Johannes Heyl from the Vereeniging SAP, Sergeant Grobler, around 15–20 African constables (all of whom live in Sharpeville when not on duty), and about the same number of White constables. Major van Zyl, their commander, expects trouble and orders them all to be well armed. The White officers have .38 revolvers; the White constables .38 revolvers and .303 rifles, as well as wooden batons; and the African police have a mix of assegais (spears) and clubs (African police in South Africa are not permitted to carry guns). Cawood issues two of the White constables, Hermanus Scheepers and J. van Rensburg, with Sten submachine guns (capable of firing 500 bullets per minute) in addition to their revolvers.[23]

They enter Sharpeville around 11:30 pm or so through the Gate and drive up Seesio to the police station. Cawood sees several hundred men walking in small groups along the main road, an unusual sight at that time of night. Directly south of the police station near Vuka – Cawood and Fourie know the direction but not the names of the neighbourhoods – they see "Africans standing there shouting 'Afrika!' ... they were just standing more or less; they did not do anything. ... I told the men [his policemen] they had better charge them and chase them ... a baton charge." This was Teketsi's meeting that was broken up. Because the phone from the police station no longer works (all phones in Sharpeville go out of service around 11 pm and remain down until the next morning), Cawood decides to return to Vereeniging (a ten-minute drive) to report in person to van Zyl. Fourie meanwhile goes out on patrol with his Vereeniging men, joined as well by an additional 15 African constables from the Sharpeville force as well as an African detective in civilian clothes, Malakia Mmotong. Within minutes of beginning the patrol, Fourie comes across Thomas More and the people gathered at the football field. Constable Khumalo had also made his own way there. He sees More approach Fourie and introduce himself and tell Fourie that those gathered intend to have a meeting. They speak a mixture of English and Afrikaans and Sesotho with Detective Malakia translating as needed (More speaks all three languages). Fourie asks whether they have permission for a meeting from the location superintendent, and when told that they are still waiting on approval, he tells them they should go home, that they can all meet again the next day when an official will be available to speak with them and then leaves with his men to return to the police station while More and his audience remain gathered at the football field.[24]

An hour later, around 12:30 am, Fourie returns, this time in the company of Captain Cawood who is back from Vereeniging with the "location superintendent," Michiel Labuschagne, and the police mood has changed. So has the size of More's audience, now about 200–300 people (Head Constable Heyl's estimate; Cawood thought it was double at 500). Again, More introduces himself to the police. Again, the leader of the police, this time Cawood, asks him if he has permission for a meeting. Again, More replies in the negative, but now adds a caveat prompted by Labuschagne's presence (the superintendent arrived in Sharpeville at midnight when he had not been able to get anyone at the police station on the phone after checking regularly on events throughout the evening). He says, "I am not holding any meeting here" – where for example was there evidence of an agenda in the hand of the person addressing the meeting? – but a *gathering*, and that is not illegal. Cawood is infuriated by the wordplay. As Mmotong recounts events, "Policemen then assaulted them with batons, i.e., sticks ... you [More] did not leave the scene as requested and then a baton charge was carried out." The crowd disperses. Mahasane Michael Thekiso remembers that night and that meeting: "We saw the police there; they beat us there; we ran away, but we had already organized ourselves for the 21st." PAC members, Thekiso among them, will distribute pamphlets to every house during the night.[25]

Cawood and Fourie and the rest of the police spend the next few hours patrolling Sharpeville in their cars and vans and attacking any group of Africans they see. When Lucas Mosheledi and his friends get to Putsoastene on Seeiso Street, they encounter a police patrol who yell out "*Wat soek julle in die nag in die straat?*" (what are you doing on the street in the night?), and without waiting for an answer – "I with my whole heart wanted to reply" – "started hitting [them] with their batons." Francis Motshoahole arriving on Seeiso Street immediately sees police with their vehicles parked in the road. The leaders of his group "requested the crowd not to run away because the Police had something to say to them." They are mistaken. The police say nothing. "At that moment, I felt a blow against my head and I fell to the ground. I do not know what struck me, whether it was a stone or piece of iron." Motshoahole loses consciousness for a few moments. On coming to and standing up, "A Native constable then came to me from the van, and he struck me with a stick across my shoulder. ... My head was covered with blood." Motshoahole goes to the Vereeniging Hospital where he receives 12 stitches. Christian Mpempe who has been woken up by people knocking and saying "Man, wake up. Why are you asleep?" goes with them as far as the post office, about a hundred yards east from where Motshoahole is assaulted. When the police find Mpempe in the street, he stated, "[T]hey did not ask us what we wanted ... but immediately they came to us they started just hitting us with sticks." He too goes to the hospital for some stitches. Inside his house, Aaron Xilishe watches through his window "vans [driven by 'Europeans'] roaming about the Location and hitting people," and hears screams that "salt ... was being sprayed on these people, and they said the salt was burning them" as they run for safety in his and other people's yards.[26]

Josephina Mofokeng's husband John, who has been woken up after midnight by some young men and goes with them, returns home before dawn and somehow tells his wife "that the Police had hurt him. I asked him what had happened, but he could no longer talk." She goes with him by taxi to the Vereeniging Hospital. He dies two days later from a skull fracture and a brain hemorrhage. He is 45 years old and leaves a widow and two sons at home, Isaac 19 and Jacob 17. An independent coal merchant with his own wagon and horses, John Kolane Mofokeng is the first person killed by the police on 21 March 1960.[27]

Even Detective Mmotong fears his police peers. Because of his civilian clothes, he thinks they may not immediately recognise him in the street and will beat him too. He spends the night hiding in a police van driven by Constable Hendrik Jan Michael Beyl. Like some others of his fellow White officers, Beyl carries a sjambok even though they are officially forbidden for the police at the time. His is an "actual" sjambok made from a strip of animal hide unlike the homemade ones carried by some of his colleagues which are fashioned from "motor-car fan belts with a stick handle at the back." Lucas Mosheledi is so discouraged by the police violence that he believes "that the plan which we had made ... was not going to work." He goes back to bed. "I thought totally that the campaign had failed."[28]

The police thought so too. The 10 to 15 men who had gathered at the police station waiting to be arrested are sent home between 2 am and 3 am. Detective Constable Edwin Litelu, who has been woken up twice earlier in the morning by people asking him to go with them, and refusing without any consequences, walks to the police station around 2:30 am and "saw nobody in the street." He does not see any White officers at the police station either and does not know if any had been there. At the other end of town near the Gate, Municipal Constable Elias Mvala who has been woken up at midnight and cannot get back to sleep, walks to the municipal offices opposite the beerhall around 2 am without seeing anything out of the ordinary. Ignatius

Ferreira, the director of *"Nie-Blanke"* ("Non-White" when written in Afrikaans, though when written in English the official translation used is "Non-European") affairs for the Vereeniging Town Council arrives alone at about 2 am, followed 45 minutes later by Major van Zyl accompanied by half a dozen White and African policemen. Ferreira and van Zyl (and his men) briefly join Cawood and Fourie on patrol and then go to the municipal offices on the northern side of Seeiso just outside the Gate for the rest of the morning. Fourie goes off duty at 3:30 am and drives home to Vereeniging.[29]

Around the same time, Cawood returns briefly to Vereeniging and phones in a report to his regional superior, Lieutenant Colonel Pienaar, who is at home in Johannesburg. Cawood tells Pienaar that there have been "skirmishes" and "clashes" with more than a dozen crowds (ranging from 50 to 500 strong) of "natives" (as was clarified in a subsequent trial, although "natives" and *"Bantu"* are the terms written down in the transcripts, the word actually spoken by the police, including in court, was normally "kaffir"), that they had fired at him, and he had chased them, "but that moment when he phoned me, things were in hand" and that he would phone again only if the situation worsened. Pienaar finds the report somewhat disturbing but nothing out of the ordinary: "I was expecting the worst demonstrations in the South-western native locations ... what is known as the South-Western Native Township." And Sharpeville? "Well, I was surprised. I was quite surprised. It was the last place that I expected it." He never got another call from Cawood that night so assumes all is under control.[30]

From Cawood's perspective, everything is indeed under control: "from half past two to five I should say it was very quiet." Others concur. Sergeant Moses Nkosi leaves his home on Zwane Street at 4:45 am and walks over to the police station to start his 5 am shift without incident. He will remain in the charge office immediately inside the public entrance to the police station on Zwane Street for the next eight hours. He doesn't see a single White officer inside the building for the first five of those hours. At 5 am, it is still over an hour to go before sunrise and, as Superintendent Labuschagne notes, "the location was completely quiet. There were no more groups of people."[31]

But all is not under control. The PAC campaign is well underway before dawn. Michael Thekiso and other PAC supporters are at the bus station at 3 am ready to tell people not to go to work and that they should instead go to the police station and surrender themselves for arrest as people not carrying passes. Labuschagne realises something is afoot when he notices at 5:30 am that no buses have arrived to take workers to the homes, stores, and factories of Vereeniging's White employers. Each day around 3:45 am a bus driven by a Mr. Uys arrives in Sharpeville from the Vereeniging Transport Company's (VTC) depot in Duncanville, near the old Top Location. At 4 am it takes the African drivers from Sharpeville, and anyone else who has an early start, to Vereeniging where each driver collects his own bus and returns for the regular commute which begins for most people around 5 am. By 5:30 am when the streets are filling with the usual morning commuters, and it is clear that

Mr. Uys is not coming, Labuschagne sends a message to the VTC asking that buses be sent in immediately with White drivers.[32]

The African bus drivers already knew there would be a problem that day. On the previous Friday, they had met with VTC management and told them that because of the PAC plans for a stop work, they did not want to drive on Monday. Partly, they were concerned that violence might arise, as had been the case with a lengthy bus strike in Evaton a couple of years earlier. More importantly, they respect the young people organising the PAC campaign – "we do respect them ... we did not want to make any trouble with them" – and some of the drivers, like Joshua Motha, "personally wanted to hear what was eventually going to be said, and what was eventually going to happen about passes." At first, the VTC management agrees not to run the service on Monday, but during the weekend changes its mind and sends messages to the drivers to come to work as usual. Perhaps Mr. Uys does not learn of the change of plans? Because when Daniel Seetsi, Edwin Mosholi, and Aaron Xilishe, who all drive for the VTC, leave their homes at around 3:30 am and walk to the local bus terminal on Seeiso fully expecting to find Mr. Uys waiting for them, they instead meet people who tell them there will be no buses and that they should go home or else go to the police station and join the campaign. For Aaron Xilishe, his reaction was more visceral given his experience earlier in the night hearing the police chase and assault people outside his home. Walking towards the bus terminal, Xilishe "saw some vans parked there, and then I went back [home]."

> I came back [home] because I knew that those people [the police] do not have laws, they do not control themselves, and they just do anything to get any person in trouble. ... I could not go near them because they hit any person who came near to them. They did not discriminate.

Some of the drivers, including Joshua Motha, do not have to risk police violence because when they answered their doors after midnight, they had been asked by their young PAC visitors to accompany them to the trees in the municipal buffer zone, just beyond the one official pathway that led west out of Sharpeville, and stay with them until dawn broke at 6:12 am. "After these people had realized that it was now after the hours that the buses should have started running, they then told us we could leave."[33]

Sharpeville's early morning commuters soon learn that there will be no going to work. Moses Shabangu gets up before 5 am and heads to the bus stop only to overhear people in the street saying. "[N]o-one was going to work today in connection with the complaint about the passes." He goes home. At around the same time, Anthony Ndaba is on his bike riding from Vuka down Zwane Street out the southern exit along the informal pathway across the open fields towards the Brick and Tile factory southeast of Sharpeville when he encounters a large crowd of PAC supporters (deployed the night before) who tell him "and others that we should go back home if we want to live, i.e. if one wanted to live long." He goes home. Johannes Seretho leaves home around 6:30 am but hears from some of his neighbours whose shifts have started earlier "that they had been assaulted" on their way past Brick and Tile "and that their lunch had been left in the street" (most of Sharpeville's commuters take packed lunches to work). He goes home. George Qtwaya half an hour later hears while outside talking to his parents that there are no buses and that people are going to drop their passes at the police station, but being a cautious person "I thought to myself, Well, let me go there, too, and see, so I went." At the bus stop, "I heard it then said that we had not to go to work." Along Seeiso Street he sees lots of people but does not know why they are there, "who did I have to ask? I do not know the people at all. Who do I have to ask?" He goes home. Just before 7 am, Alina Hlongwane's only son Thomas, who will turn 22 in 4 days time, goes "with his lunch tin as usual. ... He said that he was going to work." Just after 7 am, he returns and says that there are no buses. He goes to sleep. William and Solomon Lesito, father and son, walk to the bus stop around the same time as Thomas, but finding no buses, both return to the home in Putsoastene they share with William's wife and Solomon's six younger sisters. Twenty-seven-year-old Naphtali Tseko Maine heads to the bus terminal at 7 am for his job with a paint supplier in Vereeniging carrying his lunch tin packed, as it was every day, by his widowed mother Mirriam. He returns a couple of hours later and tells his mother, brother, and three sisters, one of them permanently disabled, that there are "no buses going to Vereeniging." He is their sole financial support.[34]

Elizabeth Setlhatlole, who has worked at the Vereeniging main post office since 1949, "asked the crowd [at the bus stop] ... where the buses were and they told me that we were not allowed to go to work that day, and I went home." Richard Molefe is starting a new job on Monday after a period of unemployment but is stopped on his way out of town and returns to his home near the football field where he lives with his pregnant wife, 19-year-old son, and five younger daughters. On the west side of town when Anna Marokoane sets off on her bicycle to her employer, Mrs. Watson, in Vanderbijlpark where she works as a maid, the same young men who have spent the night with Joshua Motha and the other bus drivers stop her at the western exit and send her back home. On the east side, just outside the Gate, another group of young men, PAC supporters deployed there the night before, tell people like Emmanuel Fantisi who are heading to work by bike that they "should stay to hear about the Passes."[35]

There are some exceptions to the stop work, but these are relatively rare. Richard Koboekae drives his own car before dawn along Seeiso to Vereeniging, taking some fellow workers with him, when almost the only private vehicles in Sharpeville are taxis. Other people use one or other of the three dirt pathways through which people are allowed to enter or exit Sharpeville besides the Gate (Anna Marokoane has gone out the western one). Philemon

Sikhosane and David Ralebese, who work for the South African Railways, walk down to the end of Zwane, along the southern official pathway and then across some vacant fields through Brick and Tile and then left up to the railyards (about 6 km). Jan Salanyane, after getting home from the police station in the middle of the night, gets on his bicycle at 6 am and makes his way "by a different route than usual" to the McKinnon Chain Factory in Vereeniging; his fellow bench warmer from the early morning, Jan Motsei, does the same thing, reaching his employer Safim at the normal start time. They may have taken the northern pathway, up Ramokhoase Street from the Gate, across the barren Escom right of way to the intersection of the Dickinsonville Industrial Area and Theunis Kruger Street, and then east along Kruger to their jobs on the eastern and north-eastern sides of Vereeniging (about 10 km). Maria Makhoba, attending a funeral out of town is allowed to pass beyond the Gate without any problem. Richard Koboekae, who like Jan Motsei and Emmanuel Fantisi, works for Safim, makes it to the factory, but his boss tells him to go back home early since only 140 of 700 employees have made it in that day, not nearly enough to keep production going. "Industry in Vereeniging was brought to a virtual standstill."[36]

By the time the manager of the VTC, Filiberto Cioffi, responds to Labuschagne's urgent message and goes with a White driver and a bus into Sharpeville at 6 am, he finds no takers for his service. Driving up Seeiso all is quiet. Parking at the bus terminal for two to three minutes, no one boards the bus. Driving back down Seeiso past the various bus stops on the way out of town, even though there were plenty of people gathering along the street, "there were no people waiting." Not one. None. "It is no working today."[37]

Monday Morning, 21 March 1960

> [A]mongst his followers there are no Non-Europeans and there are no Europeans. They are all Africans – they are as one; there is no difference. ... What the Non-European eats, the European also eats.
> (Nyakane Tsolo)[38]

Elias Lidia gets out of bed right at 6:15 am, and, leaving his mother and sister still sleeping at home, he walks over to the closest communal change house to take a shower. He sees nothing special happening in the street, but "In the shower room I heard rumours that people had been molested who had tried to go to work." Wanting to check things out for himself, he goes back home to get his bike and rides over to the bus terminal on Seeiso, "and there I found nothing of the sort. I only found that the people were more than usual, but not too much." (Only one Sharpeville resident ever makes a somewhat credible claim about being assaulted by fellow community members on 21 March 1960.) Lidia stays at the terminal for about half an hour to see what is happening and then goes home for breakfast.[39]

128   *21 March 1960*

Nyakane Tsolo rises around the same time as Lidia, showers and eats breakfast, and walks directly from his family home on the block immediately west of the school square up Seeiso heading for the police station. As he walks past the bus station, he tells those still looking for transport that he is going to the police station to surrender his pass and be the first person arrested. Further up Seeiso, he meets Khoali Teketsi and Moses Smit, a chauffeur with a Std VIII education who has lived in Sharpeville for 13 years. Teketsi and Smit are with a group of PAC supporters who they have gathered from 6 am that morning in Vuka to go to the police station. Tsolo, Teketsi, Smit, and the small groups gather on Seeiso just before the shops, take a shortcut across the field that separates the police station from Seeiso, and walk down the no-name street with the police station on their left and the library and clinic on their right. They walk past the double-gated vehicular entrance to the police station, which is almost directly opposite the clinic, and continue the 8 m to the intersection with Zwane. They turn left on Zwane and walk the 100 m to the public entrance to the police station. Tsolo opens the single gate, unlocked and unguarded as usual, and walks across the yard and up the steps to the verandah of the building. The small crowd remains outside in the police yard. Immediately after Tsolo enters the police station, he sees Sergeant Nkosi in the charge office where Nkosi has been since the start of his shift at 5 am. Tsolo tells "the Police that I personally, and the crowd that was standing outside the fence, had no reference books and that they should arrest me." "I was told by this Non-European Policeman to wait until a Policeman of a higher rank would come there and then I should speak to him about it." Nkosi remembers Tsolo telling him "to open the cells and put all the people into the cells because they have no passes" and himself in turn replying, "But the Europeans are not here." Nkosi, unable to phone since the line was still out, wants to send some of his men to Major van Zyl at the Gate to let him know Tsolo's request, but he also doesn't want to reduce his numbers since most of the Sharpeville police are still patrolling with Captain Cawood. Tsolo offers to send a couple of his people to help get the message through, and Nkosi finally decides he can spare two men (one SAP, one Municipal Police) whom he sends to the Gate after having told them first to ask all the people gathering in the yard to stay outside the fence. Tsolo's men accompany them to help encourage those inside the fence to wait outside, beyond the double gates. This was the first and only time on Monday that any police tell the crowd of people at the police station to disperse. "I was instructed to tell the crowd that they must disperse. I told them to go away but they would not listen." Those gathered to wait stay outside the fence. Tsolo's two men and the two policemen tell people as they walk down Seeiso that a European is coming to the police station to talk about passes.[40]

Tsolo is satisfied to wait and goes outside and tells the people along Zwane what he has been told by Nkosi. He then goes to the western side of the station where he meets Thomas More who is addressing the small gathering of people who have remained there while Tsolo and the others continued to the

Zwane entrance of the police station. More arrives at the police station from his home in Vuka at about the same time that Tsolo is inside talking to Nkosi. He has gone to the police station "to keep the people under proper control" and explains to those he finds already there "that seeing that I am here, they are not to create any disturbance." "They listened to what I said. I also explained to them why we had got there, and they understood ... that we had to submit in regard to the passes." More calls the passes "heart spoilers." Just as he is finishing his explanation, Tsolo arrives and tells them what he has heard from Nkosi. Then they all settle down to wait for the European, "a man of some standing," to arrive.[41]

Among those waiting with them from 8 am onwards are Brown Thabe and Thatela Benedict Griffiths. Thabe has lived in Sharpeville since 1949, married with four school-age children, and working as a salesman in a store in Vereeniging. After finding out that there were no buses that morning he is walking home when he sees a crowd of people at the police station: "Being one of Sharpeville's inhabitants, I have my family there, and I have my children there. ... I wanted to see what was going on."

> Once I got there. ... My ear heard what was being said. ... We will have to listen to what these authorities were going to tell us. ... If they arrest us, let us submit; if they say now we must go, we must all leave. But after thirty minutes we must be there again ... and come and go ... we will remain until that day and then we will go there again. ... I found that well, that is something to listen to.

Griffiths is the 17-year-old son of a Vereeniging SAP sergeant who lives with his parents in their home on Zwane a block southeast and on the same side of the street as the Sharpeville police station. Griffiths walks down Zwane to the pathways beyond Brick and Tile that morning on his way to look for work but is turned back. After going home for a bit, he walks the 200 m from his home to the police station: "I sat down for the whole morning watching what was going on."[42]

While Tsolo and More and Thabe and Griffiths and around 50 to 100 other people (Lidia estimates the number on the Zwane side at 50 looking over the road from his home as he eats breakfast) wait at 8 am at the police station either to be arrested if they support the PAC, or just to see what was happening out of curiosity, word gets out that a European officer is coming to the station to speak about passes. Other PAC members are already encouraging people throughout Sharpeville to come to the police station and hear what is to be done about their heart spoilers and have been doing so since dawn. Around the middle of Seeiso, just east of the bus terminal, Steven Lepee, the pass-burner from Friday, married with three children and a machine operator in his 20s who works for Rand Industries, gathers people. Further east near the Gate on the northern side, Dlamini (whose full name is Johannes Dlamini Monyake and who works for African Cables), the tall young man with the side whiskers and stylish haircut of Sunday night, approaches people coming out of the single men's hostels on their way to work or in some cases to buy breakfast at a café on Seeiso. At the eastern end of the houses on Seeiso, before the hostels and the Gate, Thaddea Ntoampe (also an employee of African Cables) gathers people before the exit from the town in order that they walk up Seeiso to the police station. Lucas Mosheledi who has gone to sleep that night in despair that the PAC campaign has failed wakes up around 7 am, goes out of his house on Seeiso looking for people, and is overjoyed when he "got to the Pan-Africanist group ... they had their leaders with them," including Mokgathi David Ramagole (listed in police documents as David Ramodibe), a 23-year-old single clerk who is the treasurer for the Sharpeville PAC. "There were people from the hostels, there were women, there were children ... not in the crowd but who came forward to see." They "were singing and ... going towards the Police Station."[43]

Down near the Gate, Johannes Monyake and Thaddea Ntoampe encourage people in Seeiso to call out "*Afrika!*" and "*Izwe Lethu,*" and "*Mayibuye,*" and to raise their hands in common symbols of the struggle for freedom, whether supporters of the ANC with their upraised thumb or those of the PAC with their palm facing forward. Labuschagne sees them there and concerned about the growing crowd sends a message to Cawood to return from his patrol. Van Zyl is in Vereeniging calling Pienaar to tell him about having "trouble, skirmishes" with Africans in Sharpeville. When asked if assistance is needed, van Zyl hedges; he tells Pienaar that he "might as well send reinforcements." Though no urgency is relayed by van Zyl, Pienaar decides to send reinforcements "immediately" to Sharpeville and Vereeniging from Soweto (Orlando, Newlands, and Moroka police stations) and Johannesburg (Booysens police station). While this phone conversation is taking place, Cawood arrives at the Gate a little before 7 am to find what he later claims in various court testimonies as "not less than 10,000" men, women, and children, "definitely defiant" and including "several children under five." All are calling out words and phrases he does not understand. "I don't know what language they spoke. They just shouted and screamed. I actually did not speak to anyone in particular."[44]

Lidia thinks Cawood has no reason for concern. Asked later in court to translate the terms into Afrikaans and English, he does so succinctly: "*Laat Afrika! Terugkom.* We always use it together with *Afrika*. '*Afrika! Mayebuje.*' 'Let it come back.'" And what of the supposed threat implied by a thumb pointing up? "Well, that is very, very usual; that is very, very, very, practical. It is known everywhere. Pointing thumbs up is not a very wonderful thing for the Police to have suggested anything about it."

> What would it ordinarily mean, if a motor car passes and you put up your thumb – either just put up your thumb or say "*Afrika!*"? – Well, such a sign would just give the impression that the man is giving the sign of "*Afrika!*" That is the sign used by the A.N.C. The P.A.C. sign is

raising their hand shoulder high. With palm showing to the front. What do they mean by "*Afrika*"? I don't know. I only know that Africa is a continent.[45]

Though Lidia's answer might have seemed a bit blunt in the minds of his White judicial audience, a Department of Justice official translator for the Witwatersrand Supreme Court gives a further explanation for the common usage of "*Afrika*" and the other words and gestures used by Monyake and Ntoampe.

> I know that the common word which was used by a speaker in addressing a meeting used to be "*Pula!*," which was a peaceful form of greeting. Translated "*pula*" means rain, and when the speaker has finished saying whatever he wanted to say, the listeners would in their numbers also respond by saying "*Pula!*"
> And in recent years [from about five years ago] ... the greeting "*Pula!*" has been substituted by the greeting "*Afrika!*"? – Yes ...
> [I]n the ordinary course the exchange of such a greeting between people, is [it] ... in any sense provocative? – No, it is not ...
> And what of "*Mayibuye*" in your own words? – Let it come back! ...
> And ... "*Mayibuye Africa!*" would that mean May Africa come back? – Yes ...
> [I]f a political leader uses the phrase "*Mayibuye Africa!*" as a slogan ... one of the meanings could be ... "May we also participate in the government of Africa as the people who live in Africa?" – Yes. [46]

The SB men who arrive in civilian clothes at the Gate at around the same time as Cawood have no patience for listening. The prime responsibility of the SB, nicknamed the Greys after the café on the street level of the building they occupy in central Johannesburg, is to investigate all organisations considered "a danger to the State," particularly the ANC and the PAC, and "to prevent strikes." Sergeant Wynand Wessels, who since 1954 has been the Vereeniging-based SB officer with responsibility for Vereeniging, Vanderbijlpark, and Evaton, arrives at the Gate at 6:30 am. He watches Monyake and Ntoampe with their PAC lapel badges and their call and response of *Afrika!* and *Izwe Lethu!* and *Mayibuye Africa!* with the gathering crowd until the arrival of two of his colleagues from Johannesburg, Captain Willem Willers and Sergeant Hendrik Muller at 7:15 am. Willers, confronted by a crowd that he describes as in the dozens (*duisende*) rather than the thousands of Cawood, follows the practices instilled in him by his SB boss, Colonel Spengler: identify the leaders and "get behind what is behind them." He sees Monyake and Ntoampe in the front of a crowd, which includes lots of children (none have gone to school that day). They are wearing PAC badges on the lapels on the left side of their chests and calling out *Afrika!* And *Izwe Lethu!* Willers immediately orders that they be seized, the words used are "*die vangen toe*" and "*Vang julle daardie man*" with the operative verb to catch (*vang*). Wessels grabs Ntoampe and shoves him towards a police van. Malakia Mmotong opens the van door for Wessels. It is the same van in which Mmotong has spent the night hiding. Constable Beyl is still driving the van with his sjambok on the front seat beside him. David Ntsame, the Sharpeville gatekeeper who has stayed on duty after his shift ends at 6 am, wraps his arms around Monyake's waist, lifts him up bodily with his feet off the ground, and carries him over to the police van to join Ntoampe in the back. Though Ntsame is following orders he wonders why the men are arrested (and arrest is what he understands he has been ordered to do). "He [Ntoampe] was saying '*Afrika!*' and that they did not want passes. That is all he said. ... He only kept quiet, and we took him away." Both are taken to the Vereeniging police station for interrogation by the SB men. The duty constable who processes their arrest at 8 am (it is no longer a matter of being caught or seized), Julius Pokwane, still remembers them clearly months later:

> I searched two young boys who were from Sharpeville ... on [Monyake] I found a belt ... on [Ntoampe] I found a belt as well as a torn reference book [Pokwane uses the word pass, but this is transcribed as reference book by the Court] ... inside the pass book is written T.L. Ntoampe.

The belts, Pokwane testifies, are used to hold their pants up; they don't hold them in their hands as possible weapons, as suggested by the prosecution.[47]

Just as the SB men leave, Cawood as the officer in charge (OIC) acts. Like the previous night, he has no patience when dealing with Sharpeville's residents. He "could see that they were looking for trouble, so. ... I dropped several [glass] teargas bombs in the street ... among the front portion of the crowd." There is no wind, so the gas does not dissipate quickly or blow back on the police; in fact, a slight gust takes it towards the small crowd, but it also doesn't have the effect Cawood wants of making everyone disappear entirely. The Sharpeville residents simply regroup a little further up Seeiso. Cawood's decision to use tear gas and the teargassing itself takes about ten minutes total.[48]

As the tear gas dissipates around 7:30 am, van Zyl arrives back at the Gate from Vereeniging and assumes command. He has been making and receiving calls from his equivalents in Vanderbijlpark and Evaton and reporting to his superiors in Johannesburg. Because of news that he has received from his local calls of thousands of PAC supporters in Vanderbijlpark and Evaton marching into White areas to surrender their passes and request arrest, he immediately orders Cawood with his Vereeniging men to depart for Vanderbijlpark, leaving behind with van Zyl the two Sten gunners Scheepers and van Rensburg and the Sharpeville police who had been called on duty at midnight, and also directing a head constable and an African detective (both members of the Vereeniging SAP) to go to Evaton. Then van Zyl, frustrated that some people remain in the street, decides to take more forceful action to make everyone in Seeiso go home and remove any risk, as he fears, of a march from Sharpeville into White Vereeniging and the police station there. He decides on a baton charge. According to his own telling of the story, he raises five fingers in the air to let everyone know they have five minutes to disperse. Even before the time is up, he goes over to the crowd and says (as he later claims), "Look, chaps, you might get hurt. Please go home. I am asking you nicely. Please." Not a single person there remembers hearing those words spoken.[49]

Van Zyl's 20 White and 37 African policemen charge and beat people with their batons and knobkerries. Ephraim Thaba, a Bapedi hostel dweller (he works the night shift at African Cables; his wife and five children live in Pietersburg), has just come out of the hostel gate to buy breakfast at a café at Stand No. 50 on Seeiso: "there was a crowd of people ... and just when I reached the crowd, the Police charged and hit me." He is injured so badly with lacerations to his right knee and wounds to both his hands that he has to spend the next two months in hospital. He is the first victim of police violence after the sun rises on Monday 21 March 1960.[50]

Still not satisfied that everyone has cleared the area by the Gate, van Zyl orders some of his men to chase the hostel workers back into their dormitories, and others to go up Seeiso and neighbouring streets and make every resident go back into their homes. They take violence with them wherever they go. They club and beat people in the hostels so severely that some of the residents, the night soil workers particularly – Baca municipal employees who Ntsame says were "known as people who are not full of peace" – fight back with stones picked up off the ground (Ntsame says none of these stones have been stockpiled, "I did not see any heaps of stones in the vicinity of the hostel") and force van Zyl's men to retreat. Constable Jan Hendrik Grove, driving a van to evacuate the policemen, empties his revolver magazine (six shots) firing at the hostel dwellers. Others of van Zyl's men rush in random fashion along neighbouring streets, claiming later that they have been shot at, but more likely shooting at themselves in their frantic disarray (no guns are ever found at Sharpeville, not one). The Sten-gunner van Rensburg fires short bursts at random, 12 shots in all, up Seeiso; constables Cornelius Johannes Els and Andre Thomas Kallis each empty a revolver magazine firing at houses along the main street; Constable Jakobus Nicolaas Coetzee fires one shot from his .303 rifle, a warning shot he claims. None report hitting anyone, and no bullet-related injuries or deaths are officially recorded. After this foray, van Zyl lines his men across Seeiso, effectively barring exit from and entry to the town along its only tarred entrance and waits for reinforcements to arrive. By 8 am, no one can go to work even if they want to.[51]

Senior officials in Johannesburg and Pretoria of what is known as the "Bantu Administration" and of the SAP receive the news from van Zyl and others and plan their response. Mathinus Smuts in Johannesburg, the "chief Bantu commissioner" for the entire Witwatersrand, is asked by the "Bantu" commissioner in Evaton to come; "I decided I should go to the police station at Evaton and if possible speak to the Africans gathered." Colonel J. C. Lemmer, the adjunct commissioner and head of the SAP for the Witwatersrand and Lieutenant Colonel Pienaar's immediate superior has discussions with the SB deputy head Spengler. Spengler (who is reputed to share the same birthday as Hitler) advises Lemmer that the police should never negotiate with the leader of a "mob" but only interrogate ("*ondervra*") him, do not arrest ("*nie arresteer nie*"), only catch ("*vang*"). When Smuts and Lemmer meet in Lemmer's office at 8:30 am, they have already made their respective decisions. Smuts tells Lemmer "I want to go to Evaton." Lemmer cuts short the prescheduled meeting (to discuss the upcoming Union Festival celebrating the 50th anniversary of the Union of South Africa) in order to arrange for police reinforcements to be sent to Evaton, Vanderbijlpark, and Vereeniging. Within a few minutes of their meeting ending, they both act. At 8:45 am, Smuts gets into his own car and, after informing his office where he is going, begins his drive to Evaton. At 9 am, Lemmer calls his superior, the assistant commissioner of the National SAP in Pretoria, Brigadier Cornelius Johannes Els, to let him know the situation. He calls again within a half hour and tells Els that there are 20,000 people gathered in Sharpeville. Els arranges for police reinforcements, including 10 Saracen armoured troop cars (the police had purchased 47 of these vehicles in 1959 specifically for crowd control), to be sent to Vereeniging, Vanderbijlpark, and Evaton. He also decides "definitely [to] come to Sharpeville myself at that stage to check on the circumstances and see what was happening there." The most important official dealing with African affairs on the Witwatersrand is on his way to speak to the residents of Evaton, Bophelong (where most of Iscor's African workers live), Boipatong, and Sharpeville. One of the highest-ranking police officers in South Africa has decided to go to Sharpeville, and though no one else knows it at the time, and it will never be written about (until now), he will be accompanied by the next commissioner of police, the highest-ranking SAP officer in the country, General Hendrik Jacobus du Plooy (founder of the SB). Events move so fast that Smuts passes the first group of Saracens while they are still on the road to Evaton, which he reaches at 10 am.[52]

In the meantime, the police rebuild their communications network with Sharpeville. A post office truck with short wave radio arrives at the Gate, parks near the post office on Seeiso, and Ignatius Ferreira, after finishing his breakfast at 7:30 am, takes control of relaying messages for van Zyl to his police superiors. Van Zyl no longer has to keep driving back and forth to his Vereeniging office. Before 9 am, the telephone cable outside Sharpeville has been repaired, and Ferreira again takes responsibility for arranging with the post office to have special numbers to get through to Johannesburg and Pretoria. At 9:30 am a radio car from the Johannesburg police station in Auckland Park arrives at the Sharpeville police station. Communication is now fully established between the police station and the Gate and directly with Johannesburg and Pretoria. The radio car, a 1959 Chevrolet, is staffed by three constables, two of whom, Louis Christiaan van Wyk and J. du Plessis, are armed with Sten guns. They will stay at the police station for the next four hours.[53]

As the police organise their forces, more and more of Sharpeville's residents gather at the police station to learn what is going to happen with the pass laws. Lucas Mosheledi helps Tsolo "keep order." He speaks to Sergeant Nkosi and asks to be arrested along with all the other PAC members present – he estimates there are 150 of them present – "they [the police] know them all, and they would have arrested them together." While Mosheledi is talking with Nkosi, Lidia cycles over after his breakfast. Mokgathi David Ramagole arrives from Seeiso bringing news that the young people gathered there "were being stopped from coming through by the police" and that there had been police violence and shooting at the Gate. The young people he says are angry and want "to fight." Tsolo sends two men "to go and call those people to come here" to the police station. These are the men he sends out alongside Nkosi's two African constables who walk down Seeiso together. The two men are Khoali Teketsi and Moses Smit. Smit regards his task as a matter of respect: "If one has invited the people to come, they cannot go to any place unless they hear from you, because it is through you they had come; they have been invited." Teketsi asks Lidia to join him and Smit and any others who want to go and walk down Seeiso to Putsoastene. Lidia's determination to find out what is happening and his enthusiasm for the PAC and its leaders have been growing as the day unfolds; he decides to "go and witness."[54]

Teketsi, Smit, Lidia, and others head down Seeiso to just beyond the school square. They find a crowd gathered there, at the western end of Putsoastene, of about 700 people (Lidia's estimate). The people gathered want the police (about 30 of them) who are 150 m further east on Seeiso towards the post office where Ferreira has his communications van parked, to accompany them up Seeiso to the police station; "they [people in the crowd] told us they were waiting for the Police to march together to the Police Station." Although the young people are "annoyed ... and hostile," "There was no shouting, except for the occasional shout of '*Afrika!*' ... there were no stones there. ... There were no sticks." They tell Lidia "that the Police fired shots [earlier] ... The Police just started firing, was what the people told me." Teketsi speaks first to the young people and explains "that this pass campaign was not a campaign where they were going to fight, and if they intend fighting they must go back to their homes." Then Teketsi and Smit approach a police officer holding "a little stick" (it is van Zyl with his swagger stick) and tell him that "there was no need to be afraid of these people." Smit considers it a friendly exchange. The officer tells them to go ahead and walk up Seeiso, and he and his men will follow. Khoali Teketsi calls out "Come! Come! Come! Let us march to the Police Station." Thekiso is there calling out "*Izwe Lethu*" as they march together towards the police station. The young men led by Teketsi and Smit walk slowly up Seeiso, speaking to people standing outside their houses as they pass by. It is a "very slow" march. They tell everyone that a European is coming to the police station to talk about the passes that they plan to surrender. Some in the crowd hear African policemen tell them in Sesotho to go to the police station and understand it as an official request. Lidia splits off on a shortcut to Zwane and takes his bike home before rejoining Teketsi and Smit and the others who have gone to the police station. The PAC organisers have never intended "to go out of the location" to Vereeniging; they have always planned only to go to the Sharpeville police station. By 10 am when the Seeiso people arrive at the police station and join those who have continued to gather since 8 am, they are "many."[55]

Among those already waiting is Peter Molefi who arrives at 9:30 am "to listen to what was going to be said with regard to passes. ... I went there to be arrested, that it would be explained in regard to the complaint I had [about passes]." Molefi is a sharp dresser. He wears brown shoes, brown trousers, a white shirt with a red waistcoat with black lining (he will be remembered as the man in the red shirt), and a traditional woven Basotho hat. He has been waiting to start his regular noon shift as a wine steward at the fanciest hotel in Vereeniging, the Riviera, when his grandfather tells him there are no buses, so after sitting in his yard for a while, he hears people passing by saying somebody is going to come "to address the people at the police station" so he goes there. By 10 am there are so many gathered at the police station that Constable Litelu, who has been on duty since 2:30 am, "could not count them."[56]

Elias Lidia feels he is at the police station "with a mission – on a mission." "I would never have gone away, even if they [those gathered] kept on for 17 hours, because I was there to collect some material for my book. If I had gone away, I would have gone empty-handed." He is keeping notes all the time. He hires some individuals "to collect some of the sayings of the people" and places them around the police station, including one right outside the double gates. And he treats everyone with respect, which means speaking in an indirect way. With Tsolo, "I had to befriend" him; "because I don't know anything about the P.A.C.'s policies. I was still digging for this on the 21st." "My aim was to be very friendly to him, so as to get information about their [PAC] policy. ... That is why I had to be very soft in answer. ... Because I am not entitled [to ask a direct question]. ... I was acting like a member." He has never before engaged in any political action, not for the ANC, not for the PAC, but "[i]t was the first time, on the 21st, that I took some part in it." He believes "Very much" in what they are doing.[57]

At 10 am, Colonel Lemmer orders Lieutenant Colonel Pienaar to go to Vanderbijlpark and Vereeniging to take charge of operations. Pienaar leaves Johannesburg immediately in his 1958 Chevrolet heading for Vanderbijlpark with his African driver at the wheel and a White constable in the back seat. Pienaar is in full uniform, with the blue band on his peaked cap and the blue epaulettes on his shoulders showing a senior officer. Just after 10 am, van Zyl requests more reinforcements:

> The position in which Vereeniging was placed in relation to the three places [Bophelong, Evaton, and Sharpeville] would have been extremely dangerous if the police were over-powered. ... I believed that there would be a bloodbath. I saw no other way out. That is how it looked to me and I am convinced that it would have happened.

Van Zyl also requests that aircraft be sent to all three places to intimidate the crowds, and he orders the mobilisation of the *"Skiet Commando"* – armed White citizens – in Vereeniging "with the object of having somebody on hand who could take action if anything happened." At 10:15 am, Lemmer orders Lieutenant Jakobus Johannes Claassen and three trucks containing 43 policemen to leave the police station at Hospital Hill in Johannesburg and meet Pienaar in Vanderbijlpark. Claassen has been in the SAP for 30 years and has never once used a gun. The first of the reinforcements ordered by Pienaar and approved by Lemmer and Els get to Sharpeville just before 10:30 am. Captain Frederick Jakobus Pieter Coetzee with 19 policemen from the Jeppe police station, three of them armed with Sten guns, arrives at the Gate. Sergeant Jeremiah Oosthuizen and 21 policemen from the Moroka police station in a lightly armoured truck (wire on the front and side windows), after first stopping at the Newlands police station to pick up three White officers, drive directly to the Sharpeville police station and enter the yard on the west through the double gates on the no-name street. Oosthuizen is 23 years old. He has been in the SAP since he was 18. He is armed with a Sten gun, which he has never used before other than in one training course.[58]

Tsolo waits patiently for the European promised by Nkosi to arrive at the police station. Just after 9:30 am, two hours into his wait, he talks with the men in the radio car but none of them are the officer expected. A few minutes after that conversation, he approaches Head Constable Heyl (now OIC of the police station) and Sergeant Grobler. They have just walked up Seeiso (together with four constables) after having been part of van Zyl's force that clubbed and shot at the Sharpeville residents near the Gate. Before Tsolo can speak, Heyl yells at him *"Wat is die moeilikheid?"* (What is the problem?) and tells him to get the crowd to be quiet and to keep away from the fence. Heyl doesn't mention what he and Grobler have been doing on Seeiso. Tsolo tells the crowd to be quiet, and they obey him instantly. Heyl and Grobler are impressed. The crowd is well-behaved. But neither of them is the important European that Tsolo is waiting for. Finally at 10:30 am Captain Jakobus Christiaan Visser arrives from the Vereeniging police station and walks into the Sharpeville police station through the public entry on Zwane. He is the first SAP officer that Nkosi has seen inside the police station since he came on duty over five hours earlier (the others all stay outside the building). Visser is the man "of some standing" that Tsolo has expected since before 8 am.[59]

Visser arrives in a car with the license plate TJ1980 (Lucas Mosheledi has a gift for remembering such details). As he drives up Seeiso, he notices that there are large numbers of people walking in the same direction as he is toward the police station. He is in a grey suit, grey hat, with glasses. He has driven in his own car from Vereeniging where since 1958 he has commanded the Criminal Investigation Department (CID), the detectives, two of whom are in his car with him. He is also accompanied by a truck from Johannesburg Central containing about 15 to 20 White policemen, including Pieter Machiel Saaiman, an undercover detective constable whose normal daily job is picking up what he terms "loafers" in the city. Visser comes after having conversations with van Zyl and his other superiors and knows that senior members of the "Bantu Administration" and the SAP plan to speak to the people gathered at the police station once they arrive from Johannesburg and Pretoria. He will never admit to this publicly.[60]

Nyakane Tsolo sees the arrival of the police – Oosthuizen and his men armed "with rifles and bayonettes" on the west side and officers in civilian clothes on the south side. He walks up to the verandah and speaks with the officer "who replied to me," a man in civilian clothes, "wearing a pair of spectacles, and well set." Other officers stand nearby and they, like many of the people with Tsolo, will overhear much of the conversation. Before Tsolo can start speaking, Visser tells him to get the crowd back from the fence and to have the people standing on the clinic roof watching events get down. Tsolo complies with what he considers a reasonable request and gives direction calling out and signalling with his hands, and the people move back and get down. He then speaks directly to Visser (the conversation is entirely in English), telling him "that myself and the crowd gathered there had come to surrender ourselves to be arrested because we had no passes or reference books." Visser tells him that there are not sufficient cells to accommodate all those wanting to be arrested. "There was some further discussion between myself and him," and then the "officer told me to wait for this high official to come. ... He said that we had to wait, he would be coming presently round about 2 o'clock." Peter Molefi is standing close to Tsolo; he wants "to hear ... to listen to what is going to be said"; "I heard that this official would be there at 2 pm." Nkosi standing just behind Visser listens to the end of the conversation. Tsolo talks about the innate humanness of all the people gathered there that day. When Visser asks him if, as a "Pan-Africanist ... in the event of a Non-European getting a majority ... will [they] chase the Europeans away?" Tsolo responds "amongst his followers there are no Non-Europeans and there are no Europeans. They are all Africans – they are as one; there is no difference. ... What the Non-European eats, the European also eats."[61]

Tsolo is under no misunderstanding as to what has been promised, an important police official who will talk to all those gathered about passes and a specific time for that speech. Immediately after finishing his conversation with Visser, he speaks (in Sesotho) with Thomas More, Lucas Mosheledi, Elias Lidia, Moses Smit, and then to all the people gathered on Zwane about what Visser has said to him. Mosheledi hears Visser's words repeated by Tsolo directly to him in Sesotho as "at 2 o'clock one of the high officials of the Police would come there [the football grounds] and speak to the gathering about passes." Lidia hears the same straight from Tsolo: "You shall have your answer at 2 o'clock as there was a man from Pretoria who would come and address the people. ... A senior Police Officer"; Smit also heard "we had to wait until 2 o'clock ... when a European would address them ... the Native Commissioner." Constable Litelu, eight hours after he came on duty, hears Tsolo speaking to the crowd ("when Tsolo spoke to these people they would listen to him and they would stop making a noise") on Zwane: "Tsolo said that it is said we must wait and that a high official would come and speak to them ... I heard Tsolo saying that to the people who were waiting at the fence." Tsolo's use of the passive construction "it is said" is understood by Litelu to convey to any listener that Tsolo got the information "from the Police." Joshua Motha, the bus driver who has spent the night among trees on the western side of Sharpeville and who has come to the police station to hear about passes, also hears the police officer ask the people to move to the football field and wait for the answer at 2 pm, and their response: "If anything was to be said we would listen to what was said from here, where we stand, where we are."[62]

The message is sent out, we will stay, we will wait. Brown Thabe watches Tsolo walk from the southern side of the police station to the northern side, all along the fence telling people "that we have to wait until 2 o'clock and then we will get the answer." Tsolo asks messengers to carry the news throughout Sharpeville. Lidia walks along the fence on the outside asking people to stay back; Smit tells people the same from the inside of the fence; all the way around from the single gate on Zwane to the double gate on the no-name street and back again, and again, and again for the next two hours. Mosheledi will stay with them and help open and close the double gates as police vehicles arrive and depart. Tsolo and others take a break and go to get something to eat; it is three hours to wait until 2 pm. He is exhilarated: "I had in mind that the whole of the Sharpeville village would be there ... and I was very pleased about it." With PAC members accounting by their own figures for less than half a percent of Sharpeville's residents, and about ten percent of the townspeople physically gathered at the police station, he can be confident that the opposition to passes has widespread local support. Many in the crowd sit down – it will be a long wait – and start singing *Nkosi Sikelel' iAfrika*. "It is just a hymn," says Peter Molefi, "a hymn that is sung by people who are, shall I say, in a happy mood." Tsolo says to him, "You must be happy, maybe you will get what you are waiting for"[63] (Figure 5.1).

Even though an agreement has been reached with Tsolo, and the crowd at the police station has settled down to wait, Visser and his immediate superior van Zyl still feel that more reinforcements are needed and they telephone through to Lemmer to send additional policemen. Visser thinks that the men already at the police station are tired and impatient and he thinks that even with reinforcements it will be necessary to shoot; would that be the only way to disperse the crowd? "*Ja.*"[64]

The Aerial View

A news reporter flying overhead just after 11 am takes an aerial photograph that captures clearly the situation at the police station, the no-name street, Zwane, and along Seeiso, and in the rest of the town as Tsolo goes for lunch. The chartered plane flies out of the Baragwanath airfield just southwest of

140 *21 March 1960*

Figure 5.1 Nyakane Tsolo (identified by Michael Thekiso), bottom left, with the crowd outside the police station, around 1:10 pm, 21 March 1960.

Photo by Ian Berry. Source: Ambrose Reeves, *Shooting at Sharpeville: The Agony of South Africa* (London: Victor Gollancz, 1960).

Soweto and spends 10 to 15 minutes circling back and forth a half dozen times over Sharpeville before returning to the airfield. The reporter wants to see what is happening throughout the town, and most of the time the plane is at an elevation of 500 m above the ground. At the police station, however, he wants to get a closer view and has the plane go down to 250 m where he takes three images of the police station, from the south (the one his newspaper will publish), northwest, and north. The only crowd he sees anywhere in Sharpeville is at the police station. He makes a rough estimate of their numbers – "4,000 or 5,000 people, at that point." A close examination of his photograph (Figure 5.2) using freely accessible online software suggests that his estimate is accurate. Most of the people are lined up along the double laned and tarred Zwane Street (30 m wide with no fence on the southern side of the street) in front of the public entrance to the police station; there is also a large gathering in the no-name street on the west side where the crowd collects on the tarred road bounded by a 1.4 m-high diamond mesh fence along the boundary of the police station and a similar barrier along the clinic property – essentially a fenced corridor 19 m wide. There are a few people on the northwestern side and a few on the southeastern side. Everyone is outside the fence where Lidia and Smit are walking up and down. There is a scattering of people around the shops on the northwest. There are no crowds on Seeiso, the main diagonal street to the north, nor any significant numbers of people, other than the usual daily foot traffic, on any of the pathways that crisscross the empty fields to the northwest, north, and northeast of the police

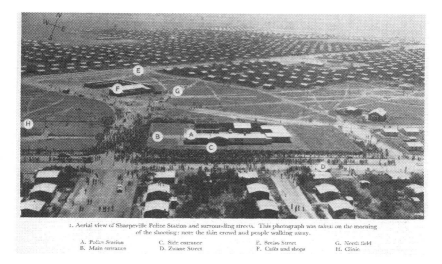

Figure 5.2 Aerial photograph of the Sharpeville police station just after 11 am, 21 March 1960.

Photo by B. J. van Beloll. Source: Ambrose Reeves, *Shooting at Sharpeville: The Agony of South Africa* (London: Victor Gollancz, 1960).

station, or on any other streets; "the rest of the location seemed to be perfectly quiet and restful." The crowd at the police station "also looked quite peaceful, from what I could see of it." Just as he leaves, the reporter sees some South African air force planes – he is not sure if they are propeller-driven Harvard Trainers or some of the Sabre Mk 6 jets recently brought into service (actually both types will be at Sharpeville) – dive down on the police station getting as close as 10 m to 20 m above the buildings. The diving has "very little effect" on the size of the crowd, "people were joining and leaving the crowd all the time," but "there was some waving from the crowd as the Jets dived."[65] The Sharpeville police station is still there almost exactly as it was in 1960 except the trees have all grown.

Notes

1 Petrus Tom, interview 12 October 2022.
2 Nancy Clark, *Manufacturing Apartheid: State Corporations in South Africa* (New Haven: Yale University Press, 1994), 150–162.
3 Ramon Lewis Leigh, *Vereeniging: South Africa* (Johannesburg: Courier-Gazette, 1968), 154.
4 Vereeniging Town Council to Secretary for Native Affairs, 19 December 1952, Native Affairs Department (NTS) 4179, 33/313(F), Part VI, Central Government Archives since 1910 (SAB).
5 Ruth First, "Give African Miners a Fair Deal!" *New Age*, 4 February 1960. The author, Ruth First, was a political activist who was accused in the Treason Trial, later imprisoned and interrogated by the SB, and ultimately assassinated in 1982

142   *21 March 1960*

      by a parcel bomb that was sent to her in exile in Mozambique by SB Officer Craig Williamson.
6 *Rand Daily Mail* (*RDM*), 29 January 1960.
7 Spengler quoted in *RDM*, 5 May 1960.
8 "Disaster at the Coalbrook North Colliery," http://mineaccidents.com.au/uploads/disaster.pdf.
9 Full text of 1950 Suppression of Communism Act can be found here: https://en.wikisource.org/wiki/Suppression_of_Communism_Act,_1950.
10 *RDM*, 22 March 1960; *New Age*, 24 March 1960.
11 Major Willem van Zyl testimony, "*Commission of Enquiry into the Occurrences at Sharpeville (and other places) on the 21st March 1960*" (hereafter Commission), 187. The Commission materials are all digitized in their entirety and freely accessible online, https://idep.library.ucla.edu/sharpeville-massacre.
12 Reporters for the Black press who were themselves in Sharpeville on 21 March 1960 published immediate text and visual accounts that differed from those in the mainstream White media. Eighteen Sharpeville residents provided eye-witness accounts within days of 21 March 1960, and these were sent directly to the United Nations in New York. Almost 130 witnesses testified to the government-established Commission of Enquiry in April, May, and June 1960, including over 30 Sharpeville residents who spoke eloquently at the hearings in Vereeniging about their experiences. One hundred and twenty people testified at the *Regina vs. Monyake and Others* trial (Case No. R. 58/1960 in the Court of the Magistrate of the Regional Division of South Transvaal, held at Vereeniging: The State against Johannes Monyake and others, hereafter referred to as Court, held in Vereeniging to prosecute Sharpeville residents for their actions on 21 March 1960, from July 1960 until June 1961), including 30 Sharpeville residents (some the same as at the Commission, some different). In addition, in making claims to the state for compensation for the deaths and injuries caused, several hundred Sharpeville residents provided detailed statements in 1961 and 1962 about their experiences on 21 March 1960, and the impact of the events on themselves and their families. Claimant files and statements for Sharpeville people with Basutoland connections are held in the British Archives. Ambrose Reeves, *Shooting at Sharpeville: The Agony of South Africa* (London: Victor Gollancz, 1960) provides a detailed description of events based on the 100 testimonies that he had collected from the Sharpeville injured still in their hospital beds during the three days immediately after the shooting. We also conducted interviews with over 30 survivors and family members in 2018, 2019, and 2022. Because much of the evidence presented here is new and is in conflict with the police stories which have dominated the existing literature, detailed footnote references are provided for each paragraph. The Court materials are also digitized in their entirety and freely accessible online, https://idep.library.ucla.edu/sharpeville-massacre.
13 Francis Motshoahole testimony, Court 2448.
14 Elias Lidia testimony, Commission 2272, 2292. Lidia testified in both English and Afrikaans.
15 Elias Lidia testimony, Commission 2292, 2293, 2294, 2333. Nyakane Tsolo knows him as Khoali Teketsi, testimony, Commission 2473. Koali Teketsi is the spelling on the death certificate (29 September 1994) shared with us by Michael Thekiso.
16 Elias Lidia testimony, Commission 2272–2273, 2291, 2292, 2334–2335.
17 Elias Lidia testimony, Commission 2272–2273, 2289–2292.
18 David Ntsame testimony, Court 1843.
19 Simon Mashelide (known as Lucas Mosheledi by Michael Thekiso) testimony, Commission 2200, 2209, 2210, 2233; Francis Motshoahole, testimony, Commission 935, 936, 937, Court 2448, 2449, 2454, 2456, 2459.

20 Richard Mtimkulu testimony, Court 2646, 2647; Mita Motsepe statement, K110 1/3/60, SAB; Izak Rampai testimony, Court 1673, 1674; Christian Nxumalo (Khumalo) testimony, Commission 1065, 1068, Court 2125; Bernard Xingwana testimony, Commission 1069; Piet Kok testimony, Court 2063, 2067; Simon Mahlase (Mahlasi) testimony, Commission 1911; Piet Mokoena testimony, Court 2568, 2578, 2579; Simon Mashelide testimony, Commission 2234; Tsolo testimony, Commission 2500.
21 Jan Nyepisi testimony, Court 2005, 2006, 2007, 2008; Jan Motsei testimony, Court 2010, 2013, 2014; Jan Salanyane testimony, Court 2017, 2018; Azael Mabote testimony, Court 2022, 2023.
22 Description of badges in evidence, Court 668–669, 697.
23 David Mokabela testimony, Court 2298; Quartus Fourie testimony, Commission 228, 229; Edward Cawood testimony, Court 645, 648, 650, 679; Johannes Heyl testimony, Commission 972.
24 Cawood testimony, Court, 650–652; Christian Nxumalo (Khumalo) testimony, Court 2130; Malakia Mmotong testimony, Court 1296; Fourie testimony, Court 2660; Heyl testimony, Court 1176.
25 Fourie testimony, Court 2660, 2661; Cawood testimony, Commission 145, Court 652–657, 665–666; Michiel Labuschagne testimony, Commission 381, 382; Heyl testimony, Commission 512, Court 1179; Thomas More cross examination of Cawood, Court 691, 692; Mmotong in response to cross examination by More, Court 1297, 1343.
26 Mashelide testimony, Commission 2210, 2211, 2212; Motshoahole testimony, Commission 938, 939, 940, Court 2450, 2451; Christian Mpempe testimony, Court 2510, 2511 2513; Aaron Exilishe (Xilishe) testimony, Court 2681, 2688, 2689; Mahasane Michael Thekiso interview, 3 October 2018.
27 Josephina Mofokeng statement, K110 1/3/60, SAB.
28 Mmotong testimony, Court 1253, 1296; Motha testimony, Court 2550; Mashelide testimony, Commission 2201, 2234. Beyl will always deny that he carried a sjambok until presented with definitive pictorial proof by Sydney Kentridge who on cross-examination suggested to him, "You see, if Policemen carry sjamboks round with them when they deal with crowds, it might give the impression that they regard the crowd as animals, might it not?" Beyl admitted he was the person in the photograph carrying a sjambok. Beyl testimony, Commission 2611, 2613, 2614.
29 Motsei testimony, Court 2014; Edwin Litelu testimony, Commission 751, 752; Elias Mvala testimony, Court 2405, 2407; Ignatius Ferreira testimony, Commission 1193; Willem van Zyl testimony, Commission 177; Fourie testimony, Court 2661. Litelu is transcribed as Dethedo at the Monyake trial, Court 2083.
30 Gideon Pienaar testimony, Court 963, 1009. On the common use by the police of "*kaffir*," see the testimony of Constable Johannes Petrus Mostert van Zyl, especially the cross-examination by Jack Unterhalter, Court 2244.
31 Cawood testimony, Court 657; Moses Nkosi testimony, 2710, 2711; Labuschagne testimony, Commission 383. When questioned in court as to whether any force had been used by the police, Ferreira replied, "No, no force," Commission 1194.
32 Labuschagne testimony, Commission 383, 384.
33 Joshua Motha testimony, Commission 1915, Court 2519, 2520, 2522–2523; Zaphenia Maphike testimony, Court 2035, 2036, 2037; Daniel Seetsi testimony, Court 2676, 2679; Edwin Mosholi testimony, Court 2029, 2030; Aaron Exilishe (Xilishe) testimony, Court, 2680, 2684, 2685, 2686, 2687, 2689, 2690.
34 Moses Shabangu testimony, Commission 1715, 1720; Anthony Ndaba testimony, Court 2570; Johannes Seretho testimony, Court 3062; George Qtwaya testimony, Commission 1991, 1992; Alina Hlongoane statement, William Lesito statement, Solomon Lesito statement, Meriam Maine statement, K110 1/3/60, SAB.

35 Elizabeth Setlhatlole statement, SAP 619 31/58/60, SAB; Martha Molefe statement, K110 1/3/60, SAB; Anna Marokoane statement, SAP 622 31/58/60, SAB; Emmanuel Fantisi statement, SAP 620 31/58/60, SAB; Isiah Monyane statement, Sharpeville Affidavits, United Nations (UN) Archives.
36 Richard Koboekae statement, SAP 620 31/58/60, SAB; Philemon Skozane (Sikhosane) testimony, Court 1670, 1671; Daniel Ralebese testimony, Court 2462, 2463; Salanyane testimony, Court 2019; Motsei testimony, Court 2010; Maria Makhoba statement, SAP 621 31/58/60, SAB; Another Safim employee, Piet Seeri, concerned about not being able to get to work, had slept Sunday night at his employer's premises, but he too was sent home early on Monday, statement SAP 619 31/58/60, SAB. The reference to industry being at a standstill is from the judgement of the magistrate in the *Regina vs. Monyake and Others* case, Court, 68.
37 Filiberto Cioffi testimony, Court, 2654, 2655; Paul Olifant testimony, Court 2566. Labuschagne would later testify that the bus was stoned by hostile crowds. Cioffi's testimony proved the falsity of that claim, Labuschagne testimony, Commission 383.
38 Nkosi testimony, Commission 2713.
39 Lidia testimony, Commission 2273, 2274. A claim of actual assault is here distinguished from references to fears of such. Aaron Mokoena said some young men on Sunday night had hit him on his head causing some bleeding, but they left him at home rather than insist he join them, and he did not need any medical attention other than from his wife. The only sign of an injury that remained nine months later when testifying in court was a "very small scar" – a quarter inch wide – on top of his head. Mokoena testimony, Court 2516, 2517, 2518. Justice Wessels wrote a very contorted description of what he claimed was widespread evidence of violence on Sunday night, but in the end had to note that "in the nature of things I can make absolutely no accurate finding in this connection." Wessels Judgement 58–59.
40 Nyakane Tsolo testimony, Commission 2486–2489; Moses Smit testimony, Commission 2016–2018, 2031–2033; Nkosi testimony, Commission 2711–2712; Constable Matthews Ngumbuxa testimony, Court 2190–2193. There are numerous witnesses who testify to hearing that a European will come. See, for example, David Khoali testimony, Commission 2736, 2738; Benjamin Maroo testimony, Commission 1701; Thomas Msimang testimony, Commission 3132.
41 More testimony, Commission 2520–2522.
42 Brown Thabe testimony, Commission 1796–1798, 1800–1801, 1808, 1810; Benedict Griffiths testimony, Commission 1948, 1949; Griffiths statement, Sharpeville Affidavits, UN.
43 The 50-person estimate comes from Elias Lidia who could see the police station from his house as he was eating breakfast, Lidia testimony, Commission 2294, 2296; Mashelide testimony, Commission 2201 2213–2215; Detective Constable Sidwell Kele testimony, Court 1373–1375, 1377–1378.
44 Cawood testimony, Court 658, 659, 673, 675, 694, 696. Pienaar testimony, Commission 1318–1319, Court 944ff; van Zyl testimony, Court 2103: "I thought I could manage. ... I asked for reinforcements. ... You did not ask for senior people? – No Sir. ... Manpower I wanted, and weapons." Labuschagne also grossly overestimated numbers, claiming that the crowd grew from 2,000 to 6,000 within a matter of minutes, Labuschagne testimony, Commission 385, 386.
45 Lidia testimony, Commission 2289, 2309, 2310.
46 Daniel Kokozela January testimony, Court 2792–2794, 2800. Lidia was not called to testify at the Monyake trial, but the prosecution called January.
47 Abraham Spengler testimony, Commission 1227ff; Pienaar testimony on Spengler's "peculiar position" in the police force and his "chief occupations,"

Court 979; Willem Willers testimony, Court 2576–2579; Wynand Wessels testimony, Commission 626–628; Mmotong testimony, Court 1255, 1262, 1297, 1299, 1300–1303; Ntsame testimony, Court 1841–1844, 1848–1849; Julius Pokwane testimony, Court 1745–1747. Ntsame explicitly recalled being ordered to arrest Monyake and Ntoampe, testimony, Court 1848–1849. Willers and Wessels and Muller, like their boss Spengler, would always deny that they had ever ordered anyone arrested; those identified as leaders would only be caught or seized ("*gevang*"). Sometimes though they would slip and acknowledge the use of "to arrest" ("*gearresteer*"). There was some confusion between the witnesses as to who was arrested first, but Monyake was processed first at the charge office and thereafter became accused No. 1 in the *Regina vs. Monyake and Others* trial of Sharpeville residents.
48 Cawood testimony, Court 659–662, 667–671, 673–674. Cawood's four tear gas bombs used up one sixth of the total number of tear gas bombs stored at the Vereeniging police station.
49 Van Zyl testimony, Court 2105; Wessels final report, 71.
50 Ephraim Thaba statement, SAP 620 31/58/60, SAB. Thaba is an exception in not being a long-term resident of Sharpeville or Top. Most of the hostel dwellers are young men from Sharpeville who are officially required to move from their family homes to the hostels once they turn 18 and live there until they marry. Many people evade this requirement.
51 Ntsame testimony, Court 1852, 1854, 1855; Jan Hendrik Grove testimony, Court 1954, 1955; Jan van den Bergh testimony, Commission 2462, 2463; Andre Thomas Kallis testimony, Court 1551,1571–1573; Heyl testimony, Court 1188, 1194–1195; Jakobus Nicolaas Coetzee testimony, Commission 357, Court 2438, 2440–2441. Coetzee testifies that he got hit by a stone and went to hospital briefly but then returned almost immediately to Sharpeville. He sustains no verifiable injury; Heyl testimony, Commission 542–544, Court 1198–1198. Sydney Kentridge representing the victims at the Wessels Commission developed the argument that the police had just shot among themselves. Philip Frankel, *An Ordinary Atrocity: Sharpeville and Its Massacre* (New Haven: Yale University Press, 2001) 86, writes that van Rensburg "felled six of the crowd on the spot," and "rifle fire" from Kallis, Coetzee, and Els "brought down several others." The only source he cites, Marius de Witt Dippenaar, *The History of the South African Police, 1913–1988* (Silverton: Promedia Publications, 1988), 277, is an official history of the police, which has no sources. Tom Lodge, *Sharpeville: An Apartheid Massacre and Its Consequences* (Oxford: Oxford University Press, 2011), 94, writes that van Rensburg killed two people and injured four after being subjected to a "shower of stones" that PAC supporters had stockpiled. Lodge provides no sources, and none of the African witnesses present recalled either the stones or the deaths and injuries, just the violence of the beatings.
52 Mathinus Smuts testimony, Court, 2600; 2606–2609; Heyl testimony, Commission 546, where he testifies that he had called Pienaar at 8:30 am on behalf of van Zyl and had been put through immediately to Lemmer; Spengler testimony, Commission 1255–1257. Spengler when asked in Court if he would only interrogate a person who was willing – "Only if he is willing?" – replies facetiously, "*As hy gewilling is, ja.*" Cornelius Johannes Els testimony, Court 2959. Els decides to go himself as soon as he hears that the additional forces are about to depart. The first of those forces leaves the Moroka police station at 9:30 am. Du Plooy established the SB in 1947, specifically to deal with the perceived threat from the Communist Party, but also with responsibility for preventing labour unrest. See Dippenaar, *The History of the South African Police*, 209–211. On Spengler's claim to share Hitler's birthday, see *Drum*, April 1957, which also

146 *21 March 1960*

has a photo of the colonel arresting one of the Treason trialists. Other journalists remembered that Spengler had a bust of Hitler on his desk, Mike Nicol, *A Good Looking Corpse* (Secker and Warburg: London, 1992), 330–332. See also Generals of the South African Police, https://issuu.com/hennieheymans/docs/00_konsep_-_sap_generaals/1; and Keith Shear, "Tested Loyalties: Police and Politics in South Africa, 1939–63," *The Journal of African History* 53:2 (2012): 187–190.

53 Ferreira testimony, Commission 1194, 1195, 1197; Paulus Maluka statement, SAP 621 31/38/60, SAB; Louis Christiaan van Wyk testimony, Court 1198–1199; Constable Andries Abraham Struwig testimony, Court 1532. How the phone lines had been damaged remains an open question. Paulus Maluka thought they had been cut; Judge Wessels assumed that had been the case when submitting his report; Magistrate P. M. O'Brien in the Monyake trial thought the cause was still unresolved.

54 Mashelide testimony, Commission 2202–2203, 2217–2218, 2221, 2236; Smit testimony, Commission 2018, 2019, 2036, 2040; Lidia testimony, Commission 2275–2276.

55 Lidia testimony, Commission 2296–2301, 2307, 2331; Lechael Musibi testimony, Commission 1892; Motshoahole testimony, Court 2454–2456; Ishmael Modise statement, Sharpeville Affidavits, UN; Smit testimony, Commission 2018–2020, 2029, 2032–2039, 2040–2041, 2048–2050; Labuschagne testimony, Commission 394–395, 421, 495. Labuschagne mistakenly thought the exchange with Teketsi took place after 11 am. He frequently got the time wrong as Judge Wessels noted. Ferreira correctly remembered it being before 10 am, testimony, Commission 1195–1196. Litelu testimony, Commission 757. Alfred Mabuya, a hostel dweller, testified that he was told to go to the police station by a European officer in khaki wearing short pants, Court 1986–1990, 1998–1999.

56 Peter Molefi testimony, Commission 1754, 1755, 1761, 1762, 1777, 1778, Court 3176, 3183–3186, 3209; Litelu testimony, Commission 757. Molefi's waistcoat has black lining so sometimes is referred to as a red shirt and sometimes as a red and black waistcoat.

57 Lidia testimony, Commission 2302, 2306, 2309, 2310.

58 Pienaar testimony, Commission 1319, 1320, Court 946; van Zyl testimony, Commission 187, 209, Court 2103, 2120; Jakobus Johannes Claassen testimony, Commission 874; Frederick Jakobus Pieter Coetzee testimony, Commission 943–944; Jeremiah Oosthuizen testimony, Commission 1002, 1007, 1030–1032; Coetzee's force is made up of 6 African policemen and 13 White; Oosthuizen's of 21 African and 3 White.

59 Heyl testimony, Commission 523–525, Court 1203–1206; Grobler testimony, Court 598–599; Jakobus Christiaan Visser testimony, Commission 2591. Heyl testifies that he and Grobler have three African and three White constables with them.

60 Mashelide testimony, Commission 2203, 2219; Visser testimony, Commission 464, 465, 467–469, 2591. Visser comes from Vanderbijlpark where he has been checking on the situation there. With the arrival of Malan's truckload of men from Johannesburg Central, and Oosthuizen's truckload from Moroka, together with the six constables with Heyl and Grobler, and the five inside (including Edwin Litelu) with Sergeant Nkosi, there are now approximately 30 African and 30 White policemen at the Sharpeville police station. Litelu testimony, Commission 755.

61 Tsolo testimony, Commission 2490, 2491, 2494, 2507; Lidia testimony, Commission 2278; Molefi testimony, Commission 1746, 1762, 1786, Court 3186, 3187; Nkosi testimony, Commission 2713–2716; Constable Matthews Ngumbuxo testimony, Court 2208; Mokabela testimony, Court 2306. Though Tsolo does not know Visser's name, he tells the court that he, like many other

African witnesses who also volunteer to do so, can identify the officers if given the chance at a police line-up. They are never given the chance.

62 Mashelide testimony, Commission 2203; Lidia testimony, Commission 2278; Smit testimony, Commission 2019; Dethedo/Litelu testimony, Commission 757, 758, 760, 761, 2683–2689; Motha testimony, Commission 1917, Court 2522–2524. On the conversation from the view of African police witnesses see also the Court testimony of Constable Dethedo/Litelu, Court 2083, 2085–2087; and Constable Matthews Ngumbuxa, Court 2199. Dethedo/Litelu mistakenly testifies that the conversation between Tsolo and Visser took place around 11:30 when in fact it occurred an hour earlier. He never informs Visser of what Tsolo tells the crowd in Sesotho. At the Monyake trial, he changes his testimony to suggest that he relied solely on Tsolo's message to the crowd to say that the words came from Visser when they may have only been Tsolo's construction, Court 2083–2086. His change of testimony is not convincing. On the football field references, see also Mashelide testimony, Commission 2203, 2220, 2221; Nkosi testimony, Commission 2716, 2717; Geelbooi Mofokeng testimony, Commission 2733, 2734. Many other people present at the conversation between Tsolo and Visser attest to the references to an important official coming at 2 pm. See the testimonies of Joshua Motha, Commission, 1917; Peter Lenyatso, Commission, 1869–1871; Anthony Ndaba, Court 2573; Samuel Mashobeni, Commission 2338; Meschack Mkwanazi, Commission, 1951, 1954–1955; Simon Lofafa, Commission 1847–1850; Isaac Tatai, Commission 2477. Many people also testify to hearing Tsolo's messengers carrying his words through the streets of Sharpeville. See, for example, the testimonies of Francis Motshoahole, Court 2453–2455; Adam Sakaone, Commission 1667–1668, 1670, Court 3139; Agnes Matshoahole, Commission 2740, 2741; Lecheal Musibi, Commission, 1897. After his conversation with Tsolo, Visser sends two constables to walk to Coetzee at the Gate and ask for reinforcements, and when none come, he goes himself, and Coetzee provides him with 12 men. P. S. Claassens, who leads the evidence for the state at the Wessels Commission, and is on leave from his regular job as attorney general for the Orange Free State, considers the testimony of Brown Thabe and Peter Molefi "the most important" that he has heard about the conversation between Tsolo and Visser, Commission 1811. Wessels himself agrees, finding Visser unreliable in his testimony.

63 Mashelide testimony, Commission 2203, 2220–2225, 2231; Lidia testimony, Commission 2279, 2304; Smit testimony, Commission 2024, 2042, 2058, 2065; Thabe testimony, Commission 1787, 1793–1795, 1798–1799; Molefi testimony, Commission 1747, 1766, Court 3187; Tsolo testimony, Commission 2504; Visser testimony, Commission 2588–2589; Heyl testimony, Commission 2601–2602, 2608.

64 Visser testimony, Commission 491, 493–494; Heyl testimony, Commission 2601–2607, Court 1210. See also Labuschagne testimony, Commission 390, 392; Theron testimony, Commission 299.

65 Barry John van Beloll testimony, Commission 1201–1210, Court 2850–2854. At the Court hearing, van Beloll raises his crowd estimate to 10,000 but when challenged by Jack Unterhalter with his previous testimony at the Wessels Commission and a request to look more closely at his own photo, he lowers his estimate to 6,000. The magistrate wonders if van Beloll has any greater expertise than anyone else looking at the photo to estimate numbers and decides likely not. On the planes, see also the *Vereeniging and Vanderbijlpark News*, 25 March 1960. Anyone can make their own reasonably accurate count of the crowd numbers (probably closer to 4,000 than van Beloll's upper estimate of 5,000) using crowd counting software such as mapchecking.com. Start with this link and develop

your own estimate using the "Reset the area" tool to adjust for crowd density from the photograph and actual street lines, https://www.mapchecking.com/#bAAAAQP-B1cFX-d5BAACYQbaA1cG0-N5BCoHVwff53kFSgdXB4fneQR2B1cEL-d5BGYLVwbj43kGrgtXBv_reQa2B1cEc-95BxYHVwXL73kEng9XB-vreQWKC1cEY-N5B.

Bibliography

Dippenaar, Marius de Witt, *The History of the South African Police, 1913-1988*. Silverton: Promedia Publications, 1988.

Frankel, Philip, *An Ordinary Atrocity: Sharpeville and Its Massacre*. New Haven: Yale University Press, 2001.

Heymans, Hennie, "Generals of the South African Police." https://issuu.com/hennieheymans/docs/00_konsep_-_sap_generaals/1.

Lodge, Tom, *Sharpeville: An Apartheid Massacre and Its Consequences*. Oxford: Oxford University Press, 2011.

Nicol, Mike, *A Good Looking Corpse*. London: Secker and Warburg, 1992.

Reeves, Ambrose, *Shooting at Sharpeville: The Agony of South Africa*. London: Victor Gollancz, 1960.

Shear, Keith, "Tested Loyalties: Police and Politics in South Africa, 1939-63." *The Journal of African History* 53:2 (2012): 173–193.

6 The Massacre

> I have explained that we all want one unity, shall I say – the feeling of Afrika!
> (Nyakane Tsolo)[1]

The Vaal Triangle, 21 March 1960

PAC supporters in the nearby African towns of Bophelong, Boipatong, and Evaton also lead marches of pass protestors to their respective local police stations (in Vanderbijlpark for the first two, in the eastern side of Evaton for the latter). In each town, as in Sharpeville, PAC people have gone house to house during the night alerting residents to their plans for Monday morning. At 6 am, the Vanderbijlpark municipal director of *"Nie-Blanke"* affairs (Ferreira's equivalent) goes to Bophelong and then to Boipatong to try and persuade those already gathered (800 and 250, respectively) not to march, but when they all insist, he tells them that he will meet them at the police station. By 7:15 am, the men, women, and children marching from Bophelong under the leadership of Sidwell Kaba have crossed the "Golden Highway" (R57) into White neighbourhoods and are approaching the Vanderbijlpark police station. By 8 am, they reach the police station and ask to be arrested. An officer phones Vereeniging for instructions. "When he came back, he said that he could not contact the big man at Vereeniging, but we must watch out for him for about fifteen minutes or so." Within less than five minutes, Captain Cawood arrives from the Gate at Sharpeville. He asks the local police who "the leader" is. Kaba is pointed out and Cawood catches him by the shoulder and instructs his men *"Sluit hom toe!"* (Lock him up). The municipal director then informs Cawood that Kaba is needed to translate instructions to the crowd to disperse. Kaba is released and stands on a chair to translate for the director. Kaba has his own message. He tells them, "If we are told to go back, we must be satisfied and we must go back and wait for the day the man would come and speak to us."[2]

Not understanding a word that Kaba has said, Cawood tells him that the crowd must disperse within five minutes. Kaba says that is impossible given the number of people gathered (3,000 to 5,000 according to inflated police

DOI: 10.4324/9781003257806-6

estimates) but starts telling the people to go home. While he is speaking and as the crowd is beginning to disperse, all before the five minutes are up, Cawood orders tear gas released, then a baton charge, then some of his police call out "Fire! Fire!": "they started hitting the people and as the people were dispersing, running away, they fired. ... Many shots." "Do you know why the Police fired? – [Kaba] I am still asking myself the same question to this day."[3]

The Bophelong residents run across the Golden Highway back towards their homes. Some of the young people, 10- to 18-year-olds, hang around near the road. They take some bananas loaded on top of a car that slows down because of the crowds crossing. They throw some stones at a passing petrol tanker. A private car comes along; it is Captain Cawood and three of his constables. Kaba sees the vehicle with uniformed men inside. "I ... saw the point of the gun out of the window of the car." Ernst Pooe, a teacher at a local school, sees the vehicle also. Kaba hears "fire" and runs off. Pooe hears "the report of a firearm ['he fired from inside the car'] and thereafter this youngster was shot, and he died." Cawood is asked if he is shooting indiscriminately. "No, I picked the man, the leader; he was running with two, big stones and I shot him." Pooe knows the victim, a 19-year-old, "He used to be one of the scholars at our school but he was finished; he had already made Std. VI." Pooe remembers his last name, "Setwanie." Another young man is shot dead by the police that morning, but he remains nameless. One is killed by a bullet to his right side, as though when turning, and the other by a bullet through the back of his neck. They are the second and third deaths caused by police violence on 21 March 1960.[4]

Events end with less violence for the Boipotong and Evaton marchers. The much smaller crowd from Boipotong, perhaps 2,500 men only (the police estimated 5,000, equivalent to almost the entire population of the town) led by PAC member Samuel Dhlamini, arrives at the Vanderbijlpark police station after Cawood has beaten, shot, and dispersed the Bophelong residents. After the municipal director speaks to them and tells them that a more important person will come to talk about passes, they agree to go home: "the people turned around and went away after that and there was no further incident." Likely the gathering of 20 to 30 White males – "All of them armed with rifles, shot guns, or both" – outside the police station has a major deterrent effect. At Evaton, the buses have stopped running, so people cannot go to work either southeast to Vereeniging (at African Metals Corporation – Amcor – for example) or northeast to the Johannesburg labour market. The crowd walking from the African side of the town on the west to the police station on the White side on the east doesn't reach its goal until 9:30 am. The police ask them to wait, while at the same time calling for reinforcements from Johannesburg. At 10:30 am, Mathinus Smuts, the "chief Bantu commissioner" for the Witwatersrand, arrives from Johannesburg and tells the police officer in command that he plans to talk to the assembled crowd.

Lieutenant van Eeden's big worry was what should be done, because it did not seem that he had very many men with him, and my advice to him was to do nothing at all for the time being until more reinforcements arrived. So we decided not to do anything. There were leaders at the gate, clamouring to be arrested, but we decided not to do anything at all.

Within a few minutes a flight of jets, the same ones that will fly over Boipatong and Bophelong, and then Sharpeville after 11 am, start flying low ("the height of two buildings") over the crowd. The aerial manoeuvres cause some people to leave, though most keep paying attention to one of the PAC men who is addressing them. He tells them how important it is to oppose the carrying of passes and reminds them of the words of the pamphlets distributed a few days before, that once they had come to the police station to surrender their passes and ask to be arrested, "we go home and don't go to work, we stay at home." One of his fellow leaders understands that means stay at home "until our demands are met." The first speaker tells the crowd that it is time to disperse, though considerable numbers remain as journalists from Johannesburg arrive. By 11 am, however, all attention is moving to Sharpeville.[5]

Sharpeville, Mid-Morning, 21 March 1960

The crowd gathered at the Sharpeville police station waits patiently as the day gets hotter. Perhaps there are around 4,000 or 5,000 men, women, and children as the newspaperman has estimated from the air; Lidia independently makes the same estimate on the ground based on his experience staging fashion shows. Thomas More, who is busy keeping people away from the fence while encouraging them to call out "*Afrika! Izwe Lethu!*" whenever "they wished to," understands that most of the people were "ordinary people coming there to listen to what was going to happen or what was going to be said ... [they] listened to what I had to say, although they were not members." They are there to get an "answer" to their question about passes. Geelbooi Mofokeng, a 21-year-old employee of Vereeniging Milling, has only been in Sharpeville for a year (before that he lived in Top Location). He has come to hear "a high official that would come and address the crowd." Petrus Mokele, a high schooler, has heard "the grown-ups" say they didn't want to carry passbooks anymore and has come "to find out if this was the truth." Azael Mabote who waited to be arrested at the police station on Sunday night, comes again because his "blood brothers" have told him a "big European" is coming. Isaac Tatai, who witnessed the police beatings on Seeiso earlier in the morning, "got amongst the people and stood amongst them and waited to hear what was going to be said, because these people were waiting for something to be said." Joseph Mochologi tells his wife that he has to be at the police station at 2 pm. He has lunch at home at 1 pm and then heads out to the police station to wait ("This was the last time I saw him alive"). Jacob Nhlapo goes to the police station "to hear good news." He is one of only two people who live outside Sharpeville who are in the town that day. Nineteen years old, Nhlapo lives with his elderly mother and younger sister and brother in Evaton and cycles to Sharpeville each day to work at the Sharpeville Cycle Works. Abraham Tinane has been waiting since 8 am for the answer, "to hear with my ears what this man had to say, not what I was being told by others." Anthony Ndaba wants "to listen to the law that was to be said at the Police Station." Thomas Msimang, dressed in clean clothes after returning from his night shift, marvels: "It was just, in other words, a nation which was standing in front of me. A what? – A nation." Meshack Mkwanazi is "prepared to wait so long" because he wants to hear "what this European had to say. ... We were all waiting for this European." By "all" Mkwanazi includes, like others in the crowd, the police as well since they understand from their conversations in Sesotho that the African police, like Constable Khumalo the previous night, also want to know what is going to be done about the passes. Solomon Dunga, an African member of the Special Branch (SB), personally considers the pass laws "unjust" and as a result "the police are burdened with the load of having to apply these laws, and so they [the police] become unpopular."[6]

The people in the crowd entertain themselves with occasional calls of *Africa!* and *Izwe Lethu!* and the singing of hymns. Isaac Tatai has his own special understanding of *Izwe Lethu*: "Seeing that there at Sharpeville was only the Africans living there at that time. ... I took it to mean that they mean that particular area belongs to us." Mkwanazi shouts out *Afrika* "[b]ecause we were born in Africa"; he holds his thumb up because "That is just the sign of '*Afrika*', that's all"; he sings the words "*Morena helaka Sechaba sahose,*" which he translates as "the Lord must guide all our people." They sing *Nkosi Sikelel' iAfrika* in isiXhosa even though not all understand the words: "It is a lovely song, a hymn [the first line] means that God should bless Africa." They sing other "church hymns" ["*Christelike lieders,*" "Abide with Me"], the anti-apartheid song *Senzeni Na,*

> *Senzeni na?* [What have we done?]
> *Sono sethu, ubumyama?* [Our sin is that we are black?]
> *Sono sethu, yinyaniso?* [Our sin is the truth?]
> *Sibulawayo!* [We are being killed!]
> *Mayibuye iAfrica!* [Let Africa return!]

and "SeSotho songs." Peter Molefi walks among the crowd joining in

> the singing of these hymns. ... They were singing these hymns, being pleased to listen to what was going to be said, although nothing had been said then. ... They were pleased because they saw that the Europeans were standing there. They seemed to look satisfied, and they were happy.[7]

Bernard Xingwana, Ferreira's senior clerk, spends an hour walking among the crowd between 11 am and noon. He also estimates that there are about 4,000 people in the crowd, most of them "singing ... in a friendly manner. ... Some of them were curious." Every so often, a person walks up to one of the African constables and "offer[s] him a reference book" and is turned away. "It was mostly singing and some slogans." Only one old man has a stick, and he is using it to shoo children away. Sergeant Grobler agrees with Xingwana's assessment of the behaviour of the crowd from 11 am until the arrival of the "three Colonels" at 1 pm: "*Ja, hulle gedrag het goed gebly*" (Yes, their behaviour remained good). After his lunch break, Tsolo is back, and whenever he asks people to step away from the fence, "[t]hey were carrying out every one of his instruction[s], every order he was giving." "When he gave the sign ... the P.A.C. sign ... they shouted '*Afrika!*' ... when he raised his hands, they would be silent." His message is inspirational: "we all want one unity, shall I say – the feeling of *Afrika!*" More and Smit and Teketsi are helping Tsolo keep order from inside the fence: "Do not come close to the fence. Do not lean against the fence. You must not cause damage to any property." Lidia too on the outside as usual. Tsolo tells them, "Whatever the Police do to me, you people must not do anything at all." Lidia has become even more committed to Tsolo and the PAC cause as the day's events unfold:

> I was still in Zwane Street, walking up and down between the people and the Police, trying to see that they would not provoke the Police. ... I did it, I can say, in moral support of the P.A.C. ... I wanted to hear what would be the outcome of the P.A.C.'s campaign and it was my duty.[8]

Xingwana sees quite a number of his friends in the crowd, "public servants" like himself. The same "respectable people" that Francis Motshoahole, still recovering from the police beating he received the night before, and the Reverend Robert Maja also observe in the crowd. All are waiting patiently. Xingwana hears one person say they are waiting for the "Bantu Commissioner to come," another person hears "Native Commissioner," another "Chief Commissioner," another "Chief Bantu Commissioner," another "an important European," another "an official from Pretoria." Marium Lepee, Steven's school-age sister (she is one month past her 16th birthday) who lives with him and their grandmother and his wife and three children (Steven and Marium's parents are deceased), seven household members in all, hears from her school friends that it might even be "Dr. Verwoerd" himself, the prime minister, not an unreasonable guess since he owns a farm on the Vaal River 10 km southwest of Sharpeville, and is scheduled to give a speech in Meyerton, 20 km northwest of Sharpeville, later that week.[9]

More officers start arriving at the police station to add to the approximately 60 already there before 11 am. Constable Saaiman comes looking for Tsolo a little after the hour but is told that he has gone to lunch. Saaiman is dressed as usual for his downtown Johannesburg duties since he was suddenly called to Sharpeville because of a need for extra drivers; somewhat dishevelled in trousers with the bottoms tucked into his socks and a white shirt, with a white handkerchief tied around his head to keep the sweat from his eyes in the increasing heat of midday. He is armed as usual with a loaded .38 revolver and has an extra 4 magazines (24 bullets) kept loose in his left trouser pocket. He buys his bullets privately and gets reimbursed at a slightly higher official rate for the shots he fires, a little scam common among the police at the time. The arrival of two armoured Saracen troop vehicles attracts a lot more attention. Captain Stephanus Jakobus van der Linde from the Moroka police station commands the Saracens. He has made a side trip to Auckland Park to pick up the vehicles and their crews of five White officers each while he sends Sergeant Oosthuizen ahead with the truckload of mostly African policemen. When van der Linde arrives at the Gate at 11:15 am with the two Saracens (part of the convoy that Smuts has seen earlier in the day on his way to Evaton), Major van Zyl orders van der Linde to escort himself and 25 reinforcements under the command of Captain Hendrik Gert Theron who have just arrived from Springs (including Constable Johannes Stephanus Joubert, armed with a Sten gun) up Seeiso directly to the western vehicular entry of the police station on the no-name street. Van der Linde reports no problems driving up Seeiso; there are no crowds on the way. Separately, van Zyl orders Captain Coetzee, who has been at the Gate since 10:30 am, to walk with his 60 men (a mix of Coetzee's Jeppe men and others from Vereeniging and Vanderbijlpark) to the public entrance of the police station on Zwane. Labuschagne walks first with van Zyl, then joins Coetzee for the rest of the trip. Just before he leaves the Gate, he sees a car which he believes is carrying African journalists trying to enter Sharpeville. Though entry is refused to them – "Get the hell out of here" – he suspects that they will try to sneak in by another way (it is Ronnie Manyosi and his colleague Bill Calder from the *Golden City Post*, and they do indeed manage to get into Sharpeville). A White journalist, however, Charles Percivale Channon, is permitted entry, and he follows van der Linde's Saracens, taking photos all the way. Calder, Manyosi and Channon will document the events that day in prose, photography, and film (most of their photographs will not survive police censorship). At the police station, Theron takes over from Heyl as OIC and stations his men in the police yard. He asks who is "the leader" of the crowd and is told that the person is at lunch. Van der Linde parks one of his Saracens inside the southwest corner, near the intersection of Zwane and the no-name street. He reconnects with one of his Moroka men who got there earlier, Sergeant Jeremiah Oosthuizen, and stations him and his Sten gun with the parked Saracen. Three more of the men with the parked Saracen are armed with Stens: Constables Frank Bernard Sneigans and J. Steynberg, and Detective Sergeant A. van der Merwe, all from the Newlands police station who arrived with Oosthuizen. Van der Linde will use his second Saracen to ferry men back and forth to the Gate for the rest of the day, and he immediately takes van Zyl back there. Adam Sakaone watches the arrivals closely and like Mosheledi pays attention to the license plates:

> I saw police coming from all over the Reef. The first troop came from Vereeniging; the next one from Boksburg and the third from Springs. I know that they came from these areas because I observed the car numbers of the vehicles.

Lidia is impressed by the arrival of the extra police and the Saracens; he thinks they have come to keep order in readiness for the arrival of the high official.[10]

The police settle in to wait. There are now approximately 100 men inside the police station on the western side and another 60 outside on the south side. Neither of their respective commanders, Captains Theron and Coetzee, will communicate with each other for the rest of the day. Coetzee describes it as "a dreadfully hot day" and the men seek whatever shade they can find. David Ntsame, the gatekeeper who has accompanied Coetzee to Zwane, goes to sleep in a police van parked in the street. Constable Jan Hendrik Grove is sleeping on the ground outside the fence in the shade along Zwane. Others are seeking any shady spot to lie down inside the police yard – because it is new, there are no trees – or inside the station itself. Soon after Theron's arrival, a Sharpeville resident drives up to the police station in a car and carries in a case of 24 bottles of cold drinks "for you people." Theron rejects the offer and will later claim that he is insulted because there are not enough drinks to go round to all his men. Neither he nor Coetzee places any guards on the gates to the police station, even though Coetzee will later claim that he keeps his men in the street because he "regarded that Police Station as a death trap, because if there was a concerted storm on it, those men would have been trampled to death, those men inside, and I wanted to maneouver." Lucas Mosheledi keeps opening and closing the double gate for vehicles like the Saracens, and Nkosi carries out his normal duties inside. Daniel Dikubo comes to the police station to complain about a stolen bike and waits to see an officer; Mischack Mareka is a complainant in a forthcoming assault trial in Vereeniging, and he comes to the police station to discuss his case with African Detective Obed. Both are told to wait outside.[11]

Mathinus Smuts arrives at the Gate at about 12:30 pm after leaving Evaton a half hour earlier. Before leaving, he phoned ahead to his local office in Vereeniging and to Major van Zyl at the Gate to report his intention to speak to the crowd gathered at the Sharpeville police station. He has also spoken about his intentions by phone with officials in his main office and with the police in Johannesburg and Pretoria and has been told that Colonel Lemmer and Brigadier Els are coming to Sharpeville and want him to delay his speech until their arrival so that as "senior people" they can all be present. He knows this information has become widespread among the African municipal and SAP employees. When he arrives at the Gate, he witnesses himself this information being conveyed to the Sharpeville police station by radio from the Saracen at the Gate to the one at the police station.[12]

All the police activity has attracted more people to the crowd gathered outside the police station, especially small children. While the diving by five planes around 11:20 am or so and then half an hour later by nine planes (which swoop up and down right above the crowds for 30 minutes, coming so low that they shake the toilet in which Minah Elizabeth Chabeli seeks refuge) has dissuaded some people, like Hophny Morobe who gets a blast of jet exhaust in his face and goes home, others are entranced. Robert Maja sees "youngsters that were throwing their hats at these aeroplanes – 'Hoorah! Hoorah!' – flinging their hats up. ... They were enjoying it." Lidia sees some people run away at first, "but as they were running away more people came out from various places." People were "attracted," like Aaron Motsoane (28) and his "little brother" 14-year-old Johannes, and 18-year-old Elliot Kubeka. Likewise with the Saracens, quite amazing looking vehicles that even the Matchbox toy company introduced as a model in 1958. Daniel Phosisi comes specifically to see them as does Meshack Pitso. Adam Sakaone is standing next to the wire of the police fence on the west side: "Amongst us there were lots of little children and women. These children had come to see the Saracens." Geelbooi Mofokeng notices a lot of these kids, little 4- and 5-year-olds playing around near the clinic on the no-name street, skipping stones – "granite chips like you pick up next to a tarmac road" – at one another.[13]

Everyday life goes on around them since the police station is situated at the major intersection of the tarred streets in Sharpeville, and the main shops and only clinic, community hall, and library in the town are in close proximity. Nor is the crowd so tightly packed that people cannot make their way through or van der Linde's Saracen enter and exit on a regular basis. Xingwana, for example, has no problem walking among the people for an hour. Normal activities include Elliot Kabi walking past the police station on his way to the post office on Seeiso to mail a letter; Selina Mazibuko's only son Abraham following the same route to pay their permit fees at the municipal offices at the Gate; David Mabaso looking for his horses in the open field northwest of the police station; John Motsoahae Mailane delivering invoices for his Vereeniging employer, a furniture store, as he did on his bicycle every Monday; George Jonah visiting the watchmen on duty at the shops as he did every day as part of his responsibilities as a municipal employee in charge of retail security. Mohauli Solomon Masilo is at home on sick leave for a skin condition and heads over to the clinic; John Phutheho, who has been asleep during the morning after having worked the night shift on Sunday at Stewarts and Lloyds, is walking over to a neighbour's house to take their daughter to the doctor since the father is at work and the mother is ill herself. Richard Koboekae and Justice Maeko are coming back from the short work shifts they did that morning (Koboekae has left his car at work).[14]

It is now the middle of the day and people are hungry and thirsty. Some go home for lunch; some head to the shops. Naphtali Maine has borrowed money from his mother so that he can buy cigarettes. Elizabeth Botha sends her husband Walter to buy food for their five young children. Anna Lethege, feeling somewhat weak as usual (she has a damaged heart valve as a result of rheumatic fever) heads over to the café to buy fish and chips for herself and her two teenage children. She is wearing bright clothes to make herself feel better: "a colourful skirt ... sort of pink-like and it had small flowers decorating it ... [and] a Basuthu hat, and a blouse ... with a white background colour, and with blue spots on it." People also start looking for their family members, especially their children. Solomon Lesito had earlier that day joined a group walking to the police station and when "the people started singing ... I also sang and pointed my thumb into the air and shouted Africa. ... I was standing at the fence of the clinic, west of the Police Station." His father, William Lesito, heads to the police station in search of Solomon; "I went there to fetch him." Makorotsoane Alinah Mokone, Elias Mtimkulu, John Nteso, Anna Motsepe, Francis Motshoahole's wife Agnes, and many other parents come looking for their children; Francis and Agnes' son and daughter are only 7 and 2½ years old, respectively, and have been playing in the street. Stephen Lehobo's mother sends him out to look for her sister's 11-year-old daughter. Christina Motsepe is looking for her mother. Peter Molefi has taken a lunch break earlier but now comes back to the police station looking for his grandfather and ends up directly in front of the double gate. The Presbyterian minister Maja is looking for his Anglican colleague Reverend Voyi to discuss a forthcoming religious event and goes over to wait for him on Voyi's stoep (porch), diagonally beyond the empty field to the northeast of the police station. He waits for his colleague while drinking tea brewed for him by Voyi's wife.[15]

It is now just before 1 pm. The crowd is waiting patiently:

> There were a few children, and there were women. They were a mixed crowd. I think I saw two or three young girls in the front. ... There were umbrellas in the crowd. Near the gate, one [woman] was standing with an umbrella in her hand; that I saw.

Between the comings and goings of people having lunch and returning to wait for the important official, and the children and others coming to see the Saracens, the crowd has remained about the same size at 1 pm as the news reporter flying over earlier at around 11 am had estimated: 4,000–5,000 people. Those gathered on the no-name street only fill about half the pavement, and all are quiet even as the Saracen convoy passes through them (Figure 6.1). Sergeant Nkosi ends his normal shift in the charge office. As he leaves to go home, certain that nothing is out of the ordinary, people outside are singing "*Afrika!*" – "Is that all? – That is all." Tsolo: "I was shouting out the word '*Afrika!*' myself and when doing so, they [the crowd] would do so,

158   *The Massacre*

7. Captain Brummer spoke of driving through a "wild" and almost impassable crowd, attempting to enter the Police Station. This photograph of the scene on the West side was taken immediately after his arrival.

Figure 6.1 Photograph of crowd on no-name street around 1:10 pm, 21 March 1960, just after the Saracen convoy passed through and entered the police station.

Photo by Jan Hoek. "Mr. S. Kentridge said the photograph ... demonstrated the mood of the crowd, and among other photographs contradicted the evidence of Captain Brummer and other officers who said that the situation was critical and dangerous when they arrived at the police station."[17] Source: Ambrose Reeves, *Shooting at Sharpeville: The Agony of South Africa* (London: Victor Gollancz, 1960).

too." Benjamin Maroo, who has been waiting to hear about passes since 11:30 am, goes home to listen, as he does every day, to the 1 pm news broadcast on SABC. He wants to find out what if anything is being reported about Sharpeville. Mathinus Smuts is sitting in the municipal offices at the Gate, preparing his speech and waiting for the arrival of Colonel Lemmer and Brigadier Els.[16]

Monday Afternoon, 21 March 1960

I never thought that they would kill, the way they did kill us.

(Nyakane Tsolo)[18]

Just after 1 pm, a convoy of five vehicles enters the police station, two cars and three Saracens. Peter Molefi gets the Sharpeville residents gathered on the no-name street to make room for the convoy; Lucas Mosheledi opens the double gate so that the vehicles can enter the police yard; Nyakane Tsolo, Thomas More, Khoali Teketsi, and Moses Smit call out from inside the yard for the crowd to make way for the new arrivals. "Look, you must open up some space here. Some of you must stand on this side and others must stand on the other side so that the men ["*die mense*"] can get through." The first car, a 1957 Ford (Moses Shabangu knows his car models) with a large radio aerial contains Colonel Prinsloo, the national head of the SB as well as his deputy, Lieutenant Colonel Spengler. The second car, a Zephyr which has piloted the convoy (Prinsloo orders the switch in lead right before the police station) from Vanderbijlpark to Sharpeville via the Parys road (now the R42) and up from the south along the old dirt farm road which becomes Zwane, contains the SB men from the morning, sergeants Muller (it is his car) and Wessels and Captain Willers. The three Saracens are commanded by Captain Andries Gottlieb Brummer (stationed at Kliptown police station) and, like van der Linde's, come from Auckland Park (also known as "Radio"). They are the other part of the convoy that Smuts has seen earlier that day, and they have spent the morning patrolling Bophelong before Prinsloo ("a little man with a tight skin which seemed to stretch like elastic around the cheek bones and the forehead") arrives and orders them to accompany him and the SB men to Sharpeville. The convoy drives up the no-name street past the police station to Seeiso and then down the paved road to the administrative offices. There, after a brief discussion with van Zyl, the convoy returns up Seeiso to the police station followed by a car with two *Rand Daily Mail* (*RDM*) reporters, Jan Hoek (a photographer) and Benjamin Pogrund. After entering the police yard, Brummer places his three Saracens in a line along the west-facing side of the police station. The turrets are left open and the browning machine guns unmanned as though no danger is expected. Each Saracen has a crew of five White officers (except one which is a man short). Seven of the men are armed with Sten guns; constables Bosch, C. Janssen, Paul Machiel Steyn, Sybrand Gerhardus van Niekerk, Johannes Petrus Mostert van Zyl, and Louis Christiaan van Wyk and J. du Plessis (the last two arrived in the radio car earlier that day and now join the Saracens). Constable Johannes Joubert is already standing with his Sten by the double gate. Sten gunners Oosthuizen, van der Merwe, Sneigans, and Steynberg from the Saracen in the southwest corner walk up and join Brummer's men.[19]

Captain Brummer uses a battery-powered loudspeaker to address the crowd on the south side. He speaks in English first, has difficulties making himself heard, then in frustration calls out *Hamba!* – Go away! – derogatory in tone and usage. Either the loudspeaker does not work, or he does not know how to use it. No one hears him; no one listens to him. He is wearing overalls and by his demeanour shows "no respect."[20]

Nyakane Tsolo, inside the police yard, as he has been all morning, approaches a man in civilian clothes and asks him if the convoy contains the important European, or if he will arrive soon. The man (it is not certain who he is, he has on a "white shirt" and "ordinary trousers," it is likely Saaiman) replies, "Fuck you." No one except Tsolo hears this.[21]

Colonel Spengler spends about four or five minutes walking around and getting the lay of the land (he doesn't talk to anyone, not to the OIC Theron, not to any police officer) and then identifies "the leader" – it is Nyakane Tsolo. Saaiman, who often works with Spengler in Johannesburg, is with him as he catches Tsolo. Spengler ("a big European who had a sporting jacket on, of fawn colour") takes Tsolo's elbow. "Before Tsolo was finished speaking, because I could still see by the movement of his mouth that he was still talking, he was taken away by this European." "I was caught hold of and pushed inside." He goes "along freely." Spengler and Saaiman walk with Tsolo through the double steel doors of the interior police yard to the southern side of the police building and take him inside to Prinsloo, "*Dit is Tsolo.*" He is then handed over to Captain Willers for interrogation. Spengler and Saaiman go back outside to look for other *aanhiteers* (agitators). When Thomas More sees Tsolo taken into the police station he "thought he [Tsolo] was going to get the answer to this chief that was going to come and address us." But then Sergeant Wessels points out More to Spengler – "*Dit is More*" – who again strides over and catches him too. Saaiman tells Mosheledi and Smit and Teketsi to get out ("*Gaan uit*"). Spengler and Wessels march More between them into the police station and hand him over to Prinsloo. "They took me in. ... No reason was given why. ... They did not speak." Wessels stays inside the police station. More sees only himself and Tsolo as prisoners inside the police station. Willers begins his interrogation of both men. Visser joins him. Lidia's "eye," the informant he has paid to watch the gate for him, tells him about the arrests of Tsolo and More. Lidia thinks that the police are testing Tsolo to determine if he really is the leader.[22]

The crowd is not disturbed by Tsolo and More being taken into the police station. Indeed, they see it as a sign of the imminent arrival of the important man and the answer to their concerns about passes. Molefi doesn't think Tsolo and More have been arrested; they have been, he explains in Sesotho, *tshoasa*, "[it] does not convey the same meaning as the European word of arrest; it means catching hold of you." Molefi is sure that Tsolo has been "taken to act as an interpreter when this speech was to be delivered." Lidia thinks the same.[23]

Outside the fence, while these developments are taking place inside the fence, between around 1:05 pm and 1:15 pm, journalists (reporters and photographers) who have followed Brummer and his Saracens from Vanderbijlpark, drive slowly through and walk among the Sharpeville residents on Zwane. Everyone they talk to is friendly, and their photographs document the crowd described by Bernard Xingwana and others – women, some with umbrellas to protect them from the midday sun, men, and children standing next to the police station fence, moving aside as asked to let vehicles through, not so densely packed that the reporters cannot walk freely among them. All are respectful and peaceful. Jan Hoek of the *RDM* takes photographs from his car window while Benjamin Pogrund is driving, along Zwane east to west, and then back west to east. In Hoek's photographs (Figure 6.1

The Massacre 161

– he will describe all his photographs in detail in subsequent official hearings), people are walking along the street, some are sitting on the kerb, others are putting their hands in the air and calling out *Africa!* Just to the east of the public entry to the police station on Zwane, Pogrund gets out of the car and approaches some residents to interview them. He "very quickly drew a big crowd." Once they know Pogrund is "from the *Rand Daily Mail*," they are eager to tell him about "their grievances – how they suffered under the pass laws and their struggle to pay rent and buy food." Ian Berry and Humphrey Tyler from *Drum* magazine also follow Brummer's Saracens to the police station (Alf Kumalo, also from *Drum*, follows them in a few minutes later). They stop behind a police lorry at the first intersection to the east of the police station on Zwane, and Berry gets out and walks through the crowd right up to the intersection with the no-name street. People speak to him as he walks among them and try to get in his pictures. All are friendly. He photographs the 1957 Ford sedan containing Prinsloo and Spengler (see Reeves, *Shooting at Sharpeville*, plate 9) as it enters through the double gates with the crowd standing politely aside, umbrellas overhead and thumbs in the air. He photographs (Figure 6.2) van der Linde's Saracen parked in the southwest corner (closed up and seemingly unmanned) and the Ford panel van alongside that was part of Brummer's convoy; here too the Sharpeville residents are all gathered peacefully along the fence on the west and southern (the immediate forefront of the photo) sides. After about ten minutes, Berry catches a

Figure 6.2 Photograph of a Saracen and a van inside the Sharpeville police station fence around 1:15 pm opposite the crowd shown in Figure 6.1 on the no-name street around 1:10 pm, 21 March 1960. Note the telegraph pole in situating your view of the two photos, Figures 6.1 and 6.2.

Photo by Ian Berry. © Ian Berry/Magnum PhotosTEST 01-Stock (Photogs).

162 *The Massacre*

lift from Hoek and Pogrund who drive him to where Tyler is parked, east along Zwane, left around the southeast corner of the police station, and up just beyond where Robert Maja is sitting having his tea across the field northeast of the station.[24]

As the four journalists drive to the other side of the police station, another convoy arrives on the no-name street and enters through the double gates into the police yard. It is about 1:25 pm. This convoy is led by Lieutenant Colonel Pienaar sitting in the front seat of his 1958 Chevrolet alongside his African driver and with Lieutenant Jacobus Johannes Claassen from Johannesburg and a Vereeniging policeman in the back seat. Pienaar is 56 years old. Claassen has met up with Pienaar in Vanderbijlpark and accompanies him to Sharpeville together with the three trucks (with Johannesburg plates, Adam Sakaone notices) containing 43 policemen (25 of them White) that he has brought from Hospital Hill (near Hillbrow in Johannesburg). On the drive from Vanderbijlpark to Sharpeville, Pienaar and Claassen sit in the back seat of the Chevrolet, and the Vereeniging policeman sits in the front beside the driver and pilots them and the three trucks of Johannesburg policemen to the Gate. When Pienaar arrives with his convoy at the Gate, he is briefed on the situation by Major van Zyl. Van Zyl tells him that a crowd of 20,000 has surrounded the police station and that tear gas and baton charges have failed to disperse them. He does not make it clear, or Pienaar does not hear, that the tear gas and baton charges have taken place at the Gate, not the police station. He tells Pienaar that he is waiting for Brigadier Els. While they are talking, a White officer arrives from the police station and tells Pienaar he is needed there immediately. Van Zyl tells Pienaar to take with him the Saracen that is waiting to accompany Brigadier Els when he arrives. The convoy is led from the Gate to the no-name street by this Saracen, one of van der Linde's, which immediately returns to the Gate to wait for Els. Pienaar thinks he is followed by "a press car or two" (it may be Channon who, after entering Sharpeville at 11:30 am and taking numerous photographs, has had his camera confiscated by the police and has to leave Sharpeville and get it back in Vereeniging before returning to the town with an ITN film crew). Right before entering the double gates Pienaar switches seats with the local policeman and gets in the front seat alongside the driver. Claassen stays in the back. As Pienaar's car approaches the double gates on the no-name street he tells the driver to speed up through the crowd; the driver swerves and hits a woman who must be pulled out of the way by another person in the crowd; she walks away limping. Pienaar walks up to Captain Theron who he, as the senior uniformed officer now replaces as OIC, and asks him what is happening. Theron replies, "*Kolonel, jy sien mos self*" (you can see for yourself) and nothing more. Pienaar tells Spengler, "Get on with your investigation." He doesn't talk to anyone else; he will later claim that he doesn't know how many policemen are at the police station (close to 300) even though they have all been sent to Sharpeville either by him or by his immediate superior Colonel Lemmer; he imagines he sees a car full of Whites being attacked as he drives in (no one else ever says they saw this "attack," no Sharpeville resident, no policeman, no one); he has no real comprehension of how many people are gathered on the no-name street or on Zwane; he doesn't even know that there are policemen on Zwane. Claassen has kept his 25 White policemen in a group together awaiting Pienaar's orders. Pienaar gives a command to the White policemen: "*tree aan en laai*" (line up and load) and does nothing else. It is now about 1:35 pm.[25]

When Pienaar drives in wearing his "striking" uniform of blue banded peaked hat and blue epaulettes, the only police officer to wear such a uniform that day, the bus driver Joshua Motha who has come back from lunch, hears the crowd around him say, "[H]ere is the big man, here is the big man," and they all draw "nearer." When he sees the police line up, all 60 to 70 of them, Motha thinks that it is an honour guard since it is nearly 2 pm. "When I immediately saw the Police being lined up there, I was then under the impression that they were saluting that big European or the important European that was arriving." "I have never seen Police saluting, but I have seen soldiers saluting, and I took it to be the same."[26]

Benjamin Maroo finishes listening to the news on his radio – "The situation in Sharpeville is calm" is the report – and as the local weather comes on, he walks back to the police station. He stands against the fence at the northern end of the clinic across the no-name street from the police station. He sees the police line up. He sees a European with a white handkerchief tied around his head. He sees a single car enter through the Gate. It is about 1:35 pm. At the same time, the three Mashiya brothers, Matthew (at home on sick leave), Peter (a schoolboy), and Isaac (the oldest of the three, a Sharpeville hostel dweller and a butcher for the Iscor butchery in Peacehaven), arrive, having decided to go to the police station to find out what is happening. They stand on the no-name street just to the north of the double gate, looking at the police line, the officers standing at ease with the butts of their guns on the ground.[27]

Things start moving very rapidly. Peter Molefi sees a European coming towards him. He makes his way through the crowd – "*Ekskuus, ekskuus, ekskuus*" – and opens the double gate (which swings both ways on its farm-style hinges) so that the man can approach him. Before he can say anything, the plainclothes officer (it is Spengler) catches "hold of the waist-coat and the shirt too and ... also pinched me on the stomach." Spengler rips Molefi's shirt and tears a button off his red waistcoat as well. He demands of Molefi "*Waar is jou bewysboek?*" (Where is your reference book?); Molefi answers in English, "I beg your pardon." "He then said 'Pass' [*Waar is jou pas?*]. I said to him, 'I am here grieving for that same book, because I have so many difficulties with this book.'" Spengler slaps Molefi on his left cheek. Molefi says, "I surrender to arrest me. You can arrest me. You can take me now." "Just at that first instant that I was seized and struck the first blow, it was then that I realized that I was in the hands of the police." Spengler gives him a "second smack ... [then a] third smack in my face." Molefi's woven

"Sesuto hat with a string round" falls on the ground, and as he picks it up, Spengler hits him again. Molefi is offended: "the way he hit me was a very unmannerly way of treating a human being." Spengler hands Molefi over to Constable Saaiman who marches him over to Sergeant Muller who attempts to frog march him into the police station. Molefi tells him he can arrest him; he doesn't need to hit him. Molefi is tall; Muller is short. Just before getting to the double steel doors, Muller attempts to trip Molefi and slap him in the face; Molefi puts his shoulder against Muller and the policeman falls over. Muller gets up and hands Molefi over to an African policeman who takes Molefi inside the police station. Molefi and the policeman (Constable Amos Daubada) stand for a few minutes at the double steel doors looking back out at the police line and the crowd of people standing behind the fence on the no-name street.[28]

Molefi sees Spengler go again to the double gate but, because of the line of police between them, he does not see what he does there. Moses Smit is standing just outside the double gate. He has seen Spengler and the man with the handkerchief (Saaiman) hit Molefi so hard ("*klapping*" him) he could have been injured and then pull him inside the gate up to the police building. At that moment, when Molefi is near the double steel doors, a uniformed policeman wearing "traffic cop" leggings and carrying a "short stick" – the man who forms the line, which likely means Lieutenant Adrian Freemantle from Boksburg (he arrives at 12:45 pm with 11 African policemen and five White) since he implements Pienaar's order to have the men line up – walks up to Smit, pushes him, strikes him with an open hand, and throws him so hard against the double gate that two of Smit's artificial teeth break, and he "nearly fainted. I was a bit dazed." Spengler is with Freemantle and trips and loses his own balance for a moment. Saaiman is there too.[29]

Benedict Griffiths, the young man whose father is a policeman and who has been sitting on the sidewalk across the road from the double gates since 8:00 am, with a break for lunch just before 1:00 pm, sees the cars and lorries and Saracens arrive. He sees the arrests of Tsolo and More. He sees the police form a line.

> They had guns and other weapons that I had seen for the first time, they were sort of like iron weapons [the Sten guns]. ... When I saw them loading the guns, then I started getting frightened. ... I got a fright when I saw ... a person ... trying to prevent the people from not standing against the fence ... [the police] putting him into the Police Station ... another one was caught hold of afterwards. ... They were jerking him about ... When the crowd saw this man [Smit] was being jerked about, they tried to run away, and it could be seen, then, that there was no-one who was going to address the gathering, but they [the police] were wanting to fight with the gathering. Did anything happen at about that time? – Yes. What happened?[30]

It is now about 1:40 pm. Joshua Motha standing near the front of the crowd two paces in front of the open double gate – Tsolo and More have given instructions that "when the big (important) [*grootmense*] people arrived the gate had to be open so that they could enter" – sees an officer with pips on his shoulders (SAP lieutenant colonels have two small metal emblems on their blue epaulettes) "and a little stick." The officer chases a young man into the crowd and threatens to throw a stone at him. He goes back inside the gate and yells at the crowd, "*Loop julle! Loop julle! Hamba*" (Go away! Go away!). Just as the officer with the pips gets back inside, Motha hears "the voice over there saying '*Skiet!*'" Samuel Mahlase also standing near the front of the crowd hears "*Skiet.*" "This one with the stick – the gentleman with the little stick. [He had his back to me]. After this gentleman had said '*Skiet!*,' the firing took place." Meschack Mkwanazi sees an officer who does the last arrests say one word, "*Skiet!*" "Just the one word '*Skiet!*'? – Yes." Though he does not know his name, Mkawanazi can identify the officer by sight (if given the chance). Benedict Griffiths sees a police sergeant – "he had a sergeant's badge [three v-shaped chevrons] here, on his arm" – coming from the police station and when near the line of policemen hears the sergeant giving the order *Skiet!* – "I could hear him when he spoke." Peter Molefi standing in the police station doorway hears a voice saying, "'Shoot!' ... I heard it in English, yes. I heard a thundering of all these things." Daniel Dikubo, the man who has come about a stolen bike and who speaks English and Afrikaans as well as Sesotho, hears "*Skiet!*" "*Hy het gese Skiet!*" "When the word '*Skiet!*' was uttered, the people turned around quickly and immediately (snaps his fingers)." Though none of the Africans who hear the order know the names of the officers, they can identify the person who first gives the order to fire if given the chance to see the White officers in an identification parade (they will never be given that opportunity). Marium Lepee, still waiting for Dr. Verwoerd with her high school friends and her young cousin Martha Masello Lepee, takes off her shoes and starts to run. "The shooting had not started."[31]

The police also hear the orders to shoot. Their line runs from the northern fence down to just below the double gate and then at a slight southeast diagonal towards Zwane. The police line is less than 40 m or 130 ft long, which means that the 77 White officers are standing shoulder to shoulder. A similar number each of White and African policemen – another 150–160 men in total – stand between the line and the double steel doors of the police station (and Peter Molefi's line of sight), not counting the 60 men lined up across Zwane under the control of Captain Coetzee. There are also Brummer's three Saracens in a line facing westward from the double steel gate of the police building towards the double gate on the no-name street. They are right behind the line of armed White policemen. Constable Gysbert Booysen standing two paces to the south of the double gate hears "someone scream *Skiet!*" He may hear it twice because apart from the scream, he also hears *skiet* spoken "in a clear voice" as a command. Constable Charles Rudolf

166 *The Massacre*

Meyer, standing immediately inside the double gate, hears an order to fire, "*Vuur!*," spoken in "a clear and distinct voice," coming from his right (i.e. slightly to the north). Constable Pieter Saaiman also standing right inside the double gate hears someone shout *Skiet!* He will always deny that he called out the word himself. There is a Sten gunner right near him facing the double gate, Constable Johannes Joubert. Just on the northern side of the double gate, Sergeant Gerhardus Petrus Nel hears "*'n bevel gegee word om to skiet*" (an order given to shoot). Constable Johannes van Zyl, standing close to the double gate in line with constables Paul Steyn, Louis van Wyk, and Sybrand van Niekerk, with another four Sten gunners close by, hears Pienaar speaking in a "clear and distinct voice" ordering them to line up and to load their weapons, and then hears an order to shoot ("*'n bevel het gekom om te skiet*"); Steyn does too. So does Constable Izak Malherbe Pretorius standing close to Pienaar. Constable Barend Johannes Theron, standing on one of the Saracens parked to the northern side of the double gate, with two Sten gunners on the same vehicle and another one standing close by, hears someone shout *Skiet!* or *Vuur!*: "did you think it was an order to fire? – *Ja*."[32]

Lieutenant Claassen standing in the police line with his group of 25 men does not personally hear the command to shoot but he does not doubt that one is given and that the order is given by Colonel Pienaar.

> I understand that among the group that were under your command there are a number of men who will say that they heard a command? – Yes, I know there are men who will say that.
>
> Are you convinced that no command was given? – No, I am not convinced that no command was given. I may not have heard it.
>
> Say a command was not given, are you able to explain why they would say that? – No; it is possible that they heard a command, if they say so.
>
> From the colonel?
>
>   – From the colonel.

> Is there a possibility that they heard a command that did not necessarily come from the colonel? – I don't believe so. The colonel was in charge and the command to fire would have come from him.[33]

All the seven White policemen (Booysen, Joel Meyer, Charles Rudolf Meyer, Nel, Pretorius, Steyn, Theron) who will testify under oath that they hear an order to fire (including those who arrived with Brummer) are under Claassen's command and are standing in the middle of the line either right behind the double gate or a pace or two to the south or north of it. Pienaar is standing immediately behind their line and slightly to the north of the double gate. Several of the men attest that they would not have fired without a command. Constable Theron, would you have fired "without an order? – *Nee.*" "I assumed it was an officer's order." Constable Booysen is sure he hears an order to fire, "otherwise I would not have fired." Likewise, Constable Charles Rudolf Meyer who stood immediately inside the double gate: "when you fired you did it, did you, in obedience to that order? – *Dit is reg.*" Constable Simon Andrew van den Bergh, armed with a Sten gun and standing the farthest away, by Brummer's own Saracen on the northwest corner of the police station, doesn't shoot. Why not? "I did not fire because whether there was an order or not, I did not hear it." Though Constable Johannes van Zyl hears Pienaar's voice – which he recognises – giving the order to line up and load, and he hears a "distinct" order to fire, he will always claim that he does not know who gave that final order. Constable Joel Meyer, standing close to Pienaar, hears an order from behind to fire but does not know at the time who gives it. He is more inquisitive than Constable van Zyl and asks among his colleagues after the event and learns from them that the person who gave the order was "*'n officier in bevel*" (an officer in command).[34]

There is only one OIC at the time of the massacre and that is Lieutenant Colonel Pienaar. Though he, and the police, and the government will always deny it, the evidence given under oath by African and White witnesses alike is overwhelming that at 1:40 pm on 21 March 1960 the OIC at Sharpeville, Lieutenant Colonel Pienaar, orders 77 White policemen armed with machine guns, rifles, and revolvers to fire directly into an unarmed and peaceful crowd. As an experienced police officer – he joined the force in 1924 – Pienaar must know that such an order will result in mass deaths. He was commissioned as an officer in 1936. He served as chief of Prime Minister Smuts' bodyguards during World War II. He commanded the police at the opening ceremonies of the Voortrekker Monument in 1949. Following the division of the SAP in 1953 along apartheid lines into units with responsibility primarily for "Europeans" or for Africans, he served as commander of the Rand Flying Squad (an early SWAT team) and as commander of the African police districts of Springs in the East Rand and Newlands in the West Rand. In 1959, he is promoted to lieutenant colonel and in 1960 appointed divisional inspector of the SAP for the Witwatersrand. On 21 March 1960, he has been given responsibility for overseeing all police actions with regard to the PAC pass protests. He has been in the SAP for 36 years and is near retirement age. He has faced crowds of African protestors and strikers many times before, people he always refers to as "mobs."

Pienaar has no respect for Africans. In 1934, as a young sergeant at the Jeppe police station in Johannesburg, he was sued for assaulting a pregnant woman and causing her to lose her unborn child. Adam Seutso sued Pienaar for assaulting his wife Martha during a police raid on the rooming house where they lived on Upper Railway Road in Doornfontein. As Pienaar and his fellow officers roughly searched their few possessions and broke some of Martha's cherished china cups,

168 *The Massacre*

she asked him not to break her things [and] he told her not to speak to a policeman and pushed her aside. ... [Adam] asked him not to push her, as she was pregnant, but he replied that he did not care because she was a Kaffir girl. He added that he did not care whether the child died or she died, or whether the child got sick.

Pienaar pushed her again, causing her to fall backwards, and she hit her head on the ground. Bedridden for two weeks, Martha lost her baby due to a miscarriage. The trial was adjourned *sine dei* and never resumed. Pienaar's contempt for Africans remained throughout his career. While he was the commander of the Springs police district, Africans told numerous stories of family members being arrested and disappearing and their bodies being discovered later. He chose whether to kill or not to kill. When groups of Zulu migrant workers and local Basotho clashed in Dube and Meadowlands in September 1957, his police fired indiscriminately and killed five Zulu. When 300 women marched on the Newlands police station in October 1958 to protest the arrests of 500 women from Sophiatown for refusing to carry passes and who demanded that they be locked up as well, Pienaar ordered them dispersed with "sticks and batons," and when later in the month, a thousand Africans gathered outside the Johannesburg magistrate's court in support of the women on trial, Pienaar ordered his 50 policemen to disperse that crowd too with tear gas bombs and batons.[35]

But on Monday, 21 March 1960, at 1:40 in the afternoon, Lieutenant Colonel Gideon Daniel Pienaar chose to kill.

What happened? "*Dit het met 'n sarsie begin*" (It started with a volley). "The first shots I heard were fired by the police. I did not hear any other shots." "Ta-ta." "*Dit was revolverskete*" (It was revolver shots). They sound like a revolver. "Ta-ta-ta." Three shots. Three shots near the double gate. They come "from the Police." "I first heard 'ta-ta;' then I heard 'trrrrrr' all of a sudden, the second time." "I heard a thundering." "There was some 'thundering.'" "I heard krrrrrr ... I heard the gewoerrrrrr, the rumbling." "Do-do-do-do-do-do." After the first thundering, the rumbling, there is a brief pause, no more than five seconds, the time it takes to reload a Sten gun, and then another "burst." "I saw something raising from inside this saracen and I heard it 'tttttt' ... it looked like the 'klavers' of a piano, it sounded like crackers. ... I saw it clearly." "I heard something sounding like a mouth organ – not like a whistling sound, but like a mouth organ. It went Pie-ie-ie-ie-ie-ieng. It kept quiet, then they were shooting at that time; and again, the same noise, and they kept quiet. When this noise was made the first time, this Pie-ie-ie-ie-ie-ieng, they fired. Pa-pa-pa! Then the second sound came." "The shots ... they were in a volley with two gaps between them. ... The last volley was not exactly a volley; it was shots – as if they were aiming. ... The first shooting, when it occurred, I remained stunned at my place." "How did you hear the shots? A volley that started all at once, or did you at first hear single shots?" Lieutenant Claassen: "the volley started all at once, a full volley ['*n volle sarsie*]." The crowd "screamed as they fled." He is also certain of the sequence of events: the police "were not attacked."[36]

"It made me think of a wheat field, where a whirlwind had shaken it. It was just like that; it was exactly like that and they were gone, and the wounded stayed behind. It happened in a flash." Petrus Tom looking onto the no-name street from the fence along the northern edge of the police station remembers that "All of a sudden the crowd had gone because they had been flattened; everyone was lying on the ground."[37]

What happened? Pieter Saaiman fires six shots from his double-action revolver directly into the people on the no-name street, empties the magazine in 3.5 seconds, reloads another six bullets individually (6 seconds), and empties a second magazine (3.5 seconds). It takes him 13 seconds to shoot 12 bullets at point-blank range (at most eight paces, more likely five). Johannes Joubert standing near Saaiman at the gate empties a magazine (a Sten gun magazine can take up to 30 bullets, most policemen load around 25) of his Sten gun into the crowd. Jeremiah Oosthuizen, a few paces north of where Saaiman and Joubert are firing, presses his finger on his Sten gun trigger and keeps the pressure on for the 3.2 seconds it takes to empty his magazine (9 mm "parabellum" ammunition, "for war"). He fires from the hip and moves the gun from side to side, spraying as many people as possible. He takes four seconds to load a new magazine and fires that in the same manner as the first, finger down and spraying bullets in an arc. "I shot without pausing." "I did not notice the effect of my shooting." He fires 64 bullets from his Sten. Johannes van Zyl a few paces northward on Oosthuizen's right empties three Sten gun magazines (75 bullets) into the crowd without looking up, and then takes his revolver out of its holster and fires a six-round magazine for good measure. Paul Steyn standing beside him does the same – three magazines of his Sten (70 bullets) spraying side to side and one magazine of his revolver (six bullets), so does J. du Plessis (65 bullets from his Sten and 6 from his revolver), so does Louis van Wyk (68 bullets from his Sten and 6 from his revolver). Constables Bosch, Janssen, and van Niekerk, all in the same row as the others, also empty their Stens (63, 35, and 45 bullets, respectively), and van Niekerk empties one magazine of his revolver (six bullets) and fires three bullets from a second magazine. Standing at the northern end of the line, Sergeant van der Merwe fires two magazines (45 bullets) into the people on the no-name street and at those running in the field to the northwest. Up on the Saracens, Constable Frank Sneigans standing on top of one of them, starts firing into the backs of people already running away across the fields between the police station and the library to the northwest, the shops to the north, and the houses to the northeast. When Sneigans starts firing, the police on the no-name street have already fired their first volley – the thundering and rumbling – while other police are beginning to fire their .303 rifles, .38 revolvers, and smaller gauge pistols (.25 carried by CID men) at the crowds on the no-name street and on Zwane. Sneigans shoots three magazines (65 bullets) into the backs of the fleeing crowd. Constable Barend Theron standing beside him fires two shots from his revolver. Constable J. Steynberg standing on the mudguard of the same vehicle empties four magazines (88 bullets) into the backs of the crowd. Constable Edward Arnold Pennekan likewise fires, "I did not aim. I shot directly into the crowd in front of me." Almost 1,400 bullets in 45 seconds, fired by every single policeman in the line (with the exception of Constable Simon Andrew van den Bergh), more than half of them by the Sten gunners firing bullets that tumble end over end tearing people apart. Sten submachine guns are much like sawed-off shotguns, with very short barrels (19.685 cm or 7.75 in compared to a rifle barrel of 76.2 cm or 30 in); much smaller 9 mm ammunition, which has a tendency to tumble unlike rifle bullets, and a wider spread of fire. These weapons are fired deliberately and persistently. It is "a firing squad"; it is, says Captain Coetzee looking out at the crowd behind the fence, like shooting "fish in a tin."[38]

Joshua Motha standing on the no-name street two paces from the fence thinks the police are firing blanks. Then he sees "flames, i.e. smoke, going up, and at the instance when I turned to look in the direction of the smoke it was then that I was hit by the bullet." "I felt a bullet grazing my trousers. ... Then I got a fright. ... Just as I lifted my leg to go forward, I was struck by a bullet here, in the right hip, and I dropped." Daniel Dikubo and Mishack Mareka, both waiting outside the police station where Detective Obed has told them to stand, are shot. Dikubo sustains a huge hole in the back of his left thigh (9 cm by 10 cm or 3.5 in by 4 in and deep); Mareka is hit by bullets in his "buttock, in the right shoulder, the right hand palm, and my private parts." Anna Lethege is walking home from the fish and chip shop because it is closed when she suddenly falls down, "I think I was shot. That caused me to fall down." John Nteso runs across Zwane glancing backwards, and as he does so, he sees a puff of smoke coming from one of the flaps in the Saracen on the southwest corner of the police station; he falls to the ground with a gunshot injury to his left foot surrounded by what he describes as "clover," the thin little bullets of the Sten guns. Elizabeth Setlhatlole, standing in a neighbour's property under a peach tree 100 m southwest of the police station on Zwane, hears a "hard bang." She thinks it sounds like lightning. Then she feels "pain in the palm of my hand and then in other places" and sees blood running from her wounds and runs into her neighbour's house. Lecheal Musibi, riding his bike north of the police station to pick up the key to the textbook case at his school, hears shots and immediately gets off his bike and lies down. Then he gets up and starts walking and suddenly hears some of his pupils calling out, "They shot you. ... Even the teacher is shot." He looks down at his leg and realises "my trousers were burst and the calf muscles were torn, and ... exposed." Benedict Griffiths starts running in a southwest direction towards his home in Vergenoeg: "Just as I was across the street [Zwane] I fell down ... Where I had fallen, I lay. ... They were still firing." Benjamin Maroo takes off running as fast as he can towards his home, off across the no-name street from where he has been standing near the clinic, south of the shops, past the three Saracens, and across the field northeast of the police station towards his home in Rooistene. Ian Berry takes photographs of the crowd running towards him (Figure 6.3); the only cameraman to capture images of the police in the act of shooting that day (three men on top of one of the Saracens, including Theron and Sneigans). Elias Lidia, who is standing near the intersection of the no-name street and Zwane when the shooting begins, takes off running along the police fence east along Zwane, and then takes a left and runs up the street on the eastern side of the police station now on a path to intersect with Benjamin Maroo. Robert Maja sitting on the Reverend Voyi's stoep drinking his tea hears the shooting begin and sees a crowd rushing across the field towards him. "I saw a woman falling just at the entrance gate [to Voyi's house]. ... Just at a short distance from her had fallen another young boy." Maroo is only 20, still a young boy to the clergyman; he sees a woman lying on the ground as he runs in the direction of Maja and a man who appears dead; he is hit twice in his left leg and falls before getting up and limping to his home. Maja decides to go towards the firing – "They were making this noise – 'Quirr! Quirr! Quirr'" – to give assistance. "There were many people lying there; some of them were dead; some of them, their intestines were protruding." He keeps running forward and hears "many bullets passing me."[39]

Like detective Malakia Mmotong, who spent Sunday night hiding in a police van for fear that other policemen might not recognise him in his

Figure 6.3 People running across the field north and northeast of the police station (building on left) and the clinic (building on right) around 1:45 pm, 21 March 1960.

Note in the back centre Constable Sneigans standing on the Saracen about to fire with his Sten gun and Constable Theron (to Sneigan's right) with his revolver. The third man in overalls remains unidentified. Photo by Ian Berry. © Ian Berry/Magnum PhotosTEST 01-Stock (Photogs).

172 *The Massacre*

civilian clothes and would beat him, his colleague detective Sidwell Kele runs to the cells in the back of the police station to hide when the shooting begins: "because I was in civilian clothing. ... I was running away from the Police because they might shoot me as well."[40]

How long was the firing? Ten seconds as Pienaar will claim? Twenty seconds as other police witnesses will claim? Forty-five seconds, as seems most likely given the type of weapons used and the duration needed to empty multiple magazines from Stens and rifles and revolvers and pistols? Lecheal Musibi has the most accurate comment: "My impression is simply this, it was too long."[41]

It has all happened so fast. Sergeant David Mokabela will later testify in a court hearing that

> The time that I have taken getting out of the witness box and pointing him out [he is identifying Peter Molefi in the courtroom], is longer than the period when he [Molefi] came in [the police station] and when I heard the firing outside.[42]

Joshua Motha lifts his head as the smoke dissipates on the no-name street right in front of the double gate. He cannot stand up because of his injury. He sees a young man he knows as "Motho" who works at an outfitter's store walk with his hand raised from the shops down to near the Saracens (this may be Edward Moloto, age 23). The police on the armoured vehicles yell at Motho, "[Y]ou must hold a white handkerchief in your hand otherwise we'll shoot you dead, like lightning." Motho doesn't speak to them but keeps walking to the double gate. When asked by the police at the gate, "[W]here are you going," he answers: "*Kyk baas, hoe die mense dood; wat het hulle gemaak? Niks*" (Look boss, how the people die; what did they do? Nothing). The police yell at him to run. He ignores them. He walks past Joshua Motha and back towards the shops. Pienaar personally orders his arrest[43] (Figure 6.4).

Elias Lidia walks westward along the northern fence across the field back towards the shops and onto the no-name street. The police tell him to leave, but he ignores them. He keeps seeing people he knows lying dead and injured. One on the northwestern corner of the police station, another who lives opposite him in Zwane lying on the no-name street, and about 30 people dead and dying between the police station and the clinic, including a "boy" he knows, Stephen Lehobo (who has been looking for his niece), with a bullet wound in his thigh. Lidia walks around the corner into Zwane and finds more dead and injured there, "two girls, one shot and one complaining that people trampled over her," (the latter is likely Agnes Motsoahole, a young mother of two), and a man he knows "almost dying," and as he walks, a White policemen yells at him in Afrikaans, "*Ja, nou gaan jy Mayebeye-toe*" (Yes, now you are going to your Mayibuye), and another policeman, Sergeant Ben Pitsi a veteran of the 1937 and 1940 Top Location "riots" yells at everyone and to no one in

The Massacre 173

Figure 6.4 Photographs taken within a few minutes of the conclusion of the shooting from inside the double gates of the police station looking out towards the intersection of the no-name street and Zwane, 21 March 1960.

The car is parked on Zwane; the clinic would be to the immediate right of the photographer, Warwick Robinson. Robinson took this photo and others before any of the police had walked outside to see what they had done.[44] Note how people have shifted position within the seconds separating the two photographs. Source: Ambrose Reeves, *Shooting at Sharpeville: The Agony of South Africa* (London: Victor Gollancz, 1960).

particular, "*Ja, ek het julle gese die Polisie sul skiet. Daar het julle dit; vat dit; dit is julle Afrika daardie*" (Yes, I told you that the police would shoot, take that, that is your Africa). Daniel Dikubo, the man who came to the police station about a stolen bike, hears a White policeman yelling out to a colleague, "There is another Kaffir; he is standing up. We haven't done anything to him yet." The police say the same thing about a woman too: "She had already been wounded, here in her side and then she tried to get up. That is when those words were used and there were shots, and then she was hit in the back of the head." Dikubo is sure he hears the policemen's words directed at the woman who is shot in the back of her head (this may be Norah Nobhekisizwe Mbhele or Paulinah Mofulatsi, both of whom will die from head wounds). None of the SAP men, White or Black, help any of the wounded. They spend their time, the Black SAP men, loading the dead into police vans, the White policemen just stand around watching. What about the injured?

> There were other people [helping] ... relatives, friends and other people. Not the Police? – No ... the greatest care was given [by the police] to the dead ... the most time was given to the people who were dead. ... They were taken away to the mortuary.

Lidia sees the arrival of ambulances after most of the dead have been picked up and wonders why all arrived at the same time and why some have Johannesburg plates. Petrus Tom will remember that he saw the ambulances already lined up at the Gate before the shooting and that they had arrived from the military base about a kilometre directly northeast of Sharpeville.[45]

As Robert Maja runs across the field toward the police station, he tries "to render assistance to these injured people." He gives water from a "big canned fruit bottle" that he fills in a yard to as many people as he can. He collects shoes and items of clothing left behind by the fleeing crowd and makes pillows for the injured; he tries to cover them as much as possible with the clothing "to protect them against the burning of the sun." He sees a man with his brains "lying out" on the ground (it is probably Joseph Morobi Mochologi; a later autopsy will find that part of his skull and half his brain are missing; though it could also have been Elias Molotsi who is shot in the back of his head "shattering a portion of the skull and brain"), and asks the police to collect the pieces of brain and preserve them with Mochologi's body. He sees some of his congregation "shot dead," "an old man, Sempampuru ... he was killed. ... A very decent man." Others of his congregation killed are adults, others are youngsters. The police try to drive him away.

> [T]he Policemen were not helping the people; I was doing the helping. ... And then, ... Residents came there ... [to] see to the wounded people. ... There were brothers and sisters of theirs that were shot, ... Everybody with sense would know that. If you are going to your brother and your brother is shot, surely everybody knows you intend to help him.

He sees three main groups of victims, most near the intersection of the no-name street and Zwane, another large group near the clinic opposite the police station, and the third group "just behind the shops" in the field to the north of the police station.⁴⁶

It is 2 pm inside the police station. The policeman guarding Peter Molefi, Constable Daubada, asks him sympathetically, "Why do these Europeans arrest you from outside there?" Sergeant Mokabela tells Daubada not to talk to the prisoner. Spengler interrogates Molefi. After asking him if he is a member of the PAC, Spengler tells Molefi, "I should be thankful for what he has done to me, i.e. by removing me from there. If he did not do that then I would have been shot." In another room of the police station, Captain Willers is interrogating Tsolo and More with the help of Sergeant Muller. The SB men insist that they sign statements that they do not agree with and which they later repudiate: "the statement which you say I signed, is the statement I was forced to sign and forced to make." In another room, Harold Sacks, the crime reporter for the *RDM* and a close personal friend of Pienaar, sits talking with Captain Theron and Captain Visser. Sacks and his *RDM* colleague Warwick Robinson left Evaton at the same time as the other journalists, but Sacks insists on stopping in Vereeniging for a cup of tea. As a result, he and Robinson arrive after the firing starts. As he sits with Theron and Visser, Sacks prepares in his mind the story that will be published in his newspaper the next day. "You were reporting the police version? – That is correct." And in yet another room, Captain Coetzee enters from his post on Zwane expecting to see his superiors from Johannesburg and Pretoria, Colonel Lemmer and Brigadier Els, but instead of Lemmer who has remained behind at his post, Coetzee finds Lieutenant General Hendrik Jacobus du Plooy, the man who established the SB right after World War II, and who before the year is out will be the commissioner of police for all of South Africa, the most senior police official in the land. Benjamin Maroo saw their car enter the police yard at around 1:35 pm. Just as Tsolo has promised his supporters, the senior men got to the police station by 2 pm.⁴⁷

Outside the police station, "the sounds of grief" fill the air. Ronnie Manyosi of the *Golden City Post*, who has been in Sharpeville since 11:30 am, sees a young boy dead on Zwane southeast of the police station, still clutching in his hands the wire toy he had been playing with when he got shot. Manyosi moves westward up Zwane to the police station.

> I came across a man ... lying face down, his whole back a mass of caking blood. I thought he was dead, his face was buried in the ground, his arms spread-eagled. When I kneeled down he lifted his head and asked in a whisper: "ARE THEY STILL KILLING US?" When I shook my head he said: "Thank God," and dropped his head again. Behind me a girl of about 15 years cupped her face suddenly in her hands and screamed "My father! My father!" then collapsed in a dead faint into the arms of a woman. In front of us a young boy clung grimly to a fence, but as we moved towards him his hands relaxed their grip and he slid to the ground. He was dead when we reached him. Thousands

stood by while hundreds gathered to assist in carrying the wounded into ambulances. ... Apart from the sounds of grief and the moans of the wounded, there was no talking, no shouting. ... [I] saw children lifting the cloths from the faces of corpses lying in the street to see whether their parents had been killed. Everywhere weeping women, children and even men shouldered their way past heavily-armed police to go among the bodies sprawled grotesquely around the police station at the Vereeniging township. Cries and wails pierced the air as they found their loved ones among the more than 200 dead and injured. Pools and trickles of blood were on every yard of ground. The wounded lay among the dead.[48]

Joe Nzingo Gqabi who has been in the township since 11 am reporting for the *New Age* walks along the no-name street:

At one stage we counted 34 bodies (including those of at least eight women) lying about the ground in front of the Sharpeville police station as though on a battleground. They seemed all dead, with bullet head wounds. Some of the injured were shot in the back, some had more than one bullet wound. ... Women wailed and sobbed over the dead and some bodies were identified by horrified relatives on the spot. Women covered their heads with their arms and wept and their cries could be heard from far off.[49]

Henri Schoup, the chief correspondent of United Press for Southern Africa who dropped off Joe Gqabi in Sharpeville at 11 am and then drove to check what was happening in Bophelong and Vanderbijlpark, has returned and arrived at the Sharpeville police station right after the shooting:

[O]n the northern side of the police station I saw a number of bodies on the ground ... [on] the piece of open ground opposite the shops lying to the northwest of the police station. I saw eleven bodies lying there ... in the roadway on the west side of [the police station] I saw many more bodies. In the roadway near the gate I saw a woman lying on her back, a hat had been placed over her face. ... There were many more in the roadway and also on the side-walk on the west side of the road. ... I saw much blood and blood-stained clothing in the roadway. ... There were certainly bodies in the roadway near the south-west corner and also in the road leading west and south away from that corner and on the side-walk on the corner diagonally opposite the south-west corner of the police station fence. ... Police were picking up dead bodies in the street near those [two police] vans and putting them in the vans. At that time wounded people were lying about in the roadway and on the open ground. Nothing was being done for them. ... Several at least of the bodies were lying face downwards with the heads pointing away from the police station. They gave me the strong impression that they had been running away from the police station. I did not see bodies with heads lying towards the police station. Many of the bodies had wounds in the back.[50]

Ronnie Manyosi, Joe Gqabi, Mohlouoa Theo Ramakatane, Alf Kumalo, Peter Magubane, Charles Channon, and Warwick Robinson document in photographs the scene immediately after the shooting. Robinson is the first to enter the police yard and takes photos from inside looking out onto no-name and Zwane streets even before any of the police walk out beyond their fence. Since he is White, the police do not bother him. In total, he takes 29 photographs of the scene on the no-name street and of the intersection with Zwane.[51]

The African photographers have to be more circumspect. One of them is arrested. Alf Kumalo uses a back entrance to Sharpeville on his way from his home in Evaton and sees

> bodies strewn all over the road. It was just minutes after the shooting. I took pictures of the bodies. ... I stayed for about two hours and had to keep changing films in case the police saw me and confiscated the one in my camera.[52]

Channon and his ITN crew also film the victims. Police photographers from the fingerprint office in Johannesburg arrive but do not take any photographs of the bodies. Lewis Nkosi and Nat Nakasa, who work for the *Golden City Post* as well as *Drum* and other publications, help lift people into the taxis and private cars and on the motorcycles owned by Sharpeville residents who speed the injured to the Vereeniging Hospital 3.25 km away with the first patients arriving at the emergency room by 1:50 pm (literally within minutes of the shooting ending), and into ambulances when these arrive 20 minutes after the shooting. Marium Lepee, who has been shot from behind in her right calf – "I fell. ... There was much pain" – is taken in a taxi by her brother Steven to the Vereeniging Hospital where she has to lie down on the ground outside and then by an ambulance to Baragwanath Hospital in Soweto where her leg below the knee is amputated the same afternoon.[53]

None of the SAP officers, White and African, help any of the wounded. The African officers are ordered to load the bodies of the dead into police vans to take to the Vereeniging police mortuary. The African municipal police (identifiable by their "pith" helmets), carry the injured roughly to the sidewalks and then load them into the ambulances once these arrive. It will take at least 40 minutes to load all the injured. Other than his command to arrest Edward Moloto. the only direct order given by Colonel Pienaar, already thinking ahead after the shooting, is to the police to collect any stones they can find on the no-name street to be used later as evidence that

178 *The Massacre*

the crowd had stoned the police station. Unfortunately for Pienaar's story, African police will later testify that no stones were ever found on the recently planted lawn within the police yard, nor any windows broken in the police station. Pienaar's only recorded comment beyond the order to pick up stones is to complain to a foreign correspondent about a dent on his car and to tell him, "If they do this sort of thing, they must learn the hard way."[54]

Abram Mofokeng, who has been waiting outside the police station for the important person to arrive at 2 pm, takes shelter behind the shops together with "four boys and three girls" (Mofokeng is only 20 years old).

> We were discussing amongst ourselves, is this serious, is it really being shot by real bullets? Some of us said no, we are not fighting, maybe they shot us with something like salt, that's how we were talking among ourselves. ... Then we started to realise that we are being shot with real bullets too, we started to see the blood coming out.

Perhaps Abram and his young friends are among the crowd that Schoup sees near the shops when he first arrives and parks his car:

> I got out of the car and walked towards them. I was at once surrounded by Africans. "What are they doing to us now?" I was asked. I replied that I did not know what was happening and I asked whether people had been killed. There was no aggressiveness among these people. Their mood was one of complete bafflement.[55]

Anna Phutheho comes looking for her husband John. A neighbour has told her that his body is lying

> on the second corner southeast of the police station. ... I ran there and arrived just in time to see them loading my husband into the police van. I do not know if he was still alive or was dead when they put him in the van.[56]

Maria Makhoba has returned from the funeral she attended outside Sharpeville earlier in the day and sits at home with her husband and their six minor children, waiting for the return home of their seventh, 14-year-old David.[57]

"[I]t rained after the shooting," "the streets have been washed clean of blood by a thundershower. Pools of water have collected where only a few hours ago there was blood." Mahasane Michael Thekiso remembers the rain as "just a small cloud for 15 minutes; it just fell; not too much of it. And it stopped. That is what happened in 1960."[58]

Pula! Afrika! Izwe Lethu! Mayibuye iAfrika!

The Intersection

The intersection of Seeiso, the no-name street, and Zwane, where on 21 March 1960 hundreds lay dead, dying, or injured, is still the physical hub of Sharpeville and the emotional heart of the community. It is still the only part of the town with a public library, the only part with a health clinic, now also the only part with a post office, and a petrol station, and a supermarket, and attractive especially to the schoolchildren and teenagers who sit on the pavement outside the Sharpeville Memorial (erected in 2010) and tap into the free Wi-Fi from the memorial to use on their cell phones to connect to the wider world. Passing through the intersection is the only way by which people can reach the community hall, still on the same site as in 1960, and beyond to get to the George Thabe stadium, where PAC leaders had gathered and been dispersed on the Sunday night before the police shooting, and where soccer matches are played on weekends, and where once a year the national government celebrates Human Rights Day on 21 March, a day local people think should be renamed Sharpeville Day. The old police station is still there, declared a National Heritage Site in 2016, where training is provided in computer and other practical skills, and a free daily lunch is provided for those who need it. Every day of the week, other than Sunday morning when most residents are in church, the intersection hums with activity as people go about their daily activities, sitting, walking, and driving on the very ground where so many hundreds of people lay dead, dying, and injured on 21 March 1960. For Sharpeville residents, the intersection itself is their memorial.

Notes

1 Tsolo testimony, *"Commission of Enquiry into the Occurrences at Sharpeville (and other places) on the 21st of March 1960"* (hereafter Commission), 2504. The Commission materials are all digitized in their entirety and freely accessible online, https://idep.library.ucla.edu/sharpeville-massacre.

2 Sidwell Kaba testimony, Commission 2567–2586; Johannes Casparus Knoetze testimony, Commission 1637–1651.

3 Kaba testimony, Commission 2572–2579. The total population of Bophelong in 1960 was approximately 8,500 men, women, and children; therefore, a crowd of 5,000 walking over 2 km to surrender their passes would have been highly unlikely.

4 Kaba testimony, Commission 2580, 2584–2586; Ernest Pooe testimony, Commission 2727–2732; Cawood testimony, Commission 175–176; Wessels Judgement, 24–37. Kaba thinks at last three people have been killed that day, but he will not provide the names of witnesses for fear that they will suffer police retribution. Dr. Hermanus Steyn, the district surgeon for Vanderbijlpark, conducts postmortems on two men killed locally, Steyn testimony, Commission 1143–1144. The name of the 19-year-old killed is recorded as Stephen Matthew by the *Drum* reporter Humphrey Tyler, *Life in the Time of Sharpeville: And Wayward Seeds of a New South Africa* (Kwela Books: Cape Town, 1995), 19. Joe Gqabi also witnesses the shooting: "A police van arrived on the scene and shot into the crowd killing a 19-year-old. His body was left lying there," *New Age*, 24 March 1960.

180   *The Massacre*

5 Knoetze testimony, Commission 1649–1651; Pienaar testimony, Commission 1322–1333; Smuts testimony, *Regina vs. Monyaki and Others* (Case No. R. 58/1960 in the Court of the Magistrate of the Regional Division of South Transvaal, held at Vereeniging: The State against Johannes Monyake and others, hereafter Court) Court 2600, 2607–2611. Harold Sacks (*RDM* reporter) testimony, Commission 1592–1594, Court 1715; Jan Zacharias Hoek (*RDM* photographer) testimony, Commission 1575, Court 1777; Warwick Robinson (*RDM* photographer) testimony, Commission 1543–1544; Ian Berry (*Drum* reporter) testimony, Commission 1818; Charles Percivale Channon (*Star* photographer) statement, Police Archives; Wessels Judgement 38–41. Evaton has a population of 50,000 Africans and 2,000 Whites. When Smuts arrives in Evaton, he finds Harold Sacks already phoning in a story from the police station to his editors and calling Colonel Lemmer to report that "the position is very bad." Sacks, who has excellent contacts in the SAP, bases his reports to the *RDM* and to Colonel Lemmer not so much on his own observations but on the information provided to him about Evaton, Boipotong and Bophelong by the OIC at Evaton, Lieutenant van Eeden. Additional information about the Evaton protest can be found in two political trials, *Regina vs. Obed Majeke, Vallance Ncomane, and Z. B. Molete*, Magistrate's Court Evaton Case 556/1960, and *Regina vs. Zachius B. Molete*, Magistrate's Court South Transvaal Case 226/1962, both available in digital form, http://historicalpapers-atom.wits.ac.za/ad1901-3-1-1-01-jpeg-pdf and http://historicalpapers-atom.wits.ac.za/ad1901-4-1-01-jpeg-pdf. The Regina vs Monyake and Others Court materials are all digitized in their entirety and freely accessible online, https://idep.library.ucla.edu/sharpeville-massacre.

6 Lidia testimony, Commission 2334–2335; More testimony, Commission 2524, 2525, 2527, 2529, 2530; Geelbooi Mofokeng testimony, Commission 1997, 1998, 2001, 2003, 2733, 2734; Petrus Mokele statement, K110 1/3/60; Mabote testimony, Court 2024; Tatai testimony, Court 2474, 2480–2482; Dora Mochologi statement, K110 1/3/60; Jacob Nhlapo statement, K110 1/3/60; Abraham Tinane testimony, Commission 2186, 2188; Anthony Ndaba testimony, Court 2573; Msimang testimony, Court 3119; Mkwanazi testimony, Commission 1957; Smit testimony, Commission 2049. Agnes Motshoahole hears people walking past her house around 11:30 am who say that "Europeans" told people to go to the police station, Commission 2739, 2741. David Morita is the second person from out of town who is identified in Sharpeville that day when he is arrested as a possible demonstrator (*betoger*) but later released. "List of Accused but Discharged after Investigation," Police Archive. Since the Sharpeville municipal police guarded the Gate as well as the three official pathways (north, south, and west) into and out of the town, and most of Sharpeville was enclosed by a fence, people who did not have a pass permitting them to enter (as, for example, if they worked there like Jacob Nhlapo and likely David Morita) could not do so. Solomon Dunga testimony, Court 304–305. All the K110 and SAP files referenced in this chapter are from the Central Government Archives since 1910 (SAB).

7 Tatai testimony, Court 2482; Mkwanazi testimony, Commission 1957; Maja testimony, Court 3003–3004; Johannes Seretho testimony, Court 3070; Thaba testimony, Commission 1792; interview with Minah Elizabeth Chabeli, Sharpeville, 14 March 2019; Molefi testimony Commission 1763, 1764–1765, 1777, 1779, 1780.

8 Xingwana testimony, Commission 1073, 1076–1077, Court 1813, 1819–1820, 1833; Grobler testimony, Court 599; Tsolo testimony, Commission 2540; Motha testimony, Court 2525–2526; Simon Mashelide (known as Lucas Mosheledi by Michael Thekiso) testimony, Commission 2239; Lidia testimony Commission 2277–2278, 2323–2324.

9 Xingwana testimony, Court 1819, 1820; Motshoahole testimony, Court 2452; Robert Maja testimony, Commission 2357, 2358; Smit testimony, Commission 2019; Musibi testimony, Commission 1879, 1897, 1898, Court 1892; Thomas Msimang testimony, Court 3126, 3127; Moses Shabangu statement, Sharpeville Affidavits, UN; Tatai testimony, Court 2474; Molefi testimony, Commission 3183–3184; Simon Mashelide testimony, Commission 2223; Miriam Lepee statements, K110 1/3/60, SAP 616 31/58/60. Shabangu hears about the Commissioner "from certain of the African Policemen."

10 Captain Jan van den Bergh testimony, Commission 2477–2478; Smit testimony, Commission 2027, 2028; Captain Stephanus Jakobus van der Linde testimony, Commission 774; Hendrik Gert Theron testimony, Commission 252, 253; Coetzee testimony, Commission 960–961; Labuschagne testimony, Commission 392; Lidia testimony, Commission 2307; Adam Sakaone statement, Sharpeville Affidavits, UN. Sidney Kentridge elicits the information about the private purchase of bullets in an extensive cross-examination, Saaiman testimony, Commission 2782–2788. Theron has 1 African sergeant and 8 African constables, 1 White head constable, 3 White sergeants, and 12 White constables. Coetzee has 60 men, 25 African constables, and 35 White officers and constables, including himself. The police vehicles arriving described by Sakaone include those of Coetzee (Vereeniging), Lieutenant Adriaan Frederick Freemantle (Boksburg), and Theron (Springs). Freemantle arrives at 12:45 pm from Boksburg with 11 African constables and 5 White, Freemantle testimony, Commission 844–845. For Manyosi's experiences, see the *Golden City Post*, 27 March 1960. Channon has already documented events in Evaton and Bophelong in a series of 20 photographs. He takes 18 following van der Linde's Saracens, and another 21 later in the day. None of his Sharpeville photos have been preserved, although copies of all of them were given to the police. Channon statement, 18 April 1960, information added 18 May 1960, Police Archive.

11 Coetzee testimony, Court 1491; Theron testimony, Court 794: Ntsame testimony, Court 1846; Jan Hendrik Grove testimony, Court 1965–1966; Smit testimony, Commission 2027, 2056–2057; Labuschagne testimony, Commission 424; Theron testimony, Commission 300–301, Court 781, 783–794; Visser testimony, Commission 485–486; Coetzee testimony, Court 1492; Daniel Dikubo testimony, Commission 2258, statement, SAP 620 31/58/60; Mischack Mareka statement, SAP 622 31/58/60.

12 Smuts testimony, Commission 2614–2616. Smuts is contradictory in his evidence, not wishing to undercut the official narrative that no official planned to speak to the Sharpeville residents gathered that day.

13 Interview with Minah Elizabeth Chabeli, Sharpeville, 14 March 2019; Hophny Morobe testimony, Court 3149, 3153; Maja testimony, Commission 2357–2358; Lidia testimony, Commission 2277, 2279, 2302–2305; Aaron Motsoane statement, K110 1/3/60; Johannes Motsoane statement, K110, 1/3/60; Elliot Kubeka statement, SAP 620 31/58/60; Daniel Phosisi statement, K110 1/3/60; Meshack Pitso statement, K110 1/3/60; Sakaone statement, Sharpeville Affidavits, UN; Mofokeng testimony, Commission 1998, 1999, 2000. See also the testimony by Maja, Commission 2366, about small children playing around in the street. Tsolo thinks that the planes are intended to scare people, but "We are not children and we are not to be frightened," Commission 2494, 2508.

14 Eric Lebeko statement concerning his relative Elliot Kabi, K110 1/3/60; Selina Mazibuko statement, K110 1/3/60; David Mabaso statement, SAP 621 31/58/60; Lydia Mailane statement, SAP 621 31/58/60; George Jonah statement, SAP 620 31/58/60; Solomon Masilo statement, SAP 622 31/58/60; Anna Phutheho

182 *The Massacre*

statement, K110 1/3/60; Koboekae statement, SAP 620 31/38/60; Justice Maeko statement, SAP 621 31/58/60.
15 Meriam Maine statement, K110 1/3/60; Elizabeth Botha statement, SAP 620 31/58/60; Anna Lethege statement, K110 1/3/60, testimony, Court 3040–3041; Dr. Albertus Lambinon testimony, Court 1048; William Lesito statement, SAP 621 31/58/60; Solomon Lesito statement, SAP 621 31/58/60; Alina Mokone statement, K110 1/3/60; Elias Mtimkulu statement, K110 1/3/60; John Nteso statement, K110 1/3/60; Anna Motsepe (55 years old) statement, K110 1/3/60; Agnes Motshoahole statement, K110 1/3/60; Stephen Lehobo testimony, Commission 1974, 1977, 1978; Anna Motsepe (63 years old) statement regarding her daughter Christina, K110 1/3/60; Molefi testimony, Commission 1747, 1779; Maja testimony, Commission 2356, 2358, Court 3008, 3012.
16 Freemantle testimony, Commission 864: *RDM*, 13 May 1960 reporting Ian Berry's testimony; Nkosi testimony, Commission 2710, 2714, 2715; Tsolo testimony, Commission 2496; Benjamin Maroo testimony, Commission 1701, 1702; Smuts testimony, Court 2616.
17 Photograph and caption from *RDM*, 15 June 1960. The photograph was taken by Jan Hoek and is described in his testimony to the Commission 1583, 1588–1589.
18 Tsolo testimony, Commission 2508.
19 Tsolo testimony, Commission 2497; Dikubo testimony, Commission 2266; Hendrik Christoffel Muller testimony, Court 835–836, 840–845; Andries Gottlieb Brummer testimony, Commission 798–802, Court 881–883; Spengler testimony, Commission 1268–1269; Jan Charles Hoek testimony, Commission 1577–1578. Bloke Modisane, *Blame Me on History* (E. P. Dutton: New York, 1963), 268.
20 Brummer testimony, Commission 804, 819, and Court 908 where Jack Unterhalter cross-examines him on the discourteous connotations of *hamba*. Lidia testimony, Commission 2302; Mkwanazi testimony, Commission 1969; Shabangu testimony, Commission 1718.
21 Molefi testimony, Commission 1748, 1749; Tsolo testimony, Commission 2492, 2495.
22 Spengler testimony, Commission, 1285, 1292–1298, 1300 (a to k); Theron testimony, Commission 304; Sakaone testimony, Commission 1662, statement Sharpeville Affidavits, UN; Litelu/Dethedo testimony, Commission 759; Lofafa testimony, Commission 1845; Tsolo testimony, Commission 2492, 2498, 2501, More testimony, Commission 2525, 2526; Wessels testimony, Commission 642–644, 651–652, Court 1084–1085; Mashelide testimony, Commission 2226–2227; Motha testimony, Commission 1929; Willers testimony, Court 2579–2580, 2589–2590; Visser testimony, Commission 501; Lidia testimony, Commission 2313, 2315, 2316. Spengler will always deny that he knows any man that day in civilian clothes and wearing a handkerchief around his head – see his testimony, Commission 1266. On Saaiman assisting Spengler, see Theron testimony, Commission 304; and Labuschagne testimony, Commission 448. Wessels and Spengler give contradictory testimony about the order of arrests. Wessels claims he arrested More first, and then Spengler arrested Tsolo. The preponderance of the testimony supports Spengler's recollection.
23 Molefi testimony, Commission 1748, 1770–1771; Lidia testimony, Commission 2315. See also Visser regarding the lack of any crowd reaction, testimony, Commission 487.
24 Jan Zacharias Hoek testimony, Commission 1777–1790, Court 1575–1591; Benjamin Pogrund, *How Can Man Die Better: The Life of Robert Sobukwe* (Jonathan Ball Publishers: Jeppestown, 1997), 132–133; Benjamin Pogrund, *War of Words: Memoir of a South African Journalist* (Seven Stories Press: New York,

The Massacre 183

2000), 83; Ian Berry testimony, Commission 1817–1843, Court 3278–3287; Shabangu testimony, Commission 1715 identifying the vehicles. Some of Hoek's and Berry's photographs are published in the order in which they are taken in Ambrose Reeves, *Shooting at Sharpeville: The Agony of South Africa* (Victor Gollancz: London, 1960), see illustrations 2–10 for those taken between about 1 pm and 1:15 pm. Alf Kumalo, *Through My Lens: A Photographic Memoir* (Cape Town: Tafelberg, 2009), 112–113.

25 Claassen testimony Commission, 874, 903, 904, 905, 907; Pienaar testimony, Commission 1327, 1328, 1330–1331, 1445–1446, Court 948, 951, 964, 998; Sakaone statement, Sharpeville Affidavits, UN; van Zyl testimony, Court 2123; van der Linde testimony, Commission 786–787; Theron testimony, Commission 305; Dikubo testimony, Commission 2258, 2267; Motha testimony, Commission 1919; Spengler testimony, Commission 1300(k); van Wyk testimony, Court 1916. After extensive cross-examination, Sydney Kentridge will note that he knows exactly what Pienaar did for the approximately 30 minutes he spent at the police station, but in fact he is being sarcastic, having elicited from Pienaar only statements about what he did not do and why he did not do it – "if only I had had the time – the time to stand on a box and say disperse? I did not have the time."

26 Motha testimony, Commission 1919, Court 2527–2528, 2542, 2552. Molefi thinks the same as Motha: "I got the impression that perhaps that [the police lined up] was a sign of respect that an important European official who perhaps was about to arrive. ... That is just what came into my mind," Court 3206.

27 Maroo testimony, Commission 1696, 1697, 1700–1704, 1707–1708, 1712–1714; statement SAP 31/58/60; Matthew Mashiya statement, Sharpeville Affidavits, UN; testimony, Commission 1728, 1734–1738; statement SAP 622 31/58/60; Elizabeth Mashiya (mother) statement, K110 1/3/60; Lofafa testimony Commission 1853; Simon Makhoba testimony, Commission 1983.

28 Molefi testifies extensively about his experiences on 21 March 1960 at both the Wessels Commission and the Monyake Trial. See his testimonies, Commission 1745–1786, Court 3175–3209. The arrest is also described by Muller in his testimony, Court 845–858. In Muller's testimony, Molefi is the aggressor. However, many people witness Molefi being assaulted by the police, including Benjamin Maroo, Moses Smit, Brown Thabe, Joshua Motha, Samuel Mahlase, Abraham Tinane, Samuel Mashobeni, Daniel Dikubo, Simon Makhoba, Isaac Tatai, Meschack Mkwanazi, George Qtwaya, Simon Mashelide, Benedict Griffiths, and Sergeant Daniel Mokabela.

29 Molefi testimony, Court 3208; Smit testimony, Commission 2025, 2026, 2044, 2067, 2068; Samuel Mahlase testimony, Commission 1902, 1903, 1913, 1914; Spengler testimony, Commission 1300(aa).

30 Griffiths statement, Sharpeville Affidavits, UN, testimony, Commission 1940–1942, 1945–1946.

31 Motha testimony, Commission 1920, 1929; Dikubo testimony, Commission 2266; Mahlase testimony, Commission 1903, 1908, 1909, 1910, 1912, 1913; Mkwanazi testimony, Commission 1969, 1970, 1971, 1973; Griffiths testimony, Commission 1942, 1946, 1947; Molefi testimony, Commission 1752, 1753, 1774, 1780–1783; Dikubo testimony, Commission 2260, 2270, 2271; Lepee statement, SAP 616 31/58/60; interview with Martha Masello Lepee, Sharpeville, 13 March 2019. Others who hear *Skiet!* shouted out include Samuel Mashobani, Commission 2339, and Isaac Tatai, Court 2478.

32 Gysbert Booysen testimony, Commission 1058, 1059, 1061, 1062, Court 1794, 1796; Charles Rudolf Meyer testimony, Court 2336; Saaiman testimony, Commission 2793, 2794; Johannes van Zyl testimony, Court 2220, 2221; Gerhardus Paulus Nel testimony, Commission 1185, 1186; Paul Machiel Sten

184 *The Massacre*

testimony, Court 2288; Izak Malherbe Pretorius testimony, Court 2268; Barend Johannes Theron testimony, Commission 2446, 2447. Constable Simon Andrew van den Bergh standing by Brummer's Saracen on the northern western corner sees the three Sten gunners, testimony, Commission 2700.

33 Claassen testimony, Commission 881–882. The original Afrikaans text quoted reads as follows:

> Ek verstaan dat onder die groep wat onder jou bevel was, daar 'n aantal manne is wat sal sê dat hulle 'n bevel gehoor het? – Ja; ek weet dat daar manne is wat dit sal sê. Is jy oortuig dat 'n bevel nie gegee is nie? – Nee, ek is nie oortuig dat 'n bevel nie gegee is nie. Dit mag gegee gewees het dat ek dit nie gehoor het nie. Veronderstel dat 'n bevel nie gegee is nie; is jy in die vermoë om te verduidelik waarom hulle dit sou sê? – Nee; dit is moontlik dat hulle so'n bevel gehoor het, as hulle so sê. Van die kolonel? – Van die kolonel. Bestaan daar 'n moontlikheid dat hulle 'n bevel gehoor het wat nie noodwendig van die kolonel afkomstig was nie? – Ek glo nie. Die kolonel was in bevel en die order om te vuur sou van hom gekom het.

34 Theron testimony, Commission, 2436, 2447; Booysen testimony, Court 1796; Charles Rudolf Meyer testimony, Court 2339; Johannes van Zyl testimony, Court 2220, 2221; Joel Meyer testimony, Commission 1180, 1181, 1182, Court 1545, 1546.
35 *RDM*, 24 March 1934, 25 October 1956, 16, 17, 18 September 1957, 22, 31 October 1958.
36 Constable Sybrandt Gerhardus van Niekerk testimony, Commission 695; Tinane testimony, Commission 2183–2185; Thabe testimony, Commission 1790; interview with Minah Elizabeth Chabeli, Sharpeville, 14 March 2019; Constable Joel Meyer testimony, Court 1545; Shabangu testimony, Commission 1718; Lofafa testimony, Commission, 1846; Molefi testimony, Commission 1752, 1784; Dikubo testimony, Commission 2260; Khaole testimony, Commission 1680, 1692–1693; Seretho testimony, Court 3068, 3069; Joseph Mojakoja statement, Sharpeville Affidavits, UN; Motha testimony, 1921, 1922; Lidia testimony, Commission 2281; Claassen testimony, Commission, 879, 912, 917, 920.
37 Labuschagne testimony, Commission 406, 416: "*Dit het my laat dink aan 'n koringland, waar 'n warrelwind hom ruk. Dit was net so; dit was net so gewees en hulle was weg, on die wat gewind was het agtergebly*"; Petrus Tom interview, 12 October 2022.
38 Saaiman testimony, Commission 2749, 2750; Johannes Stephanus Joubert testimony, Commission, 983; Oosthuizen testimony, Commission 1006, 1007, 1013–1018, 1022–1035, Court 1887–1896; Johannes van Zyl testimony, Court 2219–2230; Steyn testimony, Court 2228; van Wyk testimony, Court 1917, 1918, 1928, 1929, 1933; van Niekerk testimony, Court 698; Sergeant John Hendrik Christoffel Kok testimony, Commission 1098, 1107; Pennekan testimony, Commission 588ff, quoted in *RDM*, 26 April 1960. Some of the Sten gunners did not testify, including du Plessis, Bosch, Janssen, Steynberg, and van der Merwe. Joubert later claims he had his Sten on "single shot" and that he only fired 10 rounds, but the figures collected by van den Bergh record a magazine of 25 shots being emptied. Sneigans denies that he fired at all, even when confronted with unimpeachable visual evidence in the photographs taken by Ian Berry of the fleeing crowd with identifiable officers standing on the Saracen shooting into their backs. See Sneigans' testimony to the Wessels Commission and the cross-examination by Kentridge, Commission 2383–2428. The exact numbers of bullets shot by each policeman will never be finally determined. Judge Wessels tasked Captain Jan van den Bergh with investigating how many shots were fired, and he came up

with some tentative figures which were less than half the number later disclosed. See van den Bergh's testimony, Commission 2449–2468, 2475–2485. Phillip Frankel in 1999 found additional statistics in the Police Archive in Pretoria (*An Ordinary Atrocity*, Appendix 1, "The Police at Sharpeville," 228–241), materials that are no longer readily accessible (if they still exist; they have not been transferred to the National Archives as Frankel expected would be the case when he examined them). One complication is that according to van den Bergh, if a policeman stated that he did not fire at all, or only a certain number of bullets, then that personal testimony would be accepted as proof "beyond all doubt": "That is all you mean by 'beyond all doubt?' – Yes." Van den Bergh testimony, Commission 2479. Wessels thought that the official returns "understate the rounds fired," Commission 320. Claassen absolutely agreed that much larger figures would be forthcoming. The distance from the police line to the fence, a distance less than half that of a military firing squad (15 paces), was variously estimated by Pienaar (5 paces), Claassen (6–8), Labuschagne (3), Steyn (5), Stapelberg (5), van Wyk (3), Oosthuizen (7), and Struwig (5). Freemantle, a small arms instructor, provided detailed testimony on the fire power of all the weapons used, and especially the tremendous killing power of the Sten guns, Commission 844–873. Because of the short barrel of the Sten (like a sawed-off shotgun) and the small ammunition, the bullets fired from Sten guns "sometimes turn end over end ... tumbling ... and if it strikes the human body on the side ... it rips it right open ... if you turn the machine gun full out ... in 3.5 seconds you can cut two people to pieces, and it is not very accurate." The references to deliberate and persistent firing and to a "firing squad" are from the *Submissions* presented by the bishop of Johannesburg 132, 180–181. The best estimate of the number of shots, based on van den Bergh's original report, other testimony given to the Wessels' Commission, and Frankel's figures are at least 1,362 bullets fired, 720 of them Sten, 198 by .38 revolvers, 442 by .303 rifles, and 2 by .25 pistols (fired by two CID men). Twelve policemen fire Stens at the police station (and one earlier in the day in Seeiso), 5 of them also empty their revolvers into the crowd, another 19 fire their revolvers (and 6 of them also their rifles), and 47 men fire just their rifles, some of them emptying several magazines into the crowd. Two CID officers fire one shot each from their .25 pistols. All of the names of the officers who fired are available in these sources.

39 Motha testimony, Commission 1921–1922, 1931, Court 2531, 2542–2543; Dikubo, medical report, SAP 620 31/58/60; Mareka statement, SAP 622 31/58/60; Lethege testimony, Court 3039–3040; Nteso testimony, Commission 2353; Setlhatlole statement, SAP 619 31/58/60; Musibi testimony, Commission 1877–1878, Court 3078–3079; Griffiths testimony, Commission 1943–1944; Maroo testimony, Commission 1711, 1713–1714, statement, SAP 622 31/58/60; Maja testimony, Commission 2359–2360, 2381, Court 3000, 3016–3017. Like John Nteso, Solomon Ramohoase testifies that he was shot by a policeman who had entered a Saracen. See his testimony to the *Truth and Reconciliation Commission*, Sebokeng hearing, 5 August 1996.
40 Sidwell Kele testimony, Court 1382, 1391.
41 Pienaar testimony, Commission 1339–1340, 1485, Court; 1001; policemen van Niekerk, Stapelberg, Oosthuizen, Booysen, Commission 690, 729, 1001, 1062; Musibi testimony, Commission 1900. Labuschagne estimated 20–30 seconds, Commission 414; William Molatule thought 50–60 seconds was more likely, Commission 2076. Ian Berry reconstructed a timeline after the fact, estimating how long it took him to take each of his photos, and concluded that the shooting lasted between 40 and 45 seconds, *RDM*, 13 May 1960 summarizing his Commission testimony.

186   *The Massacre*

42 Mokabela testimony, Court 2303. Nyakane Tsolo estimates that it was only 5–6 minutes between his arrest and hearing the firing start, Commission 2494–2495.
43 Motha testimony, Commission 1922–1923, Court 2544–2545. In his Commission testimony (1924–1925) Joshua Motha says that a senior policeman in a blue uniform – the only one dressed in blue that day was Pienaar – personally orders the arrest of Motho. "Motho" may have been Edward Moloto, a 21-year-old employed by Union Steel, who later submitted a claim for false arrest. When the police seized Moloto in response to Pienaar's order, they would later claim that they had found a "formidable dagger" hidden in his clothing; the judge at the Monyake trial dismissed these police claims as "highly unsatisfactory" and found Moloto not guilty of any offences, judgement 128–129.
44 Other than one heavily cropped image that obscured all the dead bodies on the no-name street (*RDM* front page, 22 March 1960), the *RDM* editorial staff decided not to publish any of Robinson's photographs, even though they considered them "the best news photos ever taken in South Africa." One of the deputy editors described the decision making by the *RDM* as follows, "Without saying it, we all knew that it would be no more than ordinary newspaper practice and courage to print these photographs; but more important than courage at that moment was responsibility ... we knew the temper of the half-million black population which surrounded this white city of Johannesburg, and we could not print these photographs without being aware of their potentially inflammatory effect. ... After much uneasy discussion we found ourselves unhappily using a selection of the lesser pictures, leaving the grimmest for later consideration." None of Robinson's photographs of Sharpeville were ever published in apartheid-era South Africa. Lewis Sowden, *The Land of Afternoon: The Story of a White South Africa* (McGraw-Hill: New York, 1968), 201–202. Bloke Modisane in his autobiography published after Sharpeville mocked the sanctimoniousness of newspapers like the *RDM* when he wrote that "the free and courageous white press is – especially on matters of colour – more white than free and courageous," *Blame Me on History* (E. P. Dutton: New York, 1963), 147–148.
45 Lidia testimony, Commission 2284–2286, 2320–2330; Motsoahole testimony, Commission 2739-2743; Dikubo testimony, Commission 2268–2269; *RDM* summary of Dikubo's testimony, 21 May 1960; Simon Mahlase testimony, Commission 1904–1906. Mahlase heard Pitsi saying, "Yes, they have fixed you people. I have been telling you for quite some time. They have fixed you by shooting." On the ambulances, Petrus Tom interview, 12 October 2022. Separately, we have heard from acquaintances in South Africa that some of the ambulances were driven by young military recruits.
46 Maja testimony, Commission 2360–2363, 2375–78, Court 3000, 3019–24.
47 Molefi testimony, Court 3179, 3180; Daubada testimony, Court 2359; Mokabela testimony, Court 2301–2303, 2309, 2318; Tsolo and More cross examine Muller, Court 860–867. The words quoted are More's. Sacks testimony, Commission 1614–1615; Coetzee testimony, Court 1501, 1503. When they arrive at the Gate, Sacks and Robinson are not allowed to enter Sharpeville, but as the sound of firing starts, they are allowed in. As a result, all the photographs taken that day by Robinson are of the aftermath of the shooting. Du Plooy is appointed national commissioner of police on 29 June 1960 with the rank of lieutenant-general. His predecessor as national commissioner, Major-General C. I. Rademayer, was in Cape Town on 21 March 1960 and entered Langa later that night, together with the minister of justice and five Saracens. Harold Sacks wrote numerous stories for the *RDM*, relying on his personal friendship with Pienaar, with whom he often stayed. When Sacks committed suicide in 1962 after suffering a debilitating accident in 1960, Pienaar and his

wife were staying overnight at Sacks' home and Pienaar discovered the body at dawn the next morning. *RDM*, 6 April 1962.
48 *Golden City Post*, 27 March 1960. The *Post* was a weekly, thus the delayed publication date.
49 *New Age* 24 March 1960. Joe Nzingo Gqabi was assassinated by a South African government hit squad on 31 July 1981 in Harare, Zimbabwe.
50 Henri Schoup statement dated April 1960, K110.
51 For Robinson's own count of his photographs, see Commission 1552. Channon takes 21 photographs "immediately after the shooting," statement to the police dated 18 May 1960, Police Archive.
52 Manyosi's photographs were published in the *Golden City Post*, Gqabi's in the *New Age*, and Channon's in the *Star* in the week of the shooting. The *World* also had cameramen at the site of the shooting, and those photographs were published at the end of the week. Ramakatane mailed his photographs to the United Nations, but all his own copies are destroyed by a fire in his archive in the late 20-teens. The originals have not as yet been located. The *RDM* decided not to publish any of Robinson's photos apart from only one which is printed with the bodies of the dead obscured by a sub-heading. Ian Berry's photographs for *Drum* are not published in South Africa until October 1960, along with photos taken by Peter Magubane and W. Calder (Calder entered Sharpeville at 11:30 am with Manyosi). Robinson's and Berry's photographs are widely distributed outside South Africa and can be found in the 4 April 1960 issues of *Life* and *Time* magazines. The publication history of the *Drum* material (not published until the October 1960 issue of the magazine) is described by Tom Hopkinson, the editor of *Drum*, in his autobiography, *In the Fiery Continent* (Victor Gollancz: London, 1962), 255–258, 263–273. *Drum* does not include Kumalo's photograph of the bodies in the street but that image can be found in his autobiographical text, *Through My Lens*, 113. *Life*, 4 April 1960, publishes a picture of the arrested and unnamed African photographer with camera in hand being guarded by a municipal policeman.
53 Some of the ITN footage filmed on 21 March is included in episode 21, "Crisis in South Africa," of the ITN documentary news series *Searchlight*. Visser testifies about the arrival of the police photographers, Commission 504. Lewis Nkosi refers to his and Nakasa's presence in Sharpeville, "we used blankets to collect bodies," in his draft autobiography excerpted in Astrid Starck-Adler and Dag Henrichsen (eds), *The Black Psychiatrist: Flying Home: Texts, Perspectives, Homage* (Basler Afrika Bibliographien: Basel, 2021), xiv. Nkosi is interrogated by the police a few days after the shooting. Lidia accounts for the time of arrival of the ambulances, Commission 2322–2322, 2286–2287. The time of arrival of the first patients at the Vereeniging Hospital is noted in the patient records, Superintendent of Hospital Dr. P. D. Swanepoel's testimony, Commission 1151. Isiah Leroto is taken by a motorcycle to the Vereeniging Hospital and then transferred by ambulance to Baragwanath, statement SAP 619 31/58/60. For Lepee's experience see her file in K110, 1/3/60. Her amputation is performed, perhaps incorrectly as a subsequent medical examination suggests, at Baragwanath.
54 Joshua Malema testimony, Commission 2241–2246; Pienaar testimony, Commission 1340–1341, Court 958; Theron testimony, Commission 315, Court 818–820; Grobler testimony, Commission 129; Saaiman testimony, Commission 2276–2281; Mokabela testimony, Court 2323–2324; Daubada testimony, Court 2368–2369. Constable Daubada is insistent in his testimony: "The stones I picked up were lying outside the fence, outside. ... Outside, Your Worship. Outside the Police Station. ... Those are the only stones I saw which I assisted in picking up. ... Only outside there. ... I did not see stones being picked up from the lawn."

Even with all their efforts, the police only fill a single bucket with the stones they collect from the street outside the police station. That single bucket will be used again and again in the subsequent Commission of Enquiry and the trial of the Sharpeville residents, to prove stone throwing on Sunday night, Monday morning in Seeiso, and at the police station in the afternoon. The same bucket. The same stones. For Pienaar's comments, see the Commission transcript, 2801–2803. Pienaar's comments were reported by the foreign correspondent in *Time* magazine, 4 April 1960, p. 19, as, "My car was struck by a stone. If they do these things, they must learn the hard way." At the subsequent trial of Sharpeville residents, the defense counsel noted in cross-examination of a police witness "that if there were no white circles [added to a photograph presented in evidence to highlight damage] ... on this motor-car [Pienaar's], one would have to exercise one's imagination to see dents in the picture?"
55 Abram Mofokeng, interview 11 October 2018; Schoup statement April 1960, K110.
56 Phutheho statement, K110 1/3/60.
57 Makhoba statement, SAP 621 31/58/60.
58 Claassen testimony, Commission 909; Harold Sacks eyewitness testimony as reported in the *RDM*, 22 March 1960; Mahasane Michael Thekiso interview, 11 October 2018.

Bibliography

Frankel, Philip. *An Ordinary Atrocity: Sharpeville and Its Massacre*. New Haven: Yale University Press, 2001.
Hopkinson, Tom. *In the Fiery Continent*. London: Victor Gollancz, 1962.
ITN. "Crisis in South Africa." Number 21 of the documentary news series *Searchlight*. 1960.
Kumalo, Alf. *Through My Lens: A Photographic Memoir*. Cape Town: Tafelberg, 2009.
Modisane, Bloke. *Blame Me on History*. New York: E. P. Dutton, 1963.
Pogrund, Benjamin. *How Can Man Die Better: The Life of Robert Sobukwe*. Jeppestown: Jonathan Ball Publishers, 1997.
Pogrund, Benjamin. *War of Words: Memoir of a South African Journalist*. New York: Seven Stories Press, 2000.
Reeves, Ambrose. *Submissions Presented to the Commission on Behalf of the Bishop of Johannesburg*. Johannesburg, 15 June 1960a. Two volumes.
Reeves, Ambrose. *Shooting at Sharpeville: The Agony of South Africa*. London: Victor Gollancz, 1960b.
Starck-Adler, Astrid and Dag Henrichsen (eds). *The Black Psychiatrist: Flying Home: Texts, Perspectives, Homage*. Basel: Basler Afrika Bibliographien, 2021.
Truth and Reconciliation Commission, Sebokeng hearing, 5 August 1996.
Tyler, Humphrey. *Life in the Time of Sharpeville: and wayward seeds of a new South Africa*. Cape Town: Kwela Books, 1995.

7 A Family Tragedy

        Husbands killed 38   *Wives killed 2*
        Sons killed 12   *Daughters killed 2*
        Fathers killed 16   *Mothers killed 1*
        Brothers killed 1   *Sisters killed 2*[1]

Wives and mothers and daughters and sisters, sons and brothers and fathers and husbands, the familial terminology was that used by Sharpeville residents themselves in describing the pain and the loss caused by 45 seconds of the police shooting. The terms hint at the infinite variability and complexity of family relationships because no one person is one relationship; we all exist in multiple and overlapping relationships to one another in our immediate and extended families and communities. But it is in these household relationships and in plotting their connections that we can start to see the wider impact of these 45 seconds of "thundering" on an entire community.

Let Us Start with the Children

Fourteen-year-old David Makhoba was one of the first Sharpeville residents shot to death by the police on the afternoon of Monday, 21 March 1960. When his mother Maria, having waited four days for her son to return, went on Friday to the government mortuary in Johannesburg and identified his body, he had injuries to his front and back. A gunshot wound in his chest had gone through to his spinal column, injuries to his facial bones, and a bullet in his right buttock had fractured his femur (the longest and strongest bone in the body). He must have been hit in the first volley of Sten gunfire and then again as he turned to run.

    There were more children killed by the police on 21 March. James Buti Bessie, 12 years old, had gone to school, but on finding it closed and on his way back home, he had seen people going to the police station and followed them to find out what was happening. He never made it home. He may have been the dead boy seen by Ronnie Manyosi on Zwane Street, still clutching his wire toy in his hand. James' 5-year-old sister Mphonyana Annetjie Matsabu remembers to this day that after the airplanes appeared overhead,

DOI: 10.4324/9781003257806-7

she and her other siblings were told by their mother to stay inside, and they never saw their brother again. "Later on as people were called to identify the deceased, we were told he was in such a condition that we would not want to look at him." Among school-age children, the dead also included Maria Molebatsi 13, Edward Tsela 16, and three 17-year-olds, Johannes Senyalano, Zanana Nathaniel Sothoane, and Elias Masilo. Elias' father John (one of the three Masilo brothers) found his son dead on the no-name street, killed by a bullet to his head (the cause of death was "lacerations of the brain"). According to Basotho custom, the Masilo family, after mourning his death, burnt all of Elias's belongings (including his birth certificate).

Three expectant mothers lost their unborn children that day, two of them dying themselves from police bullets. Christina Motsepe, the young woman (she was 21) who was looking for her mother to tell her that lunch was ready, was shot dead from behind by a policeman (likely Constable Sneigans) standing on a Saracen on the northern side of the police station. She was between seven and eight months pregnant with a young boy. His fetus was discovered when an autopsy was carried out on her unrefrigerated body a week later. She left behind in the care of her mother her 2-year-old daughter Selina. Mamotshabi Paulina Malikoe, 21 years old and only a few months pregnant, died with her unborn child from a bullet that entered her chest, lacerating her left lung and her heart causing her to bleed to death and to leave behind in the guardianship of her father her 6-year-old daughter Elizabeth. Lydia Chalale, a 23-year-old unmarried mother of a 5-year-old daughter (Gloria) and working as a self-employed dressmaker, was standing in the yard of a friend's house on Seeiso Street, 260 m northwest of the police station, when she heard firing and saw the crowd running towards her. She tried to get in the house, but before she could do so, she was shot in the back (see Figure 7.1). The bullet tore through her body, fractured several ribs, damaged her spleen, perforated her intestines, and exited, injuring her left arm. Two weeks after the shooting, she began bleeding so severely that medical staff gave her a blood transfusion. A week later, they carried out an abortion "due to the injuries the patient suffered on March 21st."[2]

Counting the Victims

Everywhere you look, whether it be printed sources or online sites, whether it be the number of individual white plinths in the Sharpeville Memorial, or the number of gravestones in the Sharpeville Phelindaba cemetery, you will learn that 69 people were killed by the police on 21 March 1960 and approximately 180 injured. These iconic totals (police counts) are wrong, and we will explain why.

So many were killed in less than a minute, and their bodies treated with such disrespect, that the total count of the dead remains in dispute, at least in the Sharpeville community, to the present day. Immediately after the

A Family Tragedy 191

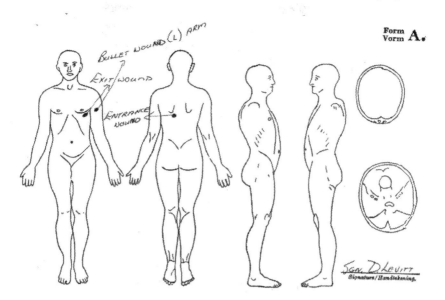

Figure 7.1 Lydia Chalale official police diagram of injuries.
Source: National Archives and Records Service of South Africa, SAP 611, SAB. Photo by authors.

shooting and before any of the bodies had been removed, Superintendent Labuschagne counted 70 dead in the vicinity of the police station – many of them people "whom I knew well." Within 20 minutes of the firing ending, almost all the bodies of the dead had been piled high in police vans and spirited away to the Vereeniging police station out of sight of the gathering photographers. When Major van Zyl arrived at the police station from the Gate at 2 pm only two to three dead still lay on the no-name street. Later in the afternoon, Captain Theron counted 53 bodies at the Vereeniging police station and 165 injured at the separate "Black section" of the Vereeniging Hospital. Most of the corpses were transferred within a day or so to the Johannesburg government mortuary and most – but not all – of the injured from the Vereeniging Hospital to the "Blacks-only" Baragwanath Hospital in Soweto. At least three of the injured in the Baragwanath Hospital and one in the Vereeniging Hospital died on March 22; subsequent deaths in the hospitals from injuries sustained on 21 March with one exception (see Walter Botha later in this chapter) remain unknown.

The official casualty figures were soon set in stone. Prime Minister Verwoerd speaking in parliament during the late afternoon of 21 March initially cited 25 killed and 50 injured. He used a particularly callous analogy comparing the actions of the police to those of doctors: "I do not believe that people should be killed unnecessarily … but there are … times when gentle doctors cause putrid wounds." Later in the evening, he reported 53 dead and 156 injured, accompanied by the supposedly reassuring statement that "Brig. Els is on the scene." The next day, his government issued an "official" count of 67 killed and 186 injured in "riots" in Sharpeville. On 5 April, the minister of justice F. C. Erasmus released an official count of injured of 186 ("138 African men, 40 women and eight children"). Two months later Captain Jan van den Bergh, tasked by Judge P. J. Wessels with making a count for the official *"Commission of Enquiry into the Occurrences at Sharpeville (and other places) on the 21st March, 1960"* of the total number of bullets used and number of people killed or injured on 21 March 1960, testified to a final official count of 69 killed and 178 injured (the number of injured has been repeated as at most 186 and usually 180), and those are the figures that have been published ever since. And yet, on 4 April 1960, *Time* magazine in its first story on Sharpeville reported, "The dead – estimates range from 72 to 90 – were carried off to makeshift morgues; more than 200 wounded overflowed the native hospital." *Time's* figures, forgotten for over half a century, are borne out by our research.[3]

Sharpeville residents didn't trust any of these counts. They knew that many of the injured either chose not to seek medical attention for fear of arrest (like Vincent Thamae's grandfather) or having received emergency treatment in the Vereeniging Hospital, like Jacob Molefe Ntjê, were helped by friends and neighbours to evade the police guards and escape back to their homes where they hid their injuries for years, sometimes for the rest of their lives. There are contemporaneous photographs of people injured who never appeared on any list of the injured, such as the Reverend Sam Hlatshwayo whose photo was taken on 21 March and captioned "he was hit on the head with a baton and struck in the ribs with a bayonet while he was standing outside his house," and of K. Lebeko, photographed the same day waiting outside the Vereeniging Hospital to be treated for a bullet wound in his leg.[4] Sharpeville family members never saw all the bodies of those killed. Perhaps because of the devastating nature of the injuries and the advanced decomposition of the bodies, government officials buried the dead using closed coffins at the two funerals held in Sharpeville, the first on 30 March, the second on 2 April. Municipal police stood guard at all entrances to the town to prevent any "unauthorised" people ("Whites, Asiatics, and non-resident Africans") entering, though several reporters got in and at least three newspapers hired planes to take aerial photographs of the first funeral (when between 32 and 34 bodies were buried in the 48 pre-dug graves – the count of graves was by the *Rand Daily Mail* (*RDM*) photographer flying overhead). The mourners sang "Abide with Me" as they had done almost ten days earlier when they had gathered before the shooting. Church leaders such as the reverends Mahabane, Maja, and Voyi (on whose stoep Maja had sat drinking tea right before the police shooting) led the thousands of mourners in prayers and hymns.

The funeral was heartbreaking. I remember a black policeman who saw his wife and children dead and resigned on the spot. It was a day of pure sorrow. All the church denominations came together and there was a massive crowd. The coffins arrived on trucks, which was normal in those days, but the sight of all these coffins arriving together was more than we could bear. Even the women helped carry the coffins off the trucks. All of them were crying. It was such a strange sight – all these coffins together being lowered with ropes into the ground. ... There is no way you can forget Sharpeville. If you saw it you will die with it.[5]

(Alf Kumalo)

Residents to this day are sure that the coffins contained more than one body, or that other bodies had already been buried in the graves before the coffins were placed over them, not farfetched since that is exactly what apartheid officials did when burying the victims of other police shootings such as those of the Mamelodi 10 in June 1986[6] (Figure 7.2).

While numbers might not always seem important to the wider public, they are viewed as extremely significant by the residents of Sharpeville who remember each and every one of the victims, so let's attempt a recount using the new documentation we discovered in the archives and incorporating people's testimonies as recorded by the Truth and Reconciliation Commission (TRC) in 1996, by the South African National Archives in 2014, and by ourselves in 2018, 2019, and 2022.

Though the official police list of the dead (official copies are still held both by the Police Archives and the National Archives in Pretoria – Document 1) and the Phelindaba gravestones each total the same number of people, some of the names differ (and we are not referring here to discrepancies accounted for by police misspellings). The police list (which we photographed at the Police Archives in 2018) has 69 names, but three of the names (as spelled by the police) on the list – Samuel Mahlele age 30, Aron Mavizela age 24, and Walter Mbatha age 35 – are not among those with gravestones. The Phelindaba gravestones, which we photographed in 2018, also have 69 names, three of which are not on the police list, Samuel Sonnyboy Moatlhodi age 34, Amos Mtimkulu age 50, and Zanana Nathaniel Sothoane age 17. Moatlhodi was the former municipal policeman (see Chapter 4) between jobs who was living with his wife and daughter in the home of his 71-year-old father the day he was shot dead. The bullet that killed him entered his back and exited slightly higher through his right lung. He must have been leaning forward slightly as he ran from the police, and he bled to death. His father identified his body the next day in Vereeniging. We have determined in discussions with community members that both Amos Mtimkulu and Zanana Nathaniel Sothoane were killed by the police on 21 March even though their names were not entered in official records.[7]

Figure 7.2 "Are there really dead bodies in those coffins? It looks as if they go into infinity."[8]
Photo by Alf Kumalo/african.pictures. © Alf Kumalo Family Trust.

Using the 69 gravestones as a baseline for those killed on 21 March or who died as a result of injuries inflicted by police bullets that day, we need to add from the police list Samuel Mahlele; Aron Mavizela, who may have been the older brother of Paulus Mabitsela (whose name was also spelled Mavizela on the police list but Mabitsela on his gravestone); and Walter Mbatha (his name is spelled Botha by the family and his granddaughter Buiswa Botha spoke with us in 2019) to the total count of the dead. As we wrote in Chapter 5, Walter's wife Elizabeth had sent him to the shops a little after noon on the 21st to buy food for their five young children. When he didn't return, she went looking for him after the shooting and found his bike lying on the no-name street. She then went to the Vereeniging Hospital where she found him shot with a bullet that had entered his back and exited his chest. He died nine days later.

Our working total is now 72 killed by the police on 21 March 1960.

The National Archives in Pretoria also contain files relating to the deaths on 21 March of Isaac Sepeng (age unknown; he left an orphaned minor daughter), police file South African Police (SAP) 31/58/60 (279); John

Mahudi (age unknown, leaving a widow Maria Mahudi and a minor child), police file SAP 31/58/60 (245); and the adult son (not named in the official records) and sole means of support for his father, Andrew Mokoena, police file SAP 31/58/60 (203), and, also without first names, the deceased husbands of Elizabeth Madeski and Evelyn Radebe, police file SAP 31/58/60 (175) and (228). In addition, *The World* newspaper published on 26 March 1960 (see Chapter 8, p. 229), an initial list of the dead including two names that do not appear anywhere else in the documentary record, T. Ramailane, "an elder of the Methodist Church," and Jerry Molapo (no ages are given). To this growing total we can add Sello Ralebakeng (whose son was a policeman) injured on 21 March, who died in police custody on 20 July 1960 when a truck taking Sharpeville prisoners from the Boksburg goal to their trial in Vereeniging rolled, and he was killed, and Joseph Morobi age 51, who spent five months in Baragwanath and whose right leg was amputated. He had to go to Johannesburg regularly to see a doctor and "when he got back from there on 12 April 1961 he said he was feeling tired and he passed away that same day." Ralebakeng left a widow and four young children; Morobi left a widow and three young children, including one with whom his wife was pregnant at the time of her husband's death (Alice, his widow, testified a year after her husband's death: "My children are small and I cannot leave them at home alone and I have no income"). Sixty years later, one of Joseph and Alice Morobi's daughters, Matshepo Maria Morobi, born after her father passed away, remembers her family as being "one of the poorest" in Sharpeville. Both Ralebakeng and Morobi were included among those officially recognised by the government Sharpeville claims committee as having died because of the police shooting on 21 March.

Our working total is now 81 killed by the police on 21 March 1960.

And let's not forget the three unborn children killed by the police on 21 March 1960: Christina Motsepe's son dying with his mother while still inside her womb, Mamotshabi Paulina Malikoe's child who also died inside her/his mother's womb, and Lydia Chalale's medically aborted child, perhaps without her knowledge. They were never listed on any police count, but their loss was their families and their community's loss as well.

Our working total is now 84 killed by the police on 21 March 1960.

We can also add Elizabeth Mookgo Ntsane, identified to TRC interviewers in 1996 as having been killed on 21 March 1960, and Khehla Mabona age 27, whose widow Konsatsama Elizabeth Mabona testified about the death of her husband when she spoke to the TRC commissioners at their hearing in Sebokeng on 5 August 1996. In addition, Philip Frankel included as an appendix to his book *An Ordinary Atrocity* a list of names of 55 "Natives who died of gun wounds" from "The Register of the Sharpeville Natives' Cemetery," and an appendix of "Names on the tombstones at the Sharpeville Natives' Cemetery." The Register is no longer accessible, and the graves have been re-dug, but discounting for names that we have already allowed for there are five additional people who should be included on the list of the dead: Pauline Madiku (age 22), Jean Mafogane (36), Elisabeth Manyane (18), Islabet Mgomezulu (30), and Enuell Mpeka (no age). (See Document 5.)

Our working total is now 91 people killed by the police on 21 March 1960, a third higher than the police count. Not 69. Never 69.[9]

And what of those who were injured on 21 March, often harmed so severely that they were left crippled for life, and who too often have been forgotten by those who write about Sharpeville but not by the residents of the town? The official figures cited earlier of between 178 and 186 injured fall well short of the numbers identified in official records later in 1960 and 1961. The actual number of verifiable injured (as distinct from generalised claims of possible anonymous victims) is considerably higher.

Initially, there was a great deal of confusion about the number of injured, and, unfortunately, that confusion has left us for decades with a severe undercount of people who were shot by the police but who survived. Different and often contradictory figures were provided at the time by the Vereeniging fire chief (reporting Red Cross numbers), the superintendent of the Vereeniging Hospital, the superintendent of the Baragwanath Hospital, and Captain van den Bergh. Even the attorneys (including Sydney Kentridge) hired by Ambrose Reeves, the Bishop of Johannesburg, to represent the victims at the Wessels Commission, initially accepted the official figures of 69 dead and 178–186 wounded.[10]

But community members themselves developed a much more accurate count later in 1960 and 1961 when, working with the attorneys in Vereeniging, Johannesburg, and Pretoria who had been retained on their behalf by the Bishop of Johannesburg or independently, they made claims for compensation against the state. These claims, for those killed and those injured, numbered (the police numbered them) at least 330 (with some repetition of names). Besides these numbered claims, the archival records contain some unnumbered files of additional victims. The numbers cannot be exact given gaps in the extant records, but discounting for those killed in Sharpeville, and for the duplicate names, and adding in the unnumbered files (as well as five African witnesses who testified in public hearings in 1960 and 1961 as being injured on 21 March but who did not file claims), we have at least 197 injured (identifiable by name, age, address, household family members, and employment) as of the time their claims were filed in early 1961. Moreover, almost hidden in the pages of *The World* newspaper (see Chapter 8, p. 229) was a list of people injured on 21 March and that list includes 8 people not identified elsewhere. After the end of the censorship of the apartheid years, the TRC solicited testimonies in 1996 of people who had been killed or injured in 1960. Of the 51 statements provided, 20 were by people who had not made a claim in 1961. The National Archives recorded 14 testimonies of Sharpeville survivors in 2014, 8 of whom had not made a claim in 1961 or given a statement to the TRC in 1996. In our own interviews, we identified at least two people (Thamae and Ntjê) who had been injured in 1960 but who had not made claims for fear of persecution by the police, and likely there are many more such individuals.

In October 2022 with the assistance of local residents, we identified another person injured on 21 March 1960, Evodia Mamatoba Phakeli, who never submitted a claim for compensation for the loss of her leg due to police bullets and therefore has never appeared in official records of the massacre. Evodia Phakeli is the woman photographed by Alf Kumalo and published (without any identifying information) in his 2009 volume, *Through My Lens*, with the caption "A victim of the Sharpeville Massacre, who was only 11 years old at the time of the tragedy, is reminded daily of her severe injuries." Although Evodia Phakeli died a decade ago, the young child on her lap, her daughter, is still alive and now (2022) aged 40, with her extended family lives in a house with a busy shoe repair business carried on in their yard over the road from local schools in the area previously known as Stands (Figure 7.3).

For now, relying solely on the number of people who can be proven by documentary or oral evidence to have been injured by the police on 21 March 1960, we have a total of at least 238 individuals (including the two injured people photographed and named in *The World*), a figure 30 percent higher than the official total reported in 1960 and repeated ever since (See Document 6).[11]

At least 91 killed, 238 and more injured by the police on 21 March 1960. Remember these numbers.

Who Were the Victims?

Not one of the individuals killed or injured, contrary to widespread belief ever since outside the community (and we were guilty of this too when we started our study), was a migrant worker. Ephraim Thaba, the Sepedi hostel dweller whose wife and five children lived in Pietersburg because they couldn't find housing in Sharpeville, and who was injured by the police on the morning of the 21st as he was going to get breakfast at a café in Stand No. 50 on Seeiso, was a long-term employee of African Cables. He was somewhat of an outlier in the hostels, most of whose inhabitants (other than the Baca night soil workers) were young men born in either Top or Sharpeville who after the age of 18 were required by location regulations (often evaded) to move out of their parents' homes and into the single men's hostels until they married. Men like Isaac Mashiya, at 31 the oldest of the three Mashiya brothers who had gone to wait on the no-name street, and the only one who did not live at home. He died from multiple bullet wounds in his back. Elliot Kabi (whose gravestone reads Sekoala Elliot Kabi, Mosekoala was the first name of his mother, Mosekoala Eusebia Kabi), the young man going to mail a letter on 21 March, worked as a clerk for the Basutoland National Treasury. He was in town briefly staying with a cousin. Elliot, who bled to death because of bullets that pierced the arteries of his neck and his chest, was the sole financial support for his widowed mother, his grandfather, and three siblings, a sister in nursing school, another sister at home with their mother, and a

198   *A Family Tragedy*

brother in boarding school, all of them living in Basutoland. Though Labuschagne, attempting to buttress police claims that the protests had been organised by outside instigators (*"aanhiteers"*), testified that 19 of the dead and 46 of the injured were "not registered as residents," in fact, every one of the claims for the over 300 dead and injured provided a Sharpeville stand address as a permanent residence, and as the documentary record shows (see Figure 7.4), official mail reached them at those addresses.[12]

All the adult (18 and above) victims, female and male alike, with less than a handful of exceptions, were employed at the time of the shooting. There were no crowds of unemployed youths, no *tsotsis* as the police (and scholars who have followed their lead) liked to claim. Of the 330 numbered claims, only 12 described the applicant as *werkloos* (unemployed), and of those 12, 6 were women and 1 was a school-aged boy (Elias Masilo, son of the panel beater). The only claimant with a criminal record was a young man who was in prison on 21 March, the day the police shot his wife in the head, leaving

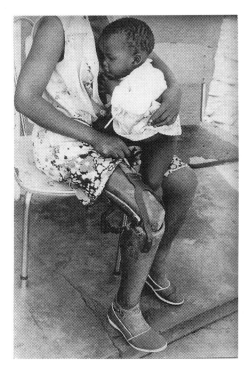

Figure 7.3 "A victim of the Sharpeville Massacre, who was only 11 years old at the time of the tragedy, is reminded daily of her severe injuries."[13]

Photo by Alf Kumalo/african.pictures. © Alf Kumalo Family Trust.

A Family Tragedy 199

Figure 7.4 Official mail received by Maine family at Stand No. 8554 in 1960 and still in their possession at the same address in 2019.
Courtesy of the Maine family. Photo by authors.

their 4-year-old son to be cared for by a maternal uncle until his father was released from prison a year later.

Like that man's wife, most of the women shot by the police worked, primarily at washing, cleaning, ironing, and cooking jobs in White private households in Vanderbijlpark and Vereeniging. People such as Christina Motsepe who had done domestic work in Vanderbijlpark, and Anna Marokoane (36) the woman on her way by bicycle to her employer in Vanderbijlpark who was turned back by PAC supporters. She was shot by the police in her right forearm and left calf and had to stay in hospital for several weeks and then in the Boksburg goal as a suspected *betoger* (protestor), leaving her six young children in the sole care of her husband. Walter Botha's wife Elizabeth (32) did washing and ironing in a Vereeniging household before and after his death. Elizabeth Mono (47) worked in the kitchen of the single men's hostel in Sharpeville before and after her husband Daniel's death (a coal seller, he bled to death internally from a bullet fired into his pelvis).

Some of the other female victims of police violence worked in a variety of better-paying jobs but all struggled to survive. Elizabeth Setlhatlole (43), the widowed 11-year post office veteran, was shot four times (in her left shoulder, left ankle, right knee, and right hand) as she stood in her neighbour's yard far from the police station. While she spent weeks in hospital, her older child Jacob had to support his sister and pay the rent all on half the income that he and his mother had earned when she was working. Anthony Ndaba's wife was not shot herself (her husband got a bullet from behind in his left thigh and was in hospital for over three months), but she did lose her job as a schoolteacher and had to support their three young children alone. Before the shooting, she had commuted 40 km roundtrip each day to Meyerton for her teaching job and had earned twice as much per month as her husband did after four years working in the local Cornelia Colliery. Anna Motsepe (a different Anna than Christina's mother) had worked at a nursery school in Sharpeville for 16 years. When the school closed early on the 21st she had gone looking for her own children after not finding them at home. The police shot her from the back in her right thigh leaving "large, jagged entrance & exit wounds" in her leg. She lost her job after her release from the hospital four months later and, walking with a limp and a great deal of pain, she and her husband (both in their 50s) had to support the four of their nine children who remained at home on his income alone.

Many of the men killed or injured by the police worked at long-term jobs for some of the leading businesses in Vereeniging (collectively the industrial base of the "company town"): 13 at African Cables (including the young man in prison), 12 at Union Steel, 11 at Stewarts and Lloyds, 9 at Brick and Tile, 9 at Safim, and 8 at Babcock and Wilcox; others worked at a variety of smaller factories and retailers in Vereeniging (Raleigh bicycles, for example, and the local branch of Johannesburg's largest wholesaler of confectionary and cigarettes, at furniture stores, and other small retailers); others carried out a variety of independent trades in and around Sharpeville, coal merchants, panel beaters, painters, plumbers, butchers, bicycle repairmen, milk sellers, scrap dealers, hawkers, metal workers and solderers (for all the household pots and pans), teachers at the nine schools in town, ministers of religion at the 18 churches, and, though they did not admit it to the police, three shebeen keepers (unlicensed liquor dealers).

Caiphus Papa Motsepe (43), for example, worked for African Cables at the time of his death. He and his wife Mita had married in the Dutch Reformed Church in Top in 1937 and raised eight children (four boys, four girls, all but one still of school age in 1960) in Top and Sharpeville, the youngest, a girl, not yet born on the day her father died (there were at least seven other married women in Sharpeville pregnant the day that they lost their husbands, not including the three pregnant women killed or injured discussed earlier). Two of Motsepe's sons already knew what they wanted to be when they grew up; one wanted to be a teacher, the other a carpenter. Caiphus was regarded as a "respectable man" by his neighbours, including by a member of the Advisory Board. Tall (1.83 m or 6 ft) and skinny (58.5 kg or 129 lbs), Caiphus was shot from behind in his lower back with the bullet exiting his abdomen near his stomach button, leaving a large hole with lacerated and irregular edges, and causing several loops of his intestines "to protrude through this exit wound." When the autopsy was performed a week after his death, his body was already in a state of "advanced decomposition." He was one of the people that the Reverend Maja saw as he ran towards the firing, dying in the field north and northwest of the police station (he must have been in one of the photographs taken by Ian Berry) with "their intestines ... protruding."

Then there were the two taxi drivers, Simon and Ezekiel Masilo. Simon (36) and his wife Ethel had seven children, all aged 15 and under on the day their father died (two wanted to become teachers, one a minister of religion, the fourth a carpenter, the others were too young to have decided). Simon Masilo was shot in his back, severing the iliac artery providing blood to his lower body and he bled to death. Ezekiel Masilo (44) and his wife Constance had five children, all brought up in Sharpeville, the youngest not born until two months after her father's death. He was shot four times, in his lungs, heart, and liver, all four bullets entering from the side as though he was turning when fired upon. Both Elias Lidia and Reverend Maja saw Ezekiel dead beside the clinic on the no-name street – "he was already gone." There was still another Masilo shot that day (besides Simon and Ezekiel and Elias), Mohauli Solomon Masilo (26) who was related to the taxi Masilos and the panel beater Masilo. He was single and lived with his father. He was the man on sick leave (he worked for African Cables) with a skin condition who went to the clinic on 21 March and found it closed and remained to see what would happen. He was shot through his right thigh and his right big toe; injuries that he did not consider too serious at the time, but as we will see later in the chapter, they became of much greater consequence for him and his family later in life.

All those killed and injured in Sharpeville on 21 March 1960 came from the town itself, from every neighbourhood, and from practically every street. We plotted on a map of the town circa. 1960 the address of every one of the several hundred people who filed claims for redress, homes in which most of them or their survivors still live, and the result can be seen in Figure 7.5. The circles are not exact locations but general indicators of the wide spread of neighbourhoods from which people came and gathered in front of the police station on 21 March. Other scholars have suggested that the people who gathered came from the newest part of town, Vuka, that they were the youngest, the most unemployed, the most disgruntled, the most likely to, in the words of the police, become a "mob."

None of that was true. The people shot on 21 March 1960 came from all over Sharpeville, most were in their 30s and married, almost all were employed, they, like everyone in Sharpeville, including the African policemen and municipal employees, disliked the *dompas*, and, as was shown clearly in Chapter 5, they were most certainly not a mob.

Trauma: Individual, Family, Community

Trauma takes many forms, physical and emotional, individual and collective. It can be short term and long term. It can have permanent effects. Sharpeville residents experienced trauma in all its forms. In this section, we want to focus on the physical and socioeconomic aspects of trauma as experienced by

202 A Family Tragedy

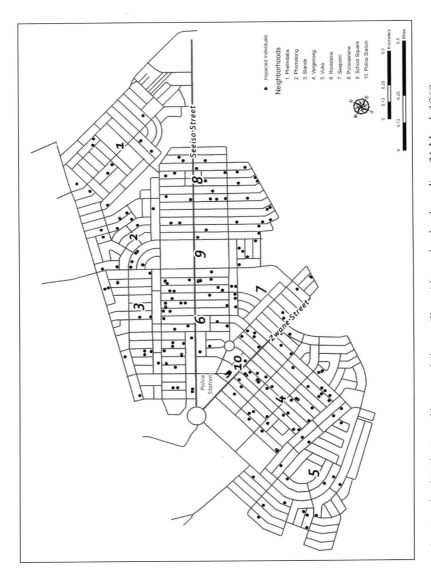

Figure 7.5 Map showing the distribution of homes of Sharpeville residents shot by the police, 21 March 1960. Map drawn by Topanga Betke based on information from Sharpeville claimants files.

individuals, by family households, and by the community at large. There will be a lot of pain discussed here, but it is necessary to do so in order to understand what people in Sharpeville suffered as an immediate consequence of the police shooting and how that suffering persisted. The emotional aspects of that physical trauma, the widespread sense of individual and collective loss, can be understood to some extent from the experiences described earlier and in the following, but we will also return to emotions and feelings in the Coda when we talk about the people of Sharpeville we have met and how they remember and still experience 21 March 1960. For now, let's focus on the impact, in the days and weeks and months after the police shooting, on what happened to people in Sharpeville in their daily lives.

Nearly all of the victims (like most of those described earlier), killed and injured alike, were shot in the back. Marium Lepee was very accurate in her recollection that as soon as the police aimed their guns at the crowd, most people turned and ran even before the shooting started. We know about the injuries in the back because autopsies were carried out on 70 of those killed, and because of detailed medical reports on many of the injured. The district surgeon of Johannesburg, watched by a medical representative of the Bishop of Johannesburg, performed autopsies on 52 of the dead, including Maria Molebatsi, David Makhoba, and James Buti Bessie: "One of the bodies was a Native female of an approximate age, or apparent age of thirteen years ... a Native youth of fourteen ... a child of twelve years." The district surgeon of Vanderbijlpark did 15 autopsies on people killed in Sharpeville (and on the two men killed by the police in his municipality), and the district surgeon of Vereeniging performed one autopsy on a Sharpeville victim. These state employees all concluded that where the direction of the bullets could be determined (a majority of the cases) most penetrated from the back, in 77 percent of the 52 autopsies carried out in Johannesburg, and 87 percent of the 16 autopsies carried out in Vereeniging (not counting the two killed in Vanderbijlpark). The medical superintendents of the Vereeniging and Baragwanath hospitals reported similar proportions of rear entry bullet wounds for the injured, 65 percent for the 38 patients in Vereeniging and 77 percent for the 128 patients in Baragwanath for whom medical records were available. Among those killed were a large number who had been shot in the head and who died of brain lacerations and internal bleeding of the skull (Gilbert Poho Dimo below; Mirriam Lekitla and John Motsoahae Mailane Chapter 5; David Makhoba and Elias Masilo above; Samuel Makhume, Ezekiel Mareletse, and Norah Nobhekisizwe Mbhele pp. 174, 213; Jan Mnguni and Joseph Mochologi Chapter 5; John Kolane Mofokeng, Paulinah Mofulatsi, Richard Molefe, Elias Molotsi, Kopano Motsega, Petros Nthoesoane, and Jacob Ramokoena – the spelling is taken from the gravestones, not from the police records).

Gilbert Poho Dimo was a small man, 1.7 m tall (5' 7") and weighing only 50.8 kilos (112 lbs). He had been born in Leribe in 1901 as Gilbert Poho but changed his last name to Dimo when he left Basutoland as a teenager to avoid his age group circumcision ritual and found long-term employment in Vereeniging with Stewarts and Lloyds. He was shot by the police in the back of his head. The entry wound was small and circular, 0.6 cm in diameter (0.25 in); the exit wound was a gaping lacerated hole, 5.7 cm (2.25 in) by 2.5 cm (1.25 in), tearing out his right eye, much of his nose, and stopping just short of his left eye. His skull was fractured in multiple places, his brain lacerated, and there was evidence of extensive bleeding (See Document 3). His wife Selina, who had given birth to all six of their children in either Top or Sharpeville and who were all living with their parents in the family home on 21 March, identified her husband's body the next day, stored in a garage at the Vereeniging police station.

Some of the victims had been shot while turning to escape with the bullets entering sideways (through their arms, shoulders, sides of chest and hips and legs), some had been shot while they were lying on the ground crawling away from the line of police (bullets entering through their feet and perineums and exiting horizontally further up out of their hips, backs or heads). More bullets entered above the waist than below, refuting the common police claim then and since that they aimed in the air or at the ground to avoid hitting people. Many of the bullets from the Stens entered bodies in a tumbling fashion causing large, lacerated entrance wounds, often splitting inside, creating massive injuries such as those of Christina Motsepe and Lydia Chalale, and also left "gross" exit wounds, large gaping holes which led to a widespread suspicion then and since that the police had used dum dums – steel-sleeved bullets with a soft lead nose that would explode upon entering the body. The issue of whether or not dum dums were used was not resolved at the time – alternative explanations of how the Sten gun bullets could spiral and tear seemed to convince most participants in the Wessels Commission that those characteristics alone could cause the terrible injuries – though the fact that many of the police, as Constable Saaiman had admitted (see Chapter 6), bought their own supplies on the private market leaves open the issue of what ammunition beyond police regulation bullets might have been used on 21 March.[14]

All these people experienced severe physical pain on 21 March whether it be the sudden sharp burning felt by Elizabeth Setlhatlole or the much longer periods endured by other victims that day, some throughout their lives. We can only imagine the pain felt by those who died, especially the ones who suffered while they bled to death, people like Naphtali Maine age 27 whose widowed mother Mirriam had watched him from their house on Zwane ("from my home I have a clear view of the police station") walking along the east side of the police station a little before 2 pm on his way to buy some cigarettes at the shops. "When I last saw him he was on his own." His body was found lying near the café. He died from a bullet wound in his pelvis. His niece, Matlakala Mauleen Maine, born after her uncle's death, remembers hearing "from my elders [that] on that day [21 March] my mother [Sheilah Mogotsi] had picked my uncle up from the street where she found him." (See Document 2.)

John Phutheho (43) was shot by the police as he was walking along Zwane Street. A neighbour had asked him to take their sick child to the doctor and because he had worked the night shift at Stewarts and Lloyds on Sunday, he had the time to do so after he woke up around noon on Monday. Like Gilbert Dimo, he bled to death, though from a bullet wound to his left lung and abdomen. When his wife Anna saw him a few minutes after the shooting being loaded into a van by the police as though he was already dead, she wondered whether he was in fact still alive.

The pain of the survivors was documented at the time. Ben Phoofolo Lechesa, for example, a 42-year-old father of five (all born in Sharpeville) who worked as a first aid assistant for Raleigh Industries in Vereeniging, was shot by the police when he was near his house, about 250 m from the police station. The bullet entered the left side of his back, fractured his spine, one of his vertebrae, and one of his ribs, and remained in his body just near his right pectoral muscle. He was according to his doctor "in excruciating pain for approximately three weeks after the shooting" because of pressure on his spinal cord. "He had no movement in his left leg and very limited movement in his right leg ... with extreme sensitivity of the left leg and severe pain down both legs." During an operation to relieve the pressure on his spinal cord, his heart stopped beating. His chest cavity was cut open so his heart could be massaged, and he was brought back to life, but no further work was done on his spine for another six weeks during which he suffered continual pain. Further surgery was completed to alleviate pressure on his spinal cord, but 18 months later, he was still in need of a spine graft to relieve his chronic pain. He could only walk with crutches and a full-length caliper on his left leg. The bullet remained in his body. His doctor concluded that his "incapacity" was 75 percent and was permanent – "I do not think Ben would be able to get a job" (Figure 7.6).

Francina Chenene was only 18 and still enrolled in school (Standard V) when she was shot in the back by the police. She had walked to the police station with some school friends "to see what was happening." The shot left her with a large lacerated wound on her left hip and a fractured femur. "Multiple metallic particles" were present in her wound and "spread throughout the muscle tissue and bone." Much of the dead muscle was surgically removed, but the area became septic causing a "huge wound over the left thigh." A year after the shooting, Francina was still in the Vereeniging Hospital. There was "no healing" between the bone ends in her femur, and she continued to suffer "considerable pain." The prognosis was not good:

[A]t some future stage a bone graft may have to be performed. ... It will be extremely lucky if these [her femur bone ends] are healed within a year ... a non-weight bearing caliper may have to be worn for the rest of her life.

Numerous other people (some discussed earlier like Anna Motsepe and in the following like Justice Maeko) had limbs amputated or suffered some form of

206 *A Family Tragedy*

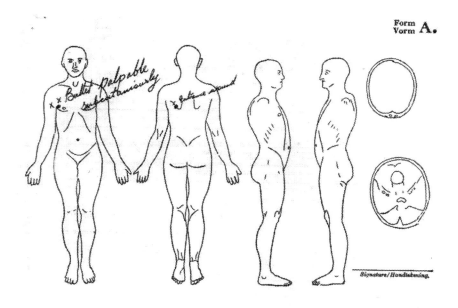

Figure 7.6 Ben Lechesa official police diagram of injuries.
Source: National Archives and Records Service of South Africa, SAP 611, SAB. Photo by authors.

permanent paralysis and disability. Joseph Tsoelipe (46) who had worked for Stewarts and Lloyds for 16 years had his right arm amputated above the elbow and could no longer find a job to support his wife and four young children at home (his oldest daughter had married). John Khota, probably the oldest victim that day – he was 73 – was a self-employed painter. His right arm was amputated, leaving him unable to work yet still responsible for his wife and his eight-year-old grandson. Elizabeth Moise (45) was shot in her right ankle on 21 March, and her leg below the knee was amputated the same day at Baragwanath. More than two years later, she still had not been fitted with a prosthesis and could only walk with crutches with difficulty. She could not do the washing and ironing that had enabled her to help support her husband and their two school-age children. Isaac Mokae (38), a road worker for the Vereeniging municipality, had the upper third of his left leg "completely shattered" by police bullets. He was injured so severely that no entrance or exit wounds could be identified. His leg was amputated, and he could not find work to support his wife, a kitchen worker who earned only R5 a month (a typical wage for female household employees), and their young son, still in school. A story published in the *RDM* a year after the shooting described an amputee, one whose personal details did not accord with any of those among the official claimants, suggesting another of the "hidden" victims of police violence. This was a man fitted with an artificial leg because of a Sharpeville injury living alone in Soweto and looking for any work he could find that would enable him to provide housing for his wife and four young children: "He has a Standard VI certificate and would prefer a job which does not entail walking or standing around for long hours."[15]

Marium Lepee, the 16-year-old schoolgirl who went to the police station at 9 am on the 21st with her school friends and her cousin Martha Masello Lepee because she had heard that "Dr. Verwoerd is coming to address us," lost her right leg that day. The amputation was carried out so quickly and poorly at Baragwanath that she was left with a considerable amount of soft tissue on her knee which prevented her from being fitted with a "below-knee type of limb" (like that of Evodia Phakeli). A medical examiner later recommended "that she be given a kneeling prosthesis ... an artificial limb in which she kneels at the knee and then has to have a pendulum action knee-joint which is controlled by a friction band," a device that he considered would allow her to return to "the open labour market" and either do "washing and ironing and kitchen work or ... do sewing and other needlework such as knitting." Two years after the police shooting and a year after the medical exam, Marium Lepee still walked with crutches: "I cannot afford a prothesis and cannot work with only one leg." Because her uncle Steven Lepee was convicted of "public violence" and sent to prison on Robben Island, Marium along with her grandmother, sister-in-law, and three cousins were all evicted from their home; she moved in first with her cousin Martha and then with other extended family members in Sebokeng. She never got a prosthesis; she could never work and support herself; eventually, she died as a result of her injury.

Many of those without amputations were so severely injured that they could never work again. Joseph Moiloa (25) spent four months in hospital because of a bullet in his right thigh fracturing his femur. A year later, he limped and could not stand on his right leg, which had shortened by almost two inches. He couldn't find a job and with his wife had to move back in with his parents. Meschack Pitso (19), along with his older brother the sole support of their widowed mother and their school-age brother, like Joseph Moloia, suffered a fractured right femur from a bullet to his back and was left, after nine months in hospital, with a two and a half inch shortened right leg. He walked with a limp and then only for short distances, and in the opinion of his doctor "cannot do physical labour." Joshua Motha (44), the bus driver we met in Chapters 5 and 6, was shot from behind in his right thigh. He spent five and a half months in Baragwanath, and when he was discharged, his right leg had shortened by an inch, and he could not drive. His medical report two years later stated, "Not fit for physical labour." He was the sole provider for his wife and their seven children. Adelina Pelaelo (26), married with three young children at home, could no longer help support her household because a bullet that entered her right elbow as she was running from the shooting left her with continual pain in her hand, arm, and shoulder. "I used to do washing, but can no longer do it since my arm hurts." Gladys Majola, 16 years old and only married for a month when the police shot her from behind in her left leg, fracturing her tibia and fibula, spent 11 months in Baragwanath and two years later still could not work "since I walk with crutches and my leg gives me a lot of trouble."

Multiply the cases described in the two preceding paragraphs by *thirtyfold* to arrive at a total of over 300 victims (killed and injured) and you get a sense of the scale of physical suffering inflicted on the residents of Sharpeville and the immediate economic impact on families and households throughout the town. Take the additional step of adding up the number of people who lived in the households from which the over 300 victims came and you get between 2,500 and 3,000 individuals, people who were intimately affected in every aspect of their daily lives by the police shooting.

Surveillance

Increased surveillance by the police; strict enforcement of township regulations; dire shortages of food, fuel to cook with, and housing; and persecution by the municipal authorities made life extremely difficult for all the residents of Sharpeville. The Saracens and their crews remained in town for a few days, along with at least 400 policemen. Thereafter, the regular police presence (SAP and municipal) was increased and everyone's movements and actions watched and controlled. Captain Cawood (who had shot dead the two young men in Vanderbijlpark) took charge of the Sharpeville police station and together with Sergeant Wessels (the SB man on duty all day on 21 March) oversaw all surveillance activities.

Mataeke Elizabeth Mokoena, 10 years old in 1960, remembers the pass law being enforced so rigorously that even a person going from their own house to a neighbour's on the same block would be asked to show their pass, and if they did not have it on their person, they would be arrested and charged for the offence. Maggie Malema, 21 years old in 1960, remembers the two years after the shooting as a period when "we were so harassed," "if they knew you were talking too much they came and arrested you." "I was not allowed to visit freely even around the township ... if I did not have the pass I would be taken to prison." "If you had a light on at night the police would shoot ... so we avoided sitting next to a window." For the residents of Sharpeville, a graphic visual reminder of the police violence remained: the "large brown blood stains" that still covered much of the no-name street months after the shooting. No amount of rain could wash those stains away.[16]

Pulane Nkhi learned the story of the killing of her grandfather Isaac Nkhi on 21 March because of constant police harassment throughout the 1960s and 1970s.

> I grew up being told the story of what happened [her grandfather had been stopped by PAC organisers while riding his bike on his way to work at Safim in Peacehaven and had been taken to join the protest at the police station where he bled to death from a police bullet that

penetrated his left lung and cut his spinal cord]. I got told the story because whites during the night would come banging and come into our homes always looking for ... what? I asked, why are we being treated like this? What have we done?

The answer was simple. Some of her male relatives were named after her grandfather,

> so time and time again the name of the grandfather would reappear in the lists of the administration offices, boys named after the grandfather. The police did not believe the grandfather was dead and thought he was still alive and a member of the PAC. So we continued being tortured. We grew up suffering.

Walter Phutheho, 2 years old when his father was shot dead by the police, told us that throughout the apartheid years, "[I]f you talked about what had happened it would put you into trouble; it would be an invitation to the police coming into your house."

The Vereeniging municipality strictly enforced the apartheid rule that in urban areas houses could only be occupied by men officially registered to work. When 20-year-old Martha Nyembezi's husband Manasi was shot dead leaving her pregnant and with two young daughters (both under 5) to care for, the municipal authorities ordered her to leave the family home. When she refused, she was arrested at the police station and sent to prison, and when she was released she found that her family had been evicted from the house and another family with a male breadwinner had been permitted to move in. Martha and her children had to move from place to place; she lost almost half her body weight in the process going from 46 kg to 26 kg (101 lbs to 57 lbs), and all of them ended up in a squatter camp in Sharpeville. As Martha Nyembezi's granddaughter Sibongile Rejoice Mgangane told us, her grandmother "suffered having no place to stay" and eventually began drinking alcohol, even though she had always abstained before. In 2019, with the remaining family still living in a squatter camp inside Sharpeville, Sibongile Mgangane told us, "We are still crying for help."

Eucalphonia Mahanjane, her brother Isaac, and their sister Dikelede Selina Monnakgotla, along with their mother Ethel, lost their family home in Vuka when Daniel Monnakgotla (36) was killed by the police (a bullet entering the back of his left thigh severing his femoral artery causing him to bleed to death). Eucalphonia was 7 years old when her father passed, Isaac 2 years old, and Dikelede still in their mother's womb. They remember the years spent with their widowed mother Ethel, "staying all over the place, hiring places from one to the other." "We struggled a lot until our mother died [in February 1990] ... we are still struggling today." Both sisters began crying as they told their stories.

Some people were able to evade the male wage earner regulation by, for example, putting the house in a son's name where the father and head of household had been killed. Gilbert Dimo's family put the house in the name of his second eldest son Nathan – the oldest was married and with a home of his own. Nathan had been studying law in Pretoria but had to return home and find work as a labourer to support his mother and five brothers and sisters. Sometimes people used the name of another male relative who did not live with them. When Salamina Thinane's daughter Martha Kaseane Thinane (24) was killed (she bled to death from three bullet wounds) leaving Salamina responsible for her own teenage son as well as Martha's two young children (her husband and her father had both already passed away), one of Salamina's younger brothers allowed her to put the house in his name so she could keep it in the family, and one of her granddaughters still lives in the house today. And there were always exceptions by which people evaded official rules. After Naphtali Maine's death, there was no other son old enough to have the house put in his name, but still, his widowed mother Mirriam and his three sisters and young brother survived on the assistance provided by close relatives and 18 months of supplies from the relief fund. Eventually, Mirriam had to sell liquor illegally to pay for the education of her children but somehow she managed to keep her house. Today, her niece Matlakala Mauleen Maine still lives in the family home, though she is the last of her grandmother's, her parents', and her own generation: "I am the only surviving one." For most families, however, who lost a male "head of household" whether by being killed or imprisoned or deemed a leader of the PAC by the police, physical displacement was a new fact of life.

Perhaps the cruellest treatment was that meted out by municipal officials like Ferreira and Labuschagne to any Sharpeville resident who they could link to Basutoland, even if those people and their families had lived all or nearly all their lives in the local community. Enuwell Monkonyane Mohlotsane, a 35-year-old auto mechanic for Raleigh Industries, was shot and killed on 21 March, bleeding to death from a bullet through the arteries in his lower rib cage. His 30-year-old widow Annakleta and her four young children were ordered by Ferreira to vacate the house registered in Enuwell's name and to go to Basutoland, even though all the children had been born in Sharpeville. Annakleta responded that "she was unwilling and has no money." Ferreira issued the same expulsion order to another widow and her four children – she too replied "that she has no money and is not willing to do so." In the case of two men whose limbs were amputated – Joseph Tsoelipe (his right arm) and Justice Maeko (his right leg below the knee) – Ferreira and Labuschagne refused to issue them with "section 12" passes, the documents that permitted them legal residence in Sharpeville. Even though their employer, Stewarts and Lloyds, was willing to rehire both men, the lack of the section 12 document meant they could not be employed nor be fitted with artificial limbs.

Though these families all fought to remain in Sharpeville, it was not without constant harassment. Maeko was imprisoned for not having his section 12 and risked being rearrested for the same offence upon his release from the first period of imprisonment. Neither Tsoelipe nor Maeko was able to find work because of their permanent disabilities; Tsoelipe had a pregnant wife and four young children, Maeko also had a wife and four young children, all of whom had to be supported. Both Tsoelipe and Maeko had to send their wives with their children to Basutoland to be educated while they tried to find work in Vereeniging.[17]

Nearly all the people who were treated at the Vereeniging Hospital and at Baragwanath, almost 200 of them, were arrested immediately upon their discharge from the hospital. They were investigated, statements taken from them, and their homes searched; they were imprisoned with the bandages and clothes they were wearing and no changes were provided. One young man, Daniel Sithole, shot in his right knee, had to make a formal request through his attorney for a pair of trousers to be brought to him from his home two months after his arrest so that he could have a change of clothes from his bloodied pants. Though the charges against 112 of them were dropped weeks and months later, an additional 85 Sharpeville residents were brought to trial. Most of these defendants eventually had their cases dismissed, but 23 (including Anna Lethege, the only female put on trial and derided by police as a "shebeen queen," and Peter Molefi, the man in the red shirt), were kept in custody for six months, then required to be in court daily for another 12 months until verdicts (not guilty for 19 of the 23) were rendered in June 1961 well over a year since their arrests in March 1960.

Those brought to trial were finally allowed to post bail in September 1960 if they could afford to do so. Some of the accused had post office savings accounts and bailed themselves out, like Matthew Mashiya, one of the three Mashiya brothers (his older brother Isaac had been killed; his younger brother Petros had been shot in the right knee; Matthew himself had been shot from behind in his right thigh and spent three months in Baragwanath before his arrest). Peter Molefi made enough at his job as a wine steward at the Riviera Hotel to have savings to pay his bail, but he needed to get out of prison and to find any time he could between court appearances to return to work because he was the sole financial support for his grandparents, his mother (his father had passed away in 1957), his sister and her 3-year-old daughter, and his brother who was a student in Thaba Nchu. Isiah Seroto, shot in the back of his right thigh and normally the only support for his widowed grandmother – "My grandmother brought me up from a young age and I am her only provider" – relied on her support at this point in his life and asked if she could "arrange for his bail."

More onerous conditions were set for PAC leaders with bail set at the equivalent of several months' wages (the PAC members at first refused to accept any bail conditions according to their slogan of "NO BAIL: NO DEFENCE: NO FINE" – see Chapter 4 – but later changed their approach).

Meeting these bail requirements meant considerable hardship for them and their families. Mokgathi David Ramagole, for example, the treasurer of the Sharpeville branch of the PAC, got his bail payment from his father, but before the police shooting, he had been the sole wage earner in a household which had consisted of himself, his elderly father and mother (to whom he normally gave his entire weekly wages), the children of his unmarried sister, and a young boy, his nephew, who had been orphaned. Who was going to support them while he was on trial? Johannes Monyake, the first PAC man arrested at the Gate on 21 March, got his bail from a friend, and though not married he was the sole financial support of his elderly parents and his sisters. Thomas More, the vice chairman of the PAC, also got his bail from the same person as Monyake. He was married and responsible for the support of his wife, his mother, and his six sisters but had "[n]othing at all" saved. Khoali Emmanuel Teketsi, the PAC man known as Qwadi by Elias Lidia, got his bail from the Defence and Aid fund (established in Johannesburg in May 1960 to provide legal aid for detainees) but still had to support his wife and three young children, and what little money he "had saved ... I have not got it now." Steven Lepee, the PAC man who had burnt his pass at the Sharpeville bus station on 18 March, was the sole support of his wife and three young children as well as his 16-year-old sister Marium and his grandmother. He had saved up some money during his regular employment, but "[i]t is finished; I do not have any now." All of the PAC organisers charged by the police – Tsolo, More, Ramagole, Monyake, Ntoampe, Teketsi, Lepee, and their families, numbering over 30 people in all – were evicted from their homes.[18]

The familial and financial burdens for all of these people were immense. How could you house and feed yourself and your family when household incomes had in so many cases dropped precipitously or ceased entirely? How could you pay your rent? How could you survive? Some immediate assistance came in the form of a truckload of supplies (two and a half tons) delivered by representatives of the United Party on the first Friday following the shooting to 103 families, and a VW minibus full of goods arranged by the Pretoria branch of the Liberal Party in the person of Adelaine Hain driving the family vehicle. Longer-term help came from a public fund initiated by the mayor of Vereeniging but without any municipal funding. The first donations to the Sharpeville Relief Fund came from overseas, from the British Labour Party (including the British Fire Brigades Union), the Quakers in Britain, and the Ghanaian Convention People's Party. Within a few weeks, more contributions came in from local businesses like Vereeniging Estates and Stewarts and Lloyds and others, and regional organisations that wanted to help like the "Indian Commercial Community" and the Transvaal African Teachers Association, and sympathetic churches and individuals. More international funds were promised by the governments of Ghana, Jamaica, and Ethiopia, and special South Africa funds were established by Christian Action in Britain, by Dutch opponents of apartheid, and by the American Committee on Africa. At the local level, religious leaders (the reverends Mahabane and Maja especially are mentioned in the statements made by Sharpeville residents at the time) arranged the distribution of supplies.[19]

Still, the total amount raised nationally and internationally by the Sharpeville Relief Fund was less than £20,000, none of the funds coming from the local or national government. The funds were barely enough to provide 156 households with 680 occupants (out of the over 300 claimant households and at least 2,500 people directly affected by the police shooting) with the "absolute necessaries" of life, food, fuel, clothing, and blankets, and for only so long as the recipients remained unable to return to work.

Who got assistance seemed a matter of chance and caprice. Jacob Mbhele, whose wife Norah Nobhekisizwe Mbhele was killed by a bullet to the back of her head, received the "weekly ration of groceries, 2 lbs of meat, and two buckets of coal" to help support him and their two young daughters (the youngest still being carried on her mother's back before Norah's death). Josiah Sefatsa, whose oldest son Samuel (28) was shot dead on 21 March and had provided half the family income for his parents and his seven siblings, got no help. Lydia Mailane (pregnant at the time of the police shooting), whose husband John was shot dead while delivering invoices for his employer, got groceries, 2 lbs of meat, and two buckets of coal every week to support herself and her four school-age children, and she thought her rent may have been paid as well – "I presume it is being paid." Groceries and rent payments were provided for Daniel Dikubo, the young man in search of his stolen bike, for the 19 months he was out of work to support him and his wife and their 4-year-old daughter. Some groceries but no rent assistance were provided for Jan Lehlokoane, whose stepson William Sedisa (19) was killed, leaving his parents with a greatly reduced household income (Jan had TB and could not work; his wife, William's mother, was unemployed; they also had their teenage daughter to support). They had to survive with some support from William's stepbrother and by gathering and selling scraps of wood. Nothing for Ephraim Thaba, the first victim of police violence at the Gate, who spent two months in hospital and whose wife and their five young children in Pietersburg had no source of income for all the time that he was hospitalised. Nothing for Anna Motsepe, the 16-year nursery school teacher who could no longer work because she walked with a painful limp. Nothing for Magdalena Khosi who lost two toes and could not walk without the aid of a crutch and was unable to contribute to the support of her husband and their 11-year-old daughter as she had before the shooting through her hotel job – "I cannot work at all. We do not receive groceries through the Sharpeville Relief Fund." Nothing for Maria Makhoba and her husband and their six children, who had lost 14-year-old David Makhoba on 21 March.

Public health options also decreased, especially for the numerous TB sufferers like Jan Lehlokoane and Makorotsoane Alinah Mokone. Mokone was a 45-year-old widow with five children living with her at home, who when looking for her children on 21 March (Chapter 6) was shot three times in her

214   A Family Tragedy

right arm, left leg, and right thigh. She was infected with TB in the Modderbee prison where she was detained after her discharge from Baragwanath. TB was highly prevalent in Sharpeville as it was throughout South Africa – "the main problem of every health department in this country" – and the town had its own TB hospital "run at a daily cost of one rand a patient." In January 1961, however, the apartheid-era "Department of Bantu Administration and Development" decreed that no further expansion could be made of TB hospitals in urban areas since, as the government phrased matters, "it is no longer necessary to extend tuberculosis hospitals in urban areas, because adequate provision of the treatment of this disease will be made in the African reserves." In Sharpeville, there was "nearly a new case every day, I (the Medical Officer of Health) have no doubt that there is more than one new case a day, because all new cases are not notified." For Jan Lehlokoane and Alinah Mokone, and, subsequently, for one of Alinah's daughters who caught TB from her mother and many other fellow sufferers, medical apartheid meant ever more hardship.[20]

Throughout this parsimonious fiscal environment, neither the Vereeniging municipality nor the national government provided any public assistance. Not a single penny of the nearly £250,000 sitting unused in the fund established for location services under the terms of the Native Services Levy Act (see Chapter 4) went to public assistance after the shooting. Though the mayor of Vereeniging had initially proposed the establishment of the relief fund, all the council members voted to prohibit any municipal funds from being spent to support the inhabitants of Sharpeville, even if those funds were primarily extracted from the residents themselves through stand rentals, brewery income, and fines for pass law offences. These same council members who in March 1960 refused to provide the £250 contribution (enough to pay for a week of food and fuel for 156 Sharpeville households) proposed by their mayor for Sharpeville Relief, didn't blink an eye in May when they voted to spend in excess of that sum to cater a single private lunch for themselves and the visiting New Zealand rugby team.[21]

Community

For most people, it was the Sharpeville community itself which enabled people to survive, even if the cost for many was a lifetime of poverty and the closing off of educational opportunities for a generation or more. Everyone who lived in Sharpeville depended on someone and at the core were the family and extended family relationships on which the community was built. Within Sharpeville, extended households – grandparents, married siblings, cousins, all manner of family connections – reached out to help their relatives survive. Anna Motsepe and Selina her granddaughter (Christina's orphaned 1-year-old child), found a home with Anna's married son (Christina's brother). Anna obtained work doing washing and provided "for myself" (she only earned R6 per week) and looked after Selina as well, but all in the household depended ultimately on her son who worked for a dentist in Vereeniging. (See Document 4.) Ben Lechesa's mother, who had long had her own home in Sharpeville, helped her permanently disabled son and his wife and their five children out as much as she could. Caiphus Papa Motsepe's widow Mita and their eight children (including the youngest with whom Mita was pregnant at the time of her husband's death) were helped by an uncle and his family in Sharpeville (a niece of Caiphus, Rosta Maratjwaneng Ramokgadi, who had been 20 in 1960, spoke to us in 2019 of her extended families' travails). Mita also found a job washing for which she earned R2 a month, and her eldest son ended his schooling early so that he could find a job to help his mother and siblings. But then he died young, and two of his brothers in their early and mid-teens (12 and 15) had to leave school and find work.

For residents of Sharpeville with extended family in Basutoland, these connections provided an avenue of support. As noted earlier, the two amputees, Joseph Tsoelipe and Justice Maeko, sent their wives and children (a total of ten people) to be looked after by relatives there. James Nkokotsane (37), who worked for Vereeniging Motors, spent seven months in hospital recovering from a bullet shot into the back of his right leg. Two months after the shooting, in May 1960, his wife died, leaving their three young children at home alone. He sent them to be looked after by his mother in Basutoland, and two years later, they were still in her care since after his release from hospital, his leg had wasted away and he could only walk with crutches. Medically he was diagnosed as "unable to do any physical labour permanently." Historina Motsega (40), whose husband Kopana (52) an employee of Babcock and Wilcox was killed by the police (a bullet to his head), sent their two children to live with her mother in Basutoland. Motseke Modise (38), who had worked for Delport Glass, was left with a crippled leg by bullets shot into the front of his left thigh and ankle. While he and his wife remained in Sharpeville, he sent their three children to live with his father in Basutoland. Anna Lethege, the woman going out for fish and chips on the 21st who the police shot and arrested and imprisoned and put on trial for 18 months, sent her two children to school in Basutoland.[22]

Most often, people in the household had to take care of themselves, which often meant children became responsible for their own upbringing and survival. Walter Botha's widow Elizabeth and her five children (ages from less than 1-year-old to 13 in March 1960) survived on her earnings from washing and ironing (R4 per month) and on groceries and rent from the Sharpeville Relief Fund, but when Elizabeth suffered a stroke, her children had to support themselves. One of Walter and Elizabeth's grandchildren, Buiswa Botha, remembers as a child that her older brother had to raise her and his other siblings, and Buiswa herself had to leave school at an early age (around 10 years old) and do "piece jobs" at home. While Emmanuel Fantisi (33) was in hospital for three months and then out of work for a year recovering – shot by the police from behind in his right buttock and hand – his mother who had her own house in Vuka helped him, his wife, and their four young children to survive until he got his old job back at Safim where he had worked for seven years. William Monedalibe Lesito (46) and his son Solomon (20), who had both been employed (William for 15 years at Broderick Engineering Works and Solomon in a job at Broderick Motors for nearly a year) at the time they were shot (William a bullet in his stomach causing a large laceration and much internal bleeding and Solomon a bullet from behind in his left thigh leaving a six inch (15.25 cm) long lacerated wound), were the only "breadwinners" for the Lesito family, which also included William's wife and Solomon's six young sisters. William spent four months in hospital, Solomon six weeks and then a period after when he was arrested and charged with incitement and public violence, and throughout all that time, William's wife (Solomon's mother) had to take care of the six young girls at home with what she made from washing and ironing. One of those girls, then 7-year-old Mahlodi Caroline Lesito, remembers still that when her father came home from the hospital, he was in much pain, especially at night when all the sisters had to help him and their mother and each other physically and emotionally, and she remembers too that her father's pain would come and go throughout the rest of his life until he died in 1997. "Father, after he was shot my life was never normal." Machabedi Mirriam Lipale, just 4 years old when her mother Martha Thinane was killed by the police on 21 March, remembers vividly to this day how difficult it was for her and her brother after the death of their mother, emotionally and financially, but also that their grandmother made sure "that they did not sleep on an empty stomach." Ephraim Masilo told us that he had to "act like a doctor" for his injured father Solomon. Solomon was single when he got bullet wounds in his right thigh and right big toe in 1960. He later married, and Ephraim was born in 1974. By then, Solomon's wounds had still failed to heal, and he was in increasing distress: he could not work; he could not walk without difficulty. Ephraim's mother had to work in a fish and chip shop to keep the family going, while Ephraim had to spend all his time with his father, "just helping." Medical treatment was too expensive, and Solomon sought help from traditional healers. But nothing worked. Though Solomon wanted Ephraim to go to technical school, he could never afford to pay for his son's education. Solomon passed away in 1999 still suffering from his injuries. Ephraim got his first job as a gardener for the superintendent at ArcelorMittal (Iscor's successor), though later was able to pay for his own technical training and get a better job at the same firm. But today, he wants his four children to go to university and cannot pay for them to do so. "Will the government help us?"

It must have been a devastatingly lonely time for Christina Mahlong, a 62-year-old widow who lost her only child, Shadrack (19), killed by a police bullet to his right leg. Each morning before work, it was Christina's habit to "ask him whether he had everything with him," and on the morning of the 21st, after she had done so as usual, he "left home ... on his bicycle ... and said he was going to work [at Babcock and Wilcox] and I never saw him again." Lonely too for Richard Mtimkulu (33), the man who had been woken up on Sunday night by "Dlamini" aka Johannes Monyake. He lost his wife Elizabeth (25) on 21 March, shot by the police through her left lung and her spleen, and though they did not have any children of their own, he was left alone with the young boy they had adopted. Perhaps it was the emotional pain of loss that caused Elliot Kaba's mother to die soon after her son's passing and was responsible for Salamina Sepampuru, the widow of the "decent" man Philemon Sepampuru who the Reverend Maja saw shot and killed, becoming paralysed down the entire left side of her body a few months after her husband's killing by the police. But at least for Salamina, her six children (aged from 11 years to 28) still lived "with me and look after me."

It was immensely sad too for the children who lost a parent. Solobatsi Ishmael Poho, Gilbert Dimo's 6-year-old youngest son, had slept every night of his life in the bed beside his father while his 2-year-old sister slept on the other side of the bed beside their mother. His older brothers and sisters slept elsewhere in their four-roomed NE 51/9 family home. Solobatsi spent a lot of time with his father – "I was used to being around him wherever he was going." The day his father died, "that is when life began changing at home." His mother Selina, who had not previously had to work, found employment doing washing and ironing in Vereeniging, hard labour for which she earned only R3 per month. His brothers and sisters all had to leave school early and find unskilled employment, as did Solobatsi, who left school in his mid-teens to support the education of his younger sister and spent most of his life as a labourer until his final job as a welder at Broderick Engineering: "The painful thing was when we imagined what would have happened if our father had still been around."

Walter Phutheho always wondered as he was growing up what had happened to his father. Others too of his generation wondered what had happened to their missing fathers. "Parents would normally tell us that our fathers worked at the mines only for us to discover that they had in fact passed on." It wasn't until the end of the 1970s when he was 21 that his mother, sister, and an uncle told him what had happened to his father. They told him that the police had shot his father once, then a second time (John Phutheho had bullet injuries in his stomach and his left lung), and then they had "pierced him through" with their bayonets as he lay on the ground. Throughout his life (he died during the pandemic), Walter never attended the 21 March commemorations because the occasion was too painful. He told us in 2019, almost 60 years after the police shooting, that "the wound is still as fresh" for him as the day it was inflicted on his father.

For all the children of the people killed and injured on 21 March 1960, the loss of educational opportunities for themselves and for their children is what they felt most keenly. There was no money in Walter Phutheho's family for education – "that was our life struggling along with our mother." Elliot Kabi's sister and brothers could not continue their studies. Simon Masilo's children who had wanted to be ministers of religion and teachers instead had to seek labouring jobs as soon as they could find an employer willing to hire them. Caiphus Motsepe's son could not train to become a teacher. Though Machabedi Mirriam Lipale did not sleep on an empty stomach, her grandmother could not afford to pay her school fees, and she had to leave school much earlier than she had hoped. Emmanuel Fantisi's second youngest daughter Amelia, 5 years old when her father was injured, recounted to us how there was no money in the family to pay for her education, and she had to leave school at an early age and work for 31 years as a cleaner in the Vereeniging Magistrates Court, the same place where so many of the Sharpeville victims would be put on trial in 1960 and 1961. Matshepo Maria Morobi and her brother and sister had to drop out of school because their mother Alice did not earn enough as a domestic worker to pay their fees. John Nteso told us that after his father, John Shabe Nteso (54) an independent businessman who sold coal and wood, was shot in his foot and crippled by the police, his older brother had to drop out of university to return home and help the family and that he (John was 11 when his father was shot) and his other four school-age siblings never got a full education. James Buti Bessie's younger sister Mphonyana Annatjie Matsabu, 5 when her 12-year-old brother was killed by the police,

> thought if our brother had been around traditionally a brother in the house would be the one helping the family, we thought had he been around our lives would have been much different, he would have helped so that we would have got an education.

But it was not to be; she and her sisters had to drop out of school. Lydia Moahloli, 10 years old when the police shot her father Elias Mtimkulu four times in his right leg as he was riding around Sharpeville collecting debts owed by customers of his "waste" business, remembers that her father never found regular work again because of his injuries and she and her seven siblings stopped attending school (all except the youngest daughter were school age). Their parents died a few years later, and her older brothers and sisters tried to find "piece jobs" just so they could all survive, "a family with no parents."

Bishop Reeves in 1960 drew attention to the calamitous impact of the police shooting and its aftermath on the Sharpeville community. He estimated that at least 216 Sharpeville family households had been "broken up" by the police shooting, "and over 500 children are paying the dreadful price of forty seconds of uncontrolled firing at Sharpeville." He drew attention to the "fate of the children of Constance and Ethel Masilo," the widows of the Masilo brothers Ezekiel and Simon who had run a taxi business ever since they moved from Top to Sharpeville in 1947. "Twenty children have lost their fathers and these two households have lost a combined income of £80 a month." He called attention also to John Khota whose "injury has cost him his livelihood," John (Joseph) Morobi who "lost a leg," Benedict Griffiths who "only has the use of his limbs by the grace of the medical staff at

Baragwanath," and Joshua Motha lying in hospital "with a broken femur which will not heal." "The toll of irresponsibility finds its expression in amputations, severe abdominal wounds, arthritic conditions, the loss of mobility and cohesion in limbs, wives left widows, and children fatherless."[23]

Sana Benjamin

Almost a year to the day after the police shooting, a young woman entered a doctor's office in Johannesburg. Sana Benjamin was 30 years old and single. On 21 March 1960, she was home from her regular employment in Vereeniging where she worked "for a Greek family, I polished floors and made beds," and was standing near the shops 200 m from the police station. The police shot her in the back of her right leg and foot. Taken first to the Vereeniging Hospital, and then to Baragwanath, she spent seven months in hospital. On her release, she had to use two crutches and a leg iron to be able to walk and kept her right knee always bandaged. She could not work.

> 25 March 1961. This woman walks into my consulting room with crutches and on the right leg she has extensive scarring on the outer side of the knee protected by an old crepe bandage and she is wearing a double below-knee iron with round heel sockets and back stops to control her drop foot.
>
> She has a dessert spoon with an angulated handle which she used to control her toes when she is putting her boot on.
>
> When she discards all her apparatus her gait is quite grotesque with her right leg abducted at the hip [the right leg moving sideways out from the body], the right knee in moderate valgus [angled outward at the knee] and the right foot in paralytic equine verus [a twisted-over foot deformity].
>
> Scars: There is gross disfigurement on the outer side of her thigh where there is an area of gross loss of tissue and multiple scars ...
>
> The lateral and anterior portion of the thigh muscles are damaged and scarred.
>
> From the nature of the loss of soft tissues one must expect the peroneal nerve [the nerve that supplies movement and sensation to the lower leg, foot and toes] to be missing also over an extensive area.
>
> The many metallic objects in the thigh cannot be removed ...
>
> She requires a stabilization operation on her foot to enable her to discard her drop foot apparatus.
>
> Such treatment would involve a major operation, 3 weeks in hospital and walking in a plaster cast ... for three months ...
>
> She could again do domestic work after completion of treatment.

Another year later, 1962, the police report that they have no address for Sana Benjamin, no record of her. Another year later, 1963, the government rejects her claim. They call her a *betoger*, a protestor. She will get no compensation. She will never get an operation.[24]

Notes

1 All the information about individuals is drawn from the police files contained in the SAP collection, in the records of the "*Commission of Enquiry into the Occurrences at Sharpeville (and other places) on the 21st of March 1960*," K110, and in the Commission testimonies (hereafter Commission), and from interviews that we have undertaken with survivors and family members. The individual files can be located by name (understanding that there are sometimes multiple spellings) by searching the online database of the South African National Archives, SAB database: http://www.national.archsrch.gov.za/sm300cv/smws/sm300gi?202302260124521EB02863%26DB%3DSABE.

2 In 1999, Carlton Monnakgotla, who had been 19 at the time of the shooting, told an interviewer that he had been getting a coke at the shops when the shooting started and when he came out of the store, he "saw the bodies and people fleeing. Right in front of me a pregnant woman was shot. Her unborn baby fell out of her stomach and the next bullet got her." Jasper van der Bliek interviewer, *Sharpeville Scars* (Tilburg-Lekoa Vaal Association: Tilburg, 2000), 19. Anna Motsepe provided two slightly different accounts of her witnessing the shooting of her daughter. The one used as a basis for the description above is undated but likely was made within a week or so of the shooting; the second, in which she stated that she "saw" her daughter shot, was made in August 1961. The difference is minor.

3 Labuschagne testimony, Commission 423; Theron testimony, Commission 316–317; Verwoerd, *Hansard*, 21 March 1960, columns 3759, 3760, 3821; *RDM* 23 March reporting on fatality figures released the previous day and 6 April reporting on injured totals released by the minister of justice; van den Bergh testimony, Commission 2484. Van den Bergh undercounted the number of bullets fired by almost 100 percent (he testified to 743 bullets fired when in fact the number used was at least 1,362) due to the false returns initially submitted by many of the policemen. The United Nations representative for India at the Security Council discussions on 30 March 1960 in New York made the following statement: "[T]he latest official version of the casualty figures which appear in this morning's papers places the number of dead at 89 and the injured at 257." We have not yet been able to identify the original source of the figures cited by the representative, United Nations, Security Council Official Records, Fifteenth Year, 852nd meeting 30 March 1960, 12. The *Time* story was based on knowledgeable sources: it included Warwick Robinson's iconic photograph of two policemen looking at dead bodies lying in the no-name street – see Reeves, *Shooting at Sharpeville*, plate 19 – and likely relied on Robinson's *RDM* colleague Harold Sacks with his intimate knowledge of his police contacts' up-to-date information.

4 *The World*, 26 March 1960. K. Lebeko may well have been related to Eric Lebeko, who was in turn related to Elliot Kabi. See Chapter 6.

5 Alf Kumalo, *Through My Lens: A Photographic Memoir* (Cape Town: Tafelberg, 2009), 114. On the prevention of entry see the *RDM*, 30 March 1960.

6 On the ground, Peter Magubane took photographs, as did Alf Kumalo, both for *Drum*, and James Soullier for the *Sunday Express*; from the air, photographers for the *RDM*, *Drum*, and *Life* each hired planes. See *RDM*, 30 and 31 March 1960; *Life*, 11 April 1960; *Time*, 11 April 1960; *Drum*, May 1960; Jurgen Schadeberg, *The Way I See It* (Picador Africa: Johannesburg, 2017), 324–325; Lesley and Terence Spencer, *Living Dangerously* (Percival Publications: Chichester, 2002 and 2012), 99; Tim Knight, 'Journalist Remembers' (*The Journalist*, 18 May 2015),

http://www.thejournalist.org.za/spotlight/sharpeville-1960-a-journalist-remembers/, and search for "Sharpeville."

7 The gravestones include one for Zaccheaus Maysiels aged 44; this is likely Ezekiel or Zaccheus Masilo aged 44, one of the Masilo brothers who owned a taxi business. There is also a gravestone with the name of Isaac Boisie Mashea aged 37; this may be the same as Izak Mashiya on the police list, although Izak is listed as only being 30 and his mother 50, too young to be the mother of Isaac Boisie Mashea if the age of Isaac is correct as placed on the gravestone.

8 Kumalo, *Through My Lens*, 115.

9 Ralebakeng's circumstances are discussed in British Basutoland correspondence, DO 119/1467, and DO 35/10585, British Archives. Ralebakeng had been born in the Free State, but he and his wife were long-term residents of Top and Sharpeville, and all their children had been born there. Morobi's police file is SAP 31/58/60 (157). There is a gravestone for Joseph Morobi Mochologi aged 46 in the Phelindaba cemetery. This is possibly a combination of two of the dead Joseph Morobi (51) and Joseph Mochologi (46), for whom there should be two gravestones instead of one. The TRC interviewers, who spoke with at least 51 individuals, also identified Joseph Kutoane as being shot dead but his SAP file, SAP 31/58/60 (165), contains a statement by him in which he confirms that he had "recovered completely" from his injuries by December 1961. See Frankel, *An Ordinary Atrocity*, 242–244 for his two appendices (2A and 2B) of people killed by bullets, and of tombstones. He also claimed (148–149) that police informants had told him that approximately two dozen corpses had been surreptitiously taken by the police and buried near the town of Parys across the Vaal River, but this seems more of a police "red herring," falsely admitting to a greater but unprovable story in order to detract attention from what can be proven. There are no stories circulating in Sharpeville of named missing people. At least 91 documented deaths are an appalling tragedy in themselves. To that total we could add the two men killed by the police in Bophelong earlier that morning since they also were part of a PAC-organized protest against pass laws, but we will leave that determination up to the Sharpeville community.

10 Dr. Phillippus Swanepoel testimony, Commission 1146; Dr. Paul Keen testimony, Commission 1164; R. P. G. van Vuuren testimony, Commission 8539; "List of injured in Vereeniging hospital," "List of injured in Baragwanath hospital," Police Archive; *Submissions Presented to the Commission on Behalf of the Bishop of Johannesburg*, 15 June 1960, vol. 1, 1; Reeves, *Shooting at Sharpeville: The Agony of South Africa* (Victor Gollancz: London, 1960), 97.

11 The list of TRC statements was provided to us by Madeleine Fullard of the Missing Persons Unit of the South African National Prosecuting Authority. Unfortunately, a subsequent Freedom of Information Act request to the National Archives, where full transcripts of the testimonies (actually preprinted questionnaires with boxes to be filled in – the completed form for Naphtali Maine is still in the possession of his survivors) were deposited by the TRC, received the reply that the records could not be found. The list of people interviewed by the National Archives in 2014 was provided to us by Nkwenkwezi Languza of the Film, Video and Sound section of the National Archives, a remarkable and underutilized resource for scholars.

12 Labuschagne testimony, Commission 129.

13 Alf Kumalo, *Through My Lens*, 114.

14 For the medical information see the testimonies by doctors Jack Friedman, Hermanus Steyn, P. D. Swanepoel, and A. Lambinon, Commission 1120–1153, 1164–1173; *Submissions Presented to the Commission on Behalf of the Bishop of Johannesburg*, 137–142, and appendix VII. Lambinon performed his one autopsy on 5 April 1960, over two weeks after the shooting. Lieutenant Adriaan Frederick

222 A Family Tragedy

    Freemantle, a police shooting instructor as well as an officer at the police station on 21 March, provided expert testimony to the Wessels Commission about the behavior of guns and ammunition, Commission 844–873. See the reporting in the *RDM* of the Monyake trial testimony about dum dums, 26 January 1961. The medical reports on several of the victims, including Sana Benjamin, Francina Chenene, Lydia Chalale, John Fani, Lefina Gamede, Marium Lepee, and Moketsi S. Mosia recorded metal particles and fragments in their bodies (as distinct from the whole bullets that remained in other victims such as Abram Mofokeng who still lives with a bullet in his lower back today). Frankel, *An Ordinary Atrocity*, 147, wrote that his police informants had told him that they had collected dum dum bullets from an army base on the morning of 21 March. While an interesting story, there is no corroboration for this account in any contemporary testimony or documentary evidence. As a possible police red herring, it takes the focus away from what can be confirmed to have happened on the day of the shooting. Unfortunately, Frankel also introduces what he terms the "shot-in-the-back" thesis as part of the "martyrology" of Sharpeville residents and then asserts, "Almost all the dead were shot in the front. The seventy percent injured from the rear were wounded" (Frankel 149). Factually, this assertion is demonstrably wrong.

15 *RDM*, 18 May 1961. Ambrose Reeves wrote in his book *Shooting at Sharpeville*, 76, that the "loss of a leg to an African labourer often means no employment and slow starvation for his remaining days."

16 Official members of the Wessels Commission and journalists visited Sharpeville on 22 April 1960 so that Judge Wessels could examine the site of violence himself. *RDM*, 22 April 1960. The continuing surveillance activities of Cawood and Wessels are reported in the *RDM*, 15 May 1961.

17 Section 12 of the Orwellian-named Natives (Abolition of Passes and Co-Ordination of Documents) Act No. 67 of 1952 regulated all particulars relating to the recording of contracts in reference books and the issuing of reference books, i.e., pass books or the *dompas* as the people of Sharpeville knew the documents.

18 Those arrested on 21 March and subsequently were denied bail at first and then bail was set at £150 each for those believed to be PAC members, a sum that none could afford. In June, the amount was reduced to £50 for nine of the defendants and to £10 for the rest. It was only in early September that the presiding magistrate agreed to a bail of £30 each for the assumed PAC members then on trial. *RDM*, 31 March, 21 June, and 8 September 1960.

19 On the truckload of supplies, see the *RDM*, 26 March 1960. On Adeline Hain see Peter Hain, *A Pretoria Boy* (Icon Books: London, 2022), 18–19.

20 On government policy and its local impact, see the *RDM*, 20 February 1961.

21 Details of the Sharpeville Relief Fund and those who contributed to it can be found in the following issues of the *RDM*, 25, 30 March and 8, 9, 14, 18, 21 June 1960, and *the Vereeniging and Vanderbijlpark News*, 25 March, 15 April, 6 May, and 3, 17 June 1960. The largest single contribution to the Fund, almost £6,000 or nearly a third of the total raised, came from the Master Diamond Cutters' Association of South Africa. The Fund spent £800 a month on "essential needs," which meant all the monies raised were exhausted by the beginning of 1962. The information on lunch costs is from the *RDM*, 16 May 1960 and 14 December 1961. The latter issue reported that the town's auditor had disallowed the All Blacks' lunch expenditure as well as R60 the town had spent on cigarettes and mineral water for the policemen on 21 March 1960.

22 Kopano Motsega's gravestone lists his age as 50, but in her 1961 statement to the police, Historina Motsega gave his age at death as 52.

23 *RDM*, 28 October 1960; *Shooting at Sharpeville*, 76–77.

24 For the medical reports and other documentation on Sana Benjamin see SAP 614 31/58/60 (164), SAP 616 31/58/60 (30), and K110 1/3/60.

Bibliography

Frankel, Philip. *An Ordinary Atrocity: Sharpeville and Its Massacre*. New Haven: Yale University Press, 2001.

Hain, Peter. *A Pretoria Boy*. London: Icon Books, 2022.

Knight, Tim. "Journalist Remembers." *The Journalist* 18 May 2015. http://www.thejournalist.org.za/spotlight/sharpeville-1960-a-journalist-remembers/.

Kumalo, Alf. *Through My Lens: A Photographic Memoir*. Cape Town: Tafelberg, 2009.

Reeves, Ambrose. *Shooting at Sharpeville: The Agony of South Africa*. London: Victor Gollancz, 1960a.

Reeves, Ambrose. *Submissions Presented to the Commission on Behalf of the Bishop of Johannesburg*. Johannesburg, 15 June 1960b. Two volumes.

Schadeberg, Jurgen. *The Way I See It*. Johannesburg: Picador Africa, 2017.

Spencer, Lesley and Terence. *Living Dangerously*. Chichester: Percival Publications, 2002 and 2012.

Van der Bliek, Jasper. *Sharpeville Scars*. Tilburg: Tilburg-Lekoa Vaal Association, 2000.

8 Sharpeville and the World

Our aim is to unite the people on the basis of African nationality; to create and assert the African personality and to restore the Black man's human dignity. That is all – I include all the people there ... From Cape to Cairo from Morocco to Alaska. (Voices from audience).

(Nyakane Tsolo, 1960)[1]

The Sharpeville murders shook public opinion for months. In the newspapers, over the airwaves, and in private conversations, Sharpeville has become a symbol. It was through Sharpeville that men and women first became acquainted with the problem of apartheid in South Africa.

(Frantz Fanon, 1961)[2]

[Y]ou have to keep in mind that the Sharpeville massacre had just happened but South Africa and the entire African continent were unknown. Africa was to the majority of the Swedish people very hot, Negroes, and paganism. Nobody knew anything.

(Peder Gowenius, 1961)[3]

This chapter is about the stories that the residents of Sharpeville told contemporaneously about their own experiences on 21 March 1960, stories that they began telling in their hospital beds in the days immediately after the shooting, and that they kept telling, to news reporters and in public hearings and in courtrooms and through other legal actions, and which were circulated around the world despite relentless police harassment for months and years after, indeed until the formal end of apartheid in 1994, and which are retold still to the present day to anyone ready to listen. Indeed, on one occasion when we stopped on Seeiso Street in October 2022 to visit a friend, a person came up to us and said, "You are not from here are you?" After we introduced ourselves, Ma Jane, as she invited us to call her, told us that anytime we wanted to listen she would be happy to tell us what happened on 21 March 1960 when she was a small girl.

DOI: 10.4324/9781003257806-8

Spread widely through the Black press in South Africa and broadcast abroad through the megaphone of the exiled liberation movements of the PAC and the ANC, both banned in South Africa by Verwoerd's government three weeks after the shooting, Sharpeville stories transformed the world's perception of apartheid and South Africa. For the first time, the international community no longer accepted the apartheid government's usual explanation of African "unrest," that the police killings throughout the 1950s of hundreds of Africans at Witzieshoek and Alexandra and Sophiatown and Port Elizabeth and East London and Sekhukhuniland and Windhoek were in every case the result of riots in which policemen faced overwhelming crowds and when attacked had to use their weapons in self-defence to protect their own lives, the usual three-part elements of police stories.[4]

Sharpeville was a watershed. It was the moment when the world, East and West, North and South, began to see South Africa and apartheid differently, not as the internal matter of a sovereign state dealing with its own urban and social problems but as a unique case of unacceptable racial discrimination, a threat to peace across the African continent and throughout the world. The United Nations (UN) highlighted this sea change when in October 1966 it proclaimed 21 March as the International Day for the Elimination of Racial Discrimination and in December of the same year defined apartheid as "a crime against humanity." Sharpeville was the beginning of the world anti-apartheid movement, and it was the beginning of the end of apartheid, but only because the residents of Sharpeville told South Africa and the world right then and there what had happened, with clarity, with precision, and with determination.

African Witness

Initially, mainstream western media followed the police story that a crowd of armed Africans had attacked the police station forcing Pienaar and his men to fire in self-defence.[5] *The Times* of London on the day after the massacre had as its main heading "Police open fire on Africans" and used the subheading "Mob stone armoured-car force." While no explanation was immediately available to its local correspondent (Charles Channon) as to the cause of the shooting, the newspaper reported that "the police station ... was virtually besieged by thousands of Africans shouting 'Africa, Africa' ... [and] some hooliganism had been going on before the crowd started stoning the armoured cars." The *New York Times* managed to conflate several stories in its issue of 22 March. On one page, the newspaper reported 50 killed "when Africans gathered at the police station ... [and] began stoning the police and armored cars that had been brought to the station"; on another page, the story was more elaborate with between 20,000 and 50,000 Africans besieging 25 policemen inside the station, until finally the "mob, which had been stoning the police, refused to disperse when ordered and police followed up with warning shots [and then] opened fire with submachine guns, mowing down the front ranks."[6]

But then Warwick Robinson's photographs (see Chapter 6), the ones he took immediately after the shooting including images of bodies lying in the no-name street before any policeman ventured out of the police station, the photographs that the *RDM* wouldn't publish in South Africa, started appearing in the international press from 22 March onward (Robinson wired them himself when his editors wouldn't publish his photographs) and those images began to change the narrative. Now there was visual evidence of an atrocity. In England, the largest mass-circulation newspaper, the *Daily Mirror*, reflected this change in an editorial published the same day as the photographs. Referring to Harold Macmillan's speech given seven weeks before (3 February 1960) in the South African parliament in Cape Town – "The wind of change is blowing through the Continent" – the *Daily Mirror* editorialist wrote that the deaths of the people of Sharpeville "lie grimly at the door of the people who willfully deny the wind of change. ... The whole civilized world is outraged by what has happened," and concluded, in underlined capitals in bold, "**YESTERDAY'S TRAGEDY COULD BE THE BEGINNING OF THE REVOLT IN SOUTH AFRICA**."[7]

The same day, 22 March, as Robinson's images began appearing in the press worldwide, the United States, for the first time in its dealings with South Africa, which it generally treated as an ally in the Cold War, officially criticised South Africa even as that meant "comment[ing] on the internal affairs of governments with which it enjoys normal relations." "The United States deplores violence in all its forms and hopes that the African people in South Africa will be able to obtain redress for their legitimate grievances by peaceful means." The statement caused a "political sensation" among the old colonial powers like Britain and France since it indicated a fundamental change of position by the United States on two matters: viewing the attack on the Sharpeville residents as racially motivated and, secondly, not solely as an internal matter of a sovereign state, a change in position that suggested that the United States could not be seen as a reliable ally in confronting demands for independence among many of the colonies remaining in Africa (only Ethiopia, Ghana, Guinea, and Liberia had independence at the beginning of 1960). Indeed, other diplomats at the UN, according to the *New York Times*, saw in the US press release "a deliberate gesture by the United States to gain the goodwill of the rising number of independent African governments and to head off the Soviet bloc's exploitation of African grievances." They may well have been right. On the same day that the United States issued its official statement deploring the actions of the police in South Africa, its State Department representative appeared before the US Senate Foreign Relations Committee and warned that international inaction would inevitably result in "increasing violence" and "massive demonstrations." "That part of Africa which lies south of the Sahara has not in the past played a prominent role in international affairs. ... But in the decade of the Sixties its role may be critical."[8]

For most of the rest of the world outside Western Europe, the USA, and the White Commonwealth (Australia, Canada, and New Zealand), condemnation of South Africa for its racial policies was already long established. India had since the end of World War II criticised vociferously South Africa's racial policies and its membership in the British Commonwealth of Nations, and other African and Asian nations had throughout the 1950s denounced the "dangerous and explosive situation" in South Africa, the "flagrant violation" apartheid posed to "the basic principles and fundamental freedoms which are enshrined in the Charter of the United Nations," and warned of the threat of those same policies to "international peace." The Bandung Conference of 29 African and Asian nations held in Indonesia in 1955 issued a communique emphasising the commitment of all the participants to the Charter of the United Nations and the UN's 1948 issuance of a Universal Declaration of Human Rights. The conference expressed "sympathy and support for the courageous stand taken by victims of racial discrimination, especially by the peoples of African and Indian and Pakistani origin in South Africa," and declared "that colonialism in all its manifestations is an evil which should speedily be brought to an end." In December 1958, Kwame Nkrumah, in one of his first acts as president of newly independent Ghana, organised in Accra the All-African People's Conference, attended by "[m]ore than 300 delegates representing 200 million Africans in 28 countries," including Patrice Lumumba, Kenneth Kaunda, Hastings Banda, and Sekou Touré. Committed to ending "racialism and discriminatory laws and practices" throughout Africa and agreeing that such racialism was the "product of colonialism," the delegates concluded that "the independence of states is the prerequisite for the end of discrimination." They condemned "the political policies of territories like South Africa which base their minority rule of the majority upon apartheid's social doctrines" and as their first action proposed the establishment of a "permanent Secretariat" to urge African states to impose economic sanctions on South Africa and boycott South African goods. This was the language that had been read in South Africa by Robert Sobukwe and others and which inspired them to establish the PAC and to plan for the pass demonstration on 21 March 1960. This was the practical action that inspired the establishment of the British Boycott Movement in 1959 at a meeting in London where one of the main speakers was Julius Nyerere.[9]

Jawaharlal Nehru, the prime minister of India, speaking to his parliament on 23 March 1960, was one of the first international leaders to criticise the Sharpeville shooting:

> Hundreds of millions of people in Asia and Africa could never accept the spirit behind the large-scale killing – the spirit of racial mastery and segregation. ... Here is Africa at the moment in a resurgent, proud and defiant mood after long centuries of suppression. Many countries have become independent and many others will become independent. On the

other side, there is this picture of people in South Africa who are practically prisoners – a whole nation excepting some groups who have settled down from Europe. ... This kind of culmination lead[s] to certain conclusions in the minds of people that this is not the end of the episode but the prelude to the future.[10]

India, along with 28 other members of the "African-Asian group" of the UN (Afghanistan, Burma, Cambodia, Ceylon, Ethiopia, Federation of Malaya, Ghana, Guinea, Indonesia, Iran, Iraq, Japan, Jordan, Laos, Lebanon, Liberia, Libya, Morocco, Nepal, Pakistan, Philippines, Saudi Arabi, Sudan, Thailand, Tunisia, Turkey, United Arab Republic, and Yemen) on 25 March 1960 called on the Security Council to schedule a hearing on the shooting of "unarmed and peaceful" protestors at Sharpeville. The question remained, however, would yet another example of an act of violence overcome the reticence of UN member nations to put aside Cold War differences and involve themselves in what was usually deemed the internal concern of a sovereign state?[11]

The international atmosphere really turned as Africans themselves told and reported their own stories about the shooting. The Black press in Johannesburg – that is, newspapers owned by Whites but staffed by African reporters and catering to an African readership – used none of the police language of the *RDM*, the *Pretoria News*, the *Star*, and other primarily White newspapers with their headline references to "riots" and "trouble." The *New Age*, whose Joe Gqabi had been in Sharpeville from 11 am onward on 21 March, headlined its front page "MASS SLAUGHTER BY POLICE," accompanied by one of Gqabi's photographs showing two bodies lying in the street with the caption "corpses littered the street." Gqabi's first-person story, under the subheading "BLOODY REPRISALS AGAINST ANTI-PASS DEMONSTRATORS," described witnessing "one of the ugliest bloodbaths ever," with "frightful reprisals from the police" on a crowd that had gathered peacefully in response "to the call to stay home from work and hand in their passes at the police station." "Women covered their heads with their arms and wept and their cries could be heard from far off." By contrast, "A police official pointed to scratched paintwork as evidence of stoning. Their attitude seemed to be: 'Demonstrate or throw stones at even our Saracens and we will teach you a lesson.'" Gqabi dismissed the police story that they had been stoned and fired upon first, noting that "by their own admission only three policemen were injured on Monday."[12]

The *Golden City Post* story on Sharpeville, written and illustrated primarily by Ronnie Manyosi who had been in the town since 11:30 am and who stayed until at least two hours after the shooting, added the voices of Sharpeville residents under its front-page headline: "'WE WERE SHOT DOWN': THE WOUNDED TALK." Here was Moses Mooi, 31 years old, "partly disemboweled by a soft-nose bullet through the back": "Before we knew what was happening, a volley of bullets from the police started and panic and confusion reigned all over." And Jacob Nhlapo, the 21-year-old mechanic who bicycled each day from his mother's home in Evaton to work in the Sharpeville Cycle Works: "the last thing he remembered was when the car [Pienaar's] knocked down the woman. 'As I watched I just felt a surge of people running on to me. The next thing, I was paralysed in the back.'" And Job Tsolo (Nyakane's older brother), the chairman of the Sharpeville branch of the PAC, whose words to Manyosi were printed by *The World* in bold caps: "**WE HAD SO CONVINCED THE PEOPLE THAT OURS WAS A NON-VIOLENT CAMPAIGN THAT EVEN WHEN POLICE MOWED THEM DOWN, NONE OF THEM LIFTED A HAND TO STRIKE BACK,**" and then continued "What other explanation could one give. Not a single cop was injured and not a single window of the police station was broken and yet 20,000 people are accused of rioting on that very spot."[13]

The third major African newspaper on the Rand, *The World*, in its weekend edition, added two more key types of evidence of the extent of the tragedy – photos of the dead and injured, some with their names, and for the first time a list of the casualties by name. The photographs included ones of the Reverend Sam Hlatshwayo with bullet and bayonet injuries, and of K. Lebeko waiting outside the Vereeniging Hospital to be treated for a bullet injury to his leg, and images of people being brought to the hospital in private vans and ambulances, and, like Lebeko, crowding outside waiting to be treated, all of them clearly in considerable pain. There was the powerful image of an unnamed young man, "His face a terrible mask of blood," shot in the face and grimly walking to get medical help. And for the first time in any newspaper, there was a list of casualties by name, information that would remain absent from the White press. We print their names in full (spellings as published) because there is no other contemporaneous list except in police records.

Here is a list of the dead people who have been identified at Sharpeville:
J. Mokoto Mazibuko, Sonnyboy Bothuli, Simon Pitikane Masilo, Paulina Madide, Ezekiel Masilo (Maisels), T. Ramailane, an elder of the Methodist church, John Mailane, Christina Motsepe, Elphas Motsepe, Sam Sefatsa, Jerry Molapo and Thomas Hlongwane.

One man who was among the crowd is missing from his home. He is Jacob Ramokoena.

Among the injured are: Abraham Khaole, Miriam Lepee, Lydia Shabalala, Emily Kambule, Samuel Moloi, Daniel Likobo, Makhoathi Senoko, Peter Molibeli, Joseph Matlaletse, Sello Ralebakang, Meshack Pitso, Miriam Diketso, Edilarno Mvubazana, Aaron Matsabu, Selina Mkwanazi, Tota Hlongwane, George Sekate, L. Setlhatlholo, Agnes Mpshe and Elizabeth Chabeli. Solomon Matogoshe, Joseph Mochulugi, Isaac Nkhi, Petrus Nteesane, Isaac Nyembezi, Dan Moera, Isaac Maboe, John Nchaupe.

Finally, here was information that had never before appeared in the South African press where, as Bloke Modisane would write in *Blame Me on History*, the "routine [police] raids are routine only in their consistency of vengeance and brutality ... [and] the hooliganism of the police is never something that gets into the newspapers."[14]

New Age, the *Golden City Post*, and *The World*, with their powerful headlines and horrific descriptions of police brutality, reached a wide audience, including among many other young Africans Dikgang Moseneke (who much later after the end of apartheid became deputy chief justice of South Africa) who as part of his daily school tasks had to read, along with his 12- and 13-year-old classmates, the morning papers. "The front page of the morning papers carried pictures of corpses lying in a street."

> Chilling fear and anxiety gripped our class. ... As we took our seats in our classroom a ghostly silence fell over us. ... Eventually the assembly bell went and we all filed outside, where the headmaster asked that we all pray for the people of Sharpeville, Langa, and Nyanga. ... My parents did not say a word to me, their eldest son, about the Sharpeville massacre, and yet a pall of pain and mourning came over our otherwise lively and jovial home.[15]

For the international audience, it was a Friday 25 March headline in the British *Daily Mirror* that alerted them to the existence of a new cache of witness testimonies: "POLICE SHOT US IN THE BACK, SAY AFRICANS." The bishop of Johannesburg, Ambrose Reeves, told a Johannesburg press conference of foreign correspondents the previous evening that three lawyers briefed by him had visited Baragwanath and at the bedsides of the Sharpeville injured, despite constant surveillance and interference by police officers, had collected "sworn statements from a hundred of the 162 Africans wounded in the shooting." These witnesses, Reeves announced to the gathered journalists, would confirm that people had gone to the police station to wait until 2 pm, at the request of the police, for "'the big white boss'... coming to the township from Pretoria to address them"; that they adhered strictly to their leaders' instructions that there was to be "no violence"; that no warning had been given before the police opened fire directly into a crowd of men, women, and children; no tear gas had been used; no baton charge; and "the overwhelming proportion of wounded were shot in the back or buttocks. Some ... were riding bicycles when hit."[16]

Eighteen of these hospital-bed narratives still exist, held in the archives of the UN where Reeves sent them by "a roundabout route" to an American, Allard Lowenstein, with a request that

> you will be able to bring them to the attention of the American people and that they will be useful to you at the U.N. [Allard was representing the African inhabitants of what was then called South West Africa in their own appeal for UN assistance].

Now digitised at our request, these 18 statements provide us with our most immediate access to eyewitness accounts told within hours or at most a few days of the police shooting. These witnesses were a cross-section of those shot by the police: they ranged in age from teenagers to people in their 50s, nearly all had been employed at the time they were shot, and they came from different addresses spread throughout Sharpeville's neighbourhoods. As Reeves noted at the time, given their injuries, the nature of their hospital conditions constantly watched by police and Special Branch (SB) men, and their individual experiences on 21 March, there was no possibility that they could have collaborated in telling their stories to his lawyers.[17]

Here is Benedict Griffiths, the 17-year-old son of an African policeman, who told one of Reeves' representatives that he had been looking for his first job that Monday but "was stopped by a group of men who were preventing people from leaving the gate." He went to the police station where people were gathering and got there by 8 am.

> I sat down for the whole morning watching what was going on. ... One of the leaders of the Pan-African movement said that we should wait until 2 o'clock when some person would tell us about Passes. After this announcement nothing happened for a while. Thereafter, the Policemen started forming into a line and started to load. When they did this one of the men who had been responsible for stopping people leaving the gates [earlier that morning] said "We are not fighting, but we have come to talk." He spoke in Sotho. ... The Police then arrested these leaders and took them into the yard. I saw no stone throwing and no stones were thrown for we had gone there to listen and not to fight. We had been told that we must not throw stones. Just before the Policemen stood in a line and started to load, reinforcements had arrived from Johannesburg, and it was these men together with the other Police who, immediately after they had arrested the leaders, started to fire. The leaders were arrested by a man who was fairly well-built with blond hair, slightly bald in front with deep-set eyes and a red face. When he arrested this man, the bald-headed man struck the leader and pushed him into the station. When the firing started, I was shot in the left thigh and right foot from behind. I fell where I was standing. The firing seemed to go on for some minutes.[18]

Griffiths' experiences were shared by other African eyewitnesses. Some added a detail or two; some spoke at less length (Griffiths' statement was two typed pages). Koti Lerolo (40 years old), married with three children and employed by Wire Works, went to listen to a "talk on Passes and to hear what we were to do with them," when "after standing quietly ... suddenly fire broke out and I was shot from behind as I ran away." Anthony Ndaba (49), married with two children and employed by the Cornelia Colliery, had gone also "to hear about passes" when suddenly police reinforcements arrived and lined up with machine guns. As he and his friends "started to walk away ... I was shot in the hip and knee from behind." Abraham Khaole (53) married with three children and employed by Safim, had come to hear about passes and "without warning, I heard the sound of firing and I turned and ran and as I ran I was shot in the back"; Moses Shabangu (19), unmarried and employed by the Central Engineering Works, saw a man raise a loudspeaker and thought he was calling the crowd forward "to hear the statement [about passes perhaps]," and "the next thing the Police fired ... [and] as I was running away, I was shot in the back of my arm."

Why did passes matter to them? Because the enforcement of the pass system limited their ability to seek better-paying jobs away from Vereeniging. Isiah Monyane (44), married with one child and employed by a jewellery store in Vereeniging, opposed the carrying of a pass because it "prevents me from seeking work wherever I wish and because I get arrested for not carrying passes"; Adam Sakaone (36), married with four children and employed in Vereeniging, thought the "[p]ass too troublesome because we get arrested if we don't carry our Passes and cannot seek work where we wish." Both were shot in the back.

None saw any stones thrown, and they were explicit in their denials: Daniel Tshabalala (35) married with five children and employed by Babcock and Wilcox, "I saw no stones being thrown"; Joseph Mokajoka (31), unmarried and between jobs, "No stones were thrown and no-one had sticks"; George Qtwaya (21), unmarried and employed by Stewarts and Lloyds, "No-one threw stones nor did anyone have a stick ... no-one told us to disperse"; Ishmael Modise (21), unmarried and working for African Cables, "I saw no stone throwing nor did we have sticks"; Joseph Mofatu (36), married with one child and employed by the Vereeniging New Consolidated Mealie Combine, "I saw no stone throwing nor did I hear any order to disperse." All five were shot in the back.

Some were not even close to the police station when they were shot. Isaai Serota (19), unmarried and employed by Central Engineering Works, was coming out of the shops when he "heard the sound of firing." Solomon Mtshali (15), a schoolboy, was also at the shops when he heard firing. Both were shot in their legs.

Beshu Mahlangu (55), married with six children and employed by the South African Railways since 1945, got shot "in the left back shoulder." Matthew Mashiya (30), unmarried and employed by Union Liquid Air, "was shot from behind." Adam Manato (59), married with three children and employed by Wire Works, "was shot in the back of the leg." Zephaniah Nchaupe (40), married with six children and employed by Stewarts and Lloyds, "had already run a good distance when I was shot from behind."

Eighteen stories, all consistent as to what happened on 21 March 1960. Waiting peaceably to hear about the pass law from a senior official who would speak to them at 2 pm. Noticing the abrupt arrival of police reinforcements in the middle of the day – Pienaar and his car forcing his way through the crowd along with trucks of police armed with machine guns (Griffiths, Khaole, Monyane, Mashiya, and Sakaone remarked on the sudden arrivals and the machine guns). No warnings to disperse. No stones thrown by the crowd. No one rushed through the double gates into the police station. Just sudden firing without warning and for longer than the police would ever admit (10 seconds, maybe 20 was the police's lengthiest estimate). Ishmael Modise fell to the ground after he was shot in the back of his leg hoping that "I would sustain no further wounds," but three more bullets flew over his head as he lay covering his head with his hands and a fourth bullet hit one of his fingers. Joseph Mokajoka lay on the ground "powerless" after he got a bullet in his leg from behind (and though he did not know it at the time, a second one entered his back as well, leaving him in hospital for four months), and a third bullet hit him in the skull but glanced off. Griffiths had thought the shooting lasted for minutes; it must have felt longer in the carnage.

None could understand why the police fired. "I don't know why they were shooting," said Beshu Mashangu; "I do not know why they fired," said Matthew Mashiya; "I do not know why the firing broke out," said Anthony Ndaba. Why, as *the Golden City Post* reporter wrote, did the police shoot to kill?[19]

Though none of the people in their hospital beds had a chance to confront the police except by telling their stories, in the streets outside, throughout the Vaal Triangle, and indeed in all of the African townships southwest of Johannesburg, people stayed away from work in the immediate aftermath of the shooting. Thousands of workers, perhaps 90 percent of the men employed in Vanderbijlpark, Vereeniging, and Evaton, stayed home that week, crippling industrial production throughout the region, including that of "the vast plant of the South African Iron and Steel Corporation."

The police responded by arresting everyone they could find who they believed was a leader of the events on 21 March (all the people hospitalised from Sharpeville, as well as those they identified as leaders in Vanderbijlpark and Evaton). But opposition only grew. On the evening of the first Monday after the massacre, 30 March, Verwoerd's government declared a state of emergency retroactive to 29 March in all urban areas of South Africa with fines of £500 (the average monthly income for urban African families at the time was £14) or five years in prison or both for men who refused to return to work "with intent to thwart the Government."[20] Yet African workers stayed home, in the Vaal Triangle, in Bloemfontein and Durban, and in small regional towns throughout the country. On the streets of Cape Town, the police whipped those they labelled "loiterers," language the same as that which Constable Saaiman used to describe his daily duties in Central Johannesburg, but what they really meant was that they were attacking people on strike. In Johannesburg, all work was brought to a halt as reported by *Time* magazine.

Johannesburg seemed strangely deserted in the bright Monday morning sun. Gone were the hordes of African delivery boys on bicycles that normally clog Commissioner Street. Gone were the black gas-station attendants, the elevator operators and the shop sweepers. That morning the boss made his own tea in the office, and the white housewife lugged her own parcels to the car after a round of shopping. For 95% of Johannesburg's Africans sat obstinately at home, mourning for the 68 hapless blacks cut down by the withering hail of police bullets in the Sharpeville massacre a week earlier.[21]

Though not a single PAC supporter responded to police violence in kind in the immediate aftermath of the 21 March shooting – they were as Job Tsolo had noted of the people in Sharpeville all following the instructions of Robert Sobukwe to withhold their labour peaceably – they did get an opportunity to speak their minds in court. In the immediate aftermath of the police shooting, 142 PAC supporters arrested on 21 March in the Soweto communities of Orlando, Mofolo, and Dube "on charges of failing to produce their reference books," together with their families and friends, "packed" the Johannesburg "Bantu Commissioners Court." Most of the people in court wore "paper slogans reading 'Africa for Africans.'" Though the accused refused to plead following the instructions of Sobukwe, they were all convicted in early April and sentenced to heavy punishments of £300 fines each, impossible for any to pay, so three years imprisonment instead. Their spokesman at sentencing took advantage of court custom to spend three hours "outlining [the] aims of the Pan-Africanist Congress." Though we don't have a record of his speech, we do have reports of others made in similar cases in Johannesburg and Pretoria and in these references were made to the laws having been made by a "White Parliament" elected by "White people" only: "We Africans played no part whatsoever in the making of these laws and we have no legal obligation to obey these laws." Four hundred and thirty Africans had died in the Coalbrook mine disaster "because they could not choose their type of work. They were compelled to go to the mines because of influx control." "Is it a government of a white minority or a black majority?"

Next the presiding officer, a member of Marthinus Smuts' (the man who had sat at the Gate preparing his speech to the Sharpeville crowd at the same time that they were being shot down by the police) "Bantu administration," spoke glowingly for two hours about apartheid policies much like his boss must have intended to do on 21 March. He spoke about the "'terrible crimes' inflicted by Africans on white South Africans"; he referred to the "torch of western civilization brought here by white South Africans and to benefits they had brought to primitive peoples"; he spoke of the "concern of white farmers for the welfare of labour sent to them under farm labour schemes," and of the "benefits Africans received from Government culminating in the Promotion of Bantu Self-Government Act"; most likely he repeated the words spoken by representatives from Smuts' office in the African townships of

Vanderbijlpark and Meyerton a few months before, that in "matters of Government you are like children today," and now, just two weeks after the 21 March shooting, he emphasised the "understanding, sympathetic and painstaking way in which the police carried out their duties."

While the people gathered at the Sharpeville police station likely would have listened politely to Smuts' proposed speech on 21 March – after all, they had come to listen not to fight on that day – the PAC members convicted for pass law offences and their supporters packing the Johannesburg courtroom in the aftermath of the shooting had no such respect for the chief "Bantu" commissioner's subordinate.

> Commissioner's peroration was frequently interrupted by derisory cries such as "rubbish" from among the accused and the public in court. After delivery of judgment accused and public joined in singing of "Sikelel Afrika" and spokesmen of accused called for few moments silence "for dead who fell at Sharpeville and other places."[22]

Framing Sharpeville: The UN's "Session of Africa"

On 30 March 1960, the same day as the first Sharpeville funeral and in response to the request five days before of the 29 African-Asian States that the Sharpeville shootings and state violence in South Africa be discussed, the Security Council of the UN, for the first time since the organisation's founding in 1945, put what had previously been deemed the internal affairs of a member state on its agenda. For three days at the UN headquarters in New York, Sharpeville, police violence, and the apartheid policies of South Africa were the agenda items for the world.[23]

The debate was led by countries which themselves had been colonised and knew intimately the type of violence recently experienced by the people of Sharpeville: by Ethiopia, whose representative noted that the 21 March South African massacre was a "sorrowful reminder of the massacre of over 30,000 Ethiopian people, by authorities of a ruthless invader, on 19 and 20 February 1937 in Addis Ababa alone"; by the representative of Guinea, who drew his colleagues' attention to the imminent admission to the UN of Madagascar "where eighty thousand people were massacred [by the French in 1947–1949]"; and by the representatives of India, Ghana, Pakistan, and Liberia, who were specially invited by the United States (which chaired the Security Council in March) to join the discussions along with the permanent members of the Council (China, France, United Kingdom, United States, USSR) and the non-permanent members (Argentina, Ceylon, Ecuador, Italy, Poland, Tunisia).

The survivors of colonialism with its long history of racism and violence wherever it had been practiced in the world, in Africa, in Asia, in the Americas, not only understood physically and emotionally what had happened to the people of Sharpeville, but they also saw in the founding principles of the UN, the 1945 Charter and the 1948 Universal Declaration of Human Rights, and in the latent power of the worldwide organisation, an opportunity to make sure that what had happened in South Africa – state-sanctioned racial discrimination – could not happen again. As the representative of Guinea noted about the deliberations, "[W]e peoples of the African-Asian countries, the stubborn foes of domination, feel that the meetings of the Security Council on the present question might be called 'the session of Africa.'"

The representative of Ceylon began the debate by stressing the moral and practical implications of their forthcoming discussion. The racial policy of South Africa, he stated, had "evoked condemnation from all men of good will as something which is ugly, almost indecent and contrary to the general concepts of Christian civilization." The circumstances of the Sharpeville shooting itself amounted to "a denial of human rights and of elementary justice." And that denial and the extent of the implementation of apartheid policies made the situation in South Africa

> one of international significance ... the fact that certain fundamental human rights have been prescribed as the inalienable rights of all Member States, and indeed of all human beings in all parts of the world, human rights which accord with the dignity and worth of the human person – must be considered as entitling us to intervene.

Over the course of the next three days of debate, the representative of Ceylon and those of the other newly independent states used their world stage to discuss in detail the Sharpeville shooting itself: the peacefulness of the crowd, the failure of the police to issue orders to disperse, Sharpeville residents "mercilessly fired upon by sub-machine guns and other automatic weapons," the mounting numbers of dead and injured (89 dead at least suggested the representative of India, perhaps over 100).

They also provided to their audience both in the Security Council itself and as reported by the world press, extensive information about life under apartheid: how Africans had no freedom of title to land; how no African could bring his wife and family to live with him in the cities; how every African, men and women alike, had to carry a pass, limiting their ability to seek work wherever they wished; how the South African economy depended on a system of government-regulated cheap Black labour; how park benches were segregated and church schools prohibited; and how the laws were enforced through harsh fines, lengthy terms of imprisonment, whippings, and forced labour on White farms. They referenced details that would have been familiar to the residents of Sharpeville if the South African newspapers had not self-censored themselves or been subjected to police raids, as they were in the case of *Drum*, the *Golden City Post*, and *New Age*, all of which had their copies for distribution confiscated and distribution itself made illegal from 31 March onward: that in Evaton "any policeman may, whenever he wishes, for any reason whatsoever, for the purpose of inspecting the dwelling occupied by a resident of the township, enter that dwelling at any time of day or night," and that in Coalbrook, the next of kin of the deceased would get a pension of £33 per month if they were White but only £3 if they were African. What this all meant in total, argued the representative for India, was that the "structure of 'apartheid' enmeshes the African in every walk of life and makes South Africa a semi-prisonhouse for the millions of its African population."

What made the South African situation different, the Security Council speakers argued, from instances of social upheaval and political violence in other countries, was that in South Africa, racial discrimination was government policy. Here was the representative of Ceylon: South Africa was "the only country in the world which has an official and Government policy of racial discrimination and racial segregation differences"; the representative of India: "[T]he killings in South Africa do not stand out in isolation. They are intimately concerned with and are indeed a culmination of the cult of racism in South Africa"; and the representative of Guinea:

> South Africa is the only country in the world in which basic questions of civil rights, justice, good and evil and, indeed, the very right to live, are determined both in law and in practice by the colour of the skin of the individual concerned.

By contrast, every other country that spoke emphasised their adherence to non-racialism. Jordan's representative took the "opportunity to say that the national and spiritual doctrines of the Arab people reject the concept of racial discrimination and can in no way tolerate it," quoted the Koran – "Thou, people of the world, all of thee, we created thee of one male and one female and made thee nations and clans to know one another and to live with one another" – and noted, "The Arab East gave birth to the three monotheistic religions, Christianity, Judaism, and Islam, which preach the brotherhood of all men before God." The representative of Ecuador spoke of coming

> from a continent and speak[ing] on behalf of a nation which are made up of a variety of races. These races have mixed with each other, and, happily for us, the people in our part of the world share alike in glory and misery, in rights and duties, without any kind of racial discrimination.

The representative of Argentina, who became the chair of the Security Council on its monthly rotation on 1 April, remarked,

> For my country, just as for the other nations of Latin America, racial prejudice is an aberration which is hard to understand. We grow up in the belief that all human beings are equal because they are all the children of the same God, and our civil laws are based on the absolute equality of all races.

Particularly significant given the timing was the Italian representative quoting Pope John XXIII who on 28 March 1960 elevated the first African as a cardinal, Laurean Rugambwa from Tanganyika, with the words "all are created equal to the Glory of God which does not know discrimination of language, origin, colour, this event being the seal of an ancient doctrine followed for two thousand years."

Although the policies and practices of apartheid ran counter to the founding principles of the UN, the representatives of the newly independent countries also recognised at the time that they could not implement the sanctions that the representative of Ceylon had embraced in his introductory speech: that "human rights which accord with the dignity and worth of the human person – must be considered as entitling us to intervene." Britain and France both had permanent seats on the Security Council, and though each emphasised their own adherence to "non-racialism" – the UK representative stated that his country "reject[ed] the idea of any inherent superiority of one race over another," and the French representative noted that the most recent French constitution, that of the Fifth Republic 1958, contained the text that all citizens "shall be equal before the law, whatever their origin, their race, and their religion" – neither country accepted that, in the words of the French representative, "the present Charter shall authorize the United Nations to intervene in matters which are essentially within the domestic jurisdiction of any State." Moreover, each could block any UN action through their veto power.

But that possibility of veto was not an impediment to the newly independent states being able to express their feelings about apartheid, and that was important in itself. The representative from Ecuador noted that "the facts themselves are so tragic that they call forth an emotional reaction"; Ethiopia's representative reported, "The recent massacre has terrified and shocked the Ethiopian people"; India's Nehru stated, "Hundreds of millions of people of Asia and Africa could never accept the spirit behind the large-scale killing – the spirit of racial mastery, the spirit of authoritarianism and segregation"; Guinea's representative stated that the UN was an appropriate place to express such feelings since it represented "the conscience of the peoples of the world." Even the representative from Ceylon who had introduced the concept of "the right to intervene," concluded that he along with other representatives "were prepared to face any resolution so long as it stated what they felt."

The resolution finally adopted by the Security Council on 1 April 1960, by a vote in favour by nine members (Argentina, Ceylon, China, Ecuador, Italy, Poland, Tunisia, USSR, and the United States), none against, and two abstaining (France and the United Kingdom), had five points, all responding to "the strong feelings and grave concern aroused among Governments and peoples of the world by the happenings in the Union of South Africa":

1. Recognised the situation in South Africa as leading "to international friction and if continued might endanger international peace and security"

2. Deplored "the loss of life of so many Africans"
3. Deplored "the policies and actions of the Government of South Africa"
4. Called upon the South African government "to abandon its policies of apartheid and racial discrimination"
5. Requested the Secretary-General "to make such arrangements as would adequately help in upholding the principles of the Charter and to report to the Security Council whenever necessary and appropriate"[24]

This resolution was, as the representative of India noted, "a historic decision." Speaking with one voice was a huge step in itself: "We are sure that the resolution will help to improve the situation in South Africa. It is certainly not going to make it worse." There would be no intervention, no sanctions, no practical steps for the moment, but the world had spoken with one voice in the UN and in doing so framed the arguments and the narrative that would mobilise and underpin the anti-apartheid struggle as it spread from the African and Asian nations to Europe, the USA, South America, and the countries of the White Commonwealth. At the end of March, for example, the British Boycott Movement renamed itself the Anti-Apartheid Movement "because of this understanding that the massacres at Sharpeville and Langa drew such widespread expressions of outrage and protest. Public opinion is wholly convinced of these facts." In the Netherlands, the South African embassy in The Hague was splashed with the slogan *Moordenaars* (murderers) and people marched through the streets of Amsterdam carrying banners proclaiming, "One race: man!," and "Human rights also in South Africa." In Sweden the immediate implementation of a widespread boycott of South African goods meant that

> hundreds of thousands of Swedes daily, for two months, in every contact with a grocery store, can not refrain from reflecting on the barbarism of race oppression. ... Making the trivial choice of dried or fresh fruit, of grapes, it is today impossible to refrain from reflecting on where the fruit has come from. A South African Brand consciously or unconsciously associated to images in newspapers and TV of coloured people who ... are met by murderous bullets from the weapons of white men of power.

In the United States, the American Committee on Africa, which had worked behind the scenes with the Security Council, organised an "Emergency Action Conference on South Africa" with the baseball player Jackie Robinson in the chair, and called on Americans to boycott South African products, stop private investment until South Africa "decides to honor the U.N. Declaration of Human Rights," and cease all cultural and sporting contacts including pressuring the International Olympic Committee to expel South Africa from the 1960 and 1964 Olympic Games. And in New Zealand, while the all-White "All Black" rugby team on tour in South Africa – the host country had insisted as always that the visiting rugby team exclude Māoris and Pacific Islanders just as the South Africans limited their team on political grounds to "Whites only" – was being treated to a lavish lunch by the Vereeniging Town Council, opposition to sporting tours was growing and no future New Zealand team would exclude players on the basis of colour.[25]

Though the number of independent African states was still small (seven only at the time of the debate) that was going to change very soon. In 1960 alone, another 16 African countries would gain independence and become members of the UN – Cameroun, Central African Republic, Chad, Congo (Brazzaville), Congo (Leopoldville), Dahomey, Gabon, Ivory Coast, Malagasy Republic, Mali, Niger, Nigeria, Senegal, Somalia, Togo, and Upper Volta. And for the moment, the session of Africa brought together all the countries of the continent in a shared feeling of unity. The representative from Guinea expressed this feeling most eloquently and in words that Robert Sobukwe and his followers like Nyakane Tsolo would have recognised and affirmed:

> For the wheel of history is turning. ... No coalition of colonialist interests, no force, no oppression, will any longer be able to stop our brothers, in South Africa or in any part of Africa, whether in North Africa, Central Africa, or South Africa. Africa will belong to the Africans.

While Robert Sobukwe would not have heard or read these words – he was arrested on 30 March and would spend the rest of his life in some form of prison or police detention – and nor would the people in Sharpeville ever hear them either, they too would have recognised the sentiments and appreciated the support of their fellow Africans, including the expression of "deepest sympathy of the Ethiopian people to the widows, widowers, and orphans of Africans massacred during the recent mass killing in South Africa." The PAC pamphlets distributed by Sobukwe and his supporters during the weekend before 21 March 1960, inspired by the example of Kwame Nkrumah and Ghana, had informed the residents of Sharpeville, "What is needed is UNITY and SACRIFICE. In 1960 we take our first step, in 1963 our last, towards freedom and independence."

What they would not have learned about at the time was the way in which Sharpeville, especially in the way it was discussed at the UN in the immediate aftermath of the massacre, had inspired African unity across the continent, and unity against apartheid and racial discrimination around the world. Nehru spoke to them even if they could not hear his words:

> Here is Africa at the present moment, proud and defiant after long centuries of suppression. ... On the other side, there is a picture of people in South Africa who are practically prisoners. ... This kind of culmination of all these events leads to certain conclusions in the minds of people that this is not an end of the episode but the prelude to the future.[26]

But could that "fitting" of the local story into the international struggle against racial discrimination and colonialism take place without the original storytellers themselves? Whose story was it? Who would tell it? Should we assume, as have so many scholars of South Africa, that because the ANC and PAC were banned two weeks after the massacre (on 7 April) that political debate about South Africa largely moved overseas for the rest of the 1960s? To answer those questions, we need to listen again to the people of Sharpeville.[27]

"Listen to My Feelings"

The reason why we can know so much about what happened on 21 March 1960, hour by hour, minute by minute, street by street, over 60 years after the massacre, is because Sharpeville residents did not hesitate to tell in public, in a straightforward manner, in detail, under oath, cross-examined, and subject to arrest if the police did not like their testimony what they saw happen and what happened to them on that day. As noted earlier, at least a hundred of the injured told their stories to Reeves and his representatives from their hospital beds. All the people the police could find and interrogate in the immediate aftermath of the massacre, Sharpeville and Bophelong and Evaton residents, as well as reporters such as Ronnie Manyosi and Lewis Nkosi, gave statements which remain to the present day in the Police Archive in downtown Pretoria. Nyakane's "deposition" (he would later refer to it as a forced interrogation) is neatly annotated, timed, and dated, 4:45 pm, 21 March 1960.

Over 70 residents of Sharpeville gave extensive testimony – days and weeks of detailed accounts of what they had seen and experienced on 21 March 1960 – to the Commission of Enquiry and to the *Regina vs. Monyake and Others* trial. The Commission hearings extended over almost three months (April, May, June 1960); the trial heard daily evidence for eight months (the end of September 1960 to mid-May 1961). Some of these witnesses were PAC members, but most were not; they were young and old, female and male, labourers and school headmasters, reverends and mechanics, and they came from every neighbourhood of Sharpeville. Lucas Mosheledi spoke for many when he said to the Commission, "I have come here to explain what I know about the happenings in Sharpeville." And he had encouraged others to testify, everyone, not just PAC: "We wanted grown-up people, most probably older than myself [Mosheledi was 21], that could come and tell the Court whatever they had to tell." Mosheledi's testimony, like all of that given by the Sharpeville residents, was subjected to cross-examination by prosecutors representing the police and detailed verbatim in the over 6,000 pages of Commission and trial records (which have been available on microfilm to researchers since the mid-1960s, but largely unread). And these testimonies were heard by hundreds, perhaps thousands, of Sharpeville residents, who filled every public space day after day in the Commission hearings and in the Monyake trial since nearly all the evidence, other than that transcribed beside hospital beds in Baragwanath, was presented in the Vereeniging magistrate's courtroom.[28]

The Sharpeville residents spoke even at risk of arrest. When the Commission began its hearings in April 1960, all in attendance were officially informed by the attorney representing the police and the state, P. S. Claassen (normally attorney general of the Free State), that the secretary of justice with instructions from the minister of justice, Erasmus, guaranteed "[t]hat no statement made by any Witness will be used against him at any criminal trial. The Attorney-General will not prosecute."[29]

But the police did not abide by that official declaration. When Lecheal Musibi, the school headmaster who had been biking to a pupil's home to get a key to his school's bookroom when he was shot by the police on 21 March, testified in May 1960 to the Commission about police "fabrication of evidence" and a report of what he said appeared on the front pages of English and Afrikaans language newspapers, he was arrested and sent to Boksburg Prison. That arrest didn't stop him from giving the same testimony about police falsification of evidence and collusion in telling their own stories when he was one of the accused at the *Regina vs. Monyake and Others* trial months later, a trial at which the judge dismissed all charges against him.[30]

Another person who was arrested after he testified, Peter Molefi, had only come forward because he was encouraged to do so by the attorney presenting the police case, Claassen. During the three months of the Commission's work, Claassen stayed at the best hotel in Vereeniging, the Riviera, just down the road from African Cables, on the Vaal River (alongside Isaac Lewis' old home, now a clubhouse for a golf course) and still open for business today. During his stay, Claassen got into conversation with the hotel's wine steward, Peter Molefi, about what had happened on 21 March, and because of these conversations, he encouraged Molefi to testify.

> Oh yes, he [Claassen] knew of [my knowledge of 21 March] because he stays where I work and we have spoken about it and he knew it perfectly well ... what he said to me is if I give evidence on what I know nothing will be done to me.

When Molefi appeared before the Commission to testify, even Judge Wessels recognised him:

> Of all the Bantus who have come to Court I think you are the only one that I know because you are a waiter at the Riviera Hotel, the Wine Steward? ... I also have the impression that you are an intelligent person ... statements which you make here in the course of your evidence, won't be used as a basis of prosecution, or for action against you. It won't be used as a ground for detention under the Emergency Regulations. Do you understand that position? – I thank you, my Lord, I do.

Though Claassen did indeed consider Molefi's testimony introduced "new and important evidence," evidence that Wessels in turn believed over some of the stories told to him by the police, neither could fulfil their personal promises to Molefi nor the guarantee of the minister of justice. "It was just a few hours after the Judge had left that I [Peter Molefi] was then arrested. I was arrested by native detectives." Judge Wessels when told of the arrests simply said, "I don't know that there is anything one can do about it." More than a year later, after spending every weekday in court, Molefi heard the judge in the *Regina vs. Monyake* case in June 1961 pronounce him "not guilty."[31]

We relied on Musibi's and Molefi's testimonies and that of their fellow Sharpeville residents to tell the story of 21 March in detail in Chapters 5 and 6. We cross-checked their testimony against that of the police, White and African officers and policemen alike, to ensure that the story that we told in their words (including those of the police) accorded as closely as we could determine with a factual and accurate account of the events of that day.

But what we did not focus on in reconstructing a narrative of 21 March were the feelings of the Sharpeville residents and that we turn to now because the feelings expressed, the ways in which the stories were told, resonated worldwide in the anti-apartheid campaigns in the 1960s and after and have kept the memories alive for the community to the present even as the storytellers themselves have been overlooked.

Reverend Robert Maja (the man sitting drinking tea on a fellow minister's porch who heard the shooting and ran to help people and gave them water and gave solace to the dead and dying and injured and spoke at the funerals) drew attention to this aspect of the testimonies when in response to what he considered yet another repetitive question about why people had gathered at the police station he replied, "I would like you to listen to my feelings first." What Maja was expressing was the feeling of perplexity held by all of Sharpeville's residents – the same feeling expressed in the 18 testimonies discussed earlier and which remains the main question of Sharpeville residents to the present day – why shoot? "The whole Sharpeville village is surprised, only to say in regard to how they feel about it – they are all surprised as to how the shooting took place; they don't know why." Why was there a police bullet in a friend's house well to the west of the police station? "You have to come across many streets before you get to that house." Why were innocent people shot? He knew of an instance "where a wife told me that her husband while lying on the lawn reading a book at his house, was shot in the foot or in the leg." Why? And as he spoke, Maja asked the audience in the courtroom to write down his testimony so that they would have a record of it in the Sharpeville community. Petrus Tom, 25 years later, wrote of hearing "a priest from the Presbyterian Church" give evidence and how, despite pressure "to agree that people were stoning the police," "he denied it."[32]

The Sharpeville residents were also affronted by the lack of respect shown to them by the police – much as Molefi had been when he was slapped in the face by Spengler – especially by police lies about evidence: about the crowd having thrown stones at them, about the crowd being armed, about the crowd having rushed into the police yard pushing over the wire fence as they rushed to attack like a crazed "mob" (in the words of Pienaar, "The mob was in a frenzied state and I feared an attack on the Police Station at any moment. ... I have had about 36 years of service ... and I have dealt with many mobs, and I know what the psychology of a mob is; they have no conscience, are capable of any rash act").

All of this was disproved by other evidence, by that of African policemen who themselves testified that there were no stones inside the police yard, by the photographs of Warwick Robinson taken immediately after the shooting that showed no weapons in the street among the bodies, that showed the fence still standing at a 90-degree angle, by the fact that if the crowd had rushed in as claimed by White policemen who testified they had to shoot to save their own lives, where were the bodies that should have been in the police yard, or at least lying on the sidewalk on the western side of the police station when in fact the closest bodies were in the middle of the no-name street where people had fallen as they were shot?[33]

But objective proof didn't stop lies being repeated – the same ones disproved at the Commission hearing were repeated by police witnesses at the subsequent Monyake trial – and that level of disrespect was what most angered people like Maja, who when asked about the crowd being armed with sticks said, "I am not speaking in terms of what might have been; but I am saying that when I handled those people with my own hands I did not see any sticks or any stones"; like Benedict Griffiths who when asked yet again whether he saw any stones thrown said, "Not a single one," and when asked again if the crowd had ever expressed any annoyance with the police replied in exasperation, "Niks! Niks!" (Nothing! Nothing!). Elias Lidia, the young fashion designer who went from being a political agnostic to a firm believer in Nyakane Tsolo and the PAC on 21 March, testified that the "evidence" presented by the police to prove that people were armed on Sunday night, and Monday morning, and Monday afternoon all consisted of exactly the same bucket of assorted "weapons" that the police claimed to have picked up on the no-name street but had in fact been taken in a subsequent raid on Sharpeville homes (including his house when they took his journals and book manuscript and never returned them) – normal personal items and household implements such as umbrellas, walking sticks, axes for cutting wood for home cooking. Meticulous in his facts as ever, he testified,

> I can even explain where they got those sticks. On the 8th April, on a Friday, between 2 and 4 o'clock, there was a very great raid in Sharpeville, from house to house, collecting hatchets, sticks and other implements. If they ever exhibited anything of that sort, it should be nothing else but that.

When the police planted a knife on one supposed suspect, the young man Edward Moloto who had walked up to the police right after the shooting and challenged them – "Look boss, how the people die; what did they do? Nothing" – and whose arrest was personally ordered by Pienaar, the case against him fell apart in court in the face of the testimony of Sharpeville witnesses. And again and again, the Sharpeville residents (including Lidia, and Maja, and Nyakane Tsolo, and others) challenged the Commission and the Court to allow them to identify the policemen whose actions they described in detail but whose names they did not know so that they could prove their stories. Neither the Commission nor the Court ever allowed them that opportunity, to their endless frustration.[34]

Some of the witnesses expressed their feelings symbolically, through their dress, as well as in their testimony. When Abraham Khaole testified at the Commission hearing, he wore the same jacket he had worn when shot by the police on 21 March, and he showed Judge Wessels the bullet hole in the back. Anna Lethege, the woman with rheumatic fever who was shot in the back of her thigh as she returned home after finding the fish and chips shop closed, wore exactly the same clothes to court that she had worn the day of the shooting and described her outfit in loving detail for the judge, whom she must have thought would not otherwise pay attention to her careful choice of items:

> I was wearing a colourful skirt. The whole colour was sort of pink-like and it had small flowers decorating it ... and a Basuthu hat, and a blouse ... with a white background colour, and with blue spots on it.

Her hat had been knocked off when she was shot, but she had picked it up and wore it a year later to the court hearing when she had painted it blue because she liked the colour. The details mattered because police witnesses had identified her on the basis of being the woman they claimed to have seen on 21 March wearing a red "*doek*" (headcovering) and a blue dress and who had thrown stones and called out to them in Afrikaans "*Vandag sal die blood loop*" (Today the blood will run). Lethege was forceful in denying their testimonies. "That is not so. In what language did I say those words if I did say them?" She had already testified that she did not speak Afrikaans.[35]

Peter Molefi too wore the same clothes to the Commission and to the Court that he had worn on the day of the shooting, brown trousers, brown shoes, a white shirt, and, especially, his red wine steward's waistcoat with black lining from which Spengler had torn a button when he seized him and slapped him and had him dragged into the police station. Molefi wanted the shirt (also torn) and waistcoat repaired, and he wanted the Basotho hat returned to him that had been knocked off his head by the SB men. He was offended at his treatment, and he was insistent. He testified to that at the Commission and then, after being arrested for that testimony, repeated it again before the court hearing months later.[36]

Thomas More and Nyakane Tsolo in their cross-examination of witnesses against them at their trial paid attention to language and how it was used in the court. They couldn't do anything about the speech of policemen like Constable Johannes Petrus Mostert van Zyl, who throughout all his testimony used the disparaging term "*kaffir*" without challenge from the Court whenever referring to Africans (even as the official written transcript was edited to make it seem as though he had used the word "*bantu*"), but they did insist on precision when it came to describing themselves and their own speech. Thomas More, for example, though described by the judge as a "delivery boy," identified himself as a "delivery man." And when Nyakane Tsolo heard a court translator using the word "*bantu*" to describe the text of the PAC pamphlets distributed in Sharpeville before Monday the 21st, he objected and cross-examined the translator, Daniel Kokozela January.

Tsolo: I want you to translate that word for me, i.e. the word "*Bantu*" in Zulu as it appears there.
Tsolo: Now you have translated which word by the word *Bantu*?
January: I have translated the word "*kumuntu ontsundu*" ... as "*Bantu*." I could not say "African."
Tsolo: Is it not true then that the meaning of the word "*Bantu*" in the true sense of it ... when the Zulus say "*Bantu*" it means "we people"? ... My objection or my quarrel is with the word "*Bantu*," because I do not believe that the P.A.C. can refer to the African people as Bantus. ... That is not then what was being said by the original pamphlet.[37]

The judge in the Monyake case clearly heard the words of Tsolo and his fellow PAC members because when he rendered judgement, Regional Magistrate P. M. O'Brien noted in his final report that all the PAC members "refused to plead on the basis that the laws, the subject of the charges, were formulated at a time when Bantu (or 'Africans' as they called themselves) were not represented in Parliament."[38]

And even as all the Sharpeville witnesses sought to adhere strictly to a factual description of what happened in their testimonies (Tsolo, for example, when asked his opinion of passes replied "If the Court wants this platform to be turned into a political platform, then I will but that is not what I came here for"), Elias Lidia, the young man who had started out on 21 March apolitical but who by the end of the day had become a committed believer in Nyakane Tsolo and the PAC, was ready to reach into his feelings and suggest a cause of the police massacre when directly asked his opinion by Judge Wessels.

THE CHAIRMAN: Did you see anything or hear anything that could have led to the shooting?
ELIAS LIDIA: In my own opinion?
THE CHAIRMAN: Yes?

ELIAS LIDIA:	Yes; I think I can. What I may say, might not be suitable to your ears, but I think I must say it, if I would be allowed.
THE CHAIRMAN:	I have told you, you are free to say anything you want to say?
ELIAS LIDIA:	Well, as far as I could judge the shooting was prejudice on a political basis, supported by hatred, *baasskap* and discrimination ...
THE CHAIRMAN:	Is that your view of perhaps underlying causes?
ELIAS LIDIA:	Yes.
THE CHAIRMAN:	... do I understand that you were of the opinion that the Police fired at the crowd just because they had a grievance against the Bantus?
ELIAS LIDIA:	Yes.
THE CHAIRMAN:	Deliberately?
ELIAS LIDIA:	Deliberately, yes.[39]

That the testimonies of the Sharpeville witnesses were deemed overwhelmingly honest and convincing at the time when subjected to cross-examination, even as details would be contested, was best demonstrated by the findings of Magistrate O'Brien in the *Regina vs. Monyake and Others* case. Of the 76 Sharpeville residents charged with public violence and incitement, he dismissed the cases against or found not guilty 70 of the 76 accused, including Musibi, Molefi, Lethege, and Moloto.

And hidden in plain sight in Judge Wessels' 200-page final report of the "*Commission of Enquiry into the Occurrences at Sharpeville*" is a sentence which suggests that he too believed the testimony of the Sharpeville witnesses, even if in his final judgement he found himself limited by his terms of reference – "namely, to collect evidence in connection with the occurrences concerned and in the light thereof to report on my findings of fact ... not ... to report on the liability of persons for their acts and omissions." Still, here is his "what if" feeling.

> Major van Zyl would have been in a ridiculous position if his superiors had found on their arrival that there was only a crowd of about 3,000 to 5,000 demonstrators and that, on top of it, they were still in a happy mood.[40]

Perhaps because of the power of the Sharpeville testimonies, perhaps because of the international outrage engendered by the international community, Verwoerd's government, though it had first passed legislation only a week after Magistrate O'Brien had found the great majority of Sharpeville accused not guilty to indemnify retroactively to 21 March 1960 every policeman, every government official right up to the president (Verwoerd) himself, from civil or criminal suit for any action they might have taken on that day, proceeded in late 1961 to allow claims for compensation to be pursued by individuals. It is because of these claims, filed by several hundred Sharpeville individuals, that we have the statements that each of them made to the police to substantiate their case for recompense. These are the claims which we used primarily in Chapter 7 (though some we relied on for Chapters 5 and 6 also), to describe the losses these people had suffered, losses of husbands and wives, of mothers and fathers, of sons and daughters. And of their enormous sense of anguish. All of these statements were made under oath, with each individual swearing to tell the truth and attesting to that statement with their signature (that of 10-year-old Charles Ramahali is particularly impressive because of his meticulous cursive) or, in many cases of people who could not read and write, their fingerprint. Most of the claims were rejected by the State, and when compensation was paid in a few cases, it was of tiny sums, sums that two survivors, brothers, David Ramohoase and Lebitsa Solomon Ramohoase, described in their 1996 testimony to the Truth and Reconciliation Commission as less than the equivalent of a hundred rand each in the form of a check, which they had to take to a bank to be cashed.

But what matters for our analysis here is that the stories that were told in 1960, and in 1961, and in 1962, always under oath, and which have been told ever since, by survivors or by their family members, have been consistent. When we have compared the interviews that we did in 2018, 2019, and 2022 with the statements given originally 60 years ago, the accounts always match up detail for detail, loss for loss, pain for pain. What happened on 21 March 1960 has left an indelible mark on the community.[41]

"Apartheid Is a Crime against Humanity"

While the words of specific Sharpeville witnesses are not remembered outside the community, and only the event is commemorated nationwide in South Africa and worldwide, the stories told by Musibi and Lidia, Lethege and Molefi, More and Tsolo did propel the world to action. Because of the experiences of Sharpeville people, their problems with passes, the way they were treated by the police, the way in which apartheid enforced White supremacy through the mechanisms of an endless state of emergency with economic privilege and democracy for a White minority and economic oppression and a police state for a Black majority their stories became embedded in the narratives of the anti-apartheid movement worldwide.

Two African journalists who had witnessed the Sharpeville massacre on 21 March and helped place the injured in ambulances reached a worldwide audience with their own retellings, not of the details of what had happened that day but in ways that as writers they got to the heart of the matter for each of them. Nat Nakasa published a lengthy article in the *New York Times* on 24 September 1961 headlined "The Human Meaning of Apartheid." The article begins with instructions on how to pronounce the word apartheid, "a-PART-hate," a careful sounding out which supporters of the South African government would for years claim was a mispronunciation by outside critics, yet it was the very same way that Verwoerd pronounced the word. Nakasa recreated a conversation between an African and a policeman which every resident in Sharpeville would have recognised:

> "*Hey wena, kom hier*" [Hey you, come here!] a policeman barks. The man stops dead on the pavement. His body goes numb as he sees the brown uniform and police boots shining. "*Waar is jou pass?*" [Where is your pass?] the policeman asks. ... "I left it at home, *baas*, in my other jacket" ... "*Jy lieg*, you're lying," and then the man is arrested, and convicted of "failing to produce" his pass, and fined and if he cannot pay the fine "he may be handed to a farmer, who will pay nine pence a day for the man's labor. In this respect the pass system is the cornerstone of apartheid. While it compels the required number of Africans to accept employment in the cities, it also helps in channeling of African labor to the white farms where wages are poorest."

Quoting from a government definition of apartheid – "It stands for the separate, orderly and systematic development of the Europeans and *Bantu*, each in his own respective, geopolitical homeland, each according to his own innate qualities, characteristics and disposition" – Nakasa "couldn't help asking myself: Is this why more than sixty Africans were shot dead during an anti-apartheid demonstration in Sharpeville last year?"[42]

And what of the police themselves, what motivated them, what explained their actions shooting point blank into the Sharpeville crowd? Lewis Nkosi, who had been interrogated by the police right after the Sharpeville massacre that he had witnessed, reimagined himself into the minds of those policemen he had encountered that day in a play he wrote for a London audience in 1963.

> *The waiting room [of the Johannesburg City Hall] has been temporarily turned into the headquarters of the South African police who are mobilized to watch the African meeting [outside] in progress. The first clue we have of this is a police hat, a machine-gun, and a revolver in a waist-strap, all lying on the bench in the empty room.*
> "There are shouts of the slogans: 'AFRICA!', 'FREEDOM IN OUR LIFETIME'" ...
> JAN [*a young policeman weighted down by a heavy machine gun*]. They drive me out of my mind! Yelling "Freedom!" "Freedom!" "Freedom!" ...
> JAN: [*nervously*]. How many of us are there?
> PIET: [*an older policeman*]. Two hundred men at the ready to shoot down any bloody-son-of-a-bitchin'-kaffir who starts trouble!
> JAN: You think that number is enough?

PIET: We are armed and the kaffirs haven't got guns …
PIET: [*nibbling at his bone again*]. Hey, Janie, you ever shot a Native before? [*Makes panning movement with the bone.*] Ta-ta-ta-ta-ta-ta-ta!
JAN [*grinning*]. Yah, it's kind-a-funny, you know, like shooting wild duck!
PIET: The first time is not easy though!
JAN: Telling me! The first time I shot a Native dead I got sick! Just stood there and threw up. His skull was ripped apart by the machine-gun! I stood over him and got sick all over his body!
PIET: Ugh, man! Got sick over him! It's not enough you rip open a kaffir's skull! You must get sick over him too!
JAN: [*pacing the floor.*] When I got home I still got sick! …
PIET: … I'm academic.
JAN: What does that mean?
PIET: Means a bloke who is a realist. No emotion. I can shoot any number of Natives without getting sick! No emotions! I shoot them academically.
JAN: Nice word … Academically.
PIET: I got it from a sergeant down at Marshall Square. He used to say, when you get into a fight with Natives don't let your feelings run away with you. Be academic. Shoot them down academically …
PIET: … Once when we were on patrol in Sophiatown THEY came! I tell you THEY came! It was night. Dark. And their shadows were darker than the dark itself. I was separated from the others! You understand that! Alone! You ever been alone with Death staring you in the eye. Well, I was! I started firing from my sten-gun. But those Natives kept on coming! It was like eternity and the dark shadows kept coming like the waves of eternal night. … Ah, but a sten-gun spits death much stronger than a thousand Natives! When it was all over I couldn't stop shooting. I was no longer in control of my fingers. The sten-gun kept barking in the dark … against shadows … anything that moved. I began to think that even if my son had appeared there I would have kept shooting away … [*He calms down at the thought.*] I don't know what I am saying …
GAMA [*a young African law student speaking to a young White friend*]:
Did you see the bodies at Sharpeville? Did you see the shoulders of children ripped off by machine-gun fire! Did you see anything! Ask Jojozi [Nkosi] to show you the pictures he and the press boys took of the whole show! A butchery, I tell you![43]

Three years after his play opened, Nkosi was one of seven "experts on apartheid" invited to prepare a background paper and attend the two-week long "Seminar on Apartheid" organised by the UN Division of Human Rights in co-operation with the government of Brazil and hosted in Brasilia, 23 August to 4 September 1966.

In the intervening years between the Sharpeville massacre and the Seminar on Apartheid, popular opposition to apartheid had grown throughout the world. More African states had become independent. Another 15 between 1961 and 1966 added to the 16 that had joined in 1960. And their voices were heard at the UN where in 1963 the General Assembly created a "Special Committee on the Policies of Apartheid" (later renamed in 1974 the "Special Committee Against Apartheid"), and the Security Council called for "all States to cease the sale and shipment of arms, ammunition and military vehicles to South Africa," the first time an arms embargo had ever been recommended against a member state (it was not mandatory until 1977). But calls for an economic boycott by the African and Asian members could not garner support from the Security Council comprised as it was of members that continued to trade with and invest heavily in South Africa, especially France, the United Kingdom, and the United States. In the same year, the International Olympic Committee gave South Africa a choice: end racial discrimination in the selection of its international teams or be excluded from the 1964 Tokyo Olympics. South Africa chose racial discrimination and exclusion. Financial support for pursuing Sharpeville legal claims against the South African government came from the International Defence and Aid Fund in England, supported in turn by considerable donations from the Dutch and Swedish governments. In December 1965, the UN adopted the "Convention on the Elimination of All Forms of Racial Discrimination," with apartheid being the only form of such discrimination that was specifically condemned as violating the Charter of the United Nations and the Universal Declaration of Human Rights.[44]

But what was missing from all these steps being taken were practical measures that would have a direct impact on the South African government. Those measures – arms and economic and sporting and cultural boycotts enforced through mandatory sanctions – were what the newly independent African states wanted to see end colonialism in South Africa, just as colonialism had ended in most of the rest of the continent (with the exception of Portuguese ruled areas of southern Africa and the White settler state of Southern Rhodesia).

The Seminar on Apartheid was an attempt to jump-start the process of mandatory sanctions. Twenty-nine countries sent formal representatives; four countries sent observers; there were also representatives of the Organization of African Unity, the League of Arab States, the International Labour Office, and UNESCO, as well as numerous other organisations such as the All-African Women's Conference, the Co-Ordinating Board of Jewish Organizations, and the Young Christian Workers. Over 300 people in all, with the Seminar chaired by the Swedish representative: "all felt that the seminar should search for new ways in which more effective and urgent pressure could be mounted against apartheid.'"

While not present, the people of Sharpeville and their stories and their suffering permeated the discussions. They would have heard the founder of the International Aid and Defence Fund, the reverend John Collins, speak of the critical financial support given by his organisation, working in collaboration with Bishop Ambrose Reeves and his 100 survivor statements and supported by the contributions of the Dutch and the Swedes to pursue compensation for the Sharpeville victims. They (especially Elias Lidia) would have relished Lewis Nkosi's reference to *baasskap* (literally boss-ship, in fact White supremacy) as the practice and policy of apartheid South Africa. They would have found comfort in the seminar participants' "unanimous ... condemnation of the policies of apartheid ... a racial tyranny ... [that] constitutes a flagrant denial of fundamental human rights." And they would have appreciated the unanimous recommendation that there be "an annual commemoration of the massacre of Sharpeville, during which funds can be collected in support of the anti-apartheid movement."[45]

Later that year, the UN adopted two major resolutions with regard to South Africa and apartheid. The first, adopted on 26 October 1966, 2142 (XII), reaffirmed the 1965 International Convention on the Elimination of All Forms of Racial Discrimination and its determination "that racial discrimination and apartheid are denials of human rights and fundamental freedoms and of justice and are offences against human dignity," and added that "21 March [should be adopted worldwide] as [the] International Day for the Elimination of Racial Discrimination." The second resolution, adopted 16 December 1966, 2202 (XXI), took "note with satisfaction of the report of the Seminar on Apartheid, Brasilia 23 August to 4 September 1966," and as its first action "*Condemns* the policies of apartheid practiced by the Government of South Africa as a crime against humanity." For African and Asian and South American states, such a description of apartheid as a crime against humanity was not an abstract concept. They had all suffered under the colonial policies of White supremacy, and they knew exactly what was at stake for the people of Sharpeville. After condemning the crime, they deplored

> the attitude of the main trading partners of South Africa, including three permanent members of the Security Council ... by increasing their collaboration with the Government of South Africa ... [which had] encouraged the latter to persist in its racial policies.

And they called for action against "the activities of foreign economic interests in southern Africa which impeded the efforts to eliminate apartheid, racial discrimination and colonialism in the region." The changes in the attitudes of the main trading partners – France, the United Kingdom, and the United States – would not come for another two decades, and the divestment campaign would also not take on steam until the mid-1980s, but the moral condemnation of apartheid was universal, and Sharpeville had started the processes, internal and external, that would bring an end to it in theory and practice.[46]

Notes

1 Tsolo testimony, "*Commission of Enquiry into the Occurrences at Sharpeville (and other places) on the 21st of March 1960,*" (hereafter Commission) 2500–2501.
2 Frantz Fanon, *Les damnés de la terre* (*The Wretched of the Earth*, 1961, 1963). "*Les meurtres de Sharpeville ont secoué l'opinion pendant des mois. Dans les journaux, sur les antennes, dans les conversations privées, Sharpeville est devenu un symbole. C'est à travers Sharpeville que des hommes et des femmes ont abordé le problème de l'apartheid en Afrique du Sud.*" Trevor Richards, *Dancing On Our Bones: New Zealand, South Africa, Rugby and Racism* (Bridget Williams Books: Wellington 1999), 23. "The massacre at Sharpeville achieved what 12 years of repressive legislation and the peaceful protest it inspired could not; it made the politics of apartheid the major story of the world's newspapers for several weeks. The events at Sharpeville introduced the world to the reality of apartheid."
3 Peder Gowenius speaking in 2018 about first going to South Africa with his wife Ulle in 1961 and soon after establishing a weaving center at Rorke's Drift, https://www.youtube.com/watch?v=ozKMa4xJGNY.
4 For a partial list of Africans killed by the police in the 1950s, see Max Coleman (ed.), *A Crime Against Humanity: Analysing the Repression of the Apartheid State* (Johannesburg: Human Rights Committee of South Africa, 1998), 262.
5 The police story was told by Verwoerd and members of his government in Parliament and through press releases, as well as narrated by police witnesses appearing before the Commission of Enquiry and the *Regina vs. Monyake and Others* trial (Case No. R. 58/1960 in the Court of the Magistrate of the Regional Division of South Transvaal, held at Vereeniging: The State against Johannes Monyake and others, hereafter Court). Verwoerd, *Hansard*, 21 March 1960, columns 3743, 3759, 3760, 3821. In his official release on 5 April of the number of Africans injured, Minister of Justice Erasmus claimed that the police had "used loudspeakers to instruct the crowd to disperse before resorting to the use of firearms." He also severely undercounted the number of police present at the Sharpeville police station at 137 men when in fact we know from more complete details the actual number in the police station grounds and in Zwane street was closer to 300 men, *Hansard*, 5 April 1960, columns 4837 and 4838. See also *RDM*, 6 April 1960. The telling and re-telling of the police story can be traced through the pages of *Nongqai*, the official news magazine of the South African police, with the latest editions subtitled "Your Security History Magazine Without Malice." The journal is available and searchable online on a site maintained by a former Afrikaner policeman, Hennie Heymans: https://issuu.com/hennieheymans. There is also an associated YouTube channel, https://www.youtube.com/channel/UC06v7Y9Niw37x0PqK6EU6LQ/featured. One of the core elements of the police story as presented by the government and repeated by some of the White police witnesses appearing before the Commission of Enquiry and at the *Regina vs. Monyake and Others* trial – none of the African police witnesses attested in support – was that some unidentified African in the crowd had fired first. No individual was ever identified at the time. In 2001,

however, Philip Frankel claimed (*An Ordinary Atrocity*, 43, 113–114, 118, 146, 171, 180) that he had learned of the identity of this individual from his police informants, and he named Geelbooi Mofokeng. Frankel sketched out an elaborate story whereby Geelbooi was an unemployed gangster who had been arrested and tortured by the police before the massacre, and seeking revenge, he had come to the police station on 21 March in a drunken state, pulled out a gun, and fired into the air, thereby precipitating the police firing in response. Frankel also claimed to have discovered an original list of the dead in the Police Archive containing Geelbooi Mofokeng's name and he published that list as Appendix 2C in his book (245–247) – "This last list has the merit of being the only one to include a 'Geelbooi' among the deceased" (151). In a review of Frankel's book, the prominent journalist Patrick Laurence suggested that this new account of Geelbooi Mofokeng and his actions finally provided a convincing explanation for what had always been unexplained – why did the police shoot? "Refracted through the prism of history, the shots from Geelbooi's pistol loom large as the final catalyst of the massacre. A constable, unnerved by the shots hears an officer shout '*skiet*!;' he shoots and his shot triggers a chain reaction and a tragedy." (*Financial Times*, 28 September 2001). Tom Lodge in his 2011 book (*Sharpeville*, 102, 105) repeats practically word for word Frankel's story of Geelbooi Mofokeng. In a footnote (# 98, p. 360) Lodge notes that "PAC veterans ... regard his story as the purest fantasy." They are right. The problem with all of this, unnoticed by any of these authors, was that Geelbooi Mofokeng gave testimony at the subsequent Commission of Enquiry and also lodged a formal claim for compensation. How could he have shot first and been killed when he was still alive afterward? Moreover, his claim for compensation, completed under oath, showed that he was employed at the time of the massacre; he was no *tstotsi* and in fact was the sole financial support of his widowed mother and four school age brothers and sisters. And in our own archival research we discovered, in both the Police Archive and the National Archive, the police list of the dead that Frankel modified. The original did not have Geelbooi Mofokeng's name on it, and the list published by Frankel substitutes (who did that we do not know) Mofokeng's name for that of an actual victim that day, Moketsi S. Mosia, who died from a bullet in the back that entered his chest and left lung. We reproduce the original police list as Document 1.

6 *The Times*, 22 March 1960; *New York Times*, 22 March 1960. An editorial in the *NYT* referred to "[t]he evil policy of apartheid" and wondered whether "South Africans think that the rest of the world will ignore such a massacre?" Håkan Thörn, *Anti-Apartheid and the Emergence of a Global Civil Society* (Palgrave Macmillan: Houndsmill, 2006), chapter 3, provides a useful survey of western media responses.

7 *Daily Mirror*, 22 March 1960. On 24 March, the *Daily Mirror* republished an enlarged section of Robinson's image overlaid with the text, "A section of the picture that shocked the world." It accompanied the reprinted photograph with an opinion piece by its political editor arguing, "South Africa is in the hands of a group of fanatical men who blindly believe that they can hold down the African majority – if necessary, by force," asking why the prime minister, Harold Macmillan, chose silence rather than repeating his warning of the winds of change, and concluding, "Must the humanity be left to the Americans, the Indians, the Labour Movement, and a bunch of young people in the sunshine in Trafalgar Square. Most of them were young. Some of them were white. Some were coloured. Some carried banners protesting against the massacre that occurred in a South African township three days ago. Those young people in the sunshine stood for the world's outraged conscience."

Sharpeville and the World   255

8   Reference to "political sensation," *The Times*, 24 March 1960; the *New York Times*, 27 March 1960, referred to the US statement as "a stunning blow" to South Africa; the language of the US statements and references to the speech by the Under Secretary of State, C. Douglas Dillon, is reported in the *New York Times*, 23 March 1960.
9   See the series of documents published in United Nations, *The United Nations and Apartheid, 1948–1994* (New York: Department of Public Information, United Nations, 1994), 221–243; "Final Communique of the Asian-African conference at Bandung, 24 April 1955," https://www.cvce.eu/en/obj/final_communique_of_the_asian_african_conference_of_bandung_24_april_1955-en-676237bd-72f7-471f-949a-88b6ae513585.html; Resolutions of the All African People's Conference, chrome-extension://efaidnbmnnnibpcajpcglclefindmkaj/https://www.jstor.org/stable/pdf/45313673.pdf?refreqid=excelsior%3Ab90621956a1ee4a7446e0c6d87b12260&ab_segments=&origin=.
10 *The United Nations and Apartheid, 1948–1994*, 223; Nehru quoted by the official representative of India at the UN Security Council meeting, on 30 March 1960. United Nations Security Council Official Records, 852nd Meeting, 30 March 1960: 17–18, https://digitallibrary.un.org/record/629458?ln=en. The UN records are available for download in English, French, Mandarin, Russian, and Spanish.
11 *The United Nations and Apartheid*, 244.
12 *New Age*, 24 March 1960. See also Chapter 6. All of the three officers were injured in the morning, none were hospitalized, and just one received some stitches for a slight head wound and immediately returned to work. See Wessels' report 70 and the testimony presented in the Monyake court case 820–821. The main Afrikaans newspaper, *Die Burger*, carried no photographs of dead or injured Africans, instead illustrating its coverage with "pictures of White women who were injured when car in which they were travelling near Langa was stoned and of White women armed with shotguns at Vanderbijlpark." Telegram, "African Riots," 22 March 1960, DO 35 10578 SAR 163/298/1, British Archives.
13 *Golden City Post*, 27 March 1960. The coverage in the newspaper also included extensive descriptions by Manyosi of the scene outside the police station, including noting that many had been shot in the back, and also reporting that the body of the man whose brain had been left lying in the street remained there for two hours before being taken away by the police.
14 *The World*, 26 March 1960; Bloke Modisane, *Blame Me on History* (E. P. Dutton: New York, 1963), 147-148.
15 Dikgang Moseneke, *My Own Liberator: A Memoir* (Picador Africa: Johannesburg, 2016), 51–52.
16 *Daily Mirror*, 25 March 1960; *Belfast Telegraph*, 25 March 1960. Reeves provided a fuller description of his actions in the days immediately after the shooting in his book, *Shooting at Sharpeville*: 47–56. He himself visited Baragwanath on the Tuesday after the shooting and kept returning each day that week. See also the *RDM*, 24 March 1960, for a description of the "seriously overcrowded" conditions at Baragwanath, "Scores of Black patients had to sleep in propped up chairs lining at least two corridors last night." The *RDM* was so irritated by the apparent exclusion of South African journalists from Reeves' press conference (he said it was not intended) that it added a "Footnote" to its own brief report of his presentation of "a really serious – and startling – allegation against the police ... [that] When the police raised their guns the crowd was taken completely by surprise." The *RDM* "footnote" reiterated the police story for its readers: "'Rand Daily Mail' reporters in all the trouble spots that day reported that the crowds were in an extremely ugly mood. Two 'Rand Daily Mail' cars were damaged by

stones and a reporter was injured," 25 March 1960. On conditions in Baragwanath and the attempts of the police to limit access to the patients (who included at least 30 women, and six children under the age of 14), see also *RDM*, 24 March 1960. The superintendent of Baragwanath, Dr. Isidore Frack, has recounted the difficult conditions at the hospital, including his own temporary suspension by apartheid authorities, in his autobiography, *Every Man Must Play a Part: Isidore Frack, The Story of a South African Doctor* (Purnell: Cape Town, 1970), 206–210.

17 UN Archives, Union of South Africa – Sharpeville Affidavits, 15/04/1960 https://search.archives.un.org/union-of-south-africa-sharpeville-affidavits; *New York Times*, 10 April 1960; *Birmingham Post*, 11 April 1960.

18 Adam Sakaone describes the SB man, Spengler, the same way as Griffiths, "At that stage one of the persons who had arrived in a car – a man in plain-clothes, well built with blond hair balding in front and a red face, arrested one of our leaders," Commission 3142.

19 *Golden City Post*, 27 March 1960.

20 For the exact contents of the state of emergency see the *Government Gazette Extraordinary*, No. 6405, dated 1 April 1960 but issued two days before. See also the *RDM*, 29, 30 and 31 March 1960.

21 *Time*, 11 April 1960.

22 For information on the continuing work stoppages after the 21 March police shooting, see the *RDM* issues of that week and the following week, as well as the *New York Times*, 24 March 1960. On the Johannesburg trial, see *The World*, 26 March 1960; Telegram 337 from Cape Town, 16 April 1960, DO 35 10578, British Archives. For the text of the talks given by "the Bantu Affairs Commissioner of Vereeniging and Vanderbijlpark" in October and November 1959, see "Self Government for the Bantu," NTS 4179 33/313(F) Part IV, SAB. Ferreira prevented the talk being given in Sharpeville. On pass law trials in Johannesburg and Pretoria in early April see the *RDM*, 9 and 15 April 1960.

23 The following discussion relies on the records of the United Nations, primarily materials that are available through their remarkable online digital library. These materials include transcripts of all the discussions of the Security Council – all material quoted comes from the 852 through 856th meetings – as well as video recordings of the sessions (see, for example, that of the 853rd meeting, https://www.unmultimedia.org/avlibrary/asset/2448/2448437/), as well as various ephemera such as the images of 3 x 5 cards noting that 3 nuns were sitting among the audience listening to the debate, chrome-extension://efaidnbmnnnibpcajpcglclefindmkaj/https://www.unmultimedia.org/avlibrary/uploads/2019/08/016-102.pdf.

24 The resolution is published in full in the UN's digital library, https://digitallibrary.un.org/record/112105?ln=en.

25 There is an excellent documentary archive of material on the British anti-apartheid movement, including the April 1960 "Programme of the Anti-Apartheid Committee" (quoted), https://www.aamarchives.org/history/1960s.html#click-here-for-documents-and-pictures-from-the-1960s. The contemporary Dutch references are from Barbara Henkes, "National Socialism, Colonialism and Anti-Fascist Memory Politics in Postwar Dutch-South African Exchanges," *South African Historical Journal* 74:1, (2022): 172–175. The Swedish reference, from a major daily Stockholm newspaper published on 3 April 1960, is cited in Thorn, *Anti-Apartheid*, 139. For the anti-apartheid struggle in Europe, see especially the remarkable collection of materials including posters held by the International Institute of Social History, https://iisg.amsterdam/en/collections/browsing/collection-guides/anti-apartheid-south-africa. For the United States, see the various publications of the American Committee on Africa held by *JSTOR*, https://www.jstor.org/site/struggles-for-freedom/southern-africa/

american-committee-on-africa/?so=old; as well as the African Activist Archive at Michigan State University, https://africanactivist.msu.edu/. On New Zealand, see Richard Thompson, "Rugby and Race Relations: A New Zealand Controversy," *The Journal of the Polynesian Society* 69:3, (1960): 285–287 (https://www.jstor.org/stable/20703837). The All Blacks did not tour South Africa again until 1970 when three Māori and Pacific Island players were allowed to enter the country as "Honorary Whites." For general studies of the origins and growth of the anti-apartheid movement see Tom Lodge, *Sharpeville: An Apartheid Massacre and Its Consequences* (Oxford University Press: Oxford, 2011), and the essays in the South African Democracy Education Trust, *The Road to Democracy in South Africa: Vol.3, Parts 1, 2, 3, International Solidarity* (University of South Africa: Pretoria, 2008 and 2018).

26 See the UN sources cited in footnote 10 for the sources of the quotations in this and the preceding paragraph.

27 The full text of the 1960 Unlawful Organizations Act can be found at https://en.wikisource.org/wiki/Unlawful_Organizations_Act,_1960.

28 Known by Michael Thekiso as Lucas Mosheledi, see Simon Mashelide testimony, Commission 2222, 2239. The Commission and Court materials are all digitized in their entirety and freely accessible online, https://idep.library.ucla.edu/sharpeville-massacre. Though Frankel (*An Ordinary Atrocity*, 190–199) claimed to have read the Commission of Enquiry testimonies, it seems his examination was cursory at best. The conscientious and extensive testimonies given by 40 Sharpeville residents to the Commission was reduced by Frankel to the following misleading summary: "Ultimately, the responses of Petrus and the other black witnesses were reduced to a monosyllabic 'ja' or 'nee baas." There is not a single "*nee baas*" in any of the Commission's voluminous records. But Frankel seems equally contemptuous of the Afrikaner SAP witnesses, referring at one point to them as "plain stupid," *An Ordinary Atrocity*, 196.

29 Claassen testimony, Commission 177.

30 See Musibi's testimony to the Commission, 1875ff, and to the Court 3074ff; and Kentridge's comments regarding his treatment and that of all others who testified, Kentridge, Commission 2252–2255.

31 See Molefi's testimony (including the comments of Claassen and Wessels), Commission 1756, 1759, 1775; Court 3182; Claassen's comment regarding the reliability of the evidence of Peter Molefi and Brown Thabe as compared with that of police witnesses, Commission 1811; and Wessel's comment on his inability to do anything with regard to the actions of the police, Commission 2014.

32 Maja testimony, Court 2363, 2364, 3002. For the fundamental question why, see also the testimonies of Simon Mashelide (Lucas Mosheledi), Commission 2239, "I am still asking that question, why did they [the police] fight?"; Moses Shabangu, Commission 1726, "I had no such thought" that the police would shoot, "I did not see what the cause was"; Matthew Mashiya, Commission 1740, "I am still putting that question to myself, as to why [the police fired]. I don't know to this day"; Joshua Motha, Court 2543, 2552, "there was not even a small thing [that justified the shooting]," "I did not see anything wrong done by the black people who were there, which could have caused the Europeans to kill." For Petrus Tom's recollection of hearing Maja's testimony, see the reprint of his 1985 autobiography in *The Story of One Tells the Struggle of All*, 120.

33 For the reference to "knowing the mob," see Pienaar's testimony, Commission 1330–1331.

34 Maja testimony, Court 3018; Griffiths testimony, Commission 1947, 1949; Lidia testimony, Commission 2320, 2335, 2336. The bucket of "weapons" – the same one used at the Commission hearings – is described in the Court transcript,

3346–3347. On Moloto see the testimonies of constables Prinsloo and Struwig, Court 1532, 1699, 1703. For statements by Sharpeville residents that they could identify policemen if given the chance to do so in a lineup see for example the testimonies of Simon Lofafa, Commission 1849; and Thaba, Commission 1799; as well as that of Labuschagne who noted that he was never asked to identify any of the policemen who had fired even though he could do so if given the opportunity. A police raid in Bophelong around the same time resulted in the confiscation from Sidwell Kaba of his copies of Alan Paton, *Cry the Beloved Country*, Booker T. Washiington, *Up From Slavery*, and copies of six PAC pamphlets and 40 single sheets with the words "Let's Forget – Lest we Forget," Kaba testimony, Commission 2580–2582.
35 Khaole testimony 1692; Lethege testimony, Court 3040–3041, 3047, 3048.
36 Molefi testimony, Commission 1751, 1753; Court 3176, 3177.
37 On the use of derogatory language by Constable van Zyl and others, see the cross examination by Advocate Unterhalter, Court 2244. More testimony, Court 2983, on insisting on being a "man," not a "boy," and for Tsolo's extended cross examination of January, see Court 2796–2800.
38 See page 2 of O'Brien's judgment, 22 June 1961, available online https://idep.library.ucla.edu/search#!/document/sharpevillemassacre:87.
39 Tsolo testimony, Commission 2498; Lidia testimony, Commission 2288, 2308.
40 Commission Report 2, 3, 134. Among his findings Wessels was not convinced by any of the police evidence that the crowd was armed (report 146ff), nor by any evidence that Tsolo and the PAC planned an attack on the police station (181).
41 For the full text of the Indemnity Act 61 of 1961, assented to on 28 June 1961, just over a week to the day that O'Brien had passed sentence, see https://en.wikipedia.org/wiki/Indemnity_Act,_1961. The TRC testimonies can be read as transcripts on the Department of Justice's website, https://www.justice.gov.za/trc/, and search for David Ramohoase, Lebitsa Solomon Ramohoase, and Konsatsama Elizabeth Mabona; or viewed and read on the website of the SABC. For David Ramohoase see https://sabctrc.saha.org.za/documents/hrvtrans/sebokeng/55901.htm; for Lebitsa Solomon Ramohoase see https://sabctrc.saha.org.za/documents/hrvtrans/sebokeng/55900.htm
42 *NYT*, 24 September 1961. For Verwoerd's pronunciation of apartheid see "Verwoerd Explains Apartheid," https://www.youtube.com/watch?v=vPCln9czoys.
43 Nkosi, *The Rhythm of Violence* (Oxford University Press: London, 1964), 1, 2, 5, 6, 14, 32. © Oxford University Press 1964. Reproduced with permission of the Licensor through PLSclear.
44 On the 1965 convention see especially Natan Lerner, *The U.N. Convention on the Elimination of All Forms of Racial Discrimination: A Commentary* (A.W. Suthoff; Leyden, 1970).
45 See the report of the Seminar, https://digitallibrary.un.org/record/849290?ln=en, esp. Nkosi, "Apartheid--Its Origins and Evolution," WP/Ex/5.
46 The UN resolutions, 2142 (XXI) and 2202 (XXI), can be found here, https://digitallibrary.un.org/record/203204?ln=en; and here: https://digitallibrary.un.org/record/203174?ln=en.ss.

Bibliography

Coleman, Max (ed.) *A Crime Against Humanity: Analysing the Repression of the Apartheid State*. Johannesburg: Human Rights Committee of South Africa, 1998.
Fanon. Frantz Fanon. *Les damnés de la terre* (*The Wretched of the Earth*). Paris: François Maspero: 1961, English translation, 1963.

Frack, Isidore. *Every Man Must Play a Part: Isidore Frack, The Story of a South African Doctor*. Cape Town: Purnell, 1970.

Frankel, Philip. *An Ordinary Atrocity: Sharpeville and Its Massacre*. New Haven: Yale University Press, 2001.

Gowenius, Peder. *The Hungry Red Lion: Art and Empowerment at Rorke's Drift, Thabana Li Mele and Oodi*. Noordhoek: Print Matters Heritage, 2021.

Henkes, Barbara. "National Socialism, Colonialism and Anti-Fascist Memory Politics in Postwar Dutch-South African Exchanges." *South African Historical Journal* Vol. 74, No. 1, (June, 2022): 160–183.

Lerner, Natan. *The U.N. Convention on the Elimination of All Forms of Racial Discrimination: A Commentary*. Leyden: A.W. Suthoff, 1970.

Lodge, Tom. *Sharpeville: An Apartheid Massacre and Its Consequences*. Oxford: Oxford University Press, 2011.

Makhoba, Mandlenkosi and Petrus Tom, *The Story of One Tells the Struggle of All: Metalworkers under Apartheid*. Auckland Park: Jacana Media, 2018.

Modisane, Bloke. *Blame Me On History*. New York: E. P. Dutton, 1963.

Moseneke, Dikgang. *My Own Liberator: A Memoir*. Johannesburg: Picador Africa, 2016.

Nkosi, Lewis. *The Rhythm of Violence*. London: Oxford University Press, 1964.

Richards, Trevor. *Dancing On Our Bones: New Zealand, South Africa, Rugby and Racism*. Wellington: Bridget Williams Books, 1999.

South African Democracy Education Trust, *The Road to Democracy in South Africa: Vol.3, Parts 1, 2, 3, International Solidarity*. Pretoria: University of South Africa, 2008 and 2018.

Sowden, Lewis. *The Land of Afternoon: The Story of a White South Africa*. New York: McGraw-Hill, 1968.

Thompson, Richard. "Rugby and Race Relations: A New Zealand Controversy." *The Journal of the Polynesian Society*, Vol. 69, No. 3 (September 1960): 285–287.

Thörn, Håkan. *Anti-Apartheid and the Emergence of a Global Civil Society*. Houndsmill: Palgrave Macmillan, 2006.

United Nations. *The United Nations and Apartheid, 1948-1994*. New York: United Nations Department of Public Information, 1994.

9 Coda
The Role of Memory

> We cannot forget. Yes, we can forgive. But we cannot forget. If we forget, we then forget about our history, and you never know where you are going.
>
> (Abram Mofokeng)[1]

The story of Sharpeville is the story of a place, a community, and an event that set off an international movement calling for the end of racial discrimination around the world and the end of apartheid in South Africa. But this is also a story of memories and how those stories and feelings have affected the community. In the years since 1960, Sharpeville itself remained frozen in time with little changed in the town's physical layout and appearance. Houses are still occupied by the same families – and often the same now elderly individuals – who moved there from Top Location in the 1940s and 1950s and endured the 1960 massacre. Residents can quickly identify the house where "Wonder Boy" Sexton Mabena's family still lives, the shebeen where Oliver Tambo's wife once sang, the house where Hugh Masekela lived for a period just down the street from that of the boxer Carlton Monnakgotla, Nyakane's Tsolo's house, and so on. History is still alive for Sharpeville's residents, but it remains unresolved.

The people of Sharpeville suffered a tragic and traumatic loss on 21 March 1960. Although they tried to tell their story, mourn their dead, and repair their community, they were muted by the government in the direct aftermath of the massacre and slowly forgotten over the years as the event – more than the victims – became an iconic symbol in the fight against racism and apartheid. In the government's rush to bury the victims, none of the families were able to attend to the preparation and burial of their loved ones or perform the rituals that normally accompany death. The immediate testimony in the 1960 and 1961 court cases, police interviews, and commission proceedings by over 400 Sharpeville residents all spoke to the shock, pain, and loss suffered as a result of the inexplicable killing of their friends and relatives, yet the victims were dismissed by the courts and officials as "*betogers*" – demonstrators – who deserved the consequences of their actions. Under apartheid rule, individuals silently and privately marked every 21st of March with their own memorials to their dead, but without a sense of recovery and closure.[2] And when the new democratically elected government came to power in

DOI: 10.4324/9781003257806-9

1994 – and Nelson Mandela signed the new constitution in Sharpeville itself in 1996 – there was an expectation that Sharpeville's trauma could finally be confronted, addressed, and even healed. But instead, in September 1994, 21 March was renamed "Human Rights Day" in South Africa, and Sharpeville became the site of festivities and celebrations recounting the heroes of the liberation struggle with little acknowledgement of the people of Sharpeville.

> It is not a nice way to commemorate that day, to go there and have a party on that day … instead it should be a mourning day, people should be mourning on that day, the priests should be called so that there are prayer sessions as opposed to what is presently taking place every year now.[3]

Today, the memory of Sharpeville is still contested by political actors, survivors, and even the perpetrators of the massacre. The South African government celebrates the Sharpeville Massacre as part of the country's triumphant liberation narrative with mostly African National Congress (ANC) victories heralded. Alternatively, former South African police who were involved in the massacre and were still alive in 2021 continued to argue that Africans threw stones and threatened violence, justifying the fear and retaliation of the police.[4] And most scholars come down in the middle, placing Sharpeville on a list of liberation battles while excusing police actions as the result of misguided fear.[5] These explanations focus on those outside Sharpeville – the liberation movements or the police – as the starring actors in this tragedy, with the people of Sharpeville in the background, as passive bystanders inadvertently destroyed by larger forces.

How do Sharpeville residents themselves remember 21 March?

> It is a very damaged society as a result of the past. There are scars within our people that are not going to be healed by time or anything … people get the history of your father, and when getting this anger, this pain is renewed within the new generation and let me tell you as black people we don't forget, particularly very painful experiences. From 1960 up until now is not a very long time to learn how to live with scars and negative thinking that will ultimately destroy not only the person that you hate, but you yourself. We are that society that is very damaged inside.[6]

Memory of the tragedy of 21 March cannot be avoided for anyone living in Sharpeville. As already noted, the massacre took place at Sharpeville's civic centre at the intersection of Seeiso and Zwane streets. It is nearly impossible to move through Sharpeville without passing this site, noting the memorial which now stands where the many victims lay dead and dying. For those who remember the events, it is a jarring reminder of the community trauma, and for their families, of the stories told. Each survivor has noted that from that day, their lives were "never the same." That event changed not only their lives, but that of their children, grandchildren, and those to come. They needed an explanation to give meaning to this pain.

It is difficult to explain such a terrible and senseless tragedy in ways that can ease community pain, lessen trauma, and bring meaning to the event. It was especially difficult for residents to develop a collective memory of the event in its immediate aftermath. The police were eager to arrest anyone who could be connected to the protest, so most residents were quiet and feigned ignorance of the political organisations; practically all declared their acquiescence to the pass laws. Following the demise of the apartheid government, Sharpeville residents have instead bitterly denounced the *"dompas"* they had to carry and admitted publicly that they were drawn that day to protest – peacefully – the hated pass laws. In a narrative of peaceful but adamant protest, the community can be proud of its actions and the courage of Nyakane Tsolo, Thomas More, and others to stand "as men" before the police. There was nothing in their actions to justify the police action. As Tsolo himself later said, "We never thought they would kill us."

So how to explain the violence? There is no community explanation but some redemption in the story that is related to events immediately following the massacre:

> The sky was so clear, without any clouds, then clouds started gathering, a very small cloud, and it started raining for about 15 minutes. God made a miracle that day, it was washing these peoples' blood, where blood flowed. Many people say that the rain was washing that people's blood, washing it to the [Dlomo] dam. But it just fell, not too much of it and it stopped. Every time on the 21st of March there is always a cloud that will rain. We've realized that happens for the last 15 years even if it does not rain on the 21st, the following day. That's why I'm saying, God makes miracles.[7]

The trauma is given meaning through God's grace to wash away the blood of the victims into a repository of sorts, the Dlomo Dam. The dam itself – the former catchment of run-off water from farms and the town of Vereeniging – has become the centre of this story with an elaborate history. But the dam takes on a different story in the retelling of the massacre. According to residents, it instead began as a small dam near a farm owned by a man named Dlomo. The size of the dam grew as the rain from Sharpeville – the rain cleansing the town of the victims' blood – flowed into the dam every year on the 21st of March. There is indeed a small underground stream that flows from the area of Zwane and Seeiso streets to the dam, which is approximately 1.6 km (one mile) from the site of the massacre. But more important than the factual accuracy of this story is that the dam itself has become an important symbol of Sharpeville's trauma, a monument to the deaths, and a sign of God's comfort. As such, it serves an important role in not only easing the pain of the deaths but also in creating a community-centred symbol of what could otherwise be seen as individual loss. And it affirms God's love for the people of Sharpeville, marking them as deserving of his mercy.

In 2022, the Sharpeville Heritage and Tourism Association was founded to "preserve the only potent heritage we have despite its painful content." The 15 to 20 members of the board of directors – all self-described entrepreneurs in Sharpeville – meet twice a week to develop ways to make Sharpeville visible once more to the world and to educate the community "in memorialising this history properly."[8] One of their first efforts is to correct the record of deaths on 21 March 1960, both at the Sharpeville memorial itself and at the national Freedom Park memorial in Pretoria, which honours all South Africans who lost their lives fighting for freedom. The Sedibeng Provincial Government also held a Social Cohesion Heritage Summit to discuss preserving and publicising the history of the Vaal region, including Sharpeville. It was evident at this meeting that it will take some time to correct the facts surrounding Sharpeville's history – from the number of dead to the origins of the Dlomo Dam – but the community is committed to disseminating "information that is equally healing but also educating us in memorializing this history properly."

> Sharpeville has been waiting for this defining moment throughout its 62 years of pain, [to put to rest] the hovering souls that never got to be brought home.[9]

Figure 9.1 Coffins of the Victims of the Massacre for burial 30 March 1960. Dlomo Dam in the distance.

Photo by Terence Spencer/Popperfoto via Getty Images.

Notes

1 Abram Mofokeng, interview by authors, Sharpeville, 5 October 2018.
2 The first Sharpeville shootings community commemoration was held in Sharpeville on 21 March 1973 at Sediba Primary School, called "Heroes' Day" by the Black Consciousness Movement family of organizations. Nkutsoeu Motsau, "AZAPO – Lest we forget," *Sedibeng Ster*, 15 March 2018.
3 Mahasane Michael Thekiso, interview by authors, Sharpeville, 19 October 2019.
4 "At Sharpeville: It was over in seconds ... and yet not," 28 March 2021, *Rapport Weekliks*.
5 Philip Frankel, *An Ordinary Atrocity: Sharpeville and Its Massacre* (New Haven: Yale University Press, 2001), 15; Tom Lodge, *Sharpeville: An Apartheid Massacre and Its Consequences* (New York: Oxford University Press, 2011), 104–105.
6 Moeletsi Vincent Thamae, interview by authors, Sharpeville, 9 October 2019.
7 Mahasane Michael Thekiso, interview by authors, Sharpeville, 3 October 2018.
8 Nicho Ntema, email message to the authors, 2 December 2022.
9 Nicho Ntema, email message to the authors, 20 December 2022.

Documents

Document 1: Official Police List of the Dead, May 1960

Police Captain Jan van den Bergh was tasked by the "Commission of Enquiry into the Occurrences at Sharpeville (and other places) on the 21st of March 1960," with making an official count of the dead and injured and this is the list that he introduced into evidence in May 1960. We photographed the original list in the Police Archive in Pretoria in 2018 and the same list in the official records of the Commission in the National Archives in Pretoria in 2022. We emphasise that this is the original official list held in the archival records because Philip Frankel in his book, An Ordinary Atrocity *(Yale University Press: New Haven, 2001), 245-247, published a typed-out misleading version in which the name of a person who was not killed on 21 March 1960, Geelbooi Mofokeng, was substituted for the name of a person who was killed, Moeketsi S. Mosia (written as entry No. 26 using the offensive term by which he was then identified by the police, Swaartbooi Mosea). Frankel then used this falsified list to spin a police story blaming the shooting on Geelbooi Mofokeng (see Chapter 8; source: authors' photograph).*

SAP 611

LYS VAN OORLEDENES.

NR.	NAAM	GESLAG	OUDERDOM
1.	William Sedisa	manlik	28
2.	John Mofokeng	manlik	44
3.	Abraham Masebuko	manlik	23
4.	Walter Mbatha5	manlik	35
5.	George Sekete	manlik	39
6.	Jacob Mafobela	manlik	35
7.	Jemina Potse	vroulik	37
8.	Petrus Ntshoasane	manlik	25
9.	David Makhoba	manlik	14
10.	Anual Mohlasane	manlik	35
11.	Shadrack Mahlong5	manlik	19
12.	Aron Mavizela	manlik	24
13.	Elliot Kabe	manlik	24
14.	Simon Masele	manlik	35
15.	Klias Maselo	manlik	17
16.	David Maphika	manlik	50
17.	Martha Tinana	vroulik	22
18.	Jeremiah Tlanyane	manlik	28

DOI: 10.4324/9781003257806-10

19.	Samuel Mokhuma	manlik	39
20.	Anna Ramothla	vroulik	22
21.	Gilbert Monyane	manlik	18
22.	Christina Motsepe	vroulik	18
23.	Kopana Mtsoga	manlik	50
24.	Gilbert Demo	manlik	58
25.	Ben Nchaupe	manlik	45
26.	Swartbooi Mosea	manlik	26
27.	Maria Molebatsi	vroulik	13
28.	Wiggi Bakela	vroulik	40
29.	Frank Makoena	manlik	34
30.	Joseph Mochologi	manlik	50
31.	Esekiel Maroletsi	manlik	33
32.	Samuel Mahlele	manlik	30
33.	Daniel Monakgotle	manlik	31
34.	Elias Moletsi	manlik	29
35.	Jan Mnguni	manlik	24
36.	Philemon Sepanpuru	manlik	48
37.	Zakia Lefakane	manlik	50
38.	Johannes Selanyane	manlik	17
39.	Edward Tsela	manlik	15
40.	Jonas Mailame	manlik	36
41.	James Besohe	manlik	12
42.	Nora Mbele	vroulik	23
43.	Paulus Mavisela	manlik	18
44.	Miriam Sekitla	vroulik	34
45.	John Phutheho	manlik	30
46.	Daniel Mono	manlik	40
47.	Malefane E. Ngwembesi	manlik	30
48.	Alfons Selepe	manlik	22
49.	Ephraim Chaka	manlik	36
50.	Ezekiel Maselo	manlik	44
51.	Naphtali Maine	manlik	25
52.	Isak Mashiya	manlik	30
53.	Richard Molefe	manlik	50
54.	Jacob Ramokoena	manlik	35
55.	Axmel Mangka	manlik	37
56.	Thomas Hlongwane	manlik	24
57.	Samuel Sefatsa	manlik	28
58.	Kaselien Matinye	manlik	45
59.	Piet Mabanjane	manlik	36
60.	Edwin Moshabate	manlik	45
61.	Elizabeth Mtimkulu	vroulik	36.
62.	Isak Rabetapi	manlik	20.
63.	Solomon Mapogeshe	manlik	36.
64.	Philemon Makoena	manlik	30.
65.	Talbert Masomba	manlik	30.
66.	Isak Nkhi	manlik	40.
67.	Kaifas Motsepe	manlik	45.
68.	Paulina Mafulatse	vroulik	25.
69.	Paulina Malikhoe	vroulik	22.

OPSOMMING : Manlik .... 58.
Vroulik .... 11.

Document 2: Meriam Maine's Claim for the Loss of Her Son Naphtali Maine

Naphtali Maine was the young man (27 years old) killed by the police as he was going to the Sharpeville shops to buy cigarettes. He bled to death from a bullet wound in his pelvis. Unmarried, he was the sole financial support of his widowed mother, his three sisters – the oldest was disabled, the other two were both school age – and one younger brother. His mother, Meriam or Mirriam (as her family spells her name), assisted by lawyers arranged by the Bishop of Johannesburg, Ambrose Reeves, lodged a claim against the State for £3,750.00 "as damages for loss of support for the wrongful and unlawful killing of her son Neptlane Maine, upon whom the Plaintiff and her children were dependent." A separate claim for £2,000 was filed on behalf of her children (Henriëtta, Sheila, Constance, and Bennet) for the loss of their brother. In support of her claim, Mirriam Maine gave a statement under oath to a policeman on 21 August 1961 detailing her family's situation and also recounting what she knew of what her son had done on 21 March 1960. Her statement was recorded in Afrikaans by the police and she attested to the truthfulness of its contents with her fingerprint. Government records in 1963 show that compensation of R312, only 1.5 percent of what was originally claimed, was authorised to be issued to the family, but whether any payment was actually made cannot be determined. Note that upon becoming a republic in 1961, South Africa changed its currency from the pound to the rand with one pound officially worth two rand (source: Claim by Meriam Maine, K110 1/3/60. See also SAP 31/58/60 (86) and (176). All are in the SAB database at the South African National Archives. Translation by Ina Roos).

Meriam Maine declares under oath:

I am a Bantu (black) woman, 53 years of age and live at #### Sharpeville Location, Vereeniging. Since my son's death [Naphtali Maine] I have not received any financial assistance from the Commissioner of Bantu Affairs. I do, however, receive some groceries weekly from the Vaal River Cash Store through the Relief Fund. Before my son's death I worked, doing washing and ironing and earned R4.50 per month. I am not working currently since I am ill.

a) Through the mediation of a lawyer's firm whose offices are behind a bank in Vereeniging I have lodged a claim against the State.
b) I received a letter from the lawyers in question, instructing me to come to their offices on a certain date and I do not know who the lawyers are.
c) Nobody advised me to consult with the lawyers in question and I went there only as a result of the letter I received. I still have the letter.
d) The lawyer in question said that he would try to get us money and that I had to pay him afterwards. He did not mention the amount I had to pay.
e) The deceased was my own child, aged 27 and was not married. I do not know where the Birth Certificate is but I will look for it.
f) The deceased provided for me, his disabled sister Henriëtta, 21 years old, Sheila, aged 15 and Constance, aged 9 [other records refer also to a son, Bennet]. My husband died a few years ago.
g) The Superintendent of Sharpeville Location can confirm that the deceased was my child.
h) The deceased worked at Vaal Paint, Vereeniging and earned R9.50 per week.

268   Documents

i) On the morning of 21 March 1960 at 7 am the deceased took his lunch tin and said he was going to work per bus as usual. At about 9.30 am he returned and said there were no buses going to Vereeniging. He did not mention to me that anyone had stopped him.

j) He stayed at home the whole day and after lunch at about 2 pm asked me for two shillings to buy cigarettes. We live about 300 yards from the Police Station and from my home I have a clear view of the Police Station and I saw that there was a crowd of people. He walked around the back, on the east side of the Police Station in the direction of the cafe when I last saw him and he was on his own.

k) He never attended meetings in the location and never indicated that he did not want to carry his passbook or did not want to work under white people. I am convinced that he never belonged to any organisation.

At present we are only surviving on the groceries we receive from the Relief Fund.

Signed by Meriam Maine (fingerprint)
Signed at Sharpeville on 29 August 1961
Signed by M.M. Kruger S/Sergeant

Witness:

1. Nelson Tshabalala
2. Signature illegible 137916 (not clear) B/Constable

Document 3: Gilbert Dimo's Autopsy

Gilbert Dimo was 59 years old when he was killed by the police on 21 March 1960, shot in the back of the head with the bullet tearing out the front of his face including part of his right eye. The bullet left a small entry wound but a large lacerated exit injury across his face leading to public claims that dum-dum bullets had been used by the police. Dimo's facial wound, like those of many others that day, inspired Don Mattera to write his poem "Day of Thunder" within two days of the shooting. Two lines are especially relevant:
"blood flowed from Black men's eyes,
when they met the Hail of Dum-Dum."
(Don Mattera, Azanian Love Song (Ravan Press: Johannesburg, 1983), 2. Dimo left behind his widowed wife Selina, and four school-age children, Albertina, Walter, Ishmael, and Elizabeth. The state authorised a payment of just under 7.5 percent of the £5,210.00 claimed by his widow and children for their loss of his household support. As was the case with 68 of those killed in Sharpeville, an autopsy was carried out on his body by a district surgeon (source: K110 1/3/60, SAP 31/58/60 (29) and (96), SAB).

GILBERT DIMO: Adult native male: 5'7" 112 lb.

Documents   269

1. *Entrance wound*: In the left posterior parietal region. 2" above the tip of the mastoid, there was a circular penetrating wound, ¼" in diameter. Beneath this, in the posterior portion of the left parietal bone, there was a horizontal wound, ½" x ¼". The outer table of the bone in this wound was cleanly cut and there was bevelling of the inner table. Radiating forwards from this wound there were numerous fissured fractures. The internal track from this wound extended forwards and to the right, emerging at the exit wound described in (2).
2. *Exit wound*: There was a gaping lacerated wound commencing near the inner angle of the right eye and extending horizontally towards the left, involving the bridge of the nose and the inner angle of the left eye. The wound measured 2¼" x 1¼". The right eye was ruptured and disorganised. The left eyeball was intact. There was deep exposure with much loss of bony tissue involving the nasal cavity to a depth of 2½" along the base of the skull. There was comminution [fragmentation] of the inner wall both the right and the left orbits. The anterior half of the base of the skull was grossly comminuted with wide exposure of the nasal cavity already described. Fractures radiated into both anterior and posterior fossae [hollows]. The brain was putrid with evidence of gross laceration and much haemorrhage.
3. Apart from the injuries and tissues described nothing abnormal was noted in the heart muscle; coronary arteries; the valves of the aorta; (There was some atheroma [degeneration] at the commencement of the aorta and there was moderate atheroma in the rest of the aorta); the respiratory tract; the liver and spleen; the kidneys (some pallor), the adrenals, the urethra and the bladder; the gastro-intestinal tract (the stomach was empty).
4. *Cause of death*: Gunshot wound of the head.

Dated 14 April 1961.

Document 4: Christina Motsepe's Life as Valued by an Actuary

Christina Motsepe (21 years old) died on 21 March 1960, along with her unborn son. She left behind her orphaned 2-year-old daughter, Selina (we interviewed her in 2018), and her widowed mother, Anna. As was the case with many of the family members who made claims for compensation, a Johannesburg actuarial firm was hired by the State to calculate the loss of income caused by her death to those dependent on her at the time of her death. The calculation relied on existing assumptions and estimates, including lower pay and shorter life expectancies for Africans as compared with Whites, and a published set of life tables. Eventually, the state Claims Committee authorised a payment of 3.2 percent of the £3,750.00 originally requested to be made to Anna on behalf of Selina. The amount authorised to be paid was slightly less (R240.00) than the amount calculated by the actuaries (R290.00; source: K110 1/3/60, SAP 31/58/60 (2), (127), and (214), SAB).

MACPHAIL & FRASER
(Consulting Actuaries, Johannesburg, 27 March 1961)

CHRISTINA MOTSEPE (DECEASED)

1. Christina Motsepe was killed at Sharpeville on 21st March 1960. In this report an estimate is given of the pecuniary loss suffered by her child by being deprived of her support.

AGES AND HEALTH

2. The ages (nearest birthday) of Motsepe and her child at the time of her death are taken as follows:

	Date of birth	Age
Deceased	1.4.1939	21
Child	12.11.1957	2

It is stated that Motsepe was in good health and it is assumed that her child enjoyed normal health.

DECEASED'S EARNINGS

3. At the time of her death Motsepe was employed as a domestic servant at Vanderbijl Park. Her earnings were R7 a month, that is R84 a year, and it is assumed that she would have continued to earn this amount until her child ceased to be dependent.

SHARES OF EARNINGS

4. It is assumed that in the future the deceased's earnings would have been apportioned so that her share was equal to twice that of her child while dependent. It is assumed that the child would have been dependent until she attained age 16.

BASIS OF CALCULATIONS

5. The expectation of life of Motsepe is based on the current Death Duty Table, that is the South African Life Table E. 4, with an addition of five years to her age to allow for the heavier mortality of the Bantu. The mortality of the child is ignored.
6. Interest is taken at 4½% a year.

PECUNIARY LOSS

7. The child's pecuniary loss is R290, being the capital value (at 4½% interest) of her share of the earnings during the mother's expectation of life while the child is under age 16, as follows:

Years after death	1–14
Mother's expectation of life	13.8 Years
Share of earnings	R28
Capital Value	R290

Document 5: Working List of Sharpeville Residents Killed by the Police on 21 March 1960

Using records that we have discovered in the Police Archive and in the National Archives in Pretoria, including materials later submitted to the Truth and Reconciliation Commission in 1996, interviews with Sharpeville survivors videotaped by the National Archives in 2014, and by ourselves in 2018, 2019, and 2022, as well as the lists of dead and injured published by The World *on 26 March 1960, and by cross checking with Frankel's appendices 2A and 2B (respectively, "'Natives who died of gunshot wounds' from the Register of the Sharpeville Natives' Cemetery," and "'Names on the tombstones at the Sharpeville Natives' Cemetery,"* An Ordinary Atrocity, *242–244), we have developed working lists of those killed and injured on 21 March 1960, or who later died as a direct result of the injuries they suffered that day. The 5 names we have taken from Frankel's two sources (which we have not seen ourselves) are printed in italics in the list below. Using these sources, we have been able to establish that at least 91 people (and likely more) were killed on 21 March 1960, and at least 238 injured, many of them very severely. But we stress that, over 60 years after the event, these are still working lists, not final counts. From 1960 until the formal end of apartheid, the South African government prevented people from speaking freely about the massacre and banned all literature about the shooting. Since 1994, the ANC government has shown no interest in re-investigating the massacre. Yet as we have discovered in our regular visits to Sharpeville, more and more information keeps being discovered as we talk with members of the community, and this process will only continue as more and more people become engaged in talking about their history. In the working list that follows, we provide alternative spellings of some of the names and alternative ages at death as recorded in the original police files. The documentary record is often replete with misspellings and misdating, and only members of the Sharpeville community will be able to develop a final record of the dead and injured. They have already established groups of "field workers," and our hope is that this list and the one following will assist them in their efforts. We have been very careful in our own estimates and our total of "at least 91 killed" accounts for the possibility that, despite different spellings and different ages, Abraham Rapule Mazibuko and Abram Mgodo Mazibuko may be the same person, so too Jemina Motsabi Motsoetsa and Jemina Potse, so too Kopano Motsega and Kopano Ntsoa, and so too Daniel Maphike/Maphika and David Mapiki. But they may not.*

WORKING LIST OF KILLED

	LASTNAME	ALT. SPELLING	FIRSTNAME	AGE
1	BAKELA		WIGGI/MAGGIE	40
2	BESCHE		JAMES BUTI	12
3	BOTHA		WALTER	38
4	CHAKA		EPHRAIM	35
5	CHALALE	CHILALE/CHIBALE	UNBORN	0
6	DIMO		GILBERT	59
7	HLANYANE	TLANYANE	JEREMIAH	28
8	HLONGWANE		THOMAS	21

9	KABI		ELLIOTT	24/25
10	LEFAKANE		ZACKIA	50
11	LEKITLA	SEKITLA	MIRRIAM	43
12	MABENYANE		PIET/PETER	30
13	MABITSELA		ARON	24
14	MABITSELA		PAULUS	18
15	MABONA		KHEHLA	27
16	MADESKI		MALE FIRSTNAME UNKNOWN	?
17	*MADIKU*		*PAULINE*	*22*
18	*MAFOGANE*		*JEAN*	*36*
19	MAFUBELU		JACOB RAMAITO	35/55
20	MAFULATSI	MOFULATSI	PAULINAH	23/25/26
21	MAHLATSANI	MOHLOTSANE/ MOHLASANI	ENUWELL MONKONYANE	35/36
22	MAHLELE		SAMUEL	30
23	MAHLONG	MATLONG	SHADRACK	19
24	MAHUDI		JOHN	
25	MAILANE		JOHN MOTSOAHAE	46
26	MAINE		NAPHTALI	25
27	MAKHOBA	MAKOBA	DAVID	14
28	MALIKOI	MADEKOI/ MOLIKOE	MAMOTSHABI PAULINA	21
29	MALIKOI		UNBORN	0
30	MANGALA		ISAIA	37
31	*MANYANE*		*ELISABETH*	*18*
32	MAPIKI		DAVID	50
33	MAPHIKE	MAPHIKA	DANIEL DIBETE	44
34	MAPOGOSHE		SOLOMON MOSALA	36
35	MARELESTSE	MARELETSA/ MAROLOTSIE	EZEKIEL	33
36	MASHIYA	MASHEYA/ MASHIEA/ MASHYA/ MASHEA	ISAAC BOISIE/BOYSIE	31
37	MASHOABATHE		EDWIN NYOLO	43
38	MASILO		ELIAS	17
39	MASILO	MASELO/ MAYSIELS	EZEKIEL	43
40	MASILO		SIMON	39
41	MATHINYE		SAMSON KHASELINE	45
42	MAZIBUKO		ABRAHAM RAPULE	23
43	MAZIBUKO		ABRAM MGODO	25
44	MAZOMBA		TALBERT	30
45	MBHELE	MBELE	NORAH NOBHEKISIZWE	21
46	*MGOMEZULU*		*ISLABET*	*30*
47	MNGUNI		JOHN/JAN	24
48	MOATLHODI	MOAHLODI	SAMUEL SONNYBOY	32
49	MOCHOLOGI		JOSEPH MOROBI	46
50	MOFOKENG		JOHN KOLANE	44

51	MOKHOMO	MOKHOMA/ MAKHOMO/ MAKHUME	SAMUEL	60
52	MOKOENA		MALE FIRSTNAME UNKNOWN	?
53	MOKOENA		PHILEMON	22/30
54	MOKOENA		SOLOMON/FRANK	34
55	MOLAPO		JERRY	?
56	MOLEBATSI		MARIA	13
57	MOLEFE		RICHARD	50
58	MOLOTSI		ELIAS	29
59	MONNAKGOTLA	MONNAKHOTLA/ MONAGOTLE	DANIEL	32
60	MONO		DANIEL KUDUMANE	48/51
61	MONYANE		GILBERT	18
62	MOROBI	MARABI/MAROBI	JOSEPH	51
63	MOSIA		MOEKETSI S./JOHN	33
64	MOTSOETSA		JEMINA MOTSABI	40
65	MOTSEGA		KOPANO	52
66	MOTSEPE		CHRISTINA	20
67	MOTSEPE		UNBORN MALE	0
68	MOTSEPE		KAIPHAS/CAIPHUS	42
69	*MPEKA*		*ENUELL*	?
70	MTHIMKULU		AMOS	50
71	MTIMKULU		ELIZABETH	25
72	NCHAUPE		BENJAMIN	56
73	NKHI		ISAAC BOISIE	46
74	NTHOESANE		PETROS	25
75	NTSANE		ELIZABETH MOOKGO	?
76	NTSOA	NTSOOA	KOPANO	52
77	NYEMBEZI		MANYASI/MANASI	27
78	PHUTHEHO		JOHN	43
79	POTSE		JEMINA MOTSABI	37
80	RABOTAPI		ISAAC BOISIE	22
81	RADEBE		MALE FIRSTNAME UNKNOWN	?
82	RALEBAKENG		SELLO	?
83	RAMAILANE		T.	?
84	RAMOHLOA		ANNA	22
85	RAMOKOEANA	RAMAKOENA/ RAMSKOENA	KHEHLA JACOB	35
86	SALANYANE	SENYALANO	JOHANNES	19
87	SEDISA		WILLIAM	19
88	SEFATSA		SAMUEL/PHEHALLO	27
89	SEKETE		GEORGE TOROKI	39
90	SELEPE		ALPHEUS	22
91	SEPAMPURU		PHILEMON	51/52
92	SEPENG		ISAAC BOISIE	?
93	SOTHOANE		ZANANA NATHANIEL	17
94	THINANE	TINANE	MARTHA KASEANE	24
95	TSELA		EDWARD	16

Document 6: Working List of Sharpeville Residents Injured by the Police on 21 March 1960

The working list of the injured, like the working list of the killed, is a work in progress. It includes names from police files in the South African National Archives, from hospital lists in the Police Archive, from the list published by The World on 26 March 1960, as well as people interviewed by the TRC, by the National Archives, and by ourselves. No previous scholars have identified the injured, but we believe it is important to memorialise their actions and their suffering on 21 March 1960. In order to provide as much information as possible to the Sharpeville community as they pursue their own research, we have included alternate spellings since in some cases these may simply be errors from the original police documentation or suggest multiple people. Though we have not printed the street addresses of all the killed and injured, we have that information and have made it available to the community to help them in their investigations since, as we have noted in the text, most families still live in the same homes that they occupied on 21 March 1960.

WORKING LIST OF INJURED

	LASTNAME	ALT. SPELLING	FIRSTNAME	AGE
1	BENGU		SARAH	?
2	BENJAMIN		SANA	29
3	BOKWA		RICHARD	23
4	BONISWA		ALICE	28
5	CHABELE	MOKWENA/ TSHABEDI	ELIZABETH MINA MATSUNYANA	5
6	CHALALE	CHILALE/ CHIBALE	LYDIA	23
7	CHENENE	CHININI/ TSHERINI	FRANCINA NTSOAKI	17
8	DANGANA	DANGANE	ISAAC	?
9	DIKETSO		MIRIAM	?
10	DIKUBO	DIKOBO/DIKOBE/ LIKOBO	DANIEL	27
11	FANI		JOHN	26
12	FANTISI	FANTISE	EMMANUEL	33
13	GAMEDE		LEFINA/LEPHINA	52
14	GRIFFITH	GRIFFITHS	THATELA BENEDICT	17
15	HLATSHWAYO		SAMUEL	?
16	HLONGWANE		JOKONIAH/JAKANIAH	?
17	JACK		EUNICE	31
18	KGOSI	KHOSI/KHOSE	MAGDELINA/ MADALENA	23
19	KHAMBULA	RAMHULA	EMILY	18
20	KHAOLE	KAHOLE	ABRAHAM RAPULE	54
21	KHOALI	KHOALE/KHAALI	DAVID	17
22	KHOBOKHOLO	KOBOKHOLO	JONAS DITATOLO	17
23	KHOTA	KNOTA	JOHN	73

24	KOBOEKAE		RICHARD	40
25	KOJOANE		JACOB	24
26	KOTERA		MAGGIE	?
27	KUBEKA		ELLIOTT	17
28	KUMALO		SOLOMON/SOLAMON	65
29	KUTOANE	KUTWANE	SEABATA AZAEL GORDON	28
30	KUTOANE	KUTANE	JOSEPH	19
31	LEBEKO		K	
32	LECHESA	LECHISA	BEN	41
33	LEHOBO	LEHABO/LEHEBO	STEPHEN	21
34	LEHOKO	LEKOKO	PHILEMON/PHILLEMON	24
35	LEPEE		MIRRIAM/MIRIAM/MERRIAM LEYA	16
36	LEROALA	LEROLO	KOTI	40
37	LESITO		SOLOMON	20
38	LESITO	LESITHO	WILLIAM	46
39	LESOANE	LESOANA/LESACANE	MICHAEL	21
40	LETHEGE	LETAGA/LETHAKHE	ANNA	47
41	LETSOENYO	LETSHOENYO	MICHAEL	32
42	LOFAFA	DHOLEFA/DHLOFAFA	SIMON	31
43	MABASO		DAVID	33
44	MACHETSE	MATHATSE	APHIA	?
45	MACHOBANE	MACHABANI/MOCHOBANE/MASHOBANI	SAMUEL	27
46	MADIKO	MODIKO	IRENE	48
47	MAEKO	MOEKO	JUSTICE	44
48	MAHABUKE		LYDIA MANTOA	14
49	MAHLANGU	MASHLANGU	BESHU	55
50	MAHLANOKO	MAHLANAKO	PHILIP/PHILLIP	60
51	MAHLASI	MAHLATSI/MAKLASI	SAMUEL	17
52	MAISI		SAMUEL	?
53	MAJOLA		GLADYS	16
54	MAKAHAJANE	MAKANJANE/MAKAHYANE/MAGAJANE	ALINA	47
55	MAKAO		TSELANE JOSEPH	?
56	MAKHOBA	MOKHOBO	SIMON	21
57	MAKOTOKO	MAKETEKE/MOKOTOKO	ELIZABETH	30
58	MAKUBI	MAKUBE/MAKUBO	JOSEPH	25
59	MALEBATSI		BEN	?
60	MALEFANE		ADAM	37
61	MALEHO	MALHEO	SEFORA/PUSELETSO ZEPHORA	21/27

62	MALEMA	MALEMO	JOSHUA	28
63	MALGAS		PAUL	?
64	MALUKA		PAULUS	41
65	MALUKO	MALUKA	PAULUS	29
66	MANATO	MANOTO	ADAM	59
67	MAOKE	MAUKE	SIMON	52
68	MAPHALIA		ADOLPHINA	?
69	MAPHELA	MAPHELE/ MOPHELA	GEORGE	47
70	MAPHISA	MAFISA/MAFETA	JOSEPH	21
71	MARABI	MARATI	ELISA	33
72	MAREKA	MOREKA	DAVID	46
73	MAREKA		MESHAK/MESHACK	32
74	MARENGANE	MORENYANE/ MOENYARE/ MOENYANE/ MANYANE	ELIAS	52
75	MARITE		DAVID	26
76	MAROKOANE	MAROEKOANE	ANNA NDOTI	36
77	MAROKOANE	MAROKWANE	EPHRAIM	22
78	MAROO		BENJAMIN	20
79	MASHIYA	MASHEYA/ MASHIEA/ MASHYA/ MASHIA/ MASCHICA	MODISE MATTHEWS/ MATTHEW	30
80	MASHIYA	MASHEYA/ MASHIEA/ MASHYA/ MASHIA	PETROS/SELEPE PETRUS	15
81	MASHOBA	MASHOBANI	SAMUEL	?
82	MASILO		MOHAULI SOLOMON	24
83	MASIMANGO	MASMANGO/ MSIMANGO/ MSIMANG/ MSIMANGA	THOMAS	60
84	MASOKOANE	MASOKHOANE	ANNA	?
85	MASUDUBELE		HILDA MATSHIDO	?
86	MATHETSE		APHATHIA	44
87	MATLALETSE		JOSEPH	?
88	MATJILA	MATJILE	JOHANNES	?
89	MATLALU	MATLALA/ MATHLALA	ALBERT	17
90	MATLHARE	MATLHAKA	ANDRIES	?
91	MATOGOSHE		SOLOMON	?
92	MATSABU	MATSABO	AARON	42
93	MEKAYOANE	MIKAYOANE/ MIKAYANE/ MILAYOANE	LEWIS	22
94	MHLAMBI		SIMON	39
95	MKHOMDANI	MKHONDENI	EDWARD	?
96	MKHUBENE	MKUMBENI/ MKHABENI	ELLIOT	19

97	MKOKOTSANE	MOKOTSANE/ NKOKOTSANE/ GAGOSANE	JAMES BUTI	37
98	MKWANAZI		ALINAH MATSHILISO	18
99	MKWANAZI		PAULUS/PAOLOS SERAME	19
100	MLAGANE	MLANGANE	MILDRED	27
101	MNGUNI		PETROS MADLAMAFA	24
102	MNGUNI	MGANE	PONTSO SELINA	18/24
103	MODIKO	MADIKO	IRENE	48
104	MOEKO	MAEKO	JUSTUS/JUSTICE	44
105	MOERA		DANIEL KOK	?
106	MOFATU	MOFOTA	JOSEPH	31
107	MOFOKENG		SEKOLOTSA ABRAM	15/20
108	MOFOKENG	-	GEELBOY/GEELBOOI	21
109	MOFOKENG	MAFOKENG	JOSEPH	43
110	MOFOKENG		SEGHEBANE/ SEGHABANE	35
111	MOGOTSI		LAZARUS MOEKETSI	18
112	MOHALI		GABRIEL/GEMUEL	27
113	MOILOA		JOSEPH	24
114	MOISI	MOISE	ELIZABETH	45
115	MOJAKOJA	MOJAKOLA/ MOKAKOJA/ MOJAKOLA	JOSEPH	32
116	MOKAE	MOKAI/MAKOE	ISAAC	38
117	MOKELE		PETROS/PETRUS	16
118	MOKHESENE	MOKHESENG	PHINEAS	34
119	MOKLEAYANE		LEEUW	?
120	MOKOENA	MOKWENA	JANTJIE PETROUS/ PETRUS	18
121	MOKOENA	MOKWENA	JOSEPH	32
122	MOKONE		ALINE/ALINAH	45
123	MOKOPOTSA	MAKOPOPO	PATRICK	28
124	MOLAMU		MANTSIOA EMMA	?
125	MOLEFE	MOLEFI	PETER	25
126	MOLEKO		DINEO ELIZABETH	9
127	MOLIBELI	MOLIBEDI/ MOTIBELI/ MODIBELI	PETER	20
128	MOLISE		BLOU JOHANNES	?
129	MOLISE	MODISE/MODESE	ISHMAEL	21
130	MOLISE	MODISE	MOTSEKE/MOTSEKI	38
131	MOLODESE		ALEDE	49
132	MOLOI		SAMUEL	31
133	MOLOTO		EDWARD	21
134	MOLOTSI		LIMAKATSO ANNA	36/37
135	MONTSI		ELIZABETH	?
136	MONYANE	MONYANI	AZAEL	45
137	MOOI	MOAI	MOSES	31
138	MORAILANA	MORIALANI/ MORAILANE	BETHUEL	42

139	MORABE		JOSEPH	?
140	MOROBE	MARABE	HOPHNY	23
141	MOSALA		SHADRACK	28
142	MOSESI		ISAAC	48
143	MOTAUNG		THABO ISAAC	22/28
144	MOTHA		JOSEPH/JOSHUE/ JOSHIAH	43
145	MOTHAKANE		MARIA MMAMOTLANYANA	36
146	MOTHEBE	MATHEBE/ MOTHEKE/ MOTHIBE	MAGGIE	44
147	MOTHIBELI	MOTHIBEDI	DANIEL KOK	34/35
148	MOTHLODISE	MOTHLODISI/ MOTLODISE/ MOTHOLIRE/ MOLIEDISE	ALIDA/ALEDE/ALIDAH	45
149	MOTIJOANE	MATYOANE	ALBERT	17
150	MOTSEPE	MOTSEPA/ MOTSIPE	ANNA	55
151	MOTSETSE	MOTSITSI	SALLY/SOLLY	23
152	MOTSOAHOLE	MOTSHOLE	AGNES	22
153	MOTSOAHOLE		FRANCIS	?
154	MOTSOAHOLE		MONICA	
155	MOTSOANE		JOHN LEHLOHONOLO	38
156	MOTSOANE	MOTSOANA	AARON	26
157	MOTSOANE	MOTSOANA	JOHANNES	13
158	MPEMPE		CHRISTIAN	41
159	MPESHE		AGNES	?
160	MSIMANGA		MAMOKETE MARIA	25
161	MTIMKULU	MTIMBULU	ELIAS	39
162	MTSHALI	MTSALI/MASHILE	SOLOMON	16
163	MUSIBI	MSIBI	LECHEAL	37
165	MVUBAZANA		EDILARNO	?
165	MVULANE		ALFRED	23
166	NARE		ELIZABETH	?
167	NCHAUPE	CHAUPE	SOPHINIA/SOPHENIA/ ZEPAHIAH	40
168	NDABA		ANTHONY	50
169	NDLOVU		ALINAH	?
170	NGATI		ISHMAIL/SEFAKO ISHMAEL/ISMAIL	31
171	NHLANGO		CHAMERLAIN	?
172	NHLAPO	NHLAPU	JACOB RAMAITO	19
173	NKPUTA		JOHN	?
174	NTEMYANE	NTIMYANE	PHILIP/PHILLIP	?
175	NTESO		JOHN	53
176	NTHE	NTLE/NTLHE	KEFILWE AGNES	46
177	NTJE		JACOB MOLEFE	?
178	NTSALA		MAPITSO LIZZIE	8

179	NTSUBA		ZABULON MOFOKENG/ ZEBULON	31
180	PEETE		MITCHELL	?
181	PELAELO	PALAELO/ PILAELO	ADELINAH/ADELINE	24
182	PHAKELI		EVODIA MAMATOBA	?
183	PHOSISI	PHOSISIE	PAPAKWE DANIEL	19/21
184	PIETERSEN	NO CLAIM	ANDREW	?
185	PITSO		MESCHACK/MISCHACK	18
186	POOE	POOL	DANIEL	66
187	POOLE	POOLO	SAMUEL	20
188	QUILE	QHILE/QINA	JOSEPH	26
189	QUTWYA	GQUTWYA/ QTWAYA/ QUTWYA/ QOTAWA	GEORGE	22
190	RABOROKO	RABOROKA	JOEL	30
191	RABOTAPI	RABATAPI/ RABATANI	VIOLET	49
192	RADEBE		MIRIAM MFAZIMNI	30
193	RADEBE	SETEBE	SOLOMON	22
194	RAHOMA		BEATRICE	?
195	RAMAHALI		CHARLES	10
196	RAMATHLOLO		ALINA	?
197	RAMOHOASE	RAMOKHOASE/ RAMAKHOASE	NTELE DAVID	28/31
198	RAMOHOASE	RAMOKHOASE/ RAMAKHOASE/ RAMOGOASE	LEBITSA SOLOMON	36
199	SAKAONE	SAKOANE/ SKAWANA	ADAM	37
200	SAKHALE		GLORINA	?
201	SECHABALA	SECHABELA	SHADRACK	21
202	SEERI	SHURI	PIET	26
203	SEFUME	SEFUMA/SEFUNE	DAVID	37
204	SEHUSI		MARTHA	?
205	SEKATE		GEORGE	?
206	SENOKO	SELEKO	MAKHOABATHE/ MAKHOATHI	39
207	SEPAMPURU		AGNES	5
208	SEPENG		DANIEL	35
209	SERETLO	SERETHO/ SERELLO/ SERETTO	JOHANNES	37
210	SEROTO	SEROTA/ SEROTHO	ESIAH/ISAAI	19
211	SETLHATLOLE	SETHATLOLE/ SETHATLOTE/ SEHLAHALE	ELIZABETH	43
212	SHABANGU		MOSES	19

213	SHASAEDI	TSOADE/SHAEDI/ TSOAELE	PETROS	63
214	SITHOLE	SETHOLE	DANIEL	21
215	SMITH		JOHANNES	23
216	SMITH	SMIT	MOSES	?
217	SPRINGKAAN		EMILY	42
218	TAMBO	MNTAMBO	MIRIAM/MERIAM/ MARIAM	32
219	TANYANE	TANYANI/ TENYANE/ MONYANE	ISIAH/AZAEL	35
220	TATAI	TETAI	ISAAC	31
221	TEKETSI		KOADI EMMANUEL	24
222	TENYANE	TANYANE/ TEMYANE/ NTIMYANEANE	PHILLIP	50
223	THABA	TLABA	EPHRAIM	35
224	THABANE	TLABANE	PETER	22
225	THAMAE		DAVID	50
226	THELETSANE	TELETSANE/ TELEKANI	LYDIA	20
227	THIPE		JOHN	62
228	TLHOPHANE	THLAPANE	JOHN	64
229	TSHABALALA	TSHAVALALA	DANIEL	32
230	TSHABALALA	SHABALALA	LYDIA	?
231	TSHABALALA		PIET	36
232	TSOAI		AGNES	14
233	TSOELIPE	SEDEPE	JOSEPH	45
234	TSONELI		PETRUS	?
235	TSUBANE	TSUBONZ/ SABANIE	EUGENE	37
236	YASSEN	MASENG	LYDIA	36
237	YONA	JONAH/JONA	GEORGE	48
238	ZONDWAYO		MAHALIO MARY	30

Index

Pages in *italics* refer to figures and pages in **bold** refer to tables.

Aerial view of Sharpeville on 21 March 139–141
African Cables 33, 45, 58, 88, 91, 94–95, 114, 118, 129–130, 133, 197, 242; labour organising at 100–102; PAC badges printed at 121; shooting victims employed by 200–201, 232
African Gas and Power Workers' Union 100
African labour, factories and 43, 94, 115–116; "Labour Bureaux" 107; South African War and "work or die" policy 12–*13*; "surplus labour" 35, 105, 107; on White farms 8–10, 15, 17, 38, 234, 236
African locations 54, 89, 93; administration 41; design 53–55, 63, 66, 68, 72, 84, 86–87; early 9–10, 53; residence requirements 35, 44, 87–88, 197; Urban Areas Act and 28
African National Congress (ANC) 39, 97, 103–105, 118, 130–131, 136, 225, 241, 261, 271
"*Afrika!*" use and meaning of 130–131, 157–158
alcohol *see* beer
All African People's Conference (1958) 227, 255
American Committee on Africa 212–213
ambulances 176–177, 187, 229; Nkosi and Nakasa place injured in 248; suspicious arrival of before massacre 174, 186

anti-apartheid struggle, Sharpeville and international 225, 236, 240, 248; "African-Asian group," 228, 235–236; Argentina 237; Ceylon 228, 236–238; Ecuador 237–238; Ethiopia 212, 228, 235, 238, 240; France 238, 251–253; Ghana 227; Guinea 226–227, 235–238; Indian origins of 220, 227–228, 236–239, 254–255; International Olympic Committee 239, 251; Italy 238; Jordan 228, 237; Netherlands 212, 239, 251–252; New Zealand 227, 239–240, 253; Sweden 225, 239, 251–253, 256; United Kingdom 238, 251–253; United States 226–227, 235, 238–239, 252–253, 256–257
apartheid, as a crime against humanity 225, 248–253; homelands 43, 99, 214, 234; laws, urban areas 43, 45, 52, 66–72; *see also* legislation
assegai (spear), used by African police 121
Assumpta Catholic private school 108
autopsies of victims of Sharpeville Massacre 174, 190, 200, 203, 221, 268–269

baasskap (boss-ship) 247, 252
Bandung Conference (1955) 227
Bantu Education Act 70, 89, 96
Baragwanath Hospital 177, 191, 196, 203, 221
Basutoland, families sent to after the Sharpeville Massacre 211, 215

beer brewing restrictions on 34–37, 39–41, 48, 54, 59, 74, 80, 89–90, 93, 102–103, 108, 110, 119, 123, 200, 210
Berry, Ian 140, 161–162, 171, 183–185, 187, 201
Black press, reporting of the massacre 142, 175–177, 225, 228–229; *see also Golden City Post; New Age; World*
Boers (Afrikaners), and Sharpeville 97–98; as farmers 17, 22, 31; political mythology of 38; republics 10, 16; and South African War 11–12, 14–15; taking of African land 7, 9
Boipatong (African township) 17, 116, 134, 149, 151
Boitso Higher Primary School 96
Bophelong (African township) 54, 68, 72, 106, 179; protest in 116–117, 134, 136, 149–151, 159, 176, 180–181, 221, 241, 258
boxing 33, 45, 97–98, 108; *see also* Mabena, Sexton; Monnakgotla, Carlton
British Fire Brigades Union 212
British Labour Party 212
bus drivers 116, 124–125, 127; *see also* Mosholi, Edwin; Motha, Joshua; Seetsi, Daniel; Vereeniging Transport Company; Xilishe, Aaron

Calder, Bill 154, 187
Calderwood, D.M. 63
Channon, Charles Percivale 154, 162, 177, 181, 187, 225
children, among the Sharpeville Massacre shooting victims 176, 189–190, 192–193, 195, 250, 256; career aspirations 200–201, 217–218; lack of economic support for after the Sharpeville massacre 121, 213, 215–216, 218, 265; left without a parent or parents 195, 199–201, 204, 209–210, 268; sent to concentration camps during the South African War 12, 14, 29; in Sharpeville 91–92, 94–96, 118, 129, 133, 153, 157, 178, 194; in the Sharpeville crowd 151, 153, 156–157, 160, 181, 230; in Top Location 32, 34–35, 48; *see also* crowd, composition of; education; schools
churches Sharpeville 59, 92, 95–97, 108–109; Top Location 32–33, 45
Cioffi, Filiberto 127, 144
Claassen, P.S. (attorney general of the Orange Free State) 147, 185, 242–243; on reliability of African witnesses as compared with police 257
Coalbrook 102; mining disaster (1960) 115, 234, 237
Collins, Reverend John 252
Coloureds (South African population group) 19; Sharpeville 58–59, 61, 68, 70, 74, 97, 104, 120; Top Location 30–31, 47, 58, 68, 70
communism/communists, official fear of 110, 116, 142, 145
Congress of the People 104
Cradle of Humankind 2–3
crowd, composition of 119–120, 129–131, 135, 153, 156–157, 160, 198; estimates of size of in Boipatong and Bophelong 116, 149–150, 179; in Evaton 150–151; Judge Wessels not convinced that the crowd was armed 258; peaceful behaviour of 122, 128, 130, 137, 139, 141, 152, 157–158, 160–161, 164, 169, 228, 236, 243–244; in Sharpeville 118, 124, 130–131, 135, 140, 144, 147–148, 151, 153, 157, 162, 225, 247; shot in the back 169–171, 174, 184, 203, 230; stereotypical references to as a "mob" 134, 167, 201, 225–226, 244, 257; waiting for a high official to address them 151–153, 160, 163, 232, 234; *see also* singing/songs

Daily Mirror coverage of Sharpeville Massacre 226, 230, 254
Daveyton (African township) 73, 75–76, 79, 84
Davidson, Herbert (Top Location superintendent) 39–41
De Certeau, Michel on "surreptitious creativities" 86, 99
Defiance Campaign (1952) 74, 103
Dhlamini, Samuel (Vanderbijlpark PAC) 150
diamonds 10, 14, 21–22, 28, 115

Die Burger, main victims of Sharpeville were Whites 255
Dimo, Gilbert Poho (husband of Selina) 96, 203–205, 210, 217; autopsy 268–269; *see also* Poho, Solobatsi Ishmael (son)
Dimo, Nathan (son of Gilbert and Selina) 210
Dimo, Selina 204, 217, 268
Dlamini, Jacob 86
Dlomo Dam 262–263
doctors *see* Lambinon, Dr. Albertus, autopsies, Steyn, Dr. Hermanus, Friedman, Dr. Jack, Swanepoel, Dr. Phillippus D.
Drum (magazine) 98, 109, 145–146, 161, 177, 179, 187, 220, 236
Duncanville 19, 42, 44–46, 95, 124

education, difficulties obtaining for victims of the massacre 206–207, 213, 215, 217–218; *see also* schools
Electricity Supply Commission (Escom/Eskom) 27, 72, 95, 100–101, 127; power stations (Klip, Highveld, Lethabo, Taaibos, Vaal) 1, 75, 114–115
emotions 193, 203, 209, 216–217, 238, 241–248, 250, 260; *see also* respect
Erasmus, F.C. (minister of justice) 192, 242, 253
Evaton 37, 44, 67–69, 74, 92, 102, 152, 177, 229, 236–237; population of 180; protest in 116–117, 125, 132–134, 136, 149–151, 154–155, 175, 180, 233, 241

Fanon, Frantz 224, 254
Fatima Industrial School 110
feelings *see* emotions, respect
Ferreira Boxing Club 98
Ferreira, Ignatius P. (Vereeniging manager of "Non-European" affairs) 74, 77, 85, 88, 98, 103, 107, 123–124, 134–135, 143, 146, 149, 153, 256; and African women 103–104, 210
First, Ruth 141
football *see* soccer
Foucault, Michel 80–81, 86
Frack, Dr. Isidore 256
Friedman, Dr. Jack 221

Funerals for Sharpeville residents killed by the police 192–193, 235, 243, 263

"Garden Cities" 54
Gate, the (entry to Sharpeville) 119, 121, 123–124, 126–134 passim, 137, 147, 149, 151, 154–156, 158, 162–163, 174, 180, 186, 191, 212–213, 234
Ghanaian Convention People's Party 212
Gqabi, Joe Nzingo 176–177, 179, 187, 228
Golden City Post 154, 175–177, 181, 187, 228–230, 233, 236, 255
Gowenius, Peder 224, 253
Greyshirts (pro-Hitler group) 38

Hain, Adelaine 212
health and sanitation 11, 29, 32, 42, 59, 63, 213–214; *see also* TB
Hertzog, J.B.M. 38
Hoek, Jan Zacharias 158–161, 182–183
Hopkinson, Tom 187
hospitals *see* Baragwanath, Vereeniging
housing 28, 31, 34–35, 42–44, 46, 54, 64, 66, 68, 72, 74, 77, 88, 90, 103; compounds 29, 42; costs and services 58–64; hostels 29–31, 42, 47, 59, 82, 130, 133, 145, 197; NE 51/9 62–65, 81–82, 217
Houtkop farm 12–13, 69, 92
Houtkop road 68; as derogatory term 84
Howard, Ebenezer 54
human rights 236, 238–239, 252; *see also* Human Rights Day; United Nations
Human Rights Day 179, 261

India and criticism of apartheid 220, 227–228, 235–239; *see also* Nehru, Jawaharlal
Indians (South African population group) 19, 30, 68, 70, 74, 99, 104, 212
industries/industry 14–15, 28, 53–54; African Metals Corporation (Amcor) 101, 150; ArcelorMittal (formerly Iscor) 2, 45, 216; Babcock and Wilcox 28, 45, 200, 215–216, 232; Broderick Engineering and Motors

92, 216–217; Central Mine 25, 55; Cornelia Colliery 22, 25, 27, 115, 200, 231; diagram of coalfields mined by 23; diagram of underground mining operations 26; Delport Glass 215; Dorman Long 116; Dunswarts 58; engineering 20; gold mines 10, 12, 14, 17, 25, 27, 37, 75, 100–101, 115; Irvine Chapman 28; Massey Ferguson 28; McKinnon Chain 45, 101, 127; Metal Box 116; mining 16–17, 115, 127; Raleigh Industries 120, 200, 205, 210; Rand Water Board (RWB) 49, 59, 75, 100, 114–115; SA Nuts and Bolts 101; Scaw Metals 45; South African Farm Implements (Safim) 88, 94–95, 101, 116, 127, 144, 200, 208, 216, 232; Union Liquid Air 232; Vecor 114; Vereeniging Brick and Tile 27, 29, 32, 55, 63, 88, 94–95, 100, 125–127, 129, 200; Vereeniging Milling 151; Vereeniging New Consolidated Mealie Combine 232; *see also* African Cables; Electricity Supply Commission; Lewis and Marks; South African, Coal, Oil and Gas Company; South African Iron and Steel Corporation; Stewarts and Lloyds; Union Steel Corporation; Vereeniging Estates
International Defence and Aid Fund 252
Iscor *see* South African Iron and Steel Corporation
ITN film crew 162, 177, 187
Izwe lethu meaning and use of 130–131, 135, 151–152

Jana, Chris (Top Location) 31–32
January, Daniel Kokozela (court translator) 144, 246

Kaba, Sidwell (Vanderbijlpark PAC) 149–150, 179, 258
Kentridge, Sydney 143, 145, 158, 181, 183, 185, 196, 257
Kimberley (and diamonds) 9, 21–22, 25, 115
Klip River 2–3, 5, 7, 12, 22, 37
Kodi, Sophia (Top Location) 48
Kumalo, Alf 161, 177, 193–194, 197–198, 220

Kwa-Thema (African township) 75–77, 84
Kweneng (African city) 4–5

Labuschagne, Michiel Andries (Sharpeville location superintendent) 88, 103–104, 122, 124–125, 130, 154, 258; effect of police shooting reminded him of a wheat field 169, 184; estimate of distance between White police and protestors 185; estimate of duration of police firing 185; false testimony of 144, 146, 198; his count of the dead 191; persecution of victims of the massacre 210
Lambinon, Dr. Albertus 221
legislation, segregation era 28, 42, 53; apartheid 70, 89, 101; *see also* pass laws
Lekoa (Basotho name for Vaal River and river basin) 7, *13*, 16, 21, 28
Lekoa Shandu High School 96, 102, 110
Leslie, T.N., Vereeniging's first mayor 27
Lethege, Anna 157, 170, 211, 215, 245, 247–248
Lewis and Marks 22, 25, 29, 42, 63; *see also* Lewis, Isaac; Marks, Sammy
Lewis, Isaac 22, 242
Lidia, Elias 118, 121, 127–129, 135–136, 138–140, 142, 155–156, 160, 248; and arrival of ambulances 174, 187; on *baasskap* 246–247, 252; can identify police 245; criticism of police evidence 244, 257–258; estimates of crowd size 135, 144, 151; explanation of words and symbols 130–131, 144; growing enthusiasm for PAC 135–136, 153; plans to write a book 118; use of paid informants on 21 March 136, 160; witnesses the massacre and aftermath 171–172, 174, 201
Lifaqane 1, 7, 21, 28
Lowenstein, Allard 230
Lynville (African township) 75–76, 78, 84

Mabena, Sexton ("Wonder Boy") 32, 98, 260
Machine guns *see* Sten gunners

Index 285

MacKenzie, Eric (assistant to superintendent Top Location) 40–41
Macmillan, Harold 226, 254
Mafube (proposed African location) 67–69
Magubane, Peter 177, 187, 220
Maja, Robert (Presbyterian minister) 97, 157, 162, 192, 213; assistance to injured 174; describes the crowd 153, 156, 244; testifies 243–245, 257; witnesses the shooting 171, 200–201, 217
Mako, Aletta (Top Location) 43
"Mamashiya" arrest of in Top Location 48
Mandela, Nelson 89, 261
Manyosi, Ronnie 154, 175–177, 187, 189, 228–229, 241, 255
Marks, Sammy 15–16, 22, 25, 27–28; see also Lewis and Marks
Masekela, Hugh 260
Matsie Steyn Lower Primary School 96
Mayibuye meaning and use of 74, 130–131, 152, 172–173
memory, consistency of 232–233, 248; redemptive role of 260–263
Methodist Mission School 33, 97
Modisane, Bloke 105, 186, 230
Moeli Higher Primary School 94
Mofokeng, Geelbooi 151, 156, 254, 265
Molefe, Reverend Philip (Assemblies of God) 108–109, 112
Molefi, Peter (the man in the red shirt) 136, 138–139, 146–147, 152, 157–158, 160, 172, 183; disrespectful police treatment of 163–165, 175, 183; testimony to Commission and to Court 183, 211, 242–243, 245, 247–248, 257
More, Thomas (PAC) 108, 120, 122, 128, 138, 151, 159–160; cross examines police witnesses at trial 143, 245–246; family responsibilities of 212; stands with Nyakane Tsolo "as men," 262; taken forcibly into police station 160
Mosheledi, Lucas Simon (PAC) 119–120, 122–123, 130, 135–136, 138–139, 155, 158, 160, 180, 241
Moshoeshoe 7–9
Municipal Police: Kok, Sergeant Piet 120; Mvala, Constable Elias 123;

Pitsi, Sergeant Ben in 1937 40; in 1960 172–173, 186
Mzilikazi 7, 9

Nakasa, Nat 177, 187, 248–249
Natives Land Act 15
Naude, D.B (Top Location superintendent) 35–36
Nehru, Jawaharlal 227–228, 238, 240
neighbourhoods, Sharpeville see Phelindaba, Phomolong, Putsoastene, Rooistene, "site and service", Stands, Vergenoeg, Vukazenzele
New Age 103–104, 116, 141, 176, 179, 187, 228, 230, 236
New York Times 225, 227, 248–249, 254–255
Nhlapo, Jacob (Evaton commuter to Sharpeville) 152, 180, 229
Nkosi, Lewis 177, 187, 241, 249–252
Nkosi Sikelel' iAfrika 139, 152
Nkrumah, Kwame 227, 240
Nyerere, Julius 227

O'Brien, P.M. (presiding magistrate in Regina vs. Monyake and Others trial) 146; finds most Sharpeville defendants not guilty 247
O'Driscoll, I.P. ("Native" commissioner Vereeniging) 75

PAC see Pan-African Congress
pain 189, 203, 248; emotional 209, 217, 230, 260–263; physical 171, 177, 200, 204–205, 207–208, 213, 216, 229; see also emotions; trauma
Pan-African Congress (PAC) 105, 107–108; attraction of 136, 153, 227, 244; badges worn 121, 131, 234; banning of 241; international anti-apartheid movement and 225; language of 246; non-violence of 229, 234–235; official retribution against 210; organisation of 21 March protest 116, 118–122, 124–126, 128–129, 135–136, 149–151, 179, 199, 208, 258; pamphlets 108, 118, 122, 151, 240, 246, 258; Sharpeville branch formed 102, 105, 108, 130, 139, 229; trial of supporters 211–212, 222, 241, 246; White fears of 103–104, 116–117, 131–132, 167, 175, 209; see also Sobukwe, Robert

286 Index

pass laws 102, 105–107, 114, 135, 152, 161, 262; arrests 41, 105–106, 208, 232, 249; *dompas* (literally stupid pass) 201, 222, 262; passbooks 74, 91–92, 105–107, 151, 268
paths/pathways, informal 33, 55–56, 87, 125–127, 129, 140, 180
Peace of Vereeniging 15–16
Phelindaba cemetery 190, 193, 221
Phelindaba (Sharpeville neighbourhood) 90, 97, 202
Phomolong (Sharpeville neighbourhood) 90–91, 97–98, 109, 202
phone, Sharpeville out of order and repaired 121–122, 128, 134, 139, 146, 155
photographers 154, 158–162, 180, 191; police 177, 187; *see also* Berry, Ian; Channon, Charles Percivale; Gqabi, Joe Nzingo; Hoek, Jan Zacharias; Kumalo, Alf; Magubane, Peter; Manyosi, Ronnie; Ramakatane, Mohlouoa Theo; Robinson, Warwick; van Beloll, Barry John
photographs of the Sharpeville massacre 143, 148, 158, 186, 220, 226, 229; by African photographers 177, 187, 192, 197, 228; available online 183; censorship of 154, 186; numbers taken 177, 181, 187; publication of by the news media 187, 226, 254, 256; showing movement of people who had been shot 175; used to prove falseness of police testimony 184, 188, 244; *see also* photographers
Pienaar, Lieutenant Colonel Gideon Daniel 115, 124, 130, 134, 136–137, 225; and aftermath of shooting 172, 178, 186, 188, 244; arrival at Sharpeville 162–163, 229, 233; career 167–168; cordial relations with White press 175, 186–187; on duration of shooting 172; estimate of distance between White police and protestors 185; orders police to search for stones as "evidence" 177–178, 188; orders White police to line up 163–164, 166; orders White police to shoot 166–168; on protestors as a "mob" 244; racist attitude to Africans 167–168; on Spengler's "peculiar position" 144–145

planes, government use of against protestors 38, 116, 141, 151, 156, 181, 189
Pogrund, Benjamin 159–162
Poho, Solobatsi Ishmael (son of Gilbert Poho Dimo) 217; *see also* Dimo, Gilbert Poho
police 36–37, 41, 73–75, 93; arrival of and numbers 118, 121, 124, 131, 137–138, 146, 153–155, 158–159, 162, 165–166, 181, 232–233; as depicted by Lewis Nkosi 249–252; bullets 40, 133; changing estimates of numbers fired by White police 170, 184–185, 220; dum dums 204, 222, 268; injuries caused by 150, 190, 197, 201, 204, 206, 215, 222, 233, 254, 265, 268; private purchase of 154; types used 121, 169–170, 185; duration of firing by 169–170, 172, 184–185, 233; false stories of Africans throwing stones and using sticks to attack 135, 144–145, 177–178, 187–188, 225, 228, 231–233, 243–245, 255–256, 261; firing squad 170, 185; label all Sharpeville residents as *aanhiteers* (agitators) 160, 198; and *betogers* (protestors) 180, 199, 220, 260; municipal 36–37, 39, 41, 120, 123, 128, 172–173, 177, 180, 187, 192–193, 208; no injuries to 117, 228, 255; no order to disperse given 128, 133, 183, 232–233, 236, 254; Officer in Charge (OIC) on 21 March (by turn Heyl, Theron, Pienaar) 132, 154, 160, 162, 167; ordered to fire (*skiet* or *vuur*) at crowd 165–167, 173, 183–184, 254; shooting considered the only way to disperse the crowd 139; use of baton charges 116, 118, 121–122, 133, 150, 162, 168, 192, 230; use of derogatory language for Africans 124, 153, 168, 173, 246, 249–250; use of language "to seize" rather than "to arrest" 131–132, 134, 145, 160; use of tear gas 116, 132, 145, 150, 162, 168, 230; usual "police story" 225, 228, 253, 255–256, 265; Wessels criticism of 247, 258; *see also* Municipal Police; Saracen; South African Police; Special Branch; Sten gunners

Pooe, Emilia Mahlodi 14, 16–17
Pooe, Ernst (Vanderbijlpark) 150
pula use and meaning of 131
Pululu, Elizabeth (Top Location) 36
Putsoastene (Sharpeville neighbourhood) 59, 61, 90–91, 94, 97–99, 109, 119–120, 122, 126, 135, 202

Quakers 212

rail/rail lines 10–12 passim, 13, 16, 25, 27–29, 42, 45, 66, 68–70, 75, 94, 115; see also South African Railways
Ramakatane, Mohlouoa Theo 177
Rand Daily Mail (RDM) reporting the "police story" 175, 255–256; self-censorship by 176, 187
Reeves, Bishop Ambrose 142, 218–219, 222, 230–231, 255; hires attorneys to represent Sharpeville victims 196, 231, 241, 252, 266
respect, concept of among Sharpeville residents 117, 119, 125, 135–136, 160, 163, 183, 235; lack of shown by Whites towards Africans 38, 122–123, 159, 163–164, 169–170, 183, 190, 243–245
Rhodes, Cecil 22
rivers see Klip, Lekoa, Suikerbosrand, Vaal
Robinson, Jackie 239
Robinson, Warwick 173, 175, 177, 186–187, 220, 226, 244, 254
Rooistene (Sharpeville neighbourhood) 61, 90–91, 97–98, 102, 119, 171; map of 202

Sacks, Harold 175, 180, 186–187, 220
Sand River Convention (1852) 8
Sapola, Jemina (Top Location) 48
Saracen armoured vehicles 134, 162, 186, 208, 228; arrival of at Sharpeville 154–157 passim, 158, 161, 164, 181; four stationed at the Sharpeville police station 117, 159–161, 165–170 passim, 171–172, 184–185, 190
Sasol see South African, Coal, Oil and Gas Company
Sasolberg 49, 72, 105–106, 114
schools and schooling 32–34, 44, 59, 70, 76, 82, 90, 94–95, 99, 102, 110, 179, 200, 236; churches and 96–97; closed on 21 March 131, 150–151, 154, 163, 165, 170, 189–190, 197–198, 200, 205, 242; School Square 62, 95–96, 108, 119, 128–129, 135, 202; White school built over Top Location after removals 16, 45; see also Assumpta Catholic private school; Boitso Higher Primary School; Fatima Industrial School; Lekoa Shandu High School; Matsie Steyn Lower Primary School; Methodist Mission School; Moeli Higher Primary School; Sediba Primary School; Sharpe Public School; St. Cyprian's Anglican School; Stewart Higher Primary School
Schoup, Henri 176–178
Sebokeng 68, 72
Sediba Primary School 264
Seminar on Apartheid (Brasilia 1966) 251–252
Senzeni Na (protest song) 152
Seutso, Adam and Martha assaulted by Gideon Daniel Pienaar 167–168
Sharpe, John Lille 28, 42, 100
Sharpe Public School 44
Sharpetown Swingsters 33, 98–99
Sharpeville Cycle Works 152
Sharpeville Heritage and Tourism Association 263
Sharpeville Memorial (erected 2010) 179, 190
Sharpeville neighbourhoods 56, 59, 61, 68–70, 72, 90, 202; see also Phelindaba; Phomolong; Putsoastene; Rooistene; "site and service"; Stands; Vergenoeg; Vukazenzele; police station in 72–75; purchase of land for 42; street layout 58–59, 61, 76–77, 81–82
Sharpeville Relief Fund 212–213, 215, 222
Sharpeville residents: Benjamin, Sana 219–220, 222; Bessie, James Buti 189–190, 203, 218; Botha, Buiswa (granddaughter of Elizabeth and Walter) 215; Botha, Elizabeth (Walter's wife) 157, 194, 199, 215; Botha (Mbatha), Walter 157, 193–194, 199; Chabeli, Minah Elizabeth 156, 229; Chalale, Lydia 190–191, 195, 204, 222; Dhlamini,

Index

Anna 103–104; Dikubo, Daniel 155, 165, 170, 173–174, 213; Fantisi, Emmanuel 95, 126–127, 215–216, 218; Griffiths, Thatela Benedict 129, 164–165, 170, 218–219, 231, 233, 244, 256; Hlatshwayo, Reverend Sam 192, 229; Hlongwane, Alina (mother of Thomas) 126; Hlongwane, Thomas 126, 229; Jonah, George 156; Kabi, Elliot (son of Mosekoala) 156, 197–198, 217; Kabi, Mosekoala Eusebia 197, 217; Khaole, Abraham 229, 232–233, 245; Khosi, Magdalena 213; Koboekae, Richard 126–127, 156; Kubeka, Elliott 156; Kutoane, Azael 92; Kutoane, Joseph 221; Lebeko, K. 192, 229; Lechesa, Ben Phoofolo 205–206, 215; Lehlokoane, Jan 213–214; Lehobo, Stephen 157, 172; Lepee, Marium (sister of Steven, cousin of Martha) 153, 165, 203, 207, 212, 222, 229; Lepee, Martha Masello 96, 165, 207; Lepee, Salanyane Steven 120–121, 129, 207, 212; Lerolo, Koti 231; Leroto, Isiah 187; Lesito, Mahlodi Caroline (daughter of William) 216; Lesito, Mohauli Solomon (son of William) 92, 126, 157, 216; Lesito, Monedalibe William 92, 126, 157, 216; Lesito family, work of 92; Lekitla, Mirriam 203; Lipale, Machabedi Mirriam 216, 218; Mabaso, David 156; Mabena, Joseph 96; Mabitsela, Paulus 194; Mabitsela (Mavizela), Aron 193–194; Mabona, Khehla (husband of Konsamatsa) 195; Mabona, Konsatsama Elizabeth 195; Mabote, Azael 120, 151; Mabuya, Alfred 146; Madeski, Elizabeth 195; Madiku, Pauline 196; Maeko, Justice 156, 205–206, 210–211, 215; Magkotse, Emily 48; Mahabane, Reverend E.E. (African Methodist Church) 97, 192, 213; Mahanjane (née Monnakgotla), Eucalphonia 211; Mahlangu, Beshu 232–233; Mahlasi, Samuel 120; Mahlele, Samuel 193–194; Mahlong, Christina (mother of Shadrack) 216–217; Mahlong, Shadrack 216–217; Mailane, John Motsoahae 156, 203; Mailane, Lydia, husband John killed 213; Maine, Matlakala Mauleen (niece of Naphtali) 204, 210; Maine, Mirriam (mother of Naphtali) 126, 204, 210, 267–268; Maine, Naphtali Tseko 126, 157, 199, 204, 210, 221, 267–268; Majola, Gladys 207–208; Makhoba, Daniel (son of Maria) 189, 203, 213; Makhoba, Maria 127, 178, 213; Makhume, Samuel 203; Malema, Maggie 86, 96, 208; Malikoe, Elizabeth (daughter of Mamotshabi) 190; Malikoe, Mamotshabi Paulina (and unborn child) 190, 195; Malotsi, Elias 92, 174, 203; Maluka, Paulus 146; Manato, Adam 232; Manyane, Elisabeth 196; Mareka, Mishack 155, 170; Mareletse, Ezekiel 203; Marokoane, Anna 126, 199; Maroo, Benjamin 158, 163, 170–171, 175; Mashiya, Elizabeth (mother of Isaac, Matthew, and Petrus) 183; Mashiya family 163; Mashiya, Isaac (brother of Matthew and Petrus) 163, 198, 211; Mashiya Matthew 163, 211, 232–233, 257; Mashiya, Peter 163, 211; Masilo, Constance (wife of Ezekiel) 201, 218; Masilo, Elias (son of John) 190, 198, 203; Masilo, Ephraim (son of Solomon), Masilo, Ethel (wife of Simon) 218; Masilo, Ezekiel (brother of Simon) 91, 201, 218, 221, 229; Masilo family 91, 94, 190, 217–218; Masilo, John 91, 190; Masilo, Mohauli Solomon 91, 105–106, 156, 201, 216; Masilo, Simon 91, 201, 217–218, 229; Mathibela, Peter 32; Mathinye family, Eva, Sampson, and Paulina 92; Matsabu, Aaron 229; Matsabu, Mphonyana Annetjie 189–190, 218; Matzumo, Eliza 43; Mazibuko, Abram Mgodo 271; Mazibuko, Abraham Rapule 271; Mazibuko, J. Mokoto 230; Mazibuko, Selina and Aaron 156; Mbhele, Jacob (husband of Norah) 213; Mbhele (Mbele), Norah Nobhekisizwe 174, 203, 213; Mgomezulu, Islabet 196; Mkwanazi, Meshack 152, 165; Mnguni, Jan 203; Mpempe, Christian 123; Moahloli,

Lydia 218; Moatlhodi, Samuel 93–94, 193; Mochologi, Joseph 151–152, 174, 203, 221; Modise, Ishmael 232–233; Modise, Motseki 215; Mofatu, Joseph 232; Mofisane, Jan 44; Mofogane, Jean 196; Mofokeng, Abram 178, 222; quoted 260, 264; Mofokeng family 90; Mofokeng, John Kolane (Josephina's husband) 123; Mofokeng, Josephina 123; Mofokeng, Minnie 40; Mofulatsi, Paulinah 174, 203; Mohlatsane, Annakleta (wife of Enuwell) 210; Mohlotsane, Enuwell Monkonyane 210; Moiloa, Joseph 207; Moise, Elizabeth 206; Mokae, Issac 206; Mokajoka, Joseph 232–233; Mokele, Petrus 151; Mokoena, Aaron 144; Mokoena, Andrew 195; Mokoena, Mataeke Elizabeth 208; Mokoena, Piet 120; Mokone, Makorotsoane Alinah 157, 213–214; Mokoteli, Michael 44; Molapo, Jerry 195, 229; Molebatsi, Maria 190, 203; Molefe family 9, 14–17; Molefe, Richard 126, 203; Moloto, Edward 172, 177, 186, 244–245, 247, 258; Molotsi, Elias 92, 174, 203; Monnakgotla, Carlton 220, 260; Monnakgotla, Daniel (father of Dikelede Monnakgotla and Eucalphonia Mahanjane) 211; Monnakgotla, Dikelede Selina 211; Mono, Elizabeth 199; Monyake, Johannes Dlamini (Qwadi) 119, 129–130, 217; Monyane, Isiah 232–233; Morita, David, lives outside Sharpeville 180; Morobe, Hophny 95, 107–108, 156; Morobi, Alice (wife of Joseph) 195, 218; Morobi, Joseph 195, 218, 221; Morobi, Matshepo Maria (daughter of Alice and Joseph) 195, 218; Mosholi, Edwin 125; Motha, Joshua 125–126, 139, 163, 165, 170, 172, 186, 207, 219, 257; Motsega, Historina (wife of Kopano) 215, 222; Motsega, Kopano 203, 222, 271; Motsei, Jan 120, 127; Motshoahole, Agnes 157, 172, 180; Motshoahole, Francis (husband of Agnes) 119–120, 122–123, 153, 157; Motsoane, Aaron 156; Mtimkulu, John 98;

Mtimkulu, Richard 119, 217; Mtshali, Solomon 232; Musibi, Lecheal 94, 170, 172, 242; Musibi family 94; Nchaupe, John 229; Nchaupe, Zephaniah 232; Ndaba, Anthony 125–126, 152, 199–200, 231–233; Nkhi, Isaac (grandfather of Pulane) 208, 229; Nkhi, Pulane Margaret 208–209; Nkokotsoane, James 215; Nteso family 90; Nteso, John Shabe 157, 170, 185, 218; Nteso, John (son of John Shabe) 218; Nthoesoane, Petros 92; Ntjê, Jacob Molefe 192, 196–197; Ntoampe, Thaddea 121, 130–132, 212; Ntsame, David (municipal gatekeeper) 119, 132–133, 145, 155; Ntsane, Elizabeth Mookgo 195; Ntsoa, Kopano 271; Nyepisi, Jan 120; Phakeli, Evodia Mamatoba 197–198, 207; Phosisi, Daniel 156; Phutheho, Anna (wife of John and mother of Walter) 178, 205; Phutheho, John 156, 178, 205, 217; Phutheho, Walter 209, 217; Pitso, Meshack 156, 207, 229; Qtwaya, George 126, 232; Raboroko, Joel 95; Radebe, Evelyn 195; Ralebakeng, Sello 93–94, 195, 221; Ralebese, David 127; Ramagole, Mokgathi David (also known as Ramodibe) 108, 130, 135, 212; Ramahali, Charles 248; Ramailane, T. 195, 229; Ramohoase, David (brother of Solomon) 248; Ramohoase, Lebitsa Solomon 187, 248, 258; Ramokgadi, Rosta Maratjwaneng 215; Ramokoena, Jacob 203, 229, 258; Rampai, Izak 119; Sakaone, Adam 155–156, 162, 232–233, 256; Salanyane, Jan 120, 127; Sedisa, William 213; Seetsi, Daniel 125; Sefatsa, Josiah, oldest son Samuel killed 213; Senyalano, Johannes 190; Sepampuru, Philemon (husband of Salamina) 174, 217; Sepampuru, Salamina 217; Sepeng, Daniel 91; Sepeng family 91–92; Sepeng, Isaac 194; Sepeng, John 91; Seretho, Johannes 126; Seroto, Isaai 232; Setlhatlole, Elizabeth 94, 126, 170, 199, 204; Setlhatlole family 94; Shabangu, Moses 125, 159, 181,

232, 257; Sikhosane, Philemon 126–127; Sothoane, Zanana Nathaniel 190, 193; Tambo (née Tshukudu), Matlala Adelaide Frances (sister of Suzan Tshukudu) 39, 48, 96, 102; Tatai, Isaac 151–152; Thaba, Ephraim 95, 133, 145, 197, 213, 258; Thabe, Brown 129, 139, 147, 257; Thabe, George 97–98, 108, 179; Thinane, Martha Kaseane (Salamina's daughter) 210, 216; Thinane, Salamina 210; Thipe, Ramarindo John and family 91; Tinane, Abraham 152; Tsela, Edward 190; Tshabalala, Daniel 232; Tshabalala family 90–91; Tshukudu, Suzan 102; Tsoelipe, Joseph 206, 210–211, 215; Voyi, Reverend 157, 171, 192; Xilishe, Aaron 123, 125; *see also* Dimo, Gilbert Poho; Lethege, Anna; Lidia, Elias; Mabena, Sexton; Maja, Robert; Mofokeng, Geelbooi; Molefe, Reverend Philip; Molefi, Peter; Monyake, Johannes Dlamini; More, Thomas; Mosheledi, Lucas; Poho, Solobatsi Ishmael; Teketsi, Emmanuel; Thamae, Moeletsi Vincent; Thekiso, Michael; Tom, Petrus; Tsolo, Job; Tsolo, Nyakane
singing/songs 74, 130, 139, 152–153, 157, 235
"site and service" (Sharpeville neighbourhood) 72, 82–83, 90, 95, 118; *see also* Vukazenzele (Vuka)
sjambok (whip), illegal use of by White police 39, 123, 132, 143
Skiet Commando (White civilian militia) 137
Smit, Moses (PAC) 128, 135–136, 138–140, 153, 158–160, 164, 183
Smuts, Mathinus (chief "Bantu" commissioner) 133–134, 150–151, 154–156, 158–159, 180–181, 234–235
Sobukwe, Robert 89, 105, 107–108, 227, 234, 240
soccer, in Sharpeville 97–98; in Top Location 32–33
Society of Young Africa (SOYA) 104
South African, Coal, Oil and Gas Company (Sasol) 27, 49, 72, 100, 114

South African Iron and Steel Corporation (Iscor) 2, 27, 49, 58, 63, 72, 100, 114, 116, 134, 163, 216, 233
South African Police (SAP), African: Daubada, Constable Amos 164, 175, 187; Kele, Detective Constable Sidwell 172; Khumalo, Constable Christian 120–122, 152; Litelu, Detective Constable Edwin 123, 136, 138–139, 143, 147; Mmotong, Detective Malakia (SAP) 122, 132, 171; Mokabela, Sergeant David (SAP) 121, 172, 175; Nkosi, Sergeant Moses (SAP) 124, 128–129, 135, 137–138, 147, 155, 157; Pokwane, Constable Julius (SAP) 132
South African Police (SAP), White: Beyl, Constable Hendrik Jan Michael 123, 132, 143; Booysen, Constable Gysbert 165–167; Brummer, Captain Andries Gottlieb 158–161, 165–167, 184; Cawood, Captain Edward 121–122, 124, 128; at the "Gate," 130–132, 145, 208; use of violence by in Vanderbijlpark 149–150; Claassen, Lieutenant Jakobus Johannes 137, 162, 166, 168–169, 184–185; Coetzee, Captain Frederick Jacobus Pieter 137, 146–147, 154–155, 165, 175, 181; like shooting "fish in a tin" 170; Coetzee, Constable Jakobus Nicolaas 133, 145; Du Plooy, General Hendrik Jacobus 117, 134, 175; Els, Brigadier Cornelius Johannes 117, 134, 155, 158, 162, 175; Els, Constable Cornelius Johannes 133, 145; Fourie, Lieutenant Quartus 121–122, 124; Freemantle, Lieutenant Adrian 164, 181; estimate of distance between White police and protestors 185; expert testimony on firearms 221–222; Grobler, Sergeant Johannes 121, 137, 146, 153; Grove, Constable Jan Hendrik 133, 155; Heyl, Head Constable Johannes 121–122, 137, 146, 154; Kallis, Constable Andre Thomas 133, 145; Lemmer, Colonel J.C. 134, 136–137, 139, 145, 155, 158, 162, 175, 180; Meyer, Constable Charles Rudolf 165–167; Meyer, Constable Joel

166–167; Pennekan, Constable Edward Arnold 170; Pretorius, Constable Izak Malherbe 166; Snyman, Head Constable 36–37; Struwig, Constable Andries Abraham 185, 258; Theron, Captain Hendrik Gert 154–155, 160, 162, 175, 181, 191; Theron, Constable Barend Johannes 166–167, 169–171; van den Bergh, Captain Jan official testimony on guns and bullets fired by the police 181, 184; van den Bergh, Constable Simon Andrew 167, 170, 184–185, 192, 196, 220, 265; van der Linde, Captain Stephanus Jakobus Saracen commander) 154–156, 159, 161–162; Visser, Captain Jakobus Christian 137–139, 146–147, 160, 175, 182, 187; *see also* Pienaar, Lieutenant Colonel Gideon Daniel; Sten gunners; Van Zyl, Major Willem

South African Railways (SAR) 32, 58, 127, 232

Special Branch (SB) 115, 152, 231; Dunga, Constable Solomon 152; Muller, Sergeant Hendrik Christoffel 131, 145, 159, 164, 175, 183; Prinsloo, Colonel Willem Carl Ernst (national head of the SB) 117, 159–161; Saaiman, Detective Constable Pieter Machiel 137–138, 153–154, 159–160, 164, 166, 233; firing by 169; purchases bullets privately 204; Wessels, Sergeant Wynand 131–132, 145, 159–160, 182, 208, 222; Willers, Captain Willem 131–132, 145, 159–160, 175; *see also* Spengler, Colonel Abraham Theodorus

Spengler, Colonel Abraham Theodorus (SB) 117; actions at Sharpeville police station on 21 March 160, 162–164, 175, 182, 243, 245; arrival at Sharpeville 159, 161, 256; on how to deal with protestors 131, 134, 145–146; on strategic importance of Vaal Triangle 115

Stands (Sharpeville neighbourhood) 88, 90, 102, 197, 202

St. Cyprian's Anglican School 99, 108

Sten gunners (all SAP): Bosch, Constable 169; du Plessis, Constable J. 134, 159, 169, 184; Janssen, Constable C. 159, 169; Joubert, Constable Johannes 154, 159, 166, 169, 184; Oosthuizen, Sergeant Jeremiah 137–138, 146, 154, 159, 169, 185; Scheepers, Constable Hermanus 121, 132; Sneigans, Constable Frank Bernard 154, 159, 169, 171, 184, 190; Steynberg, Constable J. 154, 159, 170, 184; Steyn, Constable Paul Machiel 159, 166, 169; estimate of distance between White police and protestors 185; van der Merwe, Detective Sergeant A. 154, 159, 169, 184; van Niekerk, Constable Sybrand Gerhardus 159, 166, 169; van Rensburg, Constable J. 121, 132–133, 145; van Wyk, Constable Louis Christian 159, 166, 169, 185; van Zyl, Constable Johannes Petrus Mostert 159, 166–167, 169, 246

Stewart Higher Primary School 96

Stewarts and Lloyds 28–29, 42, 58, 88, 94, 100, 156, 204–206, 212, 232; impact of protests on 21 March 114, 200, 210; labour unrest at 101

Steyn, Dr. Hermanus 179

Suikerbosrand River 2–5

Surveillance, official of Africans 39, 54, 76, 80, 86, 116, 208–214, 230

Swanepoel, Dr. Phillippus D. 187

TB (tuberculosis) 213–214; *see also* health

Teketsi, Emmanuel Khoali (PAC) 118–121 passim, 128, 135, 142, 146, 153, 158–160, 212

testimonies, National Archives 193; Truth and Reconciliation Commission (TRC) 193, 195, 197, 221, 258, **274**

Thabanetu, Anostasia (Top Location) 41, 48

Thamae, David (grandfather of Vincent) 192, 196–197

Thamae, Moeletsi Vincent 192; quoted 261

Thekiso, Mahasane Michael 104, 122, 124, 135, 140, 142, 178; quoted 262

The World list of casualties 229–230; massacre 229

Time (magazine) estimate of numbers killed and injured 192; impact of 30 March stay at home on Johannesburg 233–234; publishes photographs of Sharpeville killed and injured 187
Tom, Petrus 33, 117, 169, 174, 243; living in Top Location 30, 34–36; move to Sharpeville 83, 89–90
Top Location 20, 28–32, 47, 53, 58, 73, 101; "Asiatic Bazaar" 45; cemetery 47; churches 32; destruction of 42–45, 88–89; "riots" in 34–41, 72; three police constables killed in 1937 38–39
Transvaal African Teachers' Association 212
Transvaal Brick and Tile African Workers Union 100
trauma 201–208, 261–263; *see also* emotions; pain
Treason Trial 104
Trollope, Anthony 21
Tsirela *see* Boipatong
Tsolo family 90–91; evicted from homes 212
Tsolo, Job (brother of Nyakane) (PAC) 104, 229, 234
Tsoslo, Nyakane (PAC) 102; arranging for the important official to speak about passes 137–139, 147; cross examines police witnesses 186, 245–246, 258; and Elias Lidia 118, 136, 240, 244, 248, 260; interrogation of by police 175; legacy 260, 262; not intimidated by officials 181; opposes use of the word "Bantu" instead of "African" 246; organising protest on 21 March 108, 118–120, 128–129, 135; quoted 117, 127, 138, 149, 158, 225, 262; and PAC 102–103, 107–108; photograph of 140; at the police station 128–129, 153, 157–159, 165; seized by Spengler 160, 164, 182, 186; told "fuck you" by a White policeman 159; trade union organising 33, 102, 153, 160
Tsolo, Philemon 102
"*tsotsis*" (gangsters) no evidence of role of 99, 198, 254
Tyler, Humphrey 161–162, 179

Unions, African trade 33, 100–102, 104, 111, 116
Union Steel Corporation 27, 29, 37, 39, 45, 58, 63, 88, 94–95, 100–101, 116, 186, 200
United Nations, arms embargo of South Africa and 251; Convention on the Elimination of All Forms of Racial Discrimination (adopted 1965) 251; defines apartheid as a "crime against humanity," 225, 248, 252; economic boycott of South Africa and 251; International Day for the Elimination of Racial Discrimination (21 March) (adopted 1966) 225, 252; Security Council and debate on apartheid 228, 235–239, 251–252, 256; Seminar on Apartheid 251–252; Special Committee on the Policies of Apartheid (crated 1963) 253; sporting sanctions of South Africa and 239, 251; Universal Declaration of Human Rights (adopted 1948) 227, 236, 240, 251
United Party 66, 212
Unterhalter, Jack 143, 147, 182, 258

Vaal River Cash Store 267
Vaal River (Lekoa) 3, 7–12 passim, 13, 15–17, 20–22, 25, 27, 29, 44, 55–56, 59, 66, 94–95, 109, 221, 242; Johannesburg water supplies from 75, 100, 114; Verwoerd's farm near 66–67, 72, 153
Vaal Triangle (Vanderbijlpark, Vereeniging, and Sasolberg) 9, 20–21, 72, 114–116, 149, 233
Van Beloll, Barry John 140–141, 147
Vanderbijlpark 54, 58, 67, 70–71; *see also* Boipatong; Bophelong
Van Zyl, Major Willem (SAP) 128, 135, 191; awareness of senior officials planning to speak to the protestors at 2 pm 138, 156; beating and shooting of protestors at the Gate 132–133; certain that there would be a "bloodbath" 117, 137; fear of African protestors 116–117, 121; Judge Wessels on "ridiculous position" of 248; patrols Sharpeville Sunday night 124; requests police reinforcements 130, 136–137, 139, 144–145, 154–155; updates leaders

of SB (Prinsloo and Spengler) and uniformed branches (Pienaar) upon their arrivals in Sharpeville 159, 162

Vereeniging 20–21, 27–28, 69; African urban residence 29; coal mines 1, 9, 11–12, 14, 16–17, 21–23, 25–29, 37, 55, 100, 115; commercial origins of name 20; concentration camps 11–13; earliest African settlements 7; labour strikes 101–102; population 27, 29, 31–32, 34, 44, 67, 72, 88, 90; South African War 1, 10–12, 15, 29; Town Planning Scheme (1951) 69

Vereeniging Estates (*De Zuid Afrikaansche en Oranje Vrijstaache Koen en Mineeralen Vereeniging*: South African and Orange Free State Coal and Mineral Mining Association) 9–11, 15, 17, 20, 22, 24, 27, 42, 100, 212

Vereeniging Hospital 123, 177, 187, 191–192, 194, 196, 205, 211, 219, 221, 229

Vereeniging Town Council 41–44, 59, 67, 74, 107, 111, 115, 124, 209, 214, 240

Vereeniging Transport Company (VTC) 124–125, 127

Vergenoeg (Sharpeville neighbourhood) 61, 90–92, 94, 98, *202*

Verwoerd, Hendrik 81, 249; on African locations 66–68, 70, 72, 75–76, 81–82, 88, 99; African urban residence rights 53, 86–88; bans ANC and PAC 225; "Bantu education" 70; Bantustans 43, *71*; declares state of emergency 233, 256; ethnic zoning and 70–72; labour control of Africans 107; Marium Lepee expecting 153, 165, 207; Sharpeville Massacre 154, 165, 191–192, 207, 248

victims: claims for compensation filed by 142, 195–198, 201, 247–248, 251, 269; employment of 190, 198, 200–201, 206, 216, 231–232, 270; injuries: amputations 177, 187, 195, 205–207, 210, 219; shot in the back 150, 169–170, 174–177, 184, 189–191, 193–194, 197, 200–201, 203–205, 207, 209, 211, 213, 215, 219, 222, 228–230, 232–233, 245, 254–255, 268; shot in the head 174, 176, 189–190, 198–199, 203–204, 213, 215, 268–269; map showing distribution of homes of 202; official counts of dead and injured 82, 191–196, 253, 265–266; pregnant 48, 167–168, 190, 195, 200, 209, 220; recalculating numbers injured 196–197, 206–207, 220, **274–280**; recalculating numbers killed 193–197, 220, **271–273**; *see also* children; Sharpeville residents; women

Victoria Falls Power Company (VFPC) 25, 27, 37

Vukazenzele (Sharpeville neighbourhood), also known as Vuka 68, 83, 90, 97, 109, 118, 120, 122, 125, 128–129, 170, 201–202, 209, 216

Wessels, Judge P.J. criticisms of police actions and evidence 247, 258

Witwatersrand Native Areas Planning Committee (Mentz Committee 1952) 67

women, and Sharpeville Massacre 176, 192–193, 198–200, 228, 230; arrests of 36, 41, 48, 209, 215; employment of 12, 34–36, 39–41, 90, 198–199; immigration to urban areas 34, 90; in concentration camps 11–12, 14; killed by police 176, 192, 199; pass laws and 105, 168, 236; protests in Sharpeville 103, 130, 151, 156–157, 160; protests in Top Location 35, 39–40, 73; targeted by government officials 35–36, 39–41, 43, 48; *see also* crowd, composition of; Sharpeville residents; victims

World, The 187, 195–197, 229–230, 256, 271, **274**

Xaba's Location 10, 12, 16, 20

Xingwana, Bernard (municipal official) 120, 153, 156, 160

Printed in the United States
by Baker & Taylor Publisher Services